EXPLORATIONS IN ANTHROPOLOGY
A University College London Series
Series Editors: Barbara Bender, John Gledhill   Bruce Kapferer

HUNTERS AND GATHERERS 2

Property, power and ideology

Edited by
Tim Ingold
David Riches
James Woodburn

BERG
New York / Oxford

**Distributed exclusively in the US and Canada by
St. Martin's Press, New York**

First published in 1988 by
Berg Publishers Limited
Editorial Offices:
165 Taber Avenue, Providence, R.I. 02906, USA
150 Cowley Road, Oxford 0X4 1JJ, UK

Paperback edition 1991

British Library Cataloguing in Publication Data

Hunter and gatherers. — (Explorations in
    anthropology).
    2: Property, power and ideology
    1. Hunting and gathering societies
    I. Ingold, Tim II. Riches, David
    III. Woodburn, James IV. Series
    307.7'72   GN388
ISBN 0–85496–155–0
ISBN 0–85496–735–4 (pbk)

Library of Congress Cataloging-in-Publication Data

Hunters and gatherers.
    (Explorations in anthropology)
    Papers from the Fourth International Conference on Hunting and
Gathering Societies, held at the London School of Economics and Political
Sciences, Sept. 8–13, 1986.
    Includes bibliographies and indexes.
    Contents: v. 1. History, evolution, and social change
—2. Property, power, and ideology.
    1. Hunting and gathering societies—Congresses.
    I. Ingold, Tim, 1948– . II. Riches, David.
    III. Woodburn, James. IV. International
Conference on Hunter-Gatherers. (4th: 1986:
London School of Economics and Political
Science) V. Series.
GN388.H87 1987 306'.3 87–21216
ISBN 0–85496–155–0 (v. 2)
ISBN 0–85496–735–4 (pbk)

Printed in Great Britain by Billings of Worcester

1000339275

Cover: Some Batek youngsters hoisting a raft-load of rattan over a log while
    bringing it downstream to their Malay trading partners.
    Misk River, Kelantan, Malaysia, 1976
    Photo by Kirk Endicott

To the memory of
Glynn Isaac and Eleanor Leacock

Contents

Plates, Figures and Maps

Plates

Figures

Maps

Tables

Preface

The modern anthropological understanding of hunting and gathering societies effectively dates from 1966, when a conference was held in Chicago on the theme of *Man the hunter*, giving rise to a seminal volume with that title edited by Richard Lee and Irven DeVore (1968). Following this initial stimulus, a great deal of exciting and innovative research has been carried out among hunting and gathering peoples in many regions of the world. Twelve years later, in 1978, a major international conference was convened in Paris to review the fruits of this work. Such was the volume of interest, and the richness and quality of the work presented there, that it was resolved on that occasion to hold future conferences at regular intervals. The second international conference on hunting and gathering societies was held in Quebec in 1980, and the third in Bad Homburg, West Germany, in 1983. As at Paris, these conferences attracted contributions of outstanding quality, bringing to bear a great deal of new data and a number of revelatory theoretical insights.

At the Bad Homburg meeting, I presented a proposal for a future conference to be held, in 1986, in the United Kingdom. Following discussions with James Woodburn, an organizing committee was set up including almost all the leading specialists in hunter-gatherer studies in the country: besides Woodburn and myself, the members of the original committee were Alan Barnard, Barbara Bender, Nurit Bird-David, Signe Howell, Robert Layton, David McKnight, Brian Morris and David Riches. The committee first met in November 1983, and again on numerous occasions during the ensuing three years. There were some changes in composition: McKnight resigned at an early stage, and later on both Howell and Morris had to withdraw on account of their departure to the field. However we gained two new members: Harvey Feit, who was on sabbatical leave in London during 1985; and Howard Morphy, who arrived from Australia to take up a post at Oxford in January 1986. Representing the culmination of a lot of hard work put in by every member of the committee, the Fourth International Conference on Hunting and Gathering Societies took place, as planned, at the London School of Economics and Political Science, from Monday 8 to Saturday 13 September 1986.

1

Like its predecessors, the London conference was intended to provide a forum for the discussion of basic research on the social and
economic organization and cultural life of hunters and gatherers in all
regions of the world, as well as for the presentation of the results of
new fieldwork. Significantly marking the twentieth anniversary of the
original *Man the hunter* symposium, the conference brought together no
fewer than 114 scholars from eighteen different countries, bearing
testimony to the enormous growth in hunter-gatherer studies over the
last two decades. Its major goals were to further the comparative
understanding of hunting and gathering societies, to demonstrate the
relevance of hunter-gatherer studies to the construction of anthropological theory, to draw attention to the current status of hunting and
gathering peoples as citizens of the modern world, and to provide a
medium for presenting the results of recent empirical research. In all
these respects the conference fulfilled its purpose beyond our most
optimistic expectations, and we hope it will stimulate much further
work in what is surely a crucial area of contemporary research with
major implications for all branches of the science of humanity, including human biology and prehistoric archaeology as well as social and
cultural anthropology.

The articles published in this volume, and in its companion volume
(*Hunters and gatherers I: History, evolution and social change*), represent
only a selection of the seventy-four papers presented in the nine
sessions of the conference. On account of their uniformly outstanding
quality, the job of selection turned out to be an extremely difficult and
painful one. In order to oversee the selection and preparation of papers
for publication, the members of the original organizing committee have
continued to work together, and both volumes are the result of a joint
editorial effort. Each paper was carefully read and ranked by every
member of the committee, and these rankings — together with a
concern for balance and coherence within each volume — guided our
ultimate choice of papers. However on behalf of the committee, I
should at this point acknowledge the important and valuable contributions made by all those whose papers we have felt unable to include. I
hope that the present volumes will be seen to embody the spirit of their
work, if not its substance. I also wish to pay tribute to the dedicated
labour put in by David Riches, as co-ordinator of the editorial committee, in bringing both volumes to fruition.

There are a great many persons and organizations that we have to
thank for helping to make the conference such a resounding success.
First and foremost, of course, are those funding bodies without whose
assistance the conference would not have been possible. These include
the Economic and Social Research Council, the British Academy, the
Esperanza Trust, the Centre National de la Recherche Scientifique, and
the Maison des Sciences de l'Homme. For the funds from Esperanza we

are grateful to the Council of the Royal Anthropological Institute, and to its Director, Jonathan Benthall. Maurice Godelier was instrumental in obtaining funds from CNRS. We should also like to acknowledge the support given to us by Sir Edmund Leach and by M. Clemens Heller. One of the biggest jobs we had to cope with was the copying and precirculation of the majority of the conference papers. To save time and costs, sets of papers for Australian and North American participants were copied and circulated separately; for this we have to thank Nicolas Peterson, who undertook the Australian distribution; and Harvey Feit, who — assisted by a grant from McMaster University — produced a splendidly bound volume for distribution in Canada and the United States. However the major distribution, to remaining overseas and all UK participants, was undertaken from the University of Durham by Lesley Bailey and Robert Layton. We are specially grateful to both of them for their efforts.

The conference was sponsored by the Association of Social Anthropologists of the Commonwealth, the Royal Anthropological Institute of Great Britain and Ireland, and the London School of Economics and Political Science. We are particularly grateful to the School for allowing us to use the comfortable facilities of the Shaw Library, which provided a most congenial setting for our deliberations, and to the LSE Department of Anthropology for putting up with a week-long invasion of its premises. We also express our thanks to the Museum of Mankind for the generous loan of Andaman Islands artefacts. The Australian and Canadian High Commissions handsomely provided for a reception at the Australian Studies Centre. During the Conference itself we were all sustained by the superb catering of Lisa Woodburn, and the secretarial skills of Joan Wells, as well as receiving invaluable support from our student helpers: B.Grzimek, J. Robertson, C. Zeiske and M. Stewart.

Professor Glynn L. Isaac, of Harvard University, was to have presented a paper to the session of the conference on 'comparative studies of hunter-gatherer societies'. His tragic death, on 5 October 1985, robbed the conference of a most distinguished contributor, and is a great loss to all of us who are concerned with the ways in which studies of hunting and gathering can contribute to our overall understanding of the evolution of humanity. It is entirely appropriate that this volume should be dedicated to his memory.

Just as we were going to press we heard the sad news that Professor Eleanor Leacock had died. Remembering her major contribution to the Paris conference in 1978, and her innovatory role over many years in the development of the study of Canadian hunter-gatherers, we also dedicate this volume to her memory.

TIM INGOLD
Manchester, May 1988

1 Property, power and ideology in hunting and gathering societies: an introduction

Alan Barnard and James Woodburn

The themes

We have divided this volume into four sections. These represent not separate and distinct areas of hunter-gatherer studies, but broad themes which themselves are to a large measure interdependent. *Property rights*, arguably, are the foundation of hunter-gatherer society. *Equality and domination* stem from access to property and from rules and practices which govern its accumulation and distribution. *Symbols and representations* may at first seem the odd man out, but symbols can be property too, and their use is often the key to power as well as the foundation of ideology. *Power and ideology* bring our material full circle for, as the chapters in the last section show, these factors are truly the basis of the concepts of ownership with which the volume begins.

The themes of this book are the subject of much ongoing debate. They represent current interests among hunter-gatherer specialists and within anthropology more broadly. Together with the themes of our companion volume, *Hunters and gatherers I: History, evolution and social change*, they spell out the findings of recent studies and indicate directions for future research and discussion. The contributors to both volumes have been much influenced by the wider theoretical concerns of social anthropology in the 1970s and the early 1980s — for example, on the relation between practice and ideology, on egalitarianism and power, and on the 'post-structuralist' understanding of art, symbols and ritual, as well as on new developments in Marxist anthropology, neo-evolutionism and the study of social change.

In some ways hunter-gatherer studies have developed independently of other branches of social anthropology. Yet we believe that they are not simply in tune with social anthropology more generally: they are the backbone of the discipline. They are often much more in touch with the essence of what it is to be human than are trends in virtually any other branch of the subject. Some writers have argued that to distinguish between hunting and gathering societies and other societies is unsatisfactory. Indeed this may be true, either in the sense that it obscures similarities between hunter-gatherers and some pastoralists and cultivators (Barnard 1983) or in the sense that it cuts across the significant distinction between immediate-return societies and delayed-return ones (Woodburn 1980; 1982a). But even if the boundary between hunter-gatherers and others is an artificial one where some enquiries are concerned, the category 'hunter-gatherer' has the merit of giving focus to a set of human societies including a very high proportion of those with relatively simple forms of social organization. The comparative study of these simple forms of organization is proving highly revealing, as the present volume demonstrates. There is a resilience in hunter-gatherer studies and in the category 'hunting and gathering society', which generates very considerable interest among students, anthropologists who specialize in other areas, and scholars within other disciplines.

The present series of hunter-gatherer symposia began with the (First) International Conference on Hunting and Gathering Societies, held in Paris in June 1978. A better starting point for discussion, though, is the symposium on 'Man the hunter', which was held in Chicago in April 1966. It is interesting to note the changes that have taken place since then. In their introduction to *Man the hunter*, Lee and DeVore (1968) stressed, among other things, what they called the 'nomadic style' of hunting and gathering societies. By this they meant that hunter-gatherers can hold only a small amount of property and are relatively egalitarian, that groups are small in size, that such groups do not normally establish exclusive rights to resources (a view contested within the present volume), that food surpluses are rare, and that frequent visiting and sharing of resources are common. Several of these ideas remain current, but the emphases have changed and the sophistication of analysis has greatly increased. Not only is our knowledge, through recent fieldwork, much enhanced, but also our theoretical understanding of the 'nomadic style' has come a long way since 'Man the hunter', partly as a result of the powerful stimulus which that symposium gave to hunter-gatherer studies. The chapters in this volume bear witness to that fact.

The papers

Property rights.

Of the five chapters in this first section, two (those of Myers and of Altman and Peterson) deal with Australian Aboriginal concepts of property and exchange, while two (Scott and Burch) concern native North American property rights, and one (Endicott), property and power in a Malaysian context. Coupled with property rights, exchange emerges as a dominant interest in most of the chapters — an interest perhaps inevitably bound up with property. Social change is another subsidiary theme, discussed in all the chapters except that of Burch, who in his study of north-west Alaskan Eskimos opts instead for a detailed record and analysis of traditional concepts of exchange.

Scott couches his analysis of the Cree of northern Quebec in evolutionary-historical terms. The Cree have been the subject of much study and debate since Speck (1915; 1923) asserted the aboriginality of family hunting territories, introducing a view that many later writers came to contest. Scott's solution to the problem is to place Cree concepts of 'property' in the context of Cree ideology, rather than to employ inappropriate Western notions. The interaction between the Cree and the colonial, federal and provincial governments has yielded a complex dialectical process of power relations. Scott argues that the construction of these relations is at the root of Cree concepts of 'property'.

Myers considers property rights among the Pintupi of Western Australia in the context of identity. He argues that the Pintupi concept of the 'ownership' of 'property' represents a mechanism through which social aggregations collectively acquire identity. Property is seen not so much as an entity in itself, but as a 'sign' defined by its place in a system of exchange values. Myers analyses the complexity of property relations in such varied spheres as land, food and motor vehicles.

Altman and Peterson explore rights to resources among a group of eastern Gunwinggu in north-central Arnhem Land. At the outstation studied by Altman, strict rules, which emerged in the 1960s, govern the distribution of cash in the community. These rules are related to similar rights which govern the handling of game and the use of band resources. Although the authors classify the society as immediate-return in economic terms, there are limits to generosity; only large game is widely shared. While the accumulation of cash is theoretically possible, the goods it buys must be redistributed. Altman and Peterson argue that the general lack of material wealth and the rules of sharing together engender the exchange relationships which obtain between members of the community. For social as well as economic reasons, an accumulation of surplus is not possible.

Burch, like Scott, explores indigenous concepts of property in a North American context. His concern is with the levels of property ownership — societal (tribal), local, domestic, conjugal and individual — which characterized north-west Alaskan Eskimo societies until very recently. In some instances, 'ownership' was a matter of degree, and different kinds of property were controlled by different segmental units. Burch places particular emphasis on the indigenous categories of the language. These include mechanisms for the division of property (for example, from a hunt), types of exchange (direct exchange, buying and selling, formalized trade partnerships, 'free gifts', inheritance, and so on) and trading events (feasts and fairs). He notes that generalized reciprocity was restricted to the local family and its constituent parts, while other forms of exchange dominated the wider social context. In comparative terms, his evidence suggests that accounts of hunter-gatherer exchange emphasizing generalized reciprocity within small local groups, could be too narrowly focused. We should also explore trade networks between larger groups.

Endicott looks at property, power and conflict among the Batek, a Semang people of peninsular Malaysia. The basic social unit is the conjugal family. Parents instil in their children the values of sharing and non-aggression. All resources are regarded as unowned until they are procured, and the surplus (procured resources not needed by the family which collects them) must be shared with others. The principles of exchange and the egalitarian ethos of Batek society are characteristic of hunter-gatherers with immediate-return systems, but are not adapted to the peasant farming which the Batek are being forced to take up. The conflicts which arise as a result of the dependence on agriculture are revealing for understanding the transition from food procurement to food production.

Equality and domination

Here, as in the first section, the ethnographic spread is wide, covering examples from Canada (Guemple), Australia (Tonkinson) and the Philippines (Gibson). The chapters touch on age differentiation and socialization, which in many hunting and gathering societies are key factors in education for dominance and/or egalitarianism. Social differentiation by age, and differentiation by sex, are frequently the only dimensions in which dominance is evident in hunting and gathering societies. Tonkinson and Gibson examine ritual as an element of social interaction, while Guemple concentrates more specifically on the importance of the socialization process.

Guemple looks specifically at socialization for mutuality and reciprocity among the Qiqiqtamiut Inuit (Eskimo) of east Hudson Bay. Qiqiqtamiut teach such principles by conditioning children to accept the appropriate behaviour defined through the kinship system. There is no necessity for explicit rules to be formulated, for the conditioning process itself creates the desired effect. Through both ordinary kinship and ritual kinship, Qiqiqtamiut children learn the egalitarian ideology ever-present in their society. Guemple concludes his detailed account with a consideration of the place of socialization in the scheme of ecological adaptation.

Tonkinson examines the theme of equality and domination in a traditional Australian hunting and gathering context. The ideology of the Mardujarra of Western Australia exhibits both egalitarian and hierarchical tendencies. Yet the realization of actual social hierarchy is prevented by ideological emphases on individuality and mutual dependence, and is in particular regulated by the structure of kinship and ritual relations. Tonkinson's discussion of the principle of equality in Western Desert society is framed primarily as a reply to Bern (1979), who has argued differently, emphasizing domination rather than equality in the Australian setting.

The Buid, described in Gibson's chapter, are a part-time hunting and gathering people. Their main economic enterprise is in fact shifting cultivation. Like many full-time hunter-gatherers, they share the fruits of their labour and uphold a strong spirit of egalitarianism. Yet unlike hunter-gatherers proper, the Buid consciously avoid dyadic relations, regarding them as a source of conflict; instead, they interact primarily in groups. Groups share meat *within* the larger groups which contain them, and not specifically *with* other groups of the same order of segmentation. Augmenting Polanyi's (1968) distinctions between reciprocity, redistribution and exchange, Gibson argues that a notion of *sharing* must be introduced, as a further, distinct relationship between giver, recipient and social whole. This concept, though derived from a study of an agricultural people, may further our understanding of social and economic relationships in hunting and gathering societies.

Symbols and representations

In this section, three chapters examine the symbolic importance of animals in hunting and gathering societies. Sharp gives a North American example, while Guenther and Lewis-Williams explore the belief systems of contemporary and historical Bushman (or San) societies in Southern Africa.

Sharp discusses the Chipewyan, the easternmost northern Athapaskan group, in a regional comparative perspective. A number of ethnographers of the Subarctic region have remarked that among the Chipewyan there is an apparent absence of many of the features which characterize the culture area as a whole. Sharp's position is that it is certainly the case that public hunting ritual is absent. This, he argues, is because such ritual would be superfluous in a society in which every encounter between man and prey is itself a sacrificial event. Sharp places his discussion in a framework covering complementary aspects of the relationships between man and animal and between man and woman.

Guenther deals with the importance of the human–animal relationship in Bushman folklore and art. He points out that the animals most frequently depicted in art or described in mythology are those of symbolic and religious significance, and not those of greatest economic value. Symbolically, animals are simultaneously men and *not* men. It is this ambiguity which enables Bushmen and other hunter-gatherers to use them so resourcefully in their art, myth and ritual. In contrast to anthropologists concerned with totemic societies, Guenther puts forward the view that animals are of interest in themselves. Animals do not necessarily (and in the Bushman case certainly do not) represent mediating elements within a segmentary social structure.

Lewis-Williams's chapter also touches on the symbolic identity, or association, between animals and men. It is particularly concerned with the transformation, expressed in southern Bushman rock art, between eland and medicine man. We are given an interesting and original analysis of rock art through its possible association with concepts of 'possession' in the extinct /Xam language of the eastern Cape. Through Lewis-Williams's earlier work on Bushman rock art, the association between hunting and trance and between eland and medicine man has become well-known. The present study adds a new dimension to this already well-documented and fascinating interpretation.

Power and ideology

In this final section Kratz presents a superbly detailed study of Okiek blessings, while Morphy and Keen both, but independently, seek to understand the complexities of religious property among the Yolngu of Arnhem Land. The chapters by Morphy and Keen complement each other in that they illustrate different, but not contradictory, perspectives on the topic. All three chapters show that among these hunting and gathering peoples there is richness of thought and power in ritual, especially in the hands of elders in age-differentiated social spheres.

The Okiek (also known as 'Dorobo') are an encapsulated hunting and gathering society of the highland forests of south-western Kenya. Their blessings are a form of prayer and have a variety of uses in many social situations. In her discussion, Kratz sheds light not only on the form and context of Okiek blessings, but also on the theoretical implications of these blessings for the understanding of communication, power relations, and the ritual use of language more generally.

The Yolngu (more or less synonymous with the 'Murngin' of earlier literature) are a famous Australian Aboriginal people. Morphy focuses on the meaning of their clan designs and on the relationship between society and cosmology which these designs define. Clan designs are associated with particular parts of clan territories and refer both to ancestral beings and to social groups smaller than the clan which inhabit specific places. They express relations within the clan and between clans. Morphy analyses their significance in a dynamic framework, which itself represents an attempt to reconcile synchronic and diachronic aspects of Yolngu social relations.

Keen's account focuses more on ritual. Yolngu law, according to traditional belief, was laid down by the ancestral spirits and is administered by the elders. These elders' power derives from ownership of secret ritual knowledge. Keen's discussion, supplemented by detailed case studies, emphasizes the relationship between this knowledge and aspects of kinship and economic relations.

Some connections between property, power and ideology

The politics of property

In this section we seek to develop ideas about some of the ways in which property, power and ideology are interconnected in hunting and gathering societies. We take the view that property rights are fundamental — that in these societies it is through rights to property and the ideologies linked with such rights that structures of equality and inequality are established and maintained. Rights in property, together with other socially recognized links between people and things, are vehicles for the expression of ideals and values and other manifest concerns about the nature of human beings and the way they relate and should relate to others. Some of these ideas are politically relevant, some are not. We will be concerned here largely with those that are politically relevant, with those that affirm or deny control over other people, and with those that may have evolutionary potential for the development of such control or denial of control.

For the past hundred years one issue, more than any other, has dominated discussion of property rights in hunter-gatherer societies. This is the question of whether property in these societies is held communally or individually. The view that it is held communally is particularly associated with the work of Morgan (1877), and the view that much of it is held individually is particularly linked with Lowie (for example, Lowie 1928). Today there is a wide measure of agreement about the issue among those who have themselves carried out research in hunter-gatherer societies. Although different workers give different emphases to the data, almost all would now agree that both important group rights, guaranteeing access to land and productive resources, and important individual rights, allocating artefacts and other products of human labour to individuals, coexist. There is also wide agreement with Gluckman's position (1965: 36) that in some instances we cannot divide up sorts of property according to whether they are individually or communally held. The problem is that, often, analytically separate individual and group rights exist in the same item of property. Gluckman gives a range of illustrations of this point in relation to rights in land in agricultural tribal societies (ibid: 36–43). For hunter-gatherer societies the same issue often emerges over rights to the carcass of a successfully hunted game animal. In very many of these societies the carcass is recognized as being individually owned, and yet at the same time the various members of the camp in which the owner lives have socially recognized rights to a share in the meat which cannot be refused by the owner. In looking at the political relevance of property rights, the important question for us is not so much whether these rights are held by individuals or by groups, although this is a matter to which we will return, but the more fundamental question of the scale of equality and inequality in access by men, women and children to the range of material things that are desired and valued in hunting and gathering societies. We are concerned with the basis for the various equalities and inequalities that exist and with some of their possible historical trajectories. In our search for answers we must start with some comments about the organization of production in these societies.

Low production targets

In a famous paper at the 'Man the hunter' conference in 1966, Sahlins argued that hunter-gatherers, far from having difficulty in obtaining their material requirements and desires, obtained them rather easily and allowed themselves much leisure by setting their targets low and by limiting their material wants to those that are well within their capacity to achieve (Sahlins 1968: 85–9; 1974: 1–39). Much work has been stimulated by the theory over the years and many comments have been made, some favourable and some not. Certainly not all hunter-gatherers are willing to set their targets so low that in consequence they find tolerable the degree of hardship suggested in one of his examples (1968: 89). And again much more effort is, at some times and in some societies, made to obtain people's requirements than this theory predicts.

But, if two provisos are made, the crux of the theory has, we believe, stood up well to twenty years of additional research. The first proviso is that it applies very much better to hunter-gatherer societies with immediate-return systems — that is, in brief, with economies in which people usually obtain an immediate yield for their labour, use this yield with minimal delay and place minimal emphasis on property rights — than it does to hunter-gatherer societies with delayed-return systems — in which people place more emphasis on property rights, rights which are usually but not always linked with delayed yields on labour (for a more detailed characterization of these types of economy, see Woodburn 1980; 1982a; 1982b). Contemporary hunter-gatherers with immediate-return systems include, in Africa, the Mbuti, the !Kung, the Nharo and the Hadza; in South Asia, the Paliyan, the Hill Pandaram and the Naiken; in South-east Asia, the Batek. Most northern hunter-gatherers have delayed-return systems and so, too, do Australian Aborigines. All societies with pastoral or agricultural modes of subsistence have delayed-return systems. The second proviso is that difficulties must be recognized in the definition of material wants — those wants that according to the theory are set at a low level that is well within people's capacity to achieve. The difficulty arises because of the undoubted fact that people in these societies almost never obtain nearly as much of the more desirable foods — especially meat and honey — as they would like. And there is a clearly articulated desire for more arrows, more axes, more beads, more clothing, more tobacco, and so on. As many anthropologists who have worked in societies with immediate-return systems will testify, people's demand for food and other goods from anthropologists, as well as from members of their own society, is very great, indeed at times almost insatiable (Woodburn 1982a: 449, n.11). The point is not that *wants* are set low, but rather that *production targets* are. Demand is not focused on greater production. It does not, for example, lead to pressure to persuade those who hunt little to spend more time and effort on hunting. It is instead strongly focused on the requirement that people who at some particular moment happen to have more of something than they immediately need should carry out their moral obligation to share it out. The emphasis is on what was, at the conference from which the chapters in this volume are drawn, called demand-sharing. People do not wait meekly for their share, but make what are at times loud and explicit claims. Hunters, in some at least of these societies, are expected to deprecate their own success and may even choose to give up hunting for a while lest they be suspected of attempting to build up their status (see, for example, Lee 1984: 48–50, 151–7).

In all known hunter-gatherer societies with immediate-return systems, and in many, but not all, hunter-gatherer societies with delayed-return systems, people are almost always able to meet their nutritional needs very adequately without working long hours. In setting their production targets low, people are not normally running significant risks of endangering their health and welfare, not even, because of the emphasis on sharing, the health and welfare of the weak and potentially vulnerable.

The combination of low production targets, little difficulty for individuals in meeting their nutritional needs and strong pressures for immediate use of food and of artefacts means that, in comparison with other types of society, not many material things are held and even fewer are accumulated over time.

Definition of property rights

How, then, are property rights organized? We must first define what we mean by *property rights*.

The term is usually used for the variety of rights — especially rights of possession, of use and of disposal — that may be held in or over 'things' — for example, in land, in tools and weapons or in food. But the term is also appropriate for rights in less tangible things — rights to perform a piece of music, or to carry out a particular ritual. And we may also use the same term for rights held in or over people — rights to their labour, to their reproductive capacity and so on. Examples of such rights are the rights an English professional football club holds over its players (including the right to transfer fees if they move to another club), the right Australian Aboriginal elders may have to direct the labour of young men undergoing initiation, or the right which men in many societies exercise over their female kin — such as the right to bestow them in marriage.

Property rights exist, of course, in all societies, although in no society is everything owned. Rights are not allocated even to some things that are of such value that a supply of them is vital. Air is the most obvious example. It is not the subject of property rights for three obvious reasons — because it is not scarce, because we cannot mark out or identify with particular portions of air and, even more important, because it is not really practicable to control and parcel out access to air.

Not everything that is mine is my property. In English, possessives (my, our, your, his, her, their) are used to refer to things over which I have property rights (my pen, my car, my farm), but also to refer to people or things over which I have no property rights (my father, my name, my university). What in fact we are talking about when we refer to a property right is a particular type of association between a person and a 'thing'. The type of association is one which involves a measure of socially recognized control over the 'thing' and which necessitates some restrictions on other people's control of the same 'thing'. So, in fact, property rights (whether held individually or jointly) are held in opposition to those who do not hold such rights. Property rights may be said to mark out relations between people in respect of 'things', and our concern in what follows will be with these relations between people. However closely I am identified with something that is mine, it is not in the normal sense my property (or, more correctly, I do not have property rights in it) unless some other people are in some way restricted in their use of it. In Western culture, if I am called James or Alan, such a name is not my property because other people of the same sex have just as much right to be called by this name as I do.

Identifications between people and things are socially significant in a number of ways, but those types of identifications which can appropriately be termed property are politically much the most important. Because property rights imply some restriction or exclusion of the rights of others, they are in a sense controversial and liable to challenge by those who are restricted or excluded. They become surrounded by rules to define them, by sanctions to enforce them, and by ideologies to justify them and to establish their legitimacy. In hunting and gathering societies certain property rights provide a basis for equality and others protect inequality. But, as in other societies, if the rights reserve particular assets for privileged individuals or groups, the associated rules, sanctions and ideologies seem often to become elaborated in specific ways — typically involving secrecy and even deception of the excluded.

Types of property rights

In discussing rights in property in hunter-gatherer societies, let us distinguish between five roughly defined categories of rights:

(1) rights over land, water sources and ungarnered resources (including rights in fixed assets, if there are any — ritual sites, dwelling sites, prepared hunting sites, dams, weirs, pit traps, and so on);

(2) rights over movable property — tools and weapons, clothing, cooking pots and containers, beads and other ornaments;

(3) rights over game meat, harvested vegetable foods and other garnered food and raw materials;

(4) rights over certain capacities of specific people — over their hunting labour, over their domestic labour, over their sexual capacity, over their reproductive capacity;

(5) rights over knowledge and intellectual property — over songs, over sacred knowledge, over ritual designs, and so on.

This system of categories is not intended to cover the whole range of possible property rights in these societies, but only to draw attention to what are likely to be some of the more important rights. Nor is any particular value to be attached to the definitions of the five categories. For example, the rather widespread obligation of a son-in-law to provide meat for his parents-in-law might be treated as relating to a right over the hunting labour of the son-in-law (category 4), or simply as a particular kind of right over meat (category 3). If the parent-in-law is able to direct the son-in-law's labour, it would perhaps be better categorized in the former way; but if control is exercised only at the point where the labour yields meat, then we might talk of the right in the latter way. But such fine distinctions are really beside the point. We do not attach any particular importance to the groupings the categorization yields. Its only point is to provide a rough idea of the range of things we are concerned with and to aid exposition.

In immediate-return systems property rights of all of these sorts are *relatively* unelaborated. They are sometimes not easy to define but this is usually because there are areas of ambiguity rather than because elaborately fine distinctions are being made in the societies concerned which are difficult to sort out.

Rights over land and ungarnered resources

Certain broad principles apply. People in societies with immediate-return systems are regarded as being born, or naturally endowed, with rights of direct personal access to land and ungarnered resources of the area with which they are associated. These rights are not formally bestowed, nor can they be withheld. There is no question of the exercise of such rights in one's home area being conditional on allegiance to other individuals or to the group. People are constrained in the access that they enjoy only by their knowledge and skills as developed within a framework in which productive tasks performed by men differ in some important respects from those performed by women. But with this single important exception, access is, in principle, equal to all — married or unmarried, old or young, adult or child. Access to areas other than one's own is typically obtained easily. Permission to use such resources is never normally refused. In cases where local failure of resources is a hazard and access to areas other than one's own is of greater importance, efforts may be made to build friendly ties with kinsmen living in other areas by regular, reciprocal exchanges of small gifts (see, for example, Wiessner 1980 and 1982, on the !Kung). In societies with immediate-return systems, there are, by definition, no separate or special rights to fixed assets such as elaborately constructed trap sites. The only sort of differentiated right in land and ungarnered resources recognized in many of these societies is where an individual hunter or gatherer discovers a wild bees' nest or wild fruit tree and seeks to pre-empt the right to its yield by marking it. All that is happening is that notions of property rights in harvested food are being pushed back to the point where the food is about to be harvested. The general principle in use of land is that access to resources in one's home area is automatic and unchallengeable, untrammelled by formalities or gestures of any sort towards one's seniors, the living or the dead, who have used these resources before oneself but who are given no role in handing them on.

Endicott's chapter on the Batek, in this volume, draws attention to the important point that such rights depend on land and resources being sufficiently plentiful. Where competition over use of scarce resources becomes severe, then the principle of general access may be abrogated, rights over land and resources may be parcelled out, and access by competitors may be restricted.

In societies with delayed-return systems rights over land are typically much more complicated. In some cases, most notably in Australia, access for subsistence purposes may not be much restricted, but land serves as a template on which individuals and groups map out their social relationships to each other in terms of ritual ties. There is an elaborate ideology of mystical involvement which stresses that people and land are not separate entities: people draw their substance from their links with the land and with the Sacred Beings who in their Dreamtime wanderings created both land and people. Myers, in this volume, stresses that property rights in Australia, both in land and in movable goods, are not much concerned with use-values but are instead focused on the definition and elaboration of principles of autonomy and of shared identity.

Rights over movable property

In hunter-gatherer societies, simple movable property — weapons, tools, clothing, and so on — seems invariably to be personally owned, but in ways that are strongly constrained by custom. Typically people make their own weapons and tools, and property rights in them seem to be based on the notion that, unless overridden by some other principle, individuals are entitled to the yield of their own labour. In societies with immediate-return systems, and often also in societies with simple delayed-return systems, one such overriding principle is that people are not entitled to accumulate movable property beyond what they need for their immediate use. They are morally obliged to share it.

For a Hadza, personal ownership of a second axe or a second shirt is unlikely to last for more than a few hours or, at most, a few days. Eventually endless demands will result in the additional possession being given away or gambled away if it cannot be concealed. The strong social assertion that it is morally unacceptable to accumulate personal property is, in the Hadza case at least, highly effective in dispersing such property widely through the community. There are several important consequences of the moral obligation to share. The first is obvious. In so far as movable property represents wealth, it prevents people from differentiating themselves according to the amount of wealth that they own. Second, it gives outsiders the impression that the Hadza are propertyless and impoverished and tends to reinforce prejudice against them (Woodburn 1988). Third, it greatly reduces the possibility of using property socially, of using it carefully to build ties, to meet obligations and commitments, to pay debts. Since it has to be disposed of quickly, it is not easy to plan its use. Fourth, it tends to depress production of tools and weapons and other portable possessions beyond those needed for immediate personal use.

Rights over meat, vegetable foods and other harvested resources

Very similar principles apply to food-sharing. Again, in general, food belongs initially to the person who has worked to obtain it, but should be shared if the person has obtained more than is needed for immediate use or if anyone else in the camp is hungry.

Special rules apply to large game animals which, if hit by more than one arrow or spear, may well be allocated to the owner of one of the missiles, often the first one to hit the animal. In the case of the !Kung, hunters may hunt using arrows belonging to other people and if an animal is killed using one of these arrows, its carcass belongs not to the hunter but to the owner of the arrow. A woman can own arrows obtained through *hxaro* exchange (see later discussion), and if a hunter kills an animal using one of these arrows the woman can become the owner of a carcass. The labour of the hunter is, in such a case, disregarded in the allocation of property rights. But this is, perhaps, not so serious a loss for the hunter as might appear. The economic and political advantages of ownership are few. The meat is obligatorily shared by men, women and children throughout the camp. The owner receives much the same amount of meat as anyone else and is given minimal social recognition as a donor (Marshall 1976: 295–311; Wiessner 1982).

The Hadza have similar rules requiring that the meat of large animals be shared without expectation of return, not given as a gift for which eventual reciprocation is expected (Woodburn 1982a: 441; see also Price 1975; Gibson, this volume). Small animals and birds, however, do not have to be widely shared. Although the carcass of a large animal belongs to the hunter, he is not entitled to dispose of it as he chooses. Indeed, he often plays little or no part at all in dismembering the carcass and allocating the joints. Most of the meat is shared widely among everyone in the camp. But some special joints of the best meat are treated differently: they are rigidly reserved for the initiated men's group. The Hadza are very explicit about the fact that this meat does not belong to the hunter. Formidable sanctions protect the exclusive right of the initiated men to this meat. This exclusive right is additionally protected by deception: the men say that the meat is God's meat, not theirs, and deny that they eat it.

Hunting skill and success are very variable: some men are much more successful than others. Among the Hadza, the solidarity of the initiated men's group is elaborately protected precisely at the point where it is most vulnerable — where property rights of skilled individuals might potentially be converted into power through control over desirable 'things'. Without these sanctions a skilled and successful hunter not obliged to share might instead use his regular access to and control over desirable joints of meat to acquire dependants. Property might be converted into individual power. So here we have, within an immediate-return system in which equal access to wild food and other resources and egalitarian sharing of the produce when it is brought into camp are given much emphasis, a quite different and elaborately sanctioned rule which emphasizes a sectional privilege, the privilege of the initiated men of the camp to consume this special meat jointly. Yet there is a paradox here: the limited sharing of the meat by the initiated men in a special religious context in a sense authorizes and legitimizes the general emphasis on secular sharing of the meat of large game animals. The rules of God's meat require that it be brought back to camp from the kill site and they provide a framework for bringing back the rest of the meat, and putting it at people's disposal.

In general, in hunter-gatherer societies with delayed-return systems, sharing seems, as one would expect, to operate differently. There is still often enough an obligation to share the meat of large game animals, especially if it cannot be stored or is difficult to store, but the extensive and more or less equal and undifferentiated sharing throughout the residential unit that we find among those with immediate-return systems does not seem to be usual. It does, however, occur among the Buid (Gibson, this volume). Sharing in delayed-return systems usually follows kinship and especially affinal links (see Altman and Peterson, this volume), and tends to create reciprocal indebtedness with individuals being obliged to do their share of hunting in order to be able to repay debts of meat. Transactions mark out status positions, in particular the rights of affines and of senior men. Since individuals apparently have room for manoeuvre to use property socially in ways that they choose, we would expect some stimulus to hunting and other productive activity.

Rights over certain capacities of people

In general, in societies with immediate-return systems, people hold few rights over the capacities of other people — over, for example, their hunting labour, their domestic labour, their sexual capacity, their reproductive capacity. Individual men decide for themselves if and when they will go hunting, rather than doing so at the behest of a household head, or a camp leader or anyone else. In these societies, parents are not entitled to, or able to, control the labour of their children or of their other kinsmen. Kinship is not, in general, a vehicle for control or for the allocation of rights in or over other people.

In contrast to the situation in societies with immediate-return systems, women in societies with simple delayed-return systems are treated as jural minors. Certain rights over them and over their labour are held by their male kin and are, when they marry, formally transferred to the husband and his kin. Typically, certain rights in a woman's sexuality, in her children, in her domestic labour and in the labour she devotes to productive tasks, are held by men and are not at her own disposal. These rights are jurally defined and subject to sanctions; they can be treated as a special type of property right. Linked with the transfer of these rights from the male kin of the bride to the husband and his kin, various commitments for the transfer of specific goods and services are entered into by the different males involved — such as the giving of bride wealth, dowry or other marriage payments, the rendering of bride-service by the bridegroom to his parents-in-law, and so on.

In immediate-return systems such notions, though not absent, are minimally developed. Women usually give themselves in marriage or, where they are given in marriage by their male kin, they have a clear and unambiguous right to refuse any particular marriage. Among the !Kung, pre-adolescent girls may be given in marriage, but the majority of such marriages apparently end in failure, and women choose their own spouses in subsequent marriages. In general in societies with immediate-return systems, women are not subject to the authority of their husbands. Usually women decide for themselves what productive work they will do, when they will do it and what the destination of the yield will be. It is not passed over to the husband's control. Men in these societies typically have no rights to dispossess their wives of their children if the marriage breaks down. Children usually remain with their mothers for their early years and then decide for themselves where they will live. In these circumstances we cannot talk of men possessing property rights over women's labour or over their reproductive capacity. However, we think that there is little doubt that in all of these societies much of men's behaviour can appropriately be interpreted as indicating a desire to increase control over women, and that much of women's behaviour can be interpreted as demonstrating resistance to the imposition of such control.

Bride-service, and what may loosely be called bridewealth, do exist in some societies with immediate-return systems, but they must be distinguished from the much more elaborate forms that are found in societies with delayed-return systems. Both among the !Kung and among the Hadza, it is customary for husband and wife to live, initially at least, in the same camp as the wife's parents. Among the Hadza the husband is said to bring his bow to the marriage, that is, to hunt for his wife and his parents-in-law. But, of course, meat that he obtains is in any case widely shared among all who are in the camp, unless the animal happens to be a small one, and his wife and parents-in-law are not greatly privileged in meat distribution. He should also give marriage prestations in the form of beads and trade goods to his mother-in-law. Among the Nharo, bride-service is de-emphasized in favour of *kamane*, minor bridewealth and childbirth prestations (Barnard 1980a:

121); similar forms of gift-giving, termed *kamasi*, occur among the !Kung in combination with bride-service (Lee 1984: 76). Small though these obligations are, there are no other relationships in these societies in which as much emphasis is placed on rights and obligations, on formal commitments, between specific individuals linked by kinship, marriage or contract. It seems to be generally true of societies with immediate-return systems that the closest approximations to formal obligation, to dependence, to control are found in the marriage nexus.

Rights over knowledge and intellectual property

Lowie describes a whole range of interesting instances in which exclusive individual rights are asserted over magical formulae, over titles, over the right to sing particular songs or to perform particular dances (Lowie 1928). Such individual rights are common among societies with simple delayed-return systems, hunter-gatherers and others, but seem not to be important in societies with immediate-return systems.

In some instances in delayed-return systems, such individual rights are held by individuals on behalf of, or in consequence of, their membership of a clan or lineage or other group and can only be transferred to other people who are also members of the same group. But in other instances, to which Lowie gives particular attention, they are held by individuals on their own behalf. Lowie (ibid.: 554) cites Holm on the Greenland Eskimo, who use ancient magical formulae in hunting and when in danger. Such formulae are said to be secret and owned strictly by individuals. They are transferred from one owner to another only in return for a substantial payment of such valuables as metal dart or lance points.

In immediate-return systems, knowledge is more often freely shared. The !Kung believe that individuals possess magical powers, but these are not secret and are said to be powers of healing, powers to drive away sickness and death; these powers derive from *n/um*, a magical force that is believed to be induced in the regular trance dances which the !Kung perform. A healer's *n/um* is warmed up and made available for curing, with the help of other dancers (mainly men) and of singers (mainly women). Then, in trance, the healer lays his hands on others in the community — men, women and children — to drive out illness, real and potential. To become a healer and to acquire *n/um*, he pays no fees to the healers who teach him, and once he is qualified he shares the benefit of his skills with the community in which he lives, without fee or expectation of reciprocation. *N/um* is personally owned but shared with the community in a way that is directly analogous to the personal ownership of a game animal's carcass and its sharing with the community (Lee 1984: 109–13).

Secret knowledge may, however, even in societies with immediate-return systems, be used to differentiate men and women. We have discussed earlier how, among the Hadza, the initiated men's group maintains important privileges over certain joints of meat of large game animals. These privileges are linked with exclusive possession of secret sacred knowledge and ritual to which all women and young men are denied access.

Transmission of property between people

In the course of this review of property rights, some mention has been made of the processes of transmission of property from one person to another. These are important for the discussion that follows, and rather more must be said, especially about societies with systems of immediate return.

We have seen that in societies with immediate-return systems sharing is overwhelmingly important. Indeed the size and structure of nomadic camp units is, in some cases at least, directly related to sharing practices (Woodburn 1972). The sharing systems we find are focused mainly on food. People who obtain more food than they can immediately consume are obliged to share it, to give it to other people and to do so without making the recipients indebted to them or dependent on them. Recipients are under no obligation to reciprocate though they too must, of course, share when they in their turn obtain more food than they can immediately consume. The problem is that sharing in practice does not balance out. Often only a small proportion of men are highly successful hunters who regularly kill large game animals. Time after time, donors are again donors and recipients are again recipients. The effect of obligatory sharing is to alienate from a skilled minority part of the yield of their labour in the interests of the majority, to deny to this minority the possibility of building power for themselves by converting recipients of their meat into dependants or followers (Woodburn 1982a: 441–2).

Among the Hadza, portable, personally-owned property — arrows, knives, stone pipes, beads, and so on — is transmitted between men mainly through a traditional gambling game called *lukucuko* which maintains a constant flow of such artefacts through men's hands. Men withdraw from the game any object for which they have an immediate use and stake or restake objects for which they have no immediate use. The effect of the game is to circulate artefacts, including some that are produced only in a few localities, all over Hadza country and to give people an opportunity of meeting their needs for artefacts they cannot make for themselves without entering into commitments to other people.

The !Kung distribute artefacts among themselves mainly in a quite different way, by the system of gift-giving mentioned earlier, called *hxaro* (Wiessner 1980; 1982; Lee 1984). The Nharo have a similar system which they call *//ai* (Barnard 1978: 625–7; 1980a: 121–2).

We will describe *hxaro* at rather greater length because it is important for the discussion that follows. Unlike Hadza gambling, *hxaro* is used to build relationships. Property is put to work explicitly to develop symmetrical ties of friendship between people.

The average person among the !Kung has sixteen *hxaro* partners with whom he or she exchanges personally-owned objects such as beads, arrows, clothing or pots, but not food. All personally-owned non-consumable items can enter the system. Gifts are given, often on request, and are then reciprocated after a delay of weeks or months.

A person's *hxaro* partners include most of his or her close kin — parents, children, siblings are all eligible as well as more distant kin. In general *hxaro* relationships are superimposed on kinship relationships. As in many other societies with immediate-return systems, kinship, by itself, implies little in the way of commitment (Woodburn 1979: 257–9). By giving property to each other as gestures of friendly intent, *hxaro* exchange partners build up selected kin relationships into more committed ones, some of which will be useful in providing access to groups and to the food resources of groups in areas other than one's own. Most personally owned possessions enter into *hxaro* but, according to Marshall (1976: 308), people do not come to depend on *hxaro* for access to the type of goods which are transmitted through it.

Hxaro has a number of distinctive characteristics that differentiate it from most systems of gift-giving described in the ethnographic literature and which, taken together, tend to identify it as a product of an immediate-return system. Little emphasis is placed on the goods themselves. People ask even for things they do not need in order to perpetuate the relationship. The goods given do not have to balance: little attention is given to parity of value. The amount given is likely to relate roughly to the amount available to the donor at the time. The exchange is non-competitive, and partners are not seeking to define their relative status on any basis other than an equal one. Men and women both take part in *hxaro*, and both have partners of both sexes. The nature of the objects given is not defined by the sex of the donor or of the recipient; men can give or be given women's aprons, and women can give or be given men's arrows (Wiessner 1982:71). A recipient of a *hxaro* gift often alters it, gives it a personal touch, before passing it on. But there seems to be no mystical notion that gifts embody the donor or that such embodiment compels reciprocation.

So here we have a system of exchange which, when superimposed upon a kinship system in which people are not, in general, linked to each other by binding relationships, creates bonds. Each individual develops bonds with many others of both sexes and such bonds are all of the same sort — simple, voluntary, non-competitive, symmetrical, contractual ties in which the giving of gifts opens the way for visiting and hospitality. Unlike exchanges in many other societies, they do not mark out or confirm the status of the participants: they do not, for example, establish that individual A is a male headman while individual B, with whom he transacts, is a subordinate male household head, or that individual Y is a mother's brother and that individual Z, with whom he transacts, is his sister's son. Nor, apparently, can they be used politically to gain influence or power or wealth. Everybody, male or female, young or old, has access to the system and participates in it. The objects used are made personally or obtained from other contractual partners or obtained from outsiders: they are specifically not obtained through non-*hxaro* ties with dependants — there are no dependants to provide them.

It is important that affines do not normally become *hxaro* partners (Wiessner 1982: 66). Affinity and *hxaro* (the major form of exchange) are seen as incompatible. People are said to feel that, if affines were to become *hxaro* partners, and if a dispute over *hxaro* broke out, there would be a danger of serious conflict between the kin of the husband and the kin of the wife (ibid.: 66). *Hxaro* is given to affines but only indirectly. A man gives *hxaro* gifts to his wife, and she gives *hxaro* gifts to her kin. Each spouse maintains a separate *hxaro* network and passes on the spouse's gifts to his or her *hxaro* partners, including close kin, in whatever way seems appropriate. We would suggest that there are two other relevant factors. Firstly, giving gifts to affines would tend to convert what is essentially a means of establishing a personal tie into a tie of alliance between sets of people: it would become politically charged. Secondly, giving *hxaro* to affines would run the risk of equating people and things, of matching in some way the gift of a woman to gifts of things. If either of these outcomes were to become systematically developed, the nature of !Kung society would probably be transformed.

Principles underlying the development of property rights

What are the principles underlying the development of property rights? Clearly they are many, but one particularly important starting point is as follows: it appears that all societies operate implicitly or explicitly on the principles that whatever I, as an individual, obtain from nature or make by myself using my own labour is residually recognized as in some sense my property, that is, it is mine unless some other explicit principle overrides this basic one and the yield of my labour is alienated from me. What a person obtains or makes in combination with others will be discussed later, but basically how the object concerned is treated will depend on the allocation of authority within the set of people working in combination. Typically, in all societies, the process of alienation deprives me of part (occasionally all) of the yield of my labour, and generally this process is not wholly voluntary, nor regarded by those whom it affects as wholly benevolent in spite of ideological elaborations which may make it appear to be so. It is backed by sanctions of varying severity. For an individual man, woman or child to be left unimpeded to enjoy the entire yield of his or her labour and to use it for self-chosen purposes is rare indeed. A hermit who manages to separate himself or herself from society and lives on his or her own for a while might qualify, as might an absolute ruler, but few others would. The usual position is that I give up part of the yield of my labour in accordance with specifiable rules or obligations while any residue not subject to such rules or obligations is mine.

What I as an individual obtain or make by myself — the berries I pick, the digging stick I make — is mine on the apparently universally recognized grounds that work (including the exercise of personal skill and creativity) transforms material things into property. And this ideology has been constantly mobilized through history by radical and revolutionary movements — both those on the right seeking to promote greater inequality (who campaign against obligatory sharing and other forms of egalitarian alienation of the yield of labour), and those on the left seeking to promote greater equality (who campaign against obligatory alienation by the powerful of part of the yield of the labour of the less powerful or of the impotent).

The same ideology may be mobilized to define rights over people. In English, we call the physiological processes which lead up to birth 'labour', perhaps partly in order to define a mother's rights over her children. More generally the labour of carrying a child in pregnancy, of giving birth to it, of suckling it and nurturing it after birth, identify the child with its mother and give her rights over it. A similar recognition, but often less explicit, probably exists at least residually in all societies. Certain procedures, for example payment of bridewealth, may be carried out which alienate many of the rights and allocate them to the father of the child or to other persons. When a boy is taken from his mother's care for initiation, it is widely the case that a set of ritual procedures is used to sever his ties with the mother. They are replaced with a new ritual birth into the community of men. Indeed among Australian Aborigines the outstanding characteristic of male secret ritual is its concern with such procreation (Hiatt 1971: 77). 'Men perform these ceremonies with aggressive secrecy because the rites are contrived affirmations of male priorities in areas where women are in a naturally strong position' (ibid.: 80).

Other forms of ritual labour are also ideologically powerful and their implications for rights over people and things are important. As Bern has pointed out and as Tonkinson confirms (this volume), the dominant ideology of Australian Aborigines asserts that all wild food resources are brought into existence through men's religious practice, through ritual labour, the 'work' of ritual. 'Women only collect what men's religious practice has made available' (Bern 1979: 125).

Thus far, in discussing a salient process in the establishment of property rights, a process which because it is based on an apparently universal ideology will have recurred repeatedly through history, we have rather artificially focused attention on the individual. As we shall see, application of labour by individuals and resulting residual property rights in the yields are very important in some hunter-gatherer societies, but we also need to consider what happens when individuals combine to produce a joint yield. Food produced jointly can be eaten at a communal meal or meals but is actually far more likely to be divided out among those who produced it. The type of joint labour that takes place in a Mbuti Pygmy communal net hunt for small game, in which those who join together to hunt do so voluntarily in an *ad hoc* fashion, involves immediate, more or less equal, sharing of the yield (Turnbull 1966: 154, 157–8; Woodburn 1980: 103). In other hunter-gatherer societies, where large game animals are hunted, they are, as Dowling points out (1968), usually allocated to one owner even when more than one individual has contributed to the death of the animal. If the animal is killed by a single arrow shot by a man who is not the owner of the arrow, the ownership of the animal is more likely to be allocated to the owner of the arrow than to the hunter. But whoever it is allocated to, the consistent point is that ownership is unlikely to be divided. Single owners are the norm. In terms of meat received, the allocation of ownership of the carcass may well make little or no difference. All the hunters are, of course, likely to get a share in the general meat distribution.

Both of these arrangements are quite different from the treatment of yields of agricultural cooperation within a household, where control of the annual cycle of agricultural work and of the yields which will be stored is typically in the hands of the household head. He directs not only his own labour but also the labour of his wife or wives, his children, and perhaps other kin as well. In societies with delayed-return systems, by far the most significant alienation of the yield of the labour of individuals typically takes place within the household.

If this approach is correct, then we can readily understand the widespread rule that while the hunted carcass of a large game animal is owned individually by the hunter, he is not able to use the meat for his own chosen purposes. Most of the meat is then alienated from him, with his consent, in accordance with a rival (and again probably universal, in the sense that it is found in some contexts in every society) ideology stressing egalitarian entitlement and the importance of levelling mechanisms. This procedure has something in common with redistributive taxation in Western society (Woodburn 1982a: 441–2). Naftali

Zengu, a Hadza man present at the London conference, spoke strongly
of this moral imperative to share.

The emphasis on individual ownership of spears, bows, arrows,
clothing and other such items, combined with the strong pressure not
to accumulate them but instead to share out any for which the individual has no immediate need, can be similarly explained. There are,
however, other explanations which may also be relevant or may be
treated as alternatives. A number of writers have stressed the link
between individual property and gift-giving. Lowie, writing sixty years
ago, and citing Koppers on the Yamana of Tierra del Fuego, claimed
that the existence of reciprocated gift-giving demonstrated the existence of individual property rights: 'There was . . . a pronounced tendency to make presents, whether of food, necklaces, slings, spears or
other implements; and acceptance involved the obligation of making a
suitable return gift. The very fact of this institution constitutes proof of
individual property rights' (Lowie 1928: 553).

Dowling suggests that the individual ownership that is allocated over
the carcass of a game animal is actually the right to distribute the meat
and to gain prestige from doing so. People compete for this privilege.
To allocate ownership to one person rather than to all those who
contributed to the death of the animal is a cultural technique for
limiting conflict in a potentially disruptive situation (Dowling 1968:
506). Leacock and Lee suggest that generally in nomadic hunter-
gatherer societies 'individual ownership forms the basis for individual
gift-giving and for inter-band exchange systems that make possible
farflung networks of reciprocity' (Leacock and Lee 1982: 9). More
recently Ingold (1986:228) writes as follows:

> . . . why should it be necessary for the custodianship of collective resources to
> be vested in particular persons? Why have notions of ownership at all? The
> answer . . . has to do with their function in creating and upholding a distinc-
> tion between the categories of givers and receivers, or granters and grantees.
> Without such a distinction, there can be no basis for the extension of generos-
> ity, nor for the influence or renown that flows from it. 'To give away', as I
> have noted elsewhere, 'one must first have, and others must not. A pretence
> of appropriation has therefore to be constructed ideologically, in order that it
> may be cancelled out socially' (Ingold 1980a: 160).

Ingold goes on to emphasize that concepts of individual ownership of
game animals prior to their distribution are particularly stressed — for
example by personal identification marks on arrows — among northern
hunters. Their dependence on hunted game is far greater than it is
among tropical hunters, where vegetable foods constitute a high proportion of the diet.

To discuss these explanations, sharing of game meat and gift-giving
of artefacts should be treated separately. Important as concepts of

individual property are in providing a basis for reciprocal gift-giving of artefacts, it is doubtful whether they can be derived from this function. In some societies with immediate-return systems (for example, the Hadza), there is no system of institutionalized reciprocal gift-giving and yet individual ownership is still stressed. For sharing, which unlike gift-giving is characteristic of all immediate-return systems, the argument seems to be far less strong. In sharing, the individual donor does not, at least in theory, acquire any greater claim on future shares than he would if he had not acted as donor. So the public identification of donor as owner of what is subsequently shared cannot be explained in terms of a requirement to identify a future recipient. A good deal of evidence has accumulated to suggest that the role of successful hunter, of donor of meat to be shared, is culturally de-emphasized (Woodburn 1982a: 440–1). The owner of a kill should *not* obtain prestige through distributing it (Lee 1984: 151–7). It would seem strange to argue that individual ownership exists to define and to stress the role of donor, while at the same time other cultural practices seem designed to negate the importance of donation and the identification of the donor.

An additional problem is that a number of important personally-owned possessions are not normally given as gifts or shared. A clear instance is a Hadza man's hunting bow. Usually a Hadza man makes a bow for himself (with the help of his wife who makes the bowstring), uses it until it cracks or becomes otherwise ineffective, and then throws it away. Bows cannot be used as stakes in *lukucuko* gambling and are rarely given away, exchanged or otherwise transferred, so it can hardly be said that individual ownership here exists in order to make them available for exchange.

Ideology and the development of delayed-return systems

In this review of property rights we have so far concentrated on describing and discussing the situation in societies with immediate-return systems and have said rather little about property in societies with delayed-return systems. The aim has been to provide a kind of base line, a description and discussion of property rights in examples of societies in which such rights are less elaborated than in any other human societies.

The evolutionary status of societies with immediate-return systems has recently become somewhat controversial. It has been suggested that their egalitarian organization may be a product of their encapsulation by politically dominant neighbouring agricultural societies, and that the egalitarian values are oppositional, developed in opposition to political domination. A chapter in the companion volume to this one by one of the present authors argues that in the light of the available evidence this is implausible, and that hunter-gatherers with immediate-return organization are likely to have existed in the past as well as the present (Woodburn 1988). Assuming, then, that immediate-return organization is not just a relatively recent devolved form of organization, how plausible is it to consider such organization as in some way ancestral to simple forms of delayed-return organization such as those which are characteristic of the Australian Aborigines, or of some of the northern hunters? We think it is plausible.[1]

In an earlier paper, one of us has argued that historically there are likely to have been changes in both directions between immediate and delayed return, rather than a simple progression from one to the other (Woodburn 1980). But in the development of delayed return from immediate return 'the routes . . . are likely to be many and varied but one broad highway among them lies . . . in the intensification of control by men of rights over women who are to be given in marriage' (ibid.: 111). Any explanation for such a transition is almost certain to be multifactorial. It is also likely that the transition will have been made many times and in different ways. All we can do here is to look at some of the social and ideological factors that are likely to be relevant.

Socially, the differences between immediate- and delayed-return organization are centred on the development of corporate households, of clans, lineages and other extra-domestic forms of social grouping, and, above all, of a range of varied, committed, binding social relationships of kinship or of contract in which the participants have formal obligations to each other and are, in some sense, dependent on each other. The development of such groupings and such relationships is connected with the control and allocation of assets, usually in the form of delayed yields on labour (Woodburn 1980; 1982a).

To understand possible transitions from immediate return, in which none of these organizational forms exist, to delayed return we have to look carefully at control of women by men, especially middle-aged men, and at control of young men by middle-aged men. In delayed-return systems women and young men are dependent to a significant degree, ideologically or materially or both, on middle-aged men. The process of development of such control and dependence seems, especially in the Australian case, to work mainly from the top down, with ideological domination well developed but with economic and political control restricted to a few limited contexts (Hiatt 1971; 1986; Bern 1979; Tonkinson, this volume). Interestingly, and perhaps surprisingly, there are consistent indications that men may more readily be able to

---

1. The legitimacy of such evolutionary speculation may be queried by some social anthropologists. In reply all we can do is to draw attention to the useful contribution made to modern social anthropology by the long-standing speculative debate on the evolution of the state.

control women's destination in marriage than to control the yields of women's productive labour.

To open this possible route to delayed return, we would expect an onslaught on the considerable autonomy which women and young men enjoy in immediate-return systems. The process involves increasing incorporation of women and young men into committed kinship and affinal relationships and into structured kinship groups in which ideological control is vested predominantly in older men. This development allows increasing control by the older men over their junior female kin, who are then bestowed in marriage to other men. Sons-in-law or prospective sons-in-law provide labour for their fathers-in-law. Ideologies of domination are developed, especially in ritual contexts, in which the substantial real control that in immediate-return systems women enjoy over their own sexual and reproductive capacities and their own labour is increasingly denied. The end of this process, which is not realized in some of the simpler delayed-return systems such as those of the Australian Aborigines, comes when women and young men are fully and effectively incorporated into household units with household heads who exercise control over the yield or a significant part of the yield of women's and young men's labour.

Not enough attention has been paid to the way in which binding relationships are developed between close kin and affines. Without committed relationships there can be no real control. Committed relationship seem often to be developed through two related forms of ideological elaboration which deny the autonomy of participants. The first of these is the notion that people are mystically embodied in things, and things in people. Such a notion is fundamental to many systems of property rights and is particularly clear in the case of Australian Aboriginal land rights. The effect of such mystical involvement is not merely to tie people to things, but to tie people to other people through things. Mauss's work on the gift and Parry's recent development of Mauss's ideas explore some of the ramifications of these notions (Mauss 1954; Parry 1986).

The second form of ideological elaboration denies the autonomy of the participants more directly. In this form people are believed to be involved mystically in other people and such involvement, intentional or unintentional, affects their health or welfare. The power to bless or to curse someone, the power to bewitch them, and the power to contaminate them through pollution are all examples of such elaboration. The particular forms in which such beliefs are expressed vary widely from society to society, but what seems to be constant is that increasing commitment to other people in binding relationships is commonly linked to ideologies of mystical dependence. Kratz's chapter in the present volume gives some particularly clear cases. In immediate-return systems, such ideologies may already be present in simple forms in those relationships in which some commitment does exist. Here the Hadza data are relevant: a man is mystically involved in his wife's reproduction while she is mystically involved in his hunting. An additional ideological repertoire is probably less important in the transition to delayed return than in the operation of delayed-return systems. Things come to stand for people and their capacities. Cows stand for people and their capacities in sacrifice, bridewealth for women and their capacities in marriage transactions, bloodwealth for people and their capacities in compensation transactions for death or injury. Whatever meanings are attributed to these representations in particular societies, there is no doubt at all that they allow for far greater control and manipulation of people and their capacities than is possible in immediate-return systems.

In his discussion of the origin of the state, de Heusch plausibly suggested that in Africa 'sacred kingship . . . precedes the state and makes it possible' (1981: 24). The sacralization of leadership breaks the control of kinship over all social relations and permits the emergence of powerful centralized authorities. Our argument here has similarities with this in an entirely different context. For delayed-return kinship obligations and kinship groups to develop, female autonomy and the autonomy of young men must be broken: ideological breach seems often to be crucial. After the ideological destruction of autonomy, and the establishment of ideological domination, political and economic domination may follow. There is nothing inevitable about the process. In practice, political and economic domination may not follow, but the ground has been prepared in a way which permits their emergence.

Evans-Pritchard (1940: 89), writing about Nuer pastoralists in a much-quoted passage, suggests that

> material objects are chains along which social relationships run, and the more simple is a material culture the more numerous are the relationships expressed through it. . . . . Herds of cattle are nuclei around which kinship groups are clustered and the relationships between their members operate through cattle and are expressed in terms of cattle. A single small artefact may be a nexus between persons, e.g. a spear which passes from father to son by gift or inheritance is a symbol of their relationship and one of the bonds by which it is maintained. Thus people not only create their material culture and attach themselves to it, but also build up their relationships through it and see them in terms of it.

Evans-Pritchard's characterization is right for the Nuer and is right, too, for delayed-return hunter-gatherers including the Australian Aborigines. People build elaborate relationships with each other through symbolic elaboration of ties with and through 'things', especially, in the hunter-gatherer cases, with and through artefacts and land. These ties include various forms of identification, but property rights, with their rules of inclusion and exclusion, are of central importance.

But Evans-Pritchard was wrong, quite wrong, if he thought that symbolic elaboration is something to do with having a simple material culture. People in immediate-return systems, users of an even simpler material culture than the Nuer one, do not symbolically elaborate the relations between people and things, and between people and people through things, to any great extent except in a few restricted contexts usually linked with marriage and more generally with relations between the sexes.

Our argument is that to understand the development of political and economic complexity in hunter-gatherer societies, more attention should be given to those ideological factors which bear on crucial social relationships. A number of the chapters in this volume, even those written with very different intentions, have important things to say on this issue.

Part 1

Property rights

2. Property, practice and aboriginal rights among Quebec Cree hunters

Colin Scott

Introduction

Western categories of property are deeply implicated in anthropological perception of institutions and ideologies in hunting societies. This is apparent not just in the lineament of concepts, but in the passion they provoke. Contentious issues of Western culture's self-definition and direction are involved. Depending on context and point of view, property is seen as oppressive or liberating; as the precondition for altruistic exchange, or the privileged instrument of private accumulation. The presence, absence or kind of property in hunting societies speaks to our vision of what is humanly possible.

We would not expect to expunge such categories and oppositions as 'property', 'usufruct', and so on, of their Western socio-historical connotations. But neither would anthropologists wish to underestimate the extent to which their conceptions of these categories can be transformed through interaction with other traditions. However strewn with contradiction, this is the universal process of achieving transcultural communication. It is a process which characterizes not just professional anthropological discourse, but that of other actors too. Discourse between systems is urgently important to contemporary hunters. Lacking coercive defences, their aboriginal rights and institutions will gain recognition and consent in state systems, or will cease to exist.

In this chapter, I examine the categories used by Cree hunters of northern Quebec in speaking about the rights of individuals and groups to various objects and resources. This is done against the backdrop of some pertinent aspects of Euro-Canadian ideology, law and anthropology. It will be apparent that Cree rights are more explicitly political, in the sense of pertaining to relationships among persons, than property is admitted to be in Western systems. 'Property' is an acknowledged outcome of social and ecological practice, not a thing unto itself. The various criteria by which control of objects and resources is deemed legitimate, and hence socially sustainable, will be examined.

 I go on to discuss two periods of articulation between Cree and state systems of property: a period of increased participation by governments in the administration of 'registered traplines' in the 1930s and 1940s; and the contemporary native claims period, marked by the implementation of the James Bay Northern Quebec Agreement (Canada 1975).[1]

Concepts of property

A key issue is whether property is to be regarded merely as control of a piece of the material world, or more fundamentally as a system of relationships among persons. While social scientists may readily choose the latter alternative, the popular ideological conception of property, at least in capitalist societies, conforms more nearly to the former — property in its ideal sense connotes the absolute control, use and enjoyment of things. This view is consistent with the preoccupation of Euro-Canadian administrations in the past to obtain 'clear title' to Crown lands through the blanket extinguishment of aboriginal title via 'Indian Treaties' — a preliminary, in many cases, to selling or granting lands into private, non-native hands.

In practice, as reflected by more precise legal codifications, specific property is anything but absolute and exclusive. It is subject to a variety of limitations and claims by others. Legal specialists have fragmented the unitary conception of property into diverse 'bundles of rights', such that a thing can be 'owned' in different ways by a number of persons (Grey 1980). Property in modern capitalism lacks a necessary or unitary reference to 'things'. It has become progressively fragmented by successive contractual arrangements among legal persons, and there are no longer viable criteria for classifying its discontinuous usages as separate from other rights. Indeed, Grey argues that the law could now do just as well without the category of property, a state of affairs which would tend to unmask and undermine the moral basis of capitalism from within, revealing capitalist property for what it really is — 'a web of state-enforced relations of entitlement and duty *between persons*, some

    1. This work has benefited from the generous support of the Social Sciences and Humanities Research Council of Canada, the Direction Générale de l'Enseignement Supérieur of Quebec, the Programme in the Anthropology of Development at McGill University, and the National Museum of Civilization, Ottawa. Many individuals, at the Departments of Anthropology of McGill and McMaster Universities, the Cree community of Wemindji, the Grand Council of the Crees of Quebec/Cree Regional Authority, the Fourth International Conference on Hunting and Gathering Societies and elsewhere, have contributed through conversation to ideas developed in this chapter. Particular thanks are due to Richard Salisbury and Harvey Feit, for helpful discussion and support.

assumed voluntarily and some not' (ibid.: 79, emphasis in original).

If legal property in capitalist states has fragmented into disparate bundles of rights, it suggests that aboriginal rights are hardly an all-or-nothing proposition. State recognition of aboriginal title, in the sense of absolute and exclusive rights to traditional lands, would be politically unrealistic. But non-native 'sovereign' and 'private' interests in many capitalist systems have, by the same token, failed to disencumber themselves of aboriginal rights and claims. Native leaders and lawyers are endeavouring to 'rebundle' the rights which historically have so severely excluded indigenous nations from control of resources. The implications of this endeavour are most dramatic in northern North America, where aboriginal rights were never surrendered or extinguished. And even where central governments allegedly 'cleared title' to native lands through historical treaties, a variety of unextinguished rights are argued to have 'flowed through' treaty processes (Hutchins 1987).

Property in Cree law

In Cree, there is no substantive category either equivalent or similar to 'property' in English, and no verb 'to own'. To designate objects or resources as belonging to individuals or groups in some sense, possessive pronouns are joined to the names of the pertinent objects (e.g. *utaschiim*, 'his/her hunting grounds'); or else the verb *iiyaaw* ('he/she has') is used. In hunting, 'I' speak of 'my' personal possessions such as clothing or tools simply as *niichaakwaanim* ('my things'), or *niitaapich-taaun* ('my equipment', 'things I use').

One can identify three legitimating principles in the Cree system of property, which are very general among hunters. First, a household has certain primary or initial rights in relation to the product of its own labour — the tools and clothing it manufactures, the animals it kills and processes, and so on. High value is placed on the household's ability, through its internal division of labour, to produce the essentials of life, to make decisions about where and when to deploy its efforts, and to decide the specific recipients of gifts. Sahlins (1974) has suggested that this relative autonomy of the household is internal to the structure of societies which practice generalized reciprocity, and one line of tension which potentially develops is that between the interests of the household and those of the larger collectivity.

A second balancing principle in the Cree case refers to the rights of the collectivity, to the effect that no household may use, restrict, or accumulate resources and products in ways prejudicial to the interests of others; and as a corollary, households are expected to cooperate in particular productive contexts when collective benefit results. The

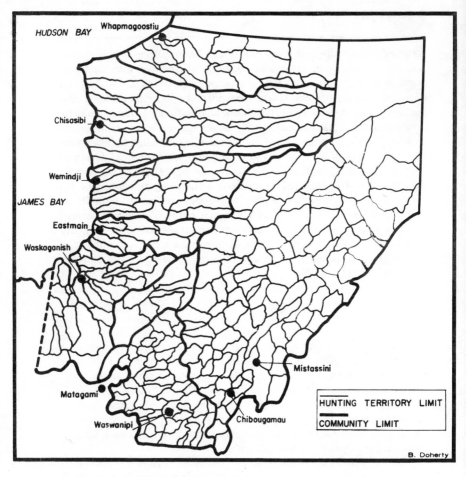

Map 2.1: Approximate hunting territories of James Bay Cree hunters.
Source: Adapted with permission from H.A. Feit, 'Hunting and the quest for power', in R.B. Morrison and C.R. Wilson (eds.), *Native peoples: the Canadian experience*, Toronto: McClelland and Stewart, 1986.

institution of hunting territories and stewards is legitimized in these terms.

The third principle is a simultaneous guarantee of the rights of households individually and collectively. It entails restrictions on the power of territory stewards who might wish to limit the use of resources to derive disproportionate benefit for themselves or immediate kin. This is the principle that ungarnered resources, 'the land', cannot be alienated for the private benefit of any privileged individual or sector of the community.

The basic unit of land tenure among eastern Cree is a hunting ground or territory (Figure 2.1) used by an extended kin network comprising as few as two but as many as a dozen households in an actual production unit. As a production unit, it is permeable, often incorporating people who are primarily or seasonally affiliated with other grounds. The leader of the group is the steward of such a ground. The relationship of the leader (*uuchimaau*) to his land (*utaschiim*, *-aschii-/* 'hunting ground', 'land', 'world', 'creation') centres on his relationship to the animals he uses from it, and to his fellow humans. *Uuchimaau* ('leader', 'boss', 'governor') refers in the subsistence context to the leader who looks after the ground or territory used by a group. The leader's activity is commonly expressed by the verb *tapaiitam* ('he decides', 'controls' or 'is in charge of it', or more literally, 'he matches it to his thinking'), a finding which also pertains to neighbouring Algonquian groups (see Vincent and Mailhot 1982).

Control is not construed as the unilateral extension of the leader's will to other beings. To be 'human' (*iiyiyuu*) connotes a sacred relationship of sharing and respect with human and non-human creatures of the world. *Iiyiyuu* in its broadest sense includes all living creatures, or 'persons' (and in its narrowest, excludes humans who are ethnically non-Indian). The leader must respect the intentions, needs, and capacities of other 'persons' — human, animal, and spiritual — if mind and world are to 'match'. By recognizing and fostering correct relations among 'persons', the leader enjoys the authority to 'decide'. *Vis-à-vis* animal populations, this responsibility includes knowledge about how many animals should be harvested by the group and at what places and times, to maximize social benefit, while maintaining optimum ecological conditions (Feit 1978; 1983; Scott 1983a). *Vis-à-vis* fellow human beings, this responsibility entails the generous sharing of opportunities to hunt. These are key legitimating criteria for the control that the 'hunting boss', or *nituuhuu uuchimaau*, exercises with respect to the land belonging to him and a network of extended kin. These criteria are heavily underscored in Cree ritual and myth, which in local knowledge encode the interdependence of sharing and effective game management (Scott 1983a).

Stewardship is typically agnatically inherited, but may also be inherited from affines. The essential criterion is that the inheritor be judged ready, in terms of knowledge and developed relationships, to assume the role. The feature of inheritance, and the fact that bilingual Cree often gloss *uuchimaau* as both 'boss' and 'owner', may have led some ethnographers to see a privatized right where collective rights are really fundamental. Cree have sometimes promoted the 'private property' analogy in speech with white men because they have perceived the European property fetish, and have hoped to improve the sacredness and legitimacy — in non-native eyes — of the Cree institution.

Internally, the Cree institution is such that if the hunting boss fails as a steward or sharer of resources, others will soon use his grounds without permission and coordination. His ability to manage resources will decline, and another territory boss will sooner or later be recognized by the hunting group and by the wider Cree community.

Chishaamintuu, the Creator, is directly implicated in these matters. Control of territory by stewards is legitimate in as much as it fosters relationships among human and non-human persons which are sacred according to the conditions of Creation. In this ultimate sense, Cree state that no one except the Creator can own the land; or that no one, *not even* the Creator, owns land.

Earlier, I referred to certain 'primary' rights in products enjoyed by virtue of households' productive efforts and autonomy. The fact is that these rights are not exclusive, and do not absolve the household in question from the imperative of sharing. Because the management and appropriation of resources is a complex matter which draws on extensive personal as well as collective inputs, it is generally recognized that the household's success seldom depends simply on its own efforts. Stewards and other senior hunters, in particular, share their more developed relationship with animals so that all hunting households may enjoy greater success.

Correspondingly, the rights of direct producers are shared at each stage of finding, killing and preparing animals. A hunter who has found a bear den or beaver lodge, for example, may 'give' those animals to other hunters to actually kill. Or a hunter who has killed an important large animal frequently gives it intact to a fellow hunter, who is then in charge of distributing the animal just as though the recipient himself had killed it. Especially when the animal is of high sacred status, as in the case of a bear, the recipient is likely to be an elder, so the giving is a gesture which underlines the acknowledged importance of elders as stewards.

To speak of Cree property, then — even 'communal' property — would be to gloss over the essential dynamic of the system. Customary rights in the land, living resources and products may be specified, but these relate to the technical and political relations of managing and sharing resources — resources in which no one, in the last analysis, retains exclusive or absolute rights.

At the same time, this system entails specific criteria for inclusion within the network of human beings who practice it. Cree, in their own view, legitimately exercise and maintain their rights as against alien claimants who fail to conform to criteria of sharing and stewardship. Historically, when white men have apparently conformed to tenets of reciprocity, and contributed to stewardship of resources, they have been accorded a measure of legitimate participation in the Cree system. Thus when white men fail these standards, evasion or opposition is deemed legitimate by Cree.

'Registered traplines' and the 'private property' analogy

By British Royal Charter, the Hudson's Bay Company was granted proprietary and gubernatorial rights over a vast expanse of subarctic North America from 1670 until Canadian Confederation in 1867. Subsequent to Confederation, Canadian federal and provincial governments, through a succession of constitutional and legislative instruments, assumed and partitioned sovereignty and proprietorship of regions occupied by the Cree and other subarctic hunters. These prerogatives over 'Crown lands' are 'burdened' by aboriginal title, until extinguished by treaty.

Until the twentieth century, these facts appear to have had limited relevance to the customary land tenure practices of Crees. For the eastern Cree region, there is little evidence that the Hudson's Bay Company was materially capable of intervening in the administration of Cree lands, except perhaps in the narrow environs of the coastal trading posts. Nor did the assumption by Canadian and Quebec governments of Crown lands after Confederation substantively impinge on Cree control of the tenure system.

Archival history (Francis and Morantz 1983) as well as oral history and myth suggest that the Cree attempted to incorporate Hudson's Bay Company traders as allies and partners in reciprocity. These strangers were accorded a measure of legitimacy by Cree as leaders in trade, albeit localized to trading posts and ships. But perceived non-egalitarian attributes also made white men into symbols of behaviour identifiable as sub-human and monstrous. Such symbolic practices (discussed in Scott 1983b) served to demarcate and insulate forest Cree social relations from exploitative premises, and similar mythical production has occurred whenever white men have threatened to impinge directly on Cree hunting lands, even up to the present.

It was not until the 1930s that Canadian provincial and federal governments became significant actors in the administration of hunting grounds around James Bay. Invasion by white trappers had led by the 1930s to depletion of beaver and other fur stocks. White trappers were heedless of Indian territories and, unlike Crees, adopted the near-sighted strategy of cleaning out whole territories, with no need or intention of returning to the same area. The Indian response was to trap out first, so that white trappers would get only what was left by the indigenous owners of the grounds. The incidence of uninvited presence of Indians on the grounds of others is also reported, as resources grew scarcer and the territory system became unworkable. The result was a general collapse of the beaver and marten populations, which sometimes meant starvation for those groups who depended primarily on beaver for food as well as fur for trade. There is broad agreement among Hudson's Bay Company managers, Indian Affairs officials, missionaries and ethnographers of the period about this account of events (for reports on this evidence, see Feit 1984; Scott, Morantz and Morrison 1986).

The government response issued from a discourse involving government and fur company officials, missionaries, Indian leadership and anthropologists. Early ethnographers of Algonquian societies (such as Speck 1915; 1923; Speck and Eiseley 1939; J. Cooper 1939) observed that families had property rights in 'family' hunting grounds, that they 'farmed' and conserved the beaver and that territories were probably aboriginal.

In the policy domain, a broad consensus developed that the prohibition of trapping by white men, permitting the restoration of the indigenous tenure system, would be in the best interests of both native people and the conservation of a 'provincial' fur resource from which governments derived royalties. This led, through the 1930s and 1940s, to the establishment of official beaver preserves in northern jurisdictions and the recognition of Indian hunting territories as 'registered traplines'. From the central government's point of view, these remained 'Crown lands', with indigenous 'owners' and their hunting partners enjoying a delegated usufruct at best.

In the reserves established around James Bay, for a period of several years any trapping of beaver was put off-limits to all — native and non-native. When the populations had regenerated, Indian hunters would have their traditional territories registered with provincial authorities, and these territories would be protected by law against intrusion by any white man or unauthorized Indian.

A succinct version of these measures, from the white administrators' point of view, is included in a letter from a deputy minister of Indian Affairs to the Royal Canadian Mounted Police in 1942 (Canada n.d.):

When an area is set aside by the Province for the exclusive use of the Indians and marked by our Branch for development as a Fur Preserve, the first step is to divide the area into band or tribal areas generally called sections. These tribal areas are further divided into family hunting areas which we call districts and one Tallyman is placed in charge of each district and charged with the following duties:

1. Count and mark — with special metal markers . . . every colony of beaver on his district
2. Indicate the location of the colonies on a map and report the location to the Supervisor
3. Report promptly to the Supervisor the presence of white trappers on his district
4. Report any case of encroachment of other Indians on his district
5. Put up posters throughout his district

When it is borne in mind that the Tallyman is the head of a family; that a district is a family trapping ground; that a section is the area trapped over by a whole tribe or band and that all boundaries are laid out by the Indians themselves, it is apparent that we have not only adhered strictly to Indian custom but have actually improved on it since, through our Supervisor, we have maps of the districts and written records, which we can use to settle future disputes over trapping grounds.

This official model failed to take into account the way that Cree land rights flowed in the exchange system. Within the Cree system, there are a range of land-use options between two poles. There are hunters who mainly confine their activities to a single customary territory, within which they rotate portions as game management requires. As an intermediate strategy, such hunters exchange hunting rights with other such families at certain times. Finally there are hunters who are exceptionally mobile, exercising links through kin and friends to hunt far and wide. Turner and Wertman's (1977) analysis shows that this flexibility is inherent in the kinship system of a closely related Algonquian group, a system which is indefinitely incorporative of both agnates and affines at the level of the production group.[2]

The poles of local affiliation and wider mobility both pertain to a unitary Cree system. Most hunters practise variations between the two poles, that is, they have a customary territory but also hunt extensively elsewhere during certain seasons, years or periods in their lives. Any effective restriction to the localized pole of use and occupancy would eventually violate the principle of equitable distribution of hunting opportunities.

The government model assumed that hunters should return perennially to their assigned registered traplines, where government officers issued them beaver quotas based on the tallyman's count of lodges. This assumption arose partly from administrators' tendency to conceive of these grounds as a Cree simile of property, and partly from their need for a bureaucratic image of control. Cree hunters worked around the rigidities of the system, either by gaining approval from white authorities to trap elsewhere from time to time, or by hunting as they would normally have done anyway, while ensuring that reported kills and tallies conformed to what was officially required.

The participation of state authorities was legitimate, from the Cree standpoint, in as much as it promoted stewardship of resources by controlling outside competition. At the same time, sustained functional dissonance between the government model and Cree practice was possible over most of Cree lands until the 1970s, because policing by non-native wildlife officers was a rarity. Non-native authorities adopted the old colonial expedient of exercising influence via indigenous leaders.

2. Relations between Algonquian kinship systems and tenure practices are addressed in Turner and Wertman (1977) and Sieciechowicz (1983).

Property and the Algonquian hunting territories debate

In academic arenas, the claim for the aboriginality of Algonquian territories was interpreted as a challenge to the evolutionist view that hunting societies were based in communal property. Leacock (1954) and Murphy and Steward (1956), among others, argued instead that private territories had developed — or were in the process of developing — only in the context of commodity production.

The characterization of Algonquian territories as 'private' bears some relation to surface appearances, but not to the underlying principles and actions which govern the Cree territory system. To be sure, some ethnography of the period explicitly recognized that Cree/Montagnais/Naskapi 'ownership' differed fundamentally from its European 'analogues' (see, for example, Lips 1947: 427–38). As Tanner (1986) points out, the Algonquian 'family hunting territory' was never an instructive test for the Marxist theory of evolution in property, because it was never sufficiently clear what kind of 'property' or what kind of territory holding 'family' one was speaking of.

Later ethnography leads to the conclusion that relations between eastern Cree trappers remained cooperative and egalitarian, and that territories never became privatized, notwithstanding fur production for trade (Rogers 1963; Tanner 1979; Feit 1979; Scott 1979; 1983a). Indeed, if one takes account of the full range of production processes in which coastal Cree hunters engage, it is where communal organization is most highly developed that the territory system reaches a climax of technical, social and ritual integration. This finding is independent of whether land-based production results in a marketable commodity (Scott 1986).

The heat generated in academic debate, it seems, was mostly symptomatic of the ideological importance of private property in Euro-North America. The significance of the 'private property' analogy in the policy arena related equally to this ideological circumstance. If Indians were seen as aboriginal proprietors of private grounds, 'farmers' of the beaver, it might enhance the legitimacy of their territories in the eyes of Euro-Canadian policy-makers and administrators. Consistent with anthropology's separation of 'pure' from 'applied' research, the theoretical implications were unacknowledged in the scholarly publications of Speck, Cooper and others, despite their policy involvement (Feit 1986).

Property in the aboriginal claims era

In the 1970s, aboriginal rights litigation and negotiations between Cree and the Governments of Quebec and Canada were precipitated by large-scale hydroelectric development at James Bay, culminating in the

James Bay and Northern Quebec Agreement (JBNQA) (Canada 1975).
The history and specifics of this process have been presented in detail
elsewhere (Feit 1980; 1982; 1984; LaRusic 1979; Salisbury 1986); here I
will focus narrowly on the implications for the property system of the
Cree.

Even where claims and negotiations lead to legal and/or legislative
codification of aboriginal rights by state institutions, a distinction between aboriginal rights and rights in native custom is important. The
description of Cree rights and practices given earlier suggests how
difficult codification by an alien legal tradition would be — as difficult
as adequate ethnography, with the risk of freezing what is really a
subtle and dynamic social process. Moreover, the rights which natives
and non-natives contest in aboriginal claims negotiations — for example, subsurface mineral rights, social programmes — may have no
specific precedents in native custom. Aboriginal rights are intersystemic and highly contested; rights in native custom are intrasystemic
and more stable. Aboriginal rights, then, are not the straightforward
translation of native customary rights into rights before the state.

Still, aboriginal rights and rights in native custom are inseparable in
the process of state-level recognition. There are two aspects to this.
First, the perceived legitimacy of aboriginal claims depends on the
demonstrable existence of rights and institutions in native custom,
either in the present, or at some time in the past. Second, interpretations of aboriginal rights involve analogies between rights in native
custom and rights bundled in our Euro-Canadian common law tradition — title in fee simple, usufruct, *profit à prendre*, sovereign jurisdiction, and so on — as courts and policy-makers strive to reconcile
aboriginal rights with European legal precedent. The ever-unfinished
analogies linking state and aboriginal systems are fundamental; they
are the discourse of institutional accommodation, to the extent that
subjects on both sides consent to terms. The separation of cultural
contexts is, at the same time, ensured through the negotiation and
exchange of rights.

The cultural relativism implicit in contracts between indigenous and
immigrant nations, together with the analogous interpretation of native
rights and institutions, establish an inherent link to anthropology as
scientific authority for such premises and interpretations. In litigation
over the James Bay hydro development, ethnological evidence about
Cree reliance on subsistence resources and the continued viability of
the territory system in game management helped to establish the
legitimacy of Cree claims. It was also key in securing the cooperation of
federal and provincial bureaucrats with this area of Cree self-
government, during negotiation of the JBNQA and its implementation
(Feit 1980; 1982; 1984). By the same token, 'acculturative' models were
exploited by opponents of the Cree, the suggestion being that the more

native people can be shown to be like Euro-Canadians, the fewer are the special rights that they enjoy.[3]

The legal composition of rights in land involves a complex bundling and partitioning under the James Bay Agreement. Both 'property' and 'governmental' rights are affected.[4] By the terms of the JBNQA, the external administrative apparatus for registered traplines, developed in the 1930s and 1940s, was largely undone. Primary rights of managing wildlife resources reverted to the traditional Cree stewards of hunting territories. The JBNQA recognizes the authority of Cree stewards and territories, but leaves their selection and definition to Cree communities. A series of bureaucratic articulations between hunters and central governments have been developed for management issues that transcend the local level (Feit 1979).

Fee-simple-style ownership by Cree communities applies only to very small tracts (so-called Category I lands) in the immediate vicinity of permanent settlements. On roughly 30 per cent of their traditional land (Category I and II lands), the Quebec Crees have exclusive rights to wildlife and other subsistence-related resources, and over the remainder of that range (Category III lands), they retain exclusive rights to some resources, and preferential rights to all others (Figure 2.2). Within this regime, the Cree retain undiminished rights to subsistence and traditional resources except on lands physically required for development; otherwise, it is unlikely that the Agreement would have been politically acceptable to Cree. The Cree did not retain subsurface rights, and in lieu of rights to royalties on industrially exploited resources, they accepted a cash settlement which, added to other compensation monies, amounted to a total of C$135 million. Compensation paid pursuant to negotiations since 1975 has increased that figure significantly.

The Quebec government, under the JBNQA, has rights of servitude and development which vary by land category, subject to certain

3. Native groups whose cultural circumstances have changed radically during the 'contact' period are, of course, the more threatened by this misuse of the acculturation model. They respond that the historical origin of their rights is clear, and that these rights have survived social change, as rights among the immigrant majority have done. Native groups who have been able to demonstrate continuities in indigenous institutions have used these facts as a political and legal resource, but seek to negotiate definitions of rights before the state which are not tied to static definitions of their social systems.

4. The distinction between rights of 'property' and rights of 'government' refers to practice in the Euro-Canadian tradition, but is somewhat artificial from the standpoint of many indigenous social systems, including that of the Cree. Under the standard-formula Indian Treaties signed between 1850 and 1923, the Crown's preoccupation was to obtain clear title to aboriginal lands. Rights of self-government, at least on lands reserved for Indians, were never explicitly extinguished. Native leaders therefore assert that indigenous nations, both signatories and non-signatories of Treaties, have never surrendered their rights of self-government. Self-government (to include control of a land base) has come to be regarded by native leadership and many observers of aboriginal rights issues as more fundamental than property *per se* (Asch 1984).

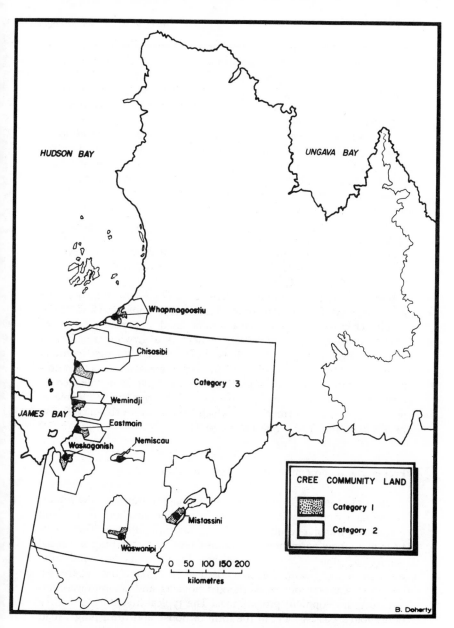

Map 2.2: Division of Cree lands under the JBNQA.

controls, safeguards and compensation. Obviously, the right to sponsor and promote industrial development results in the physical alienation of some hunting lands. In these cases, the Cree are entitled to land
replacement and/or compensation of various kinds for loss of resources
or injury to way of life.

Cree political leaders and non-native governments consented to an
agreement which transforms general and contested 'aboriginal rights'
into the guarantees and benefits specified by the JBNQA. The interpretation of rights as specified by the JBNQA is itself subject to contest, but
within much narrower legal limits. Its terms have been passed into
provincial and federal legislation and have precipitated bureaucratic
arrangements that are now fixtures of state. JBNQA-specified rights
have been the basis for litigation, and Cree have used the terms of the
JBNQA to negotiate with Quebec over subsequent industrial development not foreseen in 1975. The JBNQA, as a treaty with Canada and
Quebec, has Constitutional status.

Internally, the Cree tenure system continues to function over the
great majority of traditional lands. Significant technological and demographic changes have had to be accommodated, in part resulting from
new resources under the JBNQA. There is a growing number of
wage-earning hunters, as well as inexperienced younger hunters
whose mobility has been enhanced through increased access to motor-
ized transport. Adjustments and compromises have been managed by
stewards and other hunters, however, which appear to be viable in
terms of game management, and which have been consistent with the
principle of universal access (Scott 1983a).

Property and contemporary economic development

Pursuant to the JBNQA, there have been major inflows of new resources to Cree communities, in the form of compensation monies and
accelerated transfers under a variety of state programmes. There have
been many new permanent jobs in the Crees' self-governing and social
services administrations (amongst them the Cree Regional Authority,
the Cree School Board, the Cree Board of Health and Social Services)
and new seasonal jobs in accelerated housing and community infra-
structure development programmes. The typical inventory of a Cree
household's possessions, in the form of house and furnishings, road
vehicles, water-craft, and electronic technology, is 'middle-class' in
aspect.

There have been, as outlined earlier, ideological practices and socio-
ecological circumstances ensuring that three hundred years of fur
commodity production did not lead in the subsistence economy to the
breakdown of egalitarian principles of exchange. The Cree perception

that positive reciprocity was an inadequate model of relations with 'the white man' did not spell its demise as the model for intra-ethnic relations. On the contrary, non-egalitarian practices merely converted the white man into a more tangible symbol of what Crees were *not*. Today, none the less, one sees opportunities for accumulation by Cree which are unprecedented, and independent of the subsistence economy. Will pressures for private accumulation overtake egalitarian principles?

One apparent division which exists is that between families who are primarily wage-earners and those who are primarily subsistence-oriented (although most wage-earners also hunt, and most hunters also earn wages seasonally). Research conducted during the first few years of change following the JBNQA (Scott 1984) indicates higher incomes in both subsistence and cash goods. Several mechanisms, traditional and innovative, were promoting equitable distribution of this wealth, such that differences in access to both bush products and consumer items tended to be diminished through sharing between hunters and wage-earners, and equity in overall incomes for the two economic sectors was being maintained. Income parity between hunters and wage-earners was promoted by the Income Security Program for Cree Hunters, Fishermen and Trappers, a guaranteed income for subsistence producers negotiated as a right in perpetuity under the JBNQA, and paid for by the Quebec government over and above the cash settlement.

In the mid-1980s, any group of sibling households includes some which are primarily wage-earning, and some which are primarily subsistence-producing, so that the politics of kinship make systematic inequalities difficult. Also, just under half of the Quebec Cree population are in households whose primary occupation is hunting. If, over the longer term, there is a tendency for the sectors to become kin isolates, systematic inequalities could emerge more readily.

At the level of household income disposal, cash and consumer items are subject to sharing through kin networks, as well as some community-scale redistribution. Expenditures on Christmas, birthday and wedding gifts amount to several thousands of dollars annually for the typical household. Possessions such as vehicles, water-craft and snowmobiles are frequently given, lent and borrowed. This generalized reciprocity, however, is most intensive within a locus of near kin, so that well-to-do families can potentially emerge as sharing isolates.

Community-wide, there are other important redistributive mechanisms. Community feasts are an important symbol of sharing that transcends local kin networks. In settlements of a few hundred residents, hundreds of thousands of dollars are raised annually through bingo games and sports lotteries, in support of community projects. Several games are operated weekly. Purchase of tickets and delivery of winnings represent large and constant flows of cash. Bingos and lotteries play an important ideological function by keeping resources visibly in motion through community networks. Furthermore, the 'profit' ends up supporting community services and facilities.

While income differences are reduced in the generalized exchange network, they are not always eliminated. There are dual-income households holding down two administrative jobs, or a private business in addition to a well-paying job, resulting in family income superior to the norm. Wealth can be hidden in bank accounts and investments, so that the more unpleasant social consequences of unequal wealth can be postponed, but there are limitations on its use. Gossip about families who are 'too wealthy' can be uncomfortable, and conspicuous differences in consumption are still avoided.

The political and bureaucratic heads of Cree regional and local governments have become the stewards of collective wealth bestowed by the JBNQA. Most new jobs and services flow from these sources. The relationship between the leadership and the general Cree populace is therefore critical. As in the subsistence economy, the allocation of opportunities to earn income and share in this wealth is subject to egalitarian expectations. Elected chiefs, councils and administrators are judged accordingly. There is an important qualitative difference, however. The autonomy of the household in the cash sector, its ability to bypass stewards in the event of disagreement, is more limited.

Until now, little new wealth has been in the form of private entrepreneurial capital, although there is a handful of successful small businessmen. The most important Cree enterprises (among them Air Creebec, the Cree Construction Company, a local forestry operation, local shopping complexes) have been initiated and operated by the local and regional Cree administrations, with corporate earnings distributed in the form of salaries, or reverting to collective treasuries. But contemporary leadership is increasingly motivated to provide capital incentives for individual entrepreneurs as well, to stimulate economic development in the communities. The rapid growth in administrative, social service and community construction jobs has tapered into a plateau, while the workforce continues to expand at a rapid rate. There are pressures to concentrate assistance in the hands of individuals who have already proven themselves as administrators or entrepreneurs, because the risk of business failure is lower in such cases and non-Cree government funding is easier to arrange.

Whether cash economic development will precipitate more 'capitalistic' views of property is an open question. Cree leadership associates entrepreneurial initiative as well as bureaucratic efficiency with economic growth and self-sufficiency. There is a controversial balance still to be struck between values of sharing and the accumulation of personal wealth.

Conclusions

To describe property is to represent the entire social system of principles, expectations and coercions that shape the distribution of rights
to — and actual use of — resources. Property, in other words, is part
and parcel of social practice, and its distribution has fundamentally
political implications.

The social practice of Cree hunters, from a certain vantage point,
entails the systematic interruption of attachments between people and
things, through the sharing of rights. Analogous strategies are ad-
vanced by native leaders in dealings with the state as the basis for more
equitable exchange between aboriginal and immigrant nations. In court
and legislative arenas, aboriginal rights are aimed at interrupting definitions that have excluded native interests from property in the past,
and arriving at new social 'contracts'. In public media, 'reciprocity' is a
message both consistent with many indigenous traditions, and morally
persuasive to certain sectors of the immigrant majority.

Power exists as a distribution of abilities vested in a range of discourses of state — among them government policy, law, science, public
morality. Aboriginal claimants, as political subjects, have consolidated
around opportunities for power so distributed. Their programme consists in recognizing the import of cross-determining discourses, and the
opportunities for consent to new institutional arrangements. Consent
is critical where aboriginal people possess negligible coercive means.

A condition for consent is perceived legitimacy of aboriginal claims,
as anchored in the cultural and historical specificity of aboriginal
nations. Anthropology, as scientific authority for the relativistic interpretation of cultural 'others', is politically consequential, whether intended or not. The language of anthropology is not a neutral medium
that conveys ideas formed in the isolation of a discipline; rather, as one
vector in the field of intersystemic discourses, it directs political action
along certain paths, which become institutionalized.

3. Burning the truck and holding the country: property, time, and the negotiation identity among Pintupi Aborigines

Fred Myers

> If they are not given their shares, this denies their kinship. . . .
> A man's variegated relationships with others run through his chattels as well as his land; and the measure of how far he feels the correct sentiments in those relationships is the way he deals with his property and his produce (Gluckman 1965: 45).

The social life of objects

This chapter is concerned with the indigenous meanings attributed to a variety of 'objects' among Pintupi-speaking Aborigines of the Australian Western Desert.[1] My argument is that, for the Pintupi, 'things' (objects, ritual, land, prerogatives, duties) have meaning (that is, significance or social value) largely as expressions of both autonomy and what I have elsewhere defined as 'relatedness' or shared identity (Myers 1986). In this regard, land-ownership is not a special kind of property: it is not a special set of rights defining relationships to an ecologically necessary 'living space'.[2] Instead, it is one more form of objectifying social relationships of shared identity. This is to say that, among the Pintupi, as among many hunter-gatherers, the use-value of rights to 'things' is not at all obvious. Rather than being organised, as

1. Fieldwork with the Pintupi has been funded by NSF, NIMH, and the Australian Institute of Aboriginal Studies at Yayayi, NT (1973–5), Yayayi and Yinyilingki (1979), New Bore (1980–1), and the Central Land Council at Kintore and Kiwirrkura (1984). The present chapter is an abridged version of a longer paper, with the same title, that will appear in a volume edited by Ed Wilmsen entitled *We are here*. I am grateful to Ed and to the organizers of the Fourth International Conference on Hunting and Gathering Societies for permitting this double publication. I would like to thank Annette Weiner and Faye Ginsburg for their helpful comments in organizing and editing this chapter. They are not, of course, responsible for whatever flaws remain.

2. The focus of this chapter stresses the logic of relatedness. This is not to deny entirely the ecological significance of land-ownership, but rather to point out that the uses to which land is put for the Pintupi are equally cultural. For more detailed discussion of the relationship to foraging uses, see Myers (1982; 1986).

Radcliffe-Brown once thought, in terms of corporate groups formed around some valued property or estate, Pintupi seem to constitute social aggregations (see also Sansom 1980) and give them identity through time by projecting them into shared relationships to objects. My essay begins, then, not so much in disagreement with Gluckman's (1965) views on property, but in my discomfort with the notion of property itself: it is too concrete and specific a notion for the meanings that Pintupi give to 'objects'. Legal language may be useful for characterizing certain similarities in the relationship between persons and things, but it does not make for entirely adequate translation. To explore this theoretical problem and to search for deeper understanding of the social significance of things among hunters-gatherers, I want to focus on similarities and differences between land and other forms of property. I shall be drawing on a distinction not unlike the French contrast between *propriété* (personal property) and *immeubles* (real property), a contrast enshrined in Mauss (1954) and recently resurrected in Weiner's (1985) paper on 'Inalienable wealth'.

Two basic issues arise in this chapter. First, I ask if land tenure is different from relationships between (and among) people and other objects. Second, I address the question of the people's concerns over temporal continuity — according to Woodburn (1980) and Meillassoux (1973), a matter central to the understanding of hunter-gatherer society. Woodburn attempts to locate the source of Aboriginal concerns over enduring relationships in the 'farming' of women (in bestowal), but I see the basis of temporal continuity in the process of objectification. In articulating this process, some sorts of 'objects' have different capacities than others. I shall show that it is of critical importance that a Pintupi can 'give away' (or share) some rights to named places without losing his or her own intrinsic identity with these places. This inalienability of land — land cannot really be lost — differs from the way most other objects enter into processes of exchange.

These issues cannot be fully resolved in a short essay, but I would like to make a start by exploring the different ways in which personal identification with objects occurs in Pintupi social life. How is identity extended in the negotiation of shared rights to objects and processes of exchange? And why (for example) are 'personal effects' destroyed, effaced and given away at death — in contrast to what happens with country? What, if anything, is inherited — or what does inheritance accomplish?

Ownership and identification

A basic issue at all levels of Pintupi social organization is the fact of transaction in shared identity. What is most impressive to me about the

Pintupi conception of objects is that there is a continual negotiation about relationships to them and a willingness to include others as (for the want of a better heuristic term) 'co-owners'. Such ambiguity is deep-seated in the negotiated quality of much of Pintupi social life. Relationships among people are not totally given in the rules of a defining structure relating, say, to land-ownership, kinship or residence (Myers 1986). Instead, the relationships must be worked out in a variety of social processes. But the politics of Pintupi life should not be confused as an aim to dominate others. The roots of Pintupi politics in fact lie in the emphasis placed on shared identity with others being a basis for social interaction taking place at all.

This framework suggests a simple and obvious conclusion, namely that 'property' be viewed as a sign. The immediate material use-value of most forms of propertied objects among the Pintupi (tools, clothing, food, and so on) is not great. Such objects are clearly useful, but those that are necessary for simple production are rather easily obtained, constructed or replaced. The rapidity and ease with which things move through a network of relatives and friends shows that objects are important as opportunities to say something about oneself, to give to others, or to share. Like any signs, objects are tokens that represent an opportunity not so much to sustain exclusive use, but rather to constitute other sorts of value defined by a larger system of exchange. That these values are ultimately convertible to labor or political support, far from subtracting from the significance of a semiotic analysis, suggests that such analysis should be based on a temporal perspective that focuses on value as being constituted in the process of *reproducing* social life.

Analysis of the cultural relationships between persons and objects begins, appropriately, with Pintupi ideas of 'ownership' — a conception better translated as one of 'identification'. The Pintupi words most closely approximating 'property' are *walytja* or *yulytja*. The former may be translated as 'relative(s)' or as 'one's own personal effects' (Hansen and Hansen 1977: 152) and the latter as 'baggage and personal effects' (ibid.: 190), but the significance of identification is clearer when one understands the entire semantic range of *walytja*. In addition to objects associated with a person, it can refer to a relative, to the possessive notion of 'one's own' (such as 'my own camp' — *ngayuku ngurra walytja* — or 'my own father' — *ngayuku mama walytja*) or to reflexive conceptions like 'oneself' (such as 'I saw it myself' — *ngayulu nyangu walytjalu* — or 'he sat there by himself' — *nyinama walytja*).

This Pintupi range of meanings offers some perspective on the way legal conceptions of rights and duties are almost naturally reified in the common Western usage of 'property'. Indeed, a similar foundation of property, in rights deriving from some concept of personal identification, is suggested by the shared root of 'proper' (my proper father) and 'property' in the Latin word *proprius*, 'private or peculiar to oneself' (Partridge 1983: 529).

There is a certain ambivalence or ambiguity about Pintupi relationships to objects. In the first place, there is clearly a sense that objects might 'belong to' someone; the idea that X is the *walytja* of a person contrasts directly with the idea that X is *yapunta*, a word whose literal meaning is 'orphan' — without parents. To follow the latter linguistic usage further, one's parents are said to *kanyininpa* one, meaning 'to have', 'to hold' or, more loosely, 'to look after' one. Accordingly, an object that is *yapunta* does not belong to anyone. Yet it appears that this might also mean that it has no one holding or looking after it. This points up the question of what it means for something to 'belong to' — to be *walytja* of — someone. An object becomes *yapunta* when it is no longer 'held' but instead has been 'lost' or 'relinquished', that is, released from an active association with a subject. For objects to belong to someone, then, means that they are expressive of that person's identity as much as that they are simply identified with or related to that person. To say that something is 'one's own' implies for the Pintupi that one doesn't have to ask (or defer to) anyone about its use. Leaving aside for a moment the issue of co-owners, the right to use an object without asking — indeed, even the claim that it is 'my own' — expresses one's autonomy. By 'autonomy' I refer to self-direction, although this, we will have occasion to see, is not necessarily self-created.

Yet, for all this, rights to objects that might be regarded as personal effects still seem less exclusive among the Pintupi than, say, among Americans. The very notion of ownership as identification also provides a sense that rights to objects can and should be more widely distributed, in other words a willingness — not always ungrudging, of course — to include others with oneself, as 'co-owners'. (As I will show with motor vehicles, this can be a complex matter.) Rights to objects enter into a system of exchange that constantly negotiates the relationships of shared identity.

In the following examples, I want to show how the negotiation of the meaning of ownership rights moves within a dialectic of autonomy (as in the right to be asked) and relatedness (exemplified in the tendency to include others and to share rights with others whom one recognizes as identified). This sense of property as potentially providing a temporally extended objectification of shared identity has much in common with Basil Sansom's (1980) treatment of fringe-dwelling Aborigines in Darwin as 'people without property'.

To share, perchance to give

Let me begin with a simple and striking example of how Pintupi regard

personal possessions. Cigarettes, purchased through the cash economy, are a popular item among Western Desert Aboriginal men. Men
cadge each other's tobacco and cigarettes almost without thought. I
was not by any means the only smoker and although my Pintupi
comrades were generous with me I often found my supply all-too-
quickly depleted. Being cadged myself more often than the reverse, I
was sometimes rather cross when I ran out of cigarettes. On just such a
dyspeptic occasion, a young man came to my camp and asked if I had
any cigarettes. Aggrieved, I replied with some anger that people had
taken all of mine, more or less including him as one of those who had
taken advantage of me. Instead of taking offense (the Pintupi were
usually more tolerant of me than I of them), the young man sym-
pathized with the fact that I had been taken advantage of, and offered
me some of his cigarettes! Further, he took it upon himself to explain
that I should not give my things away so easily. Instead, I should hide
what I had — he showed me how he hid a packet of cigarettes in his
socks under his trousers — and then I could simply tell people that,
unfortunately, I had no cigarettes (but would surely give them some if I
had). Giving me a whole packet, Jimmy told me he had several buried
near his camp.

This example speaks of some common themes in Pintupi action
about sharing, owning, and asking. I interpreted Jimmy to mean, in his
way, that I did not have to refuse anyone overtly. To refuse openly, it is
clear, is something very difficult for Pintupi either to do themselves or
to accept in others. Sympathy and compassion are the appropriate and
moral response to co-residents or to relatives. Outright refusal thus
constitutes an open rejection of the other's claim to having a relationship with one (see Myers 1979): in Pintupi social life, to 'say no to
someone's face' is to do something very unusual and dangerous. Those
so denied may respond with anger and violence.

Now if Jimmy's buried cigarettes were taken by others, he would
certainly be angry — in similar cases people talk of 'theft'. Jimmy would
then say: 'Someone has taken my cigarettes, *mulyartalu*' ('thieving' —
ergative case), by which he would imply that his cigarettes had been
taken 'without asking' (*tjapintja wiya*), without a recognition that he had
rights to them. Though on the basis of their relationship he might have
been obligated to give the thief some cigarettes, he would regard the
cigarettes being taken without asking as a violation of his personal
rights to them. In support of such a view, people would often argue
that the owner of an object got it with his own money. This is to say
that the cigarettes were not a product of cooperative or joint activity
through which others could claim identification with the product.

No one else would be much exercised about such an event, as long as
their ox was not gored. Indeed, it might be claimed — in counter — that
Jimmy should not have hidden (*yarkatjunu*) his cigarettes. Or, as I

have heard it said about 'thefts' of popular radios and cassette players, that the owner should have hidden them better (so that the thief was not tempted). Jimmy's claim would be that he should have been asked. Under the latter circumstance — in which refusal is impossible — the only way to maintain one's possessions is to place them out of immediate reach. On the other hand, to give one's cigarettes in response to a request is to build one's own right to ask others because reciprocity in these matters is expected. Correspondingly, it would appear that by taking without asking one is doing more than simply taking an object; one is denying to the 'proprietor' the opportunity to give it and thus to be generous or to build thereby a debt. 'Theft', defined as taking without asking, is a serious interruption to one's ability to express the self, albeit through a gift, and to build through exchange an expanded shared identity with the other.

Finally, it is illuminating to reverse the conception offered here for a moment. Consider that one might claim a right *to be given* some object, in this way claiming either co-ownership or else a relationship with the proprietor that obligated him or her to give. While the proprietor might choose to give, for propriety's sake or to be diplomatic, he or she might still claim that the other was really 'nothing to do' (*mungutja*) — that is, had no basis for shared identity — either with the object or with the proprietor.

The exchange of food

In a short space, it is obviously not possible to circumscribe the entirety of Pintupi relationships to things. None the less, a consideration of rights in gathered or hunted food can inform us more deeply about what is at issue in the establishing of one's primary identity with 'things'.

While women frequently forage in a group for vegetable foods and for small animals, each woman has exclusive rights to what she produces — supposing that the actual productive activity is not a cooperative one. Much of the food is brought back to the residential camp for final preparation and consumption, each woman normally preparing her own produce. In camp, the product is: shared with the immediate family; given to those who looked after the children while the mother (for example) was away (B. Clark, personal communication); and/or distributed to co-residents who had not fared well. Now while all these people have claims on the producer's services, they have no special claim to the product itself. Therefore, what the woman gives is conceptualized as exchange. Co-residents in this situation are expected to share with each other, but the sharing often takes place only on request, giving the distribution a character of 'mutual taking'.

Among Pintupi men, given their technology and resources, cooperation in production is unnecessary, though often beneficial. When men
engage in cooperative drives (as they once did, hunting hare wallabies,
and occasionally still do, hunting hill kangaroos), the kill is distributed
among all who participate. Most hunting, however, takes place alone
or in small groups, and large game is distributed interdomestically to
members of the residential group who have shared with the hunter in
the past. Gifts of meat could satisfy other exchange obligations as well,
namely those to one's in-laws or parents.

Anthropologists have frequently pointed out the practical economic
benefits of such interdomestic distribution, so I need not emphasize
that point here. In any event, the preparation of large game is such as
to treat it as a social product. A hunter is supposed to give the kangaroo
he kills to others for preparation, but his part in the hunt provides him
with both the right and the responsibility to direct the disposition of the
cooked animal in exchange (if someone else's spear or rifle was used,
the actual owner of the hunting implement has this privilege). For his
services, the cook gets the tail, prized for its fat; however, the hunter
tells the cook how to distribute the parts of the cooked animal and
keeps the head (and possibly other parts) for himself. In short, success
in the hunt provides food for the hunter but this does not exhaust its
significance. Success secures a particular set of rights to the animal,
providing an opportunity to give — to engage in interdomestic exchange, which establishes or promotes a kind of moral identity with the
recipients.

In Mauss's analysis of the Eskimo winter redistribution of sexual
rights (1979: 68–70) sexuality's 'use-value' is seen as a sign for exchange. Similarly, among the Pintupi, the social value of the exchange
of meat is not simply that of calorific satisfactions. Rather, such exchange
provides a moral basis for continued and ongoing co-residence and
cooperation among members of a band. It constitutes a moment in the
reproduction of the shared identity (people who 'help each other') that
is the foundation of band organization. There are many advantages in
living with others, including the support of nonproducers, the greater
chance of band members being able to make contact with a game
animal, and the securing of protection from attack. Failure to share or
(as I would prefer to describe the activity) to exchange within such
groups has predictable consequences. The idiom of shared identity that
is sustained through exchange provides the very basis of the criticism
which may ensue: conflict arises as those who feel neglected make
accusations that they have been rejected or disregarded as 'relatives'
(*walytja*). Such neglect is understood as 'not loving' — not regarding
people as related.

The distribution of foraging produce within a large group does
present a problem. Frequently, the conflicts that develop in such

aggregations concern sharing and are brought on by the difficulty of allocating products and services among a large group of co-resident 'kin'. Since all such co-residents have claims on each other, at least to some extent, large groups place a considerable strain on individuals, producing conflicts of loyalty as well as a continuous imposition on people's generosity (not to say diminishing the incentive on people to overproduce).

Thus, the rights to the kangaroo as property are immediately involved with an exchange that is used to maintain one's relatedness to others. It is possible, of course, for a person to assert his (or her) autonomy, in other words his right to decide who gets a kangaroo. He has such rights, but what do they mean? To exercise such a 'choice' may be to defy other people's claims about their relationship with him or about his obligations, and so is likely to create a threat. Herein lies the tension between a valued autonomy and the claims and necessity of shared identity.

How Pintupi manage this tension is clear from the following 'case of the hidden meat'. In 1979, I lived at the small outstation community of Yayayi, then with a population of fifteen. Having successfully hunted kangaroos and bush bustards the previous day, we were enjoying the cooked fruits of our labor on a cold mid-morning when we heard the approaching sounds of the tractor from the nearby community of Yinyilingki. Long-time and frequent co-residents with the Yayayi people, the Yinyilingki people were close and often generous relatives who indeed were only temporarily separate. To my surprise, the male leader of Yayayi decided we should hide our cooked meat — which we did, inside the many flour drums sitting around the camp. When the Yinyilingki people arrived, they of course asked whether we had any meat, to which Tony — sitting on top of some drums — replied that unfortunately we were empty-handed. However, Ginger, his good friend from Yinyilingki, was not fooled for a minute since he could plainly see the evidence of recent cooking as well as the feathers we had plucked from the birds. Laughing and without any rancour, he opened a few flour drums until he found what he was looking for. Now, what transpired in this case is that, by identifying with the cooked meat Tony had truly spoken to the world, communicating his identity. The case is instructive about the cultural meaning of 'property' as an expression of identity — as a node of personal identity caught at once in webs of shared identity.

Materially, Tony's strategy of 'polite rejection through hiding' was a failure, although it did not lead to the conflict or antagonism that would shatter the sense of shared identity. I believe this is so because often enough he was generous. Indeed, the strategy of hiding one's property in order to avoid having either to give it away or to refuse someone overtly is a common enough practice. Ginger recognized Tony's rights to the meat, but these did not really sustain exclusive use. What Tony did with the meat was necessarily and unavoidably meaningful; it was a sign of their relationship, just as Ginger's jocular but insistent demand highlighted his sense that they were sufficiently close that he might be allowed to intrude. However, the potential dangers of such selfishness are clearly outlined in Pintupi myths, where long cycles of vengeance follow a failure to share. And conflict over food has altered the relationships in many a Pintupi camp, so it could be said that the continued identity of a community — what the Pintupi call 'the people with one camp' (*ngurra kutjungurrara*) — is essentially a temporary objectification of these relationships of exchange.

Motor vehicles as media of identification

Among the most valuable objects in contemporary Pintupi life are motor vehicles, especially the trucks and four-wheel-drive Toyotas able to carry large loads (and people) in difficult terrain. Vehicles are necessary and valuable for getting supplies from the store, for hunting expeditions and for visits near and far. Only a very small number of people have cars — few of which last beyond a month because of the hard conditions of the desert roads combined with constant use and poor maintenance. In the case of vehicles, the problem of ownership is compounded by the fact that Pintupi recognize two categories of 'property', which they call (in English) 'private' and 'community' (or 'company').

Vehicles that are 'private' are those purchased with money belonging to an individual (or, individuals — when, as occasionally, the car is bought jointly). The purchaser is understood to be the proprietor of the vehicle, and as such to have the right to decide on or determine its use and non-use. Demand, however, seems by far to exceed the supply. Also, the men or women who buy a car with the money they have saved from unemployment checks, pensions, the sale of paintings or winnings at cards often do not know how to drive. Young men (youth's love for automobiles in the Western Desert matching that in California) very commonly aggregate themselves around relatives who (temporarily) have cars, for the chance to drive or simply for the excitement of travel and visiting. It is unlikely that the proprietor will be the sole user of a vehicle but, as in the case of other personal effects, relatives and friends must ask permission to use it.

Pintupi seem to value the physical freedom of movement provided by having their own cars. Since game is often located at some distance from the settled areas of camps, the availability of transportation may be critical in getting the fresh meat that is desired and needed. Not so long ago, in their semi-nomadic past, 'footwalking' was sufficient to allow

Pintupi to hunt, but most people now regard cars as the necessary condition for this activity, which combines purpose, pleasure and freedom. Where 'movement' has always been valued, the possibility of being able to embark on a hunting expedition at will is, demonstrably, a token of people's autonomy.

Not surprisingly, such a token of possible autonomy is somewhat illusory because the possession of a car also makes one the target of requests, setting in motion a multitude of ties. Autonomy (the possibility of giving) is in itself the basis on which the extending of shared identity with others may be established. To have a car, one might say, is to find out how many relatives one has. Those without their own vehicles draw on kin relationships, especially when needing help, in this way placing those who have a car under an almost constant pressure to provide such help. Where the moral rubric of shared identity guides the relationships of those who live in the same camp, requests are difficult to refuse and open rejection is impossible. Those who refuse are said to be 'hard' or 'jealous' for the car. Anyone who has lived in a Pintupi community will recognize just how much conflict, how many fights, are occasioned by relationships to motor vehicles — conflict over misuse, and over requests for and refusals of use. Indeed, when cars break down, sometimes the owners are relieved — only then being free of demands. Disputes among kin about the use of a vehicle have, I understand, led 'proprietors' to set fire to and destroy their own cars as one desperate and angry resolution.

On the other hand, 'ownership' provides an opportunity for a person to 'give', and one who helps his relatives is not only understood to be generous but also gains a degree of respect and authority for having 'looked after' them. The demands on a proprietor are not entirely a bad thing, then, since they provide for an opportunity to 'be someone'. Proprietorship can make a person of central importance when the activities being planned require transportation.

Elders may well recognize that heavy use is detrimental to the car and, at the same time, that it is important for providing the material requirements of life in remote communities; but also they find it difficult to refuse their sons and nephews. Like us, I suspect, they take some pleasure in providing for those they love. More important is their general attitude towards personal possessions. It would appear that no matter what they cost Pintupi regard vehicles as replaceable, like spears or digging sticks. Thus, they say, even when a A$4000 car is destroyed after only a few weeks of use: 'There are plenty more motorcars; no worries'. To be sure, this reflects an expectation of long-term reciprocity — that someone else will have a car, or that another relative will help to obtain the bare necessities. But it also reflects a willingness to be rather uncomfortable if need be; Pintupi can always walk or somehow make do.

To me, this attitude to 'property' underlies much of Pintupi social life. Put in familiar terms, if faced with a choice between caring for their property or for their relatives, they prefer to invest in people rather than things. Without granting this any special moral status (although I think it deserves one), let me just say that under traditional hunter-gatherer conditions of settlement, such 'investment priorities' may be a realistic appraisal of the resources. None the less, the conception of property as replaceable guides our attention to a conception of things as being relatively transparent signs of social relationships — as 'vehicles' for another sort of value. Many Pintupi recognize a difference between their conception of the relationship between persons and things and the conception of white men. I had a long discussion with a middle-aged man which resulted in him contemplating the difference thus: 'You white people are always worrying for money. You don't think about who will cry for you when you die.' The accumulation of private objects, while not entirely ignored (Pintupi do work and save to get cars), is not the means through which one's identity is transmitted through time. This is secured, it would seem, in part, through giving such things away.

It being difficult to refuse help, 'private' cars are the basis on which a sort of shared identity is constructed; sharing the use of a car reflects an ongoing exchange. Pintupi themselves regard particular vehicles as representing a cluster of associates who, often for the life of the car, travel together: a certain blue Holden is 'that Yinyilingki motor-car', identified with a group of young men. The car is the occasion for their relationships and obligations with each other being temporarily realized. When driving past an old wreck on the road, Pintupi habitually identify it with the persons, communities and events in which it was involved. In short, it becomes an objectification of a set of social relationships.

As far as I can tell, the 'proprietor' is not held liable if a vehicle causes damage while he or she is not the operator or not present. If a vehicle crashes and people in it are killed, Pintupi seem to hold the operator and other participants responsible. However, if the operator was drunk or known to be irresponsible when he asked for the vehicle, the proprietor might be deemed to have acted irresponsibly — though this claim would most likely be made by the operator and his kin, in order that the operator might be excused and his culpability denied.

The other category of motor vehicle is the 'community' one. This has been the cause of conflict and confusion in many settlements. Such 'objects' are usually the product of government or foundation grants and not the result of a community's joint, voluntary contributions to a collective enterprise. The problem with 'community vehicles' revolves around the problem of who can actually be said to own something which belongs to a 'community'.

Ordinarily, Pintupi assimilate this problem of property to their ambiguous notion of *kanyininpa* ('to have', 'to hold', 'to look after') and recognize that Pintupi village councillors 'look after' such vehicles. Indeed, in all the cases I have seen, a particular councillor assumes responsibility for a vehicle: 'John', they might say, 'is looking after that Bedford truck'. They do not mean, of course, that he is its 'owner'. If members of the community at Yayayi (where the truck belongs) want to use it, they ask John to take them somewhere or give it to someone to drive. Should he refuse or otherwise put them off, people usually complain that the truck is not his 'private' (*walytja*) truck but that it is 'community'. They will complain that he is 'jealous' for that motor-car and that he is not 'looking afer the people properly'. Their conception, as I understand it, is that John must be asked, but that as a village councillor he *must* help them. Although he might try to explain that there are other uses for the truck and try to relate these to everyone's benefit, he cannot really refuse. Or perhaps he will explain that it is out of his hands and that he had no choice other than to allow it to be used for something else, but that as soon as it is free he will help them.

An illuminating conflict occurred when this particular councillor took the truck in his care to a distant settlement so that he could pursue one of his wives who had run away. He was gone for a few weeks, during which time Yayayi was without transport for medical or food supplies. The community was able, somewhat uncomfortably, to make do with help from government vehicles. People complained that the councillor was not looking after people properly and that he should be removed from his position. Furthermore, the truck was not 'his own (*palumpa walytja*) — that is, his to do with as he wished. He was only looking after the truck and he should have asked the other councillors about taking it away.

Such conflicts have been frequent. When a councillor has tried to be responsible about the use of vehicles and to preserve them from abuse, members of the community have argued that the vehicle was 'for everyone' and 'to help people', and that the councillor was not helping them. Being aware that the councillor was quite willing to allow the vehicle to be used when his close relatives wanted it, they interpreted his refusal as a denial of relationship or as 'selfishness'. To avoid this conundrum one strategy was to give the keys to a white person (such as me) who, it was believed, could say 'no' to people. The councillor would be able to say that he would have given the vehicle to people, but that *he* did not have the keys. He was not, then, refusing.

These 'community vehicles' are equally interesting from another point of view. To those Pintupi who are granted them, they seem to embody a recognized 'community' identity. When Pintupi refer to the Yayayi Toyota or the New Bore Toyota, they are saying more than that the vehicle belongs to that place. In a particular Pintupi sense, such objects represent the community's collective identity as an autonomous social entity. However, they do not do so legally. If the vehicle crashes, the community is not held liable collectively, and individual members will undoubtedly claim that they were 'nothing to do' (*mungutja*) with the action.

For historical reasons, Pintupi associate the founding of past outstation communities with the granting of four-wheel-drive Toyotas by the Department of Aboriginal Affairs or the Aboriginal Benefits Trust Fund. As a result of this historical association, it appears, they believe that a community's autonomy will be recognized in the granting of such a vehicle. Men often say that they are the 'boss' of an outstation at such and such a place, but they are waiting to go there because the government has not given them their Toyota yet! The attraction of gaining control over such a vehicle is possibly the very reason that people have been eager to establish outstations. The combination of a vehicle and a separate community certainly provides the men who are the 'bosses' of the outstation with a material basis to assert their capacity for self-direction and generosity.

Correspondingly, a number of outstations have split up so that men who were not 'bosses' might affiliate themselves with communities where they had more authority. A great deal of the politics of autonomy, which matters so much to men, gets worked out around the control of the motor vehicles of the community. At the first Yayayi community where I worked in 1973, there were two community vehicles, each associated with historically and geographically distinctive segments of the camp, one for the people 'from the east' and the other controlled by those whose traditional country had been further 'from the west'. The controllers of these resources became the nodes of community organization.

The ambivalence about 'proprietorship' of community vehicles is clear in the case of the death of the person who controlled the vehicle. When the 'boss' of the community at Alumbra Bore died in 1981, members had a problem of what to do with the orange Toyota that was 'theirs' from a community grant. The personal property of a deceased is always destroyed or given away to the person's 'mothers' brothers' from far away — the deceased's effects are identified with him or her, so they make close relatives sad. The Alumbra community planned initially to swap vehicles with another community, in order to remove the truck from sight — because it reminded them of the dead man. The head of the other community was rather eager, and pleased with the good deal this promised him (his truck was old), but the Alumbra people thought better of it, realizing that they would still have to see the truck quite often since it would be in the area. They planned to burn it and thus efface sad memories.

Owning the country

If the objects considered so far are recognizable as personal effects, in that they can be extended to others, land-ownership is not a special kind of property. Among Pintupi, shared identity is readily extended to others in the form of recognizing an identity with named places — this being formulated through a particular cultural logic.

Pintupi land-ownership should be understood as the negotiated outcome of individual claims and assertions (Myers 1982). An emphasis on sociability and negotiation underlies the variety of claims that individuals make in order to be affiliated not with one but with *multiple* land-owning groups. Through allowing others to become joint custodians of one's own estate, people maintain important ties with each other throughout the region. Thus, land-ownership is not primarily an ecological institution but rather a political arena in which Pintupi organize relations of autonomy and shared identity.

Ownership consists primarily in control over the stories, objects and ritual associated with the mythological ancestors of the Dreaming (*tjukurrpa*) at a particular place. Access to the knowledge of these esoterica and to the creative essence they contain is restricted, and one can acquire it only through instruction from those who have previously acquired it. Important ceremonies are conducted at some sacred sites, and other sites are associated with ceremonies in which men (particularly) give instruction on what happened during that important period in which all things took on their form (the Dreaming). Because such knowledge is highly valued and vital to social reproduction, men seek to gain it and to be associated with its display and transmission.

'Holding a country' (*kanyininpa ngurra*) — that is, ownership, as the Pintupi understand it — provides opportunities for a person to be the organizer of a significant event and to be the focus of attention, albeit in limited contexts. Owners are in a position to exercise equality with other fully adult persons, to offer ceremonial roles to others (as part of an exchange), and to share rights in ritual paraphernalia. At the same time, people view 'country' (*ngurra*) as the embodiment of kin networks and as a record of social ties that can be carried forward in time.

Various means exist by which individuals may make claims of identification with the 'country' and assert it as their 'own'. But the fundamental notion of 'identification with country', rooted in the fact that places always bear the imprint of persons, refers to the whole range of relationships which a person can claim or assert as being between him or herself and a place. These provide the cultural basis for the country's ownership,[3] and individuals have claims to more than one country. But

---

3. The multiple pathways of individual claims are based on a logic. If the place is called A, the following constitute bases for such a claim: (a) conception at the place A; (b) conception at a place B made by and/or identified with the same Dreaming ancestors as A; (c)

it is through political process that *claims* of identification are converted into *rights* over aspects of a country and *knowledge* of its esoteric qualities.

Identification is an ongoing process, subject to claim and counter-claim, dependent on validation and acceptance or invalidation and nonacceptance. The movement of the political process is along a gra-duated range of links or claims of increasing substantiality, from mere identification and residual interest in a place to the actual control of a place's sacred associations. The possession of such rights as recognized by others — called 'holding' a country — is the product of negotiation. Ultimately, ownership is not 'given' but an accomplishment, although this historicity is disguised by the fact that the cultural basis of claims is the ontological priority of the Dreaming. In the end, ownership of country, denoting close association among a set of individuals, is a projection into transhistorical time of the valued social relations of the present. But this occurs without drawing attention to the boundaries it draws.

From the Pintupi point of view, the emphasis is just as much on the social production of persons who can 'hold' the country, that is, on initiating young men and teaching them the ritual knowledge necess-ary to look after the country, as it is on getting the country. The Pintupi image of social continuity is effectively one in which 'country' as an object is passed down — 'given' (*yungu*) — from generation to genera-tion. The Pintupi regard this 'giving' as a contribution to the substance and identity of the recipient, a kind of transmission of one generation's (or person's) identity to the next. By learning about the Dreaming and seeing the rituals, one's very being is altered: people become, Pintupi say, 'different' and stronger. One cannot become adult without the help of others; no one can become a man by himself. Certainly, while younger recipients are supposed to reciprocate the gift of knowledge — hunting meat for those who give the knowledge, and deferring to them — they cannot really repay what has been given. They have received more value than they can give back; they have, as it were, acquired an obligation that they can repay only by teaching the next generation. Pintupi stress that men must hold the Law and pass it on. In fact, men are enormously concerned to pass on their knowledge and their iden-tification with places to their 'sons' and 'sister's sons'.

Ownership derives from such processes. Since knowledge and con-trol of country are already in the hands of 'owners' (my gloss for the Pintupi term *ngurrakartu* which refers particularly to custodians of a

conception at a place B whose Dreaming is associated mythologically with the Dreaming at A (the story lines cross); (d) initiation at A (for a male); (e) birth at A; (f) father conceived at A, or conditions (a)–(e) true for father; (g) mother conceived at A or conditions (b), (c), (e) true for her; (h) grandparents conceived at A or conditions (b)–(e) true; (i) residence around A; (j) death of close relatives at or near A.

named place), the conversion of *claims* in a place to an actual interest in that place means convincing the owners that one should be included in knowledge and activity. One's identification with a country must be actualized and accepted by others through a process of negotiation. Only a portion of those who claim to identify with a named place are said to 'hold' it and to control its related rituals. These primary custodians are the people who must decide whether or not to 'teach' an individual; it is they who decide on the status of claims. Men are happy to teach close kin about their country, thereby granting them an interest in the place; but the claims of remote genealogical kin and of those who are not co-residents are less persuasive.

To each significant place, then, a group of individuals can affiliate. But the corporations forming around these sacred sites, differing from place to place, are not 'closed'. Instead, there are descending kindreds of persons who have or had *primary* claims to the respective sites. The fact that men seek rights to many 'countries' leads to extended associations of individuals surrounding cores of people with primary claims. Among the Pintupi, it is common for individuals to have extensive, far-reaching estate-rights and for different individuals to have distinct personal constellations of such rights. In this sense, one's identification with a named place is at once a definition of who one is and at the same time a statement of shared identity with others. In most cases of conflict, the agreement and disagreement about who should and should not be accepted closely follow current ties of cooperation among people, who are attempting to project their associations into the past, to embody their contemporary shared identity in some objective form.

From this account, it is clear that there are two aspects to the significance of 'country' or named place as a cultural entity, both given form in processes of exchange. With its origin in the Dreaming, 'country' constitutes a form of valued knowledge that is esoteric, transmitted (or, as the Pintupi say, 'given') to younger men, but restricted in access. At the same time, 'country' constitutes an object of exchange between equal men. (And the possibility of handling 'country' in this way stems from initiation, which also underpins the possibility of two other basic forms of autonomy through exchange: marriage and fighting.) A further critical point is that for the Pintupi 'country' provides a (perhaps *the*) embodiment of identity that allows for the performance of autonomy in exchange.

If we consider how people become 'members' of land-owning groups through the politics of persuasion and exchange, it is clear that these groups represent an objectification of shared identity. That is, people's joint relationship through time to a named place represents an aspect of an identity they share, however limited. The process through which membership is established is precisely one in which people attempt to convince others that they already *are* related, that they care. Each convince others that they already *are* related, that they care. Each named place, then, commemorates, records or objectifies past and present achieved relations of shared identity among participants. Each place, however, represents a different node of relations.

The ultimate expression of this principle whereby shared identity among participants is projected out into the object world (and is seen as deriving from it) is the way Pintupi verbally extend an identification with a place, describing some important site as 'belonging to everybody, whole family' or, as they say alternatively, 'one country'. In reverse, one may and should read this as representing the Pintupi sense of themselves (they are a people with no distinctive organization as a political entity) as 'all related' (*walytja tjurta*) and as one group, although it must be noted that this is a context-dependent claim and is not to imply an identity for all time. For the Pintupi, land is a sign that can carry expressions of identity. It is critical to add that what Pintupi refer to in this fashion is not a 'community' in the sociological sense of people physically living together; rather, each place represents an aggregation of individuals from a wide area of the region in which they live. We have here a form of regional integration through individual ties.

A powerful example of the tendency towards inclusion and to the proferring of shared identity is evident in rights to 'sacred boards', the same sort of objects as the Aranda *churinga* (Strehlow 1947). As Lévi-Strauss (1966), among others, has noted, these objects may constitute title deeds for rights in land (although they are not reducible to this). Throughout central Australia, sacred boards represent (at least for men) the epitome of value; they are objects said to have been 'left by the Dreaming' (although fashioned by men) which men are permitted to know about and view only after initiation. Individual boards are always associated with particular Dreaming stories and usually with one or more named places created by that Dreaming, and rights to such objects, as with songs and stories, are part of the 'estate' associated with mythologically constituted places. I believe that a man has rights to manufacture and/or to possess the boards associated with his own conception place. Thus a number of men have described to me their conception in the following terms: such and such a Dreaming was traveling at a place, performing ceremonies, and they forgot or left behind one of their sacred objects, which (eventually) became the person.

The value of such sacred objects is constituted by their imputed indexical relationship to the Dreaming, by the restrictions on knowledge about them, by the difficulty of acquiring them and by their historical associations with the subjectivity of people who once held them and have since died. Pintupi men often emphasize how such objects were 'held' by people who are now dead ('ancestors') and how seeing the objects makes men 'sorrowful' and the objects 'dear'. In some sense, a sacred object is a powerful representation of one's identity, hidden from sight away from women and children and shown only to initiated men of one's choosing. A man keeps his sacred objects in several places, some of the objects being held jointly with other men in one place or another. Only authorized men can manufacture a sacred object — only a person who has passed through all the stages of initiation and has been granted ('has been given' — *yungu*) the right to make a board for a particular site by being taught the design by a legitimate custodian.

This is a province of Aboriginal life about which our understanding is unsatisfactory. Knowledge of such matters, as with much of religious life, is restricted in access; it is not only difficult to learn about but also problematic to publish. None the less, it is clear that, for men, the exchange and circulation of these objects is a matter of intense interest and concern. Indeed, while such boards come 'from the country' — as it were, more or less representing the country — they are detached from it and movable. In this lies part of their power. Their being exchanged among men who may live far apart constitutes a *distinctive level* of organization — a transformation of marriage exchange, ritual exchange and the like, through another medium — which has the capacity to constitute a common identity among those not in daily contact. While it is much like these other 'levels' of exchange, the negotiation of identity through sacred objects has its own properties.

Among the Pintupi, boards are frequently exchanged as a result of bestowals between a man and his male in-laws, and sometimes exchanged as a result of initiation and to settle long-standing disputes (such as murders). Access to sacred boards is obviously an important condition of autonomy and equality vis-à-vis other men. A young man must consequently rely on elder male relatives to supply him with sacred objects for marriage and so that he may begin fulfilling his obligations. But what is involved in such transactions needs further clarification. Basing his analysis on Strehlow's (1947) ethnography, Lévi-Strauss (1966) likened the exchange of such objects to loaning out one's basic identity to the care of another group — the ultimate sign of trust.

The first point to make is that a Pintupi man has rights to more than one sacred board; his total identity is not wrapped up in one alone. Second, I found it enormously difficult to discover the 'owners' of the sacred boards I was shown. This no doubt stemmed partly from the secrecy surrounding the boards, but it is also the case that boards are rarely owned by a single person. When I was shown boards, a man would tell me that this one belonged to him and also to such-and-such other men, another one belonged to him and X, and so on. Frequently, a group of 'brothers' (rarely genealogical, however) 'held' boards in common. The way I was told made me feel that, as in land-ownership, men have a tendency to extend ownership of sacred objects to others with whom they were identified. This is consistent with the way Pintupi lay stress on the enormous dangers involved should a person try to make a sacred object by himself. To do so would inevitably arouse the jealousy of other men who would kill him. It would appear that to make a sacred object oneself is to assert one's total autonomy, denying other people's relationship to oneself and to the object. One should have *kunta*, that is, 'shame' or 'respect', for others.

Thus Pintupi are inclined to share out ownership of and responsibility for sacred objects with men they regard as close. Conversely, when they plan and participate in cycles of exchange with other men this always involves a set of men who cooperate as 'brothers' as a node in the exchange, just as a group of 'brothers' will stand as a party in arranging marriage bestowals. Joint participation in exchange, then, constitutes an identity among those involved, who jointly accept a responsibility: the boards they possess in common are an objectification of their shared activity and of their joint responsibility — in other words, an objectification of who they are. Whilst failure to fulfil one's obligations in a board exchange is described as 'having trouble' (*kuun-karrinpa*), or being under threat of revenge and retaliation, and whilst fulfilling one's obligations is described as 'clearing oneself' (*kilirrinpa*), or being free, joint participation may reduce the danger of failure.

What happens in the exchange itself is equally illuminating. Men often described how they had lived in other people's country for some time (as young novices or in bride-service) and how, when they made ready to return to their own country, 'owners' of the host country 'gave' them sacred boards. This meant that such 'owners' drew designs on a fashioned board, which a young man then carved, the finished object being taken by him on his return. Effectively, the young man had been taught the design and given the right to reproduce it — although not, it appears, the right to teach other people. His possessing the board from the host country was a recognition of his prolonged residence and shared identity with the people of that country, converting residence and cooperation through time into an identity projected into land ownership. It is important to recognize, too, that in 'giving' the board, the original owner had not actually lost anything. He recognized or granted to another both rights in the country and shared identity (as embodied in the object), but he retained his own identification with the place.

Death, memory and the social transmission of identity

I have argued that there is much similarity between the extension of rights to property through exchange and the extension of rights in land. As objects, land and other forms of property have the capacity to embody the relationships among people in outward form. Proprietorship, then, provides a basis on which identity can be built through exchange, both by establishing one's autonomy through the possibility of taking part in an exchange and by creating the possibility of expanding that identity to include others. Both such possibilities are encoded in the meaning of *walytja*, as 'relative', 'oneself', and 'something owned'. None the less, these various objects have very different potentials as regards constituting identity through time. This becomes clear when we consider how the Pintupi deploy them in the case of a proprietor's death.

In death, the accumulation of personal effects throughout a lifetime is denied; they are transmitted neither as an estate nor as personal mementos to the heirs most closely identified with the deceased. In the Pintupi view, because things associated with the identity of a dead person make his or her relatives sad, such things are effaced. All of a person's *yulytja* (or *walytja*) are given away to distant relatives, preferably of the mother's brother kin category. Typically, these effects include a person's blankets and 'swag' (the bedroll in which he or she camped), his or her hair (which is cropped close at death), his or her tools and personal items — even including a motor-car if they own one. Objects are given away or destroyed. In the 'finishing up' ceremonies, as Pintupi call the distribution at death, the carefully rolled-up dead person's 'swag' seems to stand for the body, placed as it is out in front of the mourners as the silent and untouched focus of attention. attention.

For one such ceremony at least, it was the dead man's wife who oversaw the 'swag', while it was women mourners who carried it about preparatory to each performance of 'finishing up' (that is, upon each arrival of groups of kin from other places, whose willingness to take part shows they are not guilty of ill-will). Invoking the identity of the dead, the 'swag' occasions elaborate expressions of grief and anger at loss. The camp or house the deceased inhabited is abandoned; relatives in other communities may move their own camps as well if they remind them of the dead person. (In semi-nomadic, traditional times, the places of death and burial were avoided for years until all traces of the dead were gone.) For similar reason, the personal name(s) of the dead person — and anything sounding like it — are avoided, and substituted for in everyday speech by synonyms or the avoidance term *kunmarnu*. The deceased is referred to subsequently by the name of the place where he or she died. As an example of the degree to which such effacement may be extended, when L died his relatives proposed burning the nearly-new truck that had been granted to the outstation community which he led. The sight of the truck, even if it were given to distant relatives, would cause them grief.

Despite the dramatically enacted grief at the loss of a relative, the symbolic effect of these practices is quite the opposite of commemorating the dead through inheritance. Relatives of the deceased's own generation (not parents or children but, as in the case with which I was best acquainted, the deceased's close younger brothers) are responsible for collecting his or her goods and for seeing to their dispersal among other distant relatives. As far as I could tell from the activity surrounding L's death, the sending off of the *yulytja* is the primary responsibility and activity for close relatives; the funeral, albeit a Christian one now, could not take place until this had been completed. L's brothers collected his 'bag' (which I presume contained some of his personal ritual paraphernalia — hair string, arm bands, small sacred objects), and his close mother's brothers (who in fact had been living with him) seem to have overseen the planning and organization of the 'sorry business' distribution of goods. During such occasions, the sense of obligation is pressing. It was important, L's mother's brothers told me, to send this bag off to the mother's brothers in Yuendumu quickly, lest people begin to talk about them (*wangkakuturripayingka*, 'to avoid moving towards talk').

In a sense, these goods are not allowed to carry the deceased's identity forward in time. A person's identity is instead carried forward in the grief and in the lives of those whom he or she 'held' (or looked after), especially those whom he or she 'grew up'. The Pintupi man who criticized the concerns of white men with money and accumulation, by asking: 'Who will cry for you when you die?' was pointing to this alternative form of accumulation — of investing identity in and increasing the social value of people through caring for them as a relative. This is the focus of Pintupi social reproduction which so much emphasizes the role of seniors as 'nurturing' those who come after. Pintupi often explain their grief at loss by referring to the way the person 'held' them; further, the people who have been looked after by the same person consider themselves related as if they share substance by that contribution. It is through such links to some predecessor, as well, that groups of people formulate their shared identity, referring to themselves as 'real siblings', for example, because 'we have one father' or 'one grandmother'.

Unlike the personal effects (related to a transient historical identity) that are dispersed at death, men particularly strive to pass on to their successors an identity formulated through ties to named places. Maantja Tjungurrayi, as a case in point, constantly put pressure on his son, Ray, to attend his ceremonies, and to learn, so that he could 'pass on' his country. As Maantja and a number of other Pintupi explained to me, the process they desire is one in which '*Mamalu wantintja, katjapir-tilulpi witininpa*', that is, 'the fathers having lost (relinquished) it, the group of sons grab it'. What they pass on, or transmit, in this way is not a personal property that they have created or accumulated themselves, but an identity that is already objectified in the land. Recipients acquire rights to a named place that has pre-existing relationships with other named places on its Dreaming track; through rightful possession of this knowledge inheritors gain the possibility of taking part in equal exchange with other men and the capacity to nurture the coming generation of men with the gift of their knowledge.

This knowledge of country, and the rights to place represented in knowledge, is a form of 'inalienable wealth', as Weiner (1985) describes it. Unlike the spear one has made or the kangaroo one has hunted and cooked, one can 'give' one's country to others — take part in exchanges — without really losing it. Thus, as represented in a shared relationship to an object, others are accepted as sharing identity; but one does not thereby lose the ability to give the object away again. Indeed, by including more people as 'co-owners' one to some extent increases the value and importance of a place, as long as recognition as principal custodian continues. As Munn (1970) has clearly realized, Western Desert Aborigines perceive the country as symbolically bearing an identity which those who take it on (or 'hold' it) come to possess as their identity. When one dies, these special 'objects', with which one has come to be associated in the course of one's life, remain in the landscape, and the people to whom one contributed by 'growing' them up and by teaching, are those able — even obligated — to carry on the responsibility for this country. This is the identity that endures and is reproduced through time in the social production of persons, an identity that is taken on by each generation from its forebears, mediated through the 'inheritance' of place.

I believe that the freedom with which Pintupi are willing to part with their personal possessions owes something to this enduring dimension of identity. Spears, rifles, clothing, food, even the costly motor-car — these are all, in the Pintupi view, replaceable. There are always 'plenty more motor-cars'. So long as such objects provide a basis through which identity can be created and extended, the Pintupi take part in such exchanges with an assured foundation. Everyone, according to their conception beliefs, comes into the world with an association with the Dreaming at a place. In some critical way, Pintupi regard themselves as having an assured identity no matter what happens to personal possessions. This is different indeed from a world in which accumulated personal property constitutes the only medium in which identity can be realized. Several years ago the Native American activist, Vine DeLoria, spoke to a class I was teaching, and a student with a beginner's ethnocentric background in psychology tried to question him about the way in which some Indian religious concepts provided for them a sense of self. 'The Self', DeLoria snorted, 'is not an Indian problem. That's something white people worry about.'

A hierarchy in the organization of relationships to objects takes us away from the simple notion of 'property rights' as legal problems and suggests that objects, as property or not, have meanings for people that cannot be limited to the analytic domains in which Western notions too often restrict us. For the Pintupi, I would maintain, one's identification with place as an object assures an identity in the world on which the more transient exchanges of daily life can take place without threatening to reduce participants to the emptiness of pure despair that economic failure too often brings to people in the Western world.

4. Rights to game and rights to cash among contemporary Australian hunter-gatherers

Jon Altman and Nicolas Peterson

Introduction

Reports of land ownership, tool ownership and kill ownership in hunting and gathering societies have long been taken as evidence that there is private property in resources in these societies rather than collective access and ownership. Recently, however, it has been suggested that this view is in error. In the case of land, it is argued that what has been reported as ownership of resources is really a regulation of hunting practice to prevent competition and improve efficiency, and as such is simply part of the forces of production (Ingold 1980b). Correspondingly, where tools are concerned, 'ownership' is primarily a mechanism for identifying the killer of an animal, thus providing for an incentive to hunt — a necessity with an ethic of sharing because otherwise people would be sitting around waiting for other people to do the work, knowing they would be provisioned in the event of a kill. By identifying a killer who has the right to distribute the kill and consequently secure the prestige of having made it, ownership of tools motivates hunters to hunt (ibid.).

More generally, Woodburn (1982a) maintains that in those hunter-gatherer societies which he classifies as 'immediate-return', there is a general disengagement from property and so from its potential for creating interpersonal dependency. Among the mechanisms securing this egalitarianism are the ability of individuals to use resources freely without reference to other people, to share as equals in game meat brought into camp and to obtain personal possessions without entering into dependent relationships. Taken together these views suggest that property is of almost inconsequential significance in many hunting and gathering societies.

Australian Aborigines are interesting in respect of these general observations because, although in subsistence terms they fit the category of immediate-return societies, Woodburn classifies them as 'delayed-return'. This is not because of their developed notions of property but because of their long-term betrothal arrangements associated with affinal payments and developed polygyny. In fact, notions of material and intellectual property are well developed in Australia, in the one case associated with land and in the other with rights in songs, myths, paintings, dances and esoteric knowledge (see Keen and Morphy, both in this volume). Nevertheless both the relative ease with which people can attach and detach themselves from residential groups and the economic independence of the household serve as radical constraints on the emergence of inequality — in line with what Woodburn suggests for immediate-return societies.

In the domain of kill ownership, there is, in the Australian material, long-standing evidence that has been taken to suggest that game is collectively appropriated rather than individually owned. Writing of the Aborigines of Victoria in 1881, Dawson reports:

> There are strict rules regulating the distribution of food. When a hunter brings game to the camp he gives up all claim to it, and must stand aside and allow the best portions to be given away, and content himself with the worst. If he has a brother present, the brother is treated in the same way, and helps the killer of the game to eat the poor pieces which are thrown to them such as the forequarters and ribs of the kangaroos, oppossums, and small quadrupeds, and the backbones of birds. The narrator of this custom mentioned that when he was very young he used to grumble because his father gave away all the best pieces of birds and quadrupeds, and the finest eels, but he was told that it was a rule and must be observed. This custom is called *yuurka baawhaar*, meaning 'exchange' (1881: 22).

Similar accounts of the game being taken off the hunter can be found from throughout the continent. In this chapter we provide evidence that this kind of generalized statement obscures an important distinction between two kinds of game: large game and small game. A hunter's rights in large game are typically diluted in a number of ways — though the distribution of such game is neither automatic nor uncontentious. In the case of small game, however, the hunter's control is complete. We compare these rights in game with those in items bought with cash.

The information presented here was collected while one of us (Altman) resided with a group of eastern Gunwinggu at an outstation (a small satellite Aboriginal community) in north-central Arnhem Land. The land over which these people forage varies dramatically, from the tidal reaches of rivers that flow into the Arafura Sea to the rocky outliers and escarpments of the Arnhem Land plateau. Over a 296-day period, in 1979 and 1980, the subsistence activities and returns, work effort, expenditure and consumption patterns of one band (the Momega band) were monitored. During this period the band averaged thirty-one persons divided into ten households and grouped into three household clusters. In the wet season (November to April) the monitored group was the entire band but during the dry season (May to October) the band divided into smaller household-cluster groups and the activities of the main cluster were recorded (Altman 1987).

Arnhem Landers today use introduced technology in the food quest, particularly shotguns, nylon fishing lines, steel hooks and lures and metal digging sticks. Nevertheless the social relations of subsistence production appear little altered from traditional conditions. The critical economic change has been the introduction of the cash economy. Today these people receive social security benefits as if they were urbanized Australians: these include unemployment benefits, pensions of various types and family allowance (child endowment) payments. In recent years, people in Arnhem Land have also adapted artefact manufacture for market exchange, and this today is the most important source of non-welfare cash.[1]

In 1979–80, it was estimated that the market replacement value of subsistence production accounted for 64 per cent of the outstation's total (cash and imputed) income.[2] Meanwhile, social security payments amounted to 26 per cent of total income (but 70 per cent of cash income) and artefact production to 10 per cent of total income and 30 per cent of cash. Cash is used primarily to procure market goods. Subsistence production currently provides 46 per cent of calories and 80 per cent of protein intake at the outstation. In time allocation terms, people spend 72 per cent of materially productive work effort in the subsistence sector, 22 per cent in manufacturing artefacts for market exchange and 6 per cent in a variety of miscellaneous activities. About 90 per cent of subsistence return is game hunted by men. This is partly as a result of the men adopting and adapting modern technology. The decline in women's contribution to subsistence is associated with the availability of cheap market carbohydrates like flour and sugar which are procured with social security cash (Altman 1984).

Rights to game

In Arnhem Land people cannot hunt anywhere they please. Rights to use the food sources of a range (band territory) are secured when people are accepted into the band occupying it. On entering the range of another band people always seek out the resident group to announce their presence. Failure to do this would be taken as evidence of being in

---

1. The economic changes that have resulted at the outstation after monetization and welfare-state intervention are examined elsewhere (Altman 1987).

2. Imputed income is the estimated market replacement value of the returns from hunting, fishing and gathering activities (for a detailed discussion of the outstation's social accounts, see Altman 1987).

the area with evil intent — in the past with intent to kill. Once accepted into the group, visitors have access to all normal food resources. In eastern Arnhem Land people in an area for the first time should be cautious and reserved in respect of appropriating resources and may even hold off (Williams 1982: 147) because of hostility emanating from the land. Food resources found near sacred localities will be restricted, and substantial areas of a range may be closed off if there has been a recent death, until such time as the senior land-owner has raised the prohibition (Altman 1987). People may, however, kill game that they come across on their way to visit the residing band, but they would be expected to give the game to the senior land-owner, especially if it were a person's first kill in the area.

The Gunwinggu distinguish between large game, *maih nagimuk* (such as all macropods, crocodiles, emus and feral buffaloes, together with pigs and cattle), and small game, *maih yawut* (such as fish, lizards and birds), although a large quantity of any of the latter caught at one time may be classed with the former. Game belongs to the person who first disables it. This person is known as *welenggeng*, which Gunwinggu translate as 'winner'. All people actively participating in the hunt receive some meat unless under some taboo. If the weapon with which the animal has been killed belongs to a person other than the hunter its owner has a right to meat and expects to be able to claim a better cut than might have been received otherwise.

After cooking, animals are butchered into the appropriate cuts for the particular species. Macropods, for instance, are cut into eight basic pieces: the head, two forequarters, rump, tail, two hindquarters and offal (see Figure 4.1). The hunter always takes the head but, depending on the number of people among whom the animal has to be divided, he may also take half or all the forequarters, sharing them with his hunting partners and/or brother. The much-valued rump and tail, which may be divided into three pieces, is given to actual or classificatory wife's brothers. The hindquarters and offal will go to senior men.

A person out hunting alone is at liberty to kill an animal and bring back only a small section for his household. This is frowned upon, however, and unless there is some good reason for not bringing the meat back and reaping the social benefit that accrues, it is unlikely that this will be done. On occasions people shoot an animal or catch fish which, proving on inspection to be lacking in fat, is abandoned in the expectation that better-quality game will be obtained later in the day — although this does not always happen. Where the kill is very large, such as a buffalo or crocodile, a person will either carry as much as possible back to camp or people will move to camp near the carcass.

Given that there is an expectation that large game will be shared and that in the absence of storage such sharing makes sense in terms of creating or meeting obligations, the sense in which large game can be

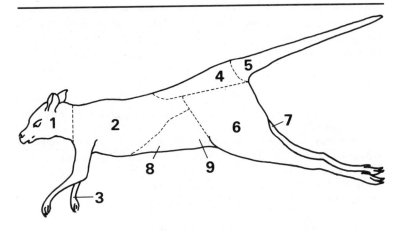

Figure 4.1: Rules for sharing macropods among the eastern Gunwinggu.

Main portion	Gunwinggu name	European name	Average weight (%) Wallaby[1]	Average weight (%) Kangaroo[2]	Recipient
1	Gun.goitj	Head	8	10	Hunter
2	Gunbel	Forequarter	8	11	Hunter
3	Gunbel	Forequarter	8	11	Hunter's companion or brother
4	Dumeno	Rump	10	6	Hunter's MBS or MMBDS[3]
5	Gunbet	Tail	9	10	Hunter's MBS or MMBDS
6	Gundat	Hindquarter	19	15	Senior man
7	Gundat	Hindquarter	19	15	Senior man
8	Duduno, malkno, nukno etc.	Heart, liver tripe etc. (offal)	6	4	Hunter and senior (or present) men
9	Nutno	Gut/waste	13	18	—

1. *Macropus agilis* (agile wallaby);
   Lagochestes conspicillatus (spectacled hare wallaby);
   Petrogale brachyotis (short-eared wallaby);
   Peradorcas concinna (little rock wallaby).
2. *Macropus antilopinus* (antilopine kangaroo);
   Macropus robustus (euro);
   Macropus bernardus (black or Woodward's wallaroo).
3. For the explanation of this nomenclature, p. 88 n. 4.

said to be owned is limited. Such 'ownership' extends only so far as being able to allocate the cuts. If the hunter is a young unmarried man he may, having cooked the animal, give it over to his father or to another senior male relative for it to be distributed. If an older man has killed the animal he will distribute it himself but may allocate the task of cooking to a younger male relative. Since not all of the animal is spoken for there are, at times, real decisions to be made and people often feel free to make claims for particular cuts. The pattern of distribution is for a senior man in each of the household clusters to be given portions which he then redistributes between the households of the cluster. Each hunter is likely to give the meat to a different senior man in a given cluster, according to his own particular kin ties. Once the meat is at the household level it cannot be claimed by anyone outside the household.

These rules for sharing may be modified by a complex set of taboos, called *djamun*. These taboos are broadly linked to three factors:

— *The ritual status of the hunter.* Sections of the band population can be restricted access to the game that has been hunted by junior men. Such game is most frequently shared only by ritually senior men and by uninitiated males and females.

— *The type of game.* Certain types of totemically significant game are not available to certain sections of the community such as ritually junior men, lactating women, pregnant women and menstruating women. At times these restrictions are size-related rather than species-related.

— *The seasonal cycle.* Some restrictions are seasonally determined, and this in general results in the non-exploitation of species. These restrictions usually apply for ecologically sound reasons during the breeding season of the species concerned. If such game is accidentally caught (for example, river shark or sawfish) only senior men may consume them.

These restrictions often apply to the successful hunter. Today, if a hunter is not allowed access to the game he has secured, he is frequently given market foods, which in the profane context are never restricted. Thus while the hunter may end up with no control over the distribution of game, he will always acquire prestige. People are acutely aware of who the successful hunters are and of the frequency of their success.

Rights in cash

The Gunwinggu have been involved in the cash economy only since the 1960s. In contrast to the use-production domain, there are few clearly articulated rules about rights to cash or to the goods it can buy.

Nevertheless there are clear parallels between the treatment of game and traditional material culture, and of cash and its products. When game is brought into camp it is at its most public and most vulnerable to claims. Similarly, when people are paid their pensions every fortnight on the arrival of a supply vehicle (or boat during the wet season) they are likewise open to claims.

The extent to which individuals are able to restrict claims to their cash by relatives is dependent primarily on the degree of income variability throughout the band. If cash is inequitably bestowed then it is widely redistributed (like surplus game); if cash is equitably bestowed then there is only limited redistribution beyond the household. With cash, as with game, there are anti-surplus forces at work which require the generalized distribution of immediate surpluses. However, as will be demonstrated, mechanisms have been adopted that result in cash accumulation, in marked contrast to game, which is never stored.

With cash, as with game, rights vary with different distribution rounds. Just as game, once cooked and divided, is regarded as restricted to the household (or in some cases the household cluster), the goods bought with cash are regarded as household property. When households have spent their cash allocations on goods such as flour, sugar, tea, tobacco and shotgun cartridges, rights to these goods lie with the household. The fact that someone else's cash was used to procure the goods is of limited significance, except in rare cases of dispute.

However, it is important to note that people tolerate household failure where budgeting with bought goods is concerned. If a household runs out of the staples (flour, sugar or tea), a second-round redistribution may occur from households which have surpluses of these goods. Such redistribution generally occurs after a request for goods from kinsfolk (and all camp co-residents are kin) that is difficult to refuse. In such circumstances people are entitled to ask for repayment when supplies arrive again, and the original transfer can therefore be regarded as a loan. There is a limit to people's tolerance of poor budgeting in the longer run; continual mismanagement of resources can result in disputes.

People spend cash not only on consumables but also on a limited range of personal items including clothes, hunting and fishing equipment, cooking equipment, axes, knives and smoking pipes. Rights to these goods are similar to people's rights in non-sacred items of traditional material culture: they are personal property. Similarly, shelters (today made from corrugated iron as well as from the traditional bark) are recognized as the private property of households. If a shelter is unoccupied and its owners residing elsewhere, their permission will generally be sought prior to occupation by others.

Both traditional and non-traditional items may be marked with designs (Thomson 1939a) or other personal marks which today include the items being carved with initials or first names. More significantly, however, small game may also be marked to indicate that it is accounted for if it seems possible that there may be confusion about ownership such as at large-scale fire drives. In the case of magpie geese this is frequently done by pulling feathers from the wings or rump.

Close kinsmen are constantly making requests for the use, loan or gift of goods. While requests for access to goods are frequently difficult to deflect, acceptable counter-strategies are available to those willing to miss out on the social credit which meeting obligations provides. For example, lying is acceptable, and greatly preferred to straight refusal. The most common strategy, though, is to claim prior need to an item; one can maintain control of one's shotgun, for example, by stating that one was just about to use it. This, of course, commits one to the stated action and at times such a ploy is used to 'encourage' junior hunters to use their equipment.

Given that there is continual pressure on individuals to share game and cash it is interesting that cash accumulation can occur. The main modes of accumulation are via gambling (Altman 1985) and by saving in bank accounts, usually with the assistance of a white broker. Saving can also occur for the common good via pooling, and at times large items such as vehicles or boats are bought with pooled cash. However, such pooling requires someone to have a great deal of organizational ability.

If an individual devises a strategy to accumulate cash to procure what is in local terms a 'large capital item' such as a vehicle, stereo cassette-recorder or even a video, he or she is greatly respected, for people recognize that there are powerful anti-accumulation forces at work in the society. If someone can surmount the social hurdles to saving, they acquire prestige as a resource manager. However, once a large item is procured, the nominal owner can rarely limit access to it. Hence, while vehicles or videos can be procured by individuals, usufruct rights to these goods end up being communal. In some cases, the owner becomes a vehicle's only driver (dependent on him being able to drive), but such a person's ability unilaterally to control the vehicle is very limited, since demands for transportation are incessant and can only be denied at considerable social cost.

This expected egalitarianism in the sharing of cash and goods is in part a function of assimilating the handling of cash to traditional practices but also partly a function of most cash income being a welfare transfer. An individual's rights to cash earned either from producing for market exchange or from wage employment at nearby townships is more strongly controlled than a pension income. However, if individuals accumulate such cash (by target saving for a vehicle, for example), then the resulting object is treated no differently than if it were purchased with pooled funds or accumulated social security payments. The complex set of kin relations and obligations in this society make it impossible to maintain exclusive control of large items which, by definition, are nearly always in short supply.

Distribution of game and cash: case studies

In Figure 4.2 (p. 84), a sketch genealogy of the Momega band is presented. The band, comprising three household clusters,[3] consisted of the households of a man (household 1A), his sister (household 2B) and six of their married children (1B — daughter; 1C, 1D, 1E, 2A, 3A — sons), together with two related households of visitors (1F, 3C). (The nomenclature differentiates clusters [CL] by numbers and households [H] by letters.) Table 4.1 (p. 85) sets out details of seventeen cases of meat-sharing in a four-week period over January to February 1980. Three hundred and ninety-one kilograms of meat were produced in this period, and accurate details of the distribution of 68 per cent of this amount were collected. All comments on 'first-round' meat distribution refer to this Table.

The senior man's household (1A) and that of the elderly visitor (1F) produced no game in this period, but in the first-round distributions 1A's household received the second highest amount of meat. This related directly to his responsibility of overseeing the redistribution in a second round to the members of his household cluster. Another point is that while distribution evens out inequalities between households in production, there is no compensation made for the size of households or for dependency ratios. Thus cluster 3 received twice as much game per capita as cluster 1. This is in part a reflection of success in hunting, which always assures the hunter's household of a share, and is also because the more successful hunters tend to be young and to come from smaller households. Thus redistribution has its limits, so there is some correlation between contribution to production and consumption.

Information on the distribution of cash between households is presented in Table 4.2 (p. 87). It was collected during three months when the band was relatively isolated because of seasonal flooding affecting

3. The notion of household cluster, mentioned in the cases which follow, needs some elaboration (cf. Figure 4.2). Household clusters are evident in the physical distribution of households at a camp — all households in a cluster reside close together and share a communal hearth or 'kitchen'. Clusters are not permanent residential arrangements and their compositions change from time to time because of the domestic development cycle, the seasonal factor or the movement of individual households to another location. Clusters are loose economic alliances; the rationale for their composition is analysed elsewhere (Altman 1987).

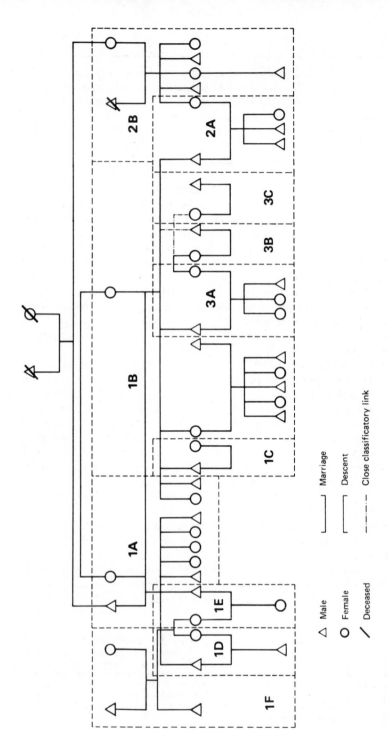

△ Male   ⌐ Marriage

○ Female   ⌐ Descent

／ Deceased   –·–·– Close classificatory link

Figure 4.2: Kinship composition of the Momega band.

Table 4.1: Seventeen cases of first-round sharing of game, January and February 1980.

| Date | Kilos of game received per household (H) and household cluster (CL) | | | | | | | | | | | | | Total |
	H/1A	H/1B	H/1C	H/1D	H/1E	H/1F	CL/1	H/2A	H/2B	CL/2	H/3A	H/3C	CL/3	
20 Jan.	9.0	11.0			9.0			8.0	13.0		11.0[1]	7.0		68.0
2 Feb.		9.9[1]						2.6			1.1			13.6
4 Feb.					6.3[1]						6.7			13.0
4 Feb.	4.8	1.9						3.8[1]	4.6		4.8			19.9
7 Feb.	6.8											0.0[1]		6.8
7 Feb.								1.8				5.0[1]		6.8
8 Feb.								3.9[1]			3.9			7.8[2]
9 Feb.		9.1[1]												9.1
9 Feb.								2.9			6.6[1]			9.5
9 Feb.												4.5[1]		4.5
10 Feb.	6.1							1.9[1]	1.9[1]		8.3			18.2
11 Feb.	12.4	3.1	2.8[1]					3.4	2.8		2.8			27.3[2]
13 Feb.	4.3	2.8[1]						3.3			3.4			13.8[2]
13 Feb.				9.1[1]										9.1
13 Feb.					5.7							1.2		6.9[2]
15 Feb.		4.3[1]						5.7	1.4		5.7	7.1[1]		24.2[2]
15 Feb.					2.5				2.5[1]		1.9			6.9[2]
Total	43.4	42.1	2.8	9.1	23.5	0.0	120.9	37.3	26.2	63.5	56.2	24.8	81.0	265.4
Game per capita (CL)[3]							5.5			6.8			11.7	

1. Household affiliation of successful hunter.
2. Some game consumed at men's hunting camp.
3. Average population: CL/1: 21.9 persons; CL/2: 9.4 persons; CL/3: 6.9 persons.

overland links to the regional service centre seventy kilometres away. All cash and supplies to the outstation were delivered by a boat that visited a nearby landing every fortnight. This was a point of contact with the market economy, where artefacts were bought, social security cheques delivered and cashed, and supplies sold. The total duration of the market contact amounted to about two hours on each occasion.

Table 4.2 provides some summary information on income and expenditure by household, the amounts presented being net household cash incomes after expenditure. In many cases, these net incomes are negative. Since the regional retailer did not allow credit at the mobile store, these negative sums indicate transfers from other members of the band. In general, these transfers occurred within clusters; hence as can be seen, for clusters 1 and 3, net income was close to zero, in marked contrast to the high variability in individual household incomes. Cluster 2, on the other hand, had a net saving of several hundred dollars. This was a result, primarily, of a high one-off payment of pension back-pay to a woman in household 2B, the pool of cash leading to a prolonged gambling bout which extended over a period of four weeks. The cash surplus eventually circulated round the community several times, with various households syphoning off portions of the total pool.

Although open conflict over the sharing of food is rare, there were a number of disputes which related to food. Actual dispute over food-sharing was observed on only one occasion. This was between two sisters.

Case 1

A group had gone by vehicle from Gurror camp to Gunbatgarri to fish for barramundi. It was early May and beyond Mangodbehgayo the road was still boggy; from there on the people had to walk to Gunbatgarri. A large quantity of fish was caught, and fifty-nine kilograms were brought back to camp. Thirteen fish were left behind at Gunbatgarri by Aga. Next day Aga's 'sister', Gon, publicly accused her of being lazy. Aga claimed that the fish were too heavy; that her husband had brought back a large load; and there was enough fish for all anyway. But she was visibly upset by the attack and said that she would go and camp elsewhere, with her patrikin. No one else at Gurror took part in the argument; though interested in every word the two sisters were screaming they politely pretended that nothing out of the ordinary was happening.

Generally disputes over food are indirect, resulting in ill-feeling and gossip rather than in direct confrontation. Although the wet season is the period when bush food is scarcest, the fact that people have to spend several months together in permanent encampments means that

Table 4.2: Receipts less expenditure for Momega households, February to May 1980.

Household	Net income from each supply boat delivery (dollars)								Total[1]	Total[2]
	2 Feb.	16 Feb.	19 Feb.	15 Mar.	28 Mar.	11 Apr.	25 Apr.	9 May		
1A	−70	−126	−50	−61	−74	n/p	n/p	n/p	−381	
1B	+58	+199	+73	+83	+64	+211	n/p	n/p	+688	
1C	−154	−20	−26	–[3]	−42	−26	–[3]	−71	−339	
1D	+15	+63	n/p	n/p	n/p	n/p	n/p	n/p	+78	
1E	+1	+5	−50	with 1A	−28	n/p	n/p	n/p	−72	
1F	+3	−48	n/p	n/p	n/p	n/p	n/p	n/p	−45	−71
2A	+48	−24	+42	−70	−20	−82	–[3]	n/p	−106	
2B	−57	+52	+56	+532	+33	+102	+80	+71	+869	+763
3A	+12	−60	0	−60	−46	−43	–[3]	−28	−225	
3B	n/p	n/p	n/p	n/p	n/p	n/p	n/p	+101	+101	
3C	n/p	+12	+16	+3	+46	n/p	n/p	n/p	+77	−47
Total	−144	+53	+61	+427	−67	+162	+80	+73	+645	

1. Household total.
2. Household cluster total.
3. No cash income and no expenditure.
4. n/p = Not present.

people work to resolve disputes as quickly as possible. An example is provided by a case of inequitable distribution of game, a problem that occurred on three other occasions.

Case 2

7 February 1980: Gab, a visitor from Barridjowgeng camping with cluster 3 (CL/3), shot two wallabies. But distribution was far from ideal; CL/2 received only one hindquarter. This was due to collusion between CLs/1 and 3 who had decided that CL/2 was not contributing enough — partly because it was headed by an artist who spent long hours producing for exchange.

8 February 1980: The head of CL/2 was convinced that his 'mother' was the instigator of the dispute and retaliated by going hunting with his brother (household [H] 3A) and his FZS[4] (H/2B). They shot a wallaby, ate as much as they could at the day hunting camp, and distributed nothing to CL/1 or the visitors.

9 February 1980: The dispute was in the process of being resolved. A team of hunters from CLs/1 and 3 shot two wallabies. One was shared by CL/1 (six households) and the other by CLs/2 and 3 (four households).

10 February 1980: The dispute flared again. Mar, from H/1A, took too large a portion of a wallaby shot by Dju (H/2B) as a reprisal for not getting any meat on the 8th. Because she was a close FZ and he was a young man, he accepted this.

11 February 1980: Dji from H/1A shot a large male wallaby. This was distributed strictly and regularly ('proper custom way'): the tail went to his FZS and ZH; an arm to his FZS: a leg each to his father and older brother; an arm (forequarter) to another older brother; and Dji kept the head. This equitable distribution seemed to resolve the dispute.

In the dry season people are more mobile and dispersed. At this time of year it is not uncommon for people to either hide, or lie about, their success rate in hunting. This behaviour is most commonly directed against people from other bands, often with the collusion of co-resident members of the band. But sometimes people get caught out.

Case 3

In November 1979, there was a mortuary ceremony at Marrgulidban, and en route to the ceremony two Momega men, Maw and Dja, shot thirty-four ducks and a wallaby. They openly presented half the ducks to their father-in-law, Kod, and the rest they consumed or

4. This chapter uses standard anthropological abbreviations for more complex kinship relations: M = mother; F = father; B = brother; Z = sister; S = son; D = daughter; C = child; W = wife; H = husband; w = woman; m = man. Thus FZS = father's sister's son.

gave away more generally. The wallaby was hidden, to be cooked later. But a child discovered the wallaby under some blankets in the back of the Toyota in which they were travelling. Kod heard of this and immediately demanded that the young men cook the wallaby. The hunters complied with his wish somewhat shamefacedly.

Case 4

In October 1980, there was a large ceremony held at Manmoyi. Some Momega men travelled to Gubumi to enquire when some close kinsmen were coming to the ceremony. Two kangaroos were shot on the way. They were taken off the vehicle near Gubumi and hidden behind some rocks. According to Momega men, Gubumi men were renowned for their greed for meat; the hunters were proud of their guile in the deception.

Case 5

In March 1980, Dju and Mar, two young brothers aged 24 and 17, went fishing at Mangalgadjurmi. They were extremely successful and between them they caught twelve large barramundi and a sarratoga. These were cooked at Mangalgadjurmi and carried back to Momega wrapped in paperbark. The bundles of fish were hidden in the bushes near Momega, and the young men walked into camp empty-handed; they had not felt up to the responsibility of distributing the fish. Later their mother went and collected the bundles and arranged distribution.

At other times, however, people may go to great lengths to share surplus foodstuffs with kinsmen in other bands. This usually happens during the dry season.

Case 6

In September 1980 Nyi, of CL/2, was camped with a small group at Yadar. He shot an emu, which is food surrounded with rigid taboos. Next day his mother, Wur, and his mother-in-law (and FZ), Gai, co-residents in his camp, carried ten kilograms of emu to Gal, their husband and brother (respectively), who was camped at Nakorro, five kilometres away.

Case 7

In October 1980, Gur shot a male euro near Gubumi. Gub, camp boss of the outstation, brought part of his share (the tail and rump, for he was Gur's brother-in-law) to Gal, his 'cousin' and long-standing friend, as a gift. Gal was camping at Miwalaber, about five kilometres from Gubumi outstation.

But there are other ways in which the norms of sharing may be breached — by loitering around a household cluster's hearth while food is cooking, or by stealing.

Case 8
Lam, of CL/1, saw some fish brought into CL/2. He went and loitered around this cluster's hearth while the fish cooked. When it was obvious that he had no intention of leaving, his patrilateral half-brother, Nyi, reluctantly offered him a small fish. Lam accepted this and left.

Case 9
Jil, of CL/2, went to see her MM, Lin, in CL/3, where some fish was cooking. She asked for some fish for her young son. Lin begrudgingly gave her some but commented she should go fishing herself. Next day Lin responded in the same manner and asked Jil for some long-necked turtle she had caught.

Case 10
Everyone from CL/3 was out hunting and gathering. Nag, a visitor at Momega who was being cared for by this cluster, took a cooked leg of wallaby from a storage platform and greedily consumed it. When people came back they were mildly cross. But Nag was *bengwar* ('crazy') — it was their fault for leaving the meat accessible.

Thus there are four types of dispute over food-sharing: open disputes, which are rare; disputes that result in ill-feeling within the community rather than in open aggression, which are more common during the wet season; devious behaviour generally directed towards outsiders (non-co-residents) but also towards kinsmen when obligations seem too burdensome; and, finally, inappropriate behaviour running counter to norms of sharing.

Cash creates several distinctive kinds of dispute: those arising out of failure to budget properly; those arising from new forms of property, notably vehicles; and those arising from gambling. Disputes over market foods were not common and were usually fairly private.

Case 11
During the 1979/80 wet season there were a number of arguments about the redistribution of market foodstuffs. The instigator of these often seemed to be Mar, Gal's co-resident younger wife. On one occasion she argued with Wur, Gal's senior wife (and Mar's full sister) who was living in H/1B with Mib. Wur, defending the interests of her daughter and daughter's husband against those of her sister and husband, felt that Mar was asking for too much flour and

sugar. At another time Mar was refused a request for sugar by CL/2. Gai and Nyi, the two household heads in CL/2, felt she should manage her affairs better: they complained that when the supply truck or boat arrived Mar was too busy buying soft drinks and tinned desserts — she should have bought flour and sugar first.

This case indicates the basis of arguments about sharing market foods: arguments occur when people regard claims as excessive or inappropriate. People also argue about the various obligations of vehicle owners. During fieldwork at Momega there was a vehicle in working order for only two months. This was Nyi's Land Rover. While the vehicle was functioning life was extremely hectic for Nyi, for all his kinsmen pressured him to meet their various transport requirements. Some people at Momega facetiously termed him 'taxi driver'. When the Land Rover broke down in early June, Nyi was quite relieved: an artist, he had not been able to paint for over two months. But by July he was saving up again to have the vehicle repaired. Arguments about vehicle use are very common and often result in the division of the band when they become intolerable and counter-productive. Meanwhile, gambling creates disputes as people try to syphon off their winnings, or when people feel they have been let down.

Case 12
Naw won A$450 in a card game at Momega. He decided to try and escape with these winnings, and set out for Maningrida. But he got word that his older patrilateral half-brother, Dal, was displeased about this and that he should return to continue the game. Naw was not happy about the implicitly threatening tone of this message; he was angry and confused. None the less, he returned to Momega almost immediately.

Case 13
Fifteen-year-old Nam was playing cards at Miwalaber with his older brother, Iyu. Iyu warned Nam not to gamble recklessly with the fifteen dollars he had given him but Nam did not heed his brother's advice. Eventually he lost the fifteen dollars, and when Iyu would not help him out he became enraged. First he went for a shotgun, but was prevented from putting a cartridge in the chamber. Next he got hold of a hatchet and proceeded to perforate a number of billycans. People let Nam vent his rage for a few moments; most found it all very amusing. Eventually his older patrilateral half-brother, Maw, disarmed him.

Analysis

In general, the strongest form of property ownership is when a single individual has the unilateral right to decide the use and disposal of the object concerned. In many cases this right is diluted because it is shared with others and/or constrained by collective interests that define and limit what may or may not be done with the property. Ownership, in the strong sense, appears to be common enough in many hunting and gathering societies where it relates to the smaller items of material culture acquired or made for personal use. Rights in game, however, are more difficult to delineate because food is a crucial medium of exchange, sustaining social relationships — and anyone who feels they have been stinted will conclude that the right sentiments towards them are absent.

The crucial distinction made by the Gunwinggu between large and small game hinges on the illegitimacy of making claims on the latter. Small game is owned and, as Cases 8 and 9 make clear, there is strong disapproval even of demanding it non-verbally. Such control is underlined by a person having the right not to bring back what he had killed by his own efforts. Nobody but a very close relative would dare to challenge this right (see Case 1). While it could be argued that ownership exists simply to create the possibility of exchange, in fact it is items least likely to be exchanged that are owned, specifically the items which are the focus of household subsistence. It may thus be argued that the essential function of the ownership of the kill is to protect the economic viability of the basic economic unit in society, the household. This is supported by Cases 2 and 11, which make it clear that Gunwinggu feel individuals have an obligation to act responsibly in the provisioning of their own households. In Case 2 an artist was failing to do this since, although a capable hunter, he was pursuing his own personal financial gain and relying on game produced by others. In Case 11 people were highly critical of the woman who failed to budget responsibly. The other side of the coin is that households may be subject to pressures, which can create problems. This emerges clearly from Cases 3 and 4 where knowing the extent of demands from affines and other relatives led people to conceal food, either because they felt they had adequately met their obligations or because they felt such obligations did not apply.

The Gunwinggu rules relating to sharing are not directed to the small game essential for provisioning the household but to occasions when there is an immediate surplus to household needs. Though there may be voluntary giving of small game outside the household, it is only when large game is involved that the formal sharing rules come into play. It is highly significant, however, that such rules only specify the destination of less than half the maximum number of basic cuts, leaving as much as 50 per cent by weight unallocated. The specified cuts safeguard the hunter's (or hunters') rights and the rights of those primary affinal kin most likely to be of an age when they are active hunters (that is, WBs), leaving the rest to discretionary distribution. Case 5 underlines the extent to which people are sensitive to the way such discretionary distribution takes place: the unmarried young men chose to leave the fish outside camp and let their mother allocate it. Had they brought such 'large game' (in this case, large quantities of small game) into camp, its public display could not have been avoided, and the household would have laid itself open to claims. For the hunter the benefit of public recognition is offset by the radical reduction in rights in the game.

As Gluckman suggests (1965: 45), to understand the claims and obligations relevant to the distribution of immediate surplus, it is necessary to have regard to the system of status relationships. At the most general level there are restrictions enforced by mystical sanctions on particular categories of people in respect of certain kinds of food. Thus for substantial periods of time subsequent to the beginning of induction into adult religious life, young unmarried Gunwinggu hunters are deprived of most of the game they hunt, which they may not eat and which they have to give to senior men as payment for the religious instruction they have received. Affines always have strong claims on a person's production: Cases 3, 6 and 7 deal with the rights and obligations in respect of these people which can never totally be satisfied. Whereas these relatives have strong expectations and can frequently be demanding, only the elder brother and father have direct authority over a hunter. Figure 4.2 and Table 4.1 make clear the flow of meat and cash to the senior man in 1A, mainly from his sons (although much of the cash appears to have come from his son-in-law in 1B). This is not so much for personal consumption but in recognition of the paternal authority, which makes this man the appropriate person to redistribute within the household cluster. In the gambling disputes the authority of the elder brother emerges clearly.

Conclusion

In terms of their subsistence economy the Gunwinggu can be classified as an immediate-return society, and as in other such societies there is a pervasive emphasis on sharing and generosity. Yet there are limits to the demand for generosity. These limits are found at the household level. The household's rights in the produce necessary to ensure its own provisioning are a property right which receives explicit recognition in the distinction made between small and large game. Even in the case of large game the essential rights of the married hunter are recognized, although the control over the greater portion depends on his status and the specific set of co-residents present. It is not that the notion of property is alien in such societies but that there is no mechanism for the accumulation of material wealth. Although the advent of cash creates the possibilities for accumulation, because it is concealable, the goods it buys are not. The disinclination to share appears to have been 'commonly felt and sometimes acted upon', as Hiatt observes (1982: 23), but the ethic of generosity and the paucity of material possessions draws all such possessions into the constant exchanges that create and sustain social relations.

5 Modes of exchange in north-west Alaska

Ernest S. Burch, Jr.

Introduction

That hunters 'share' is part of the received wisdom of anthropology. Although a few authors (e.g. Gould 1982) have suggested that modifications of this view are in order, I believe it fair to say that most students of the subject would accept without objection Dowling's (1968: 503) assertion that, among hunters, 'generosity is almost universally valued, inculcated in the young, and sanctioned by myth and tradition'. This view was echoed by Service (1979: 18), who stated that 'sharing is an expectation of the moral order and a rule of etiquette, as well as the keynote of the value system. A man shares simply because it is the right thing to do.' The clear impression conveyed by these and the many similar statements in the literature is that generalized reciprocity (Sahlins 1965: 147) is not only present in all hunter-gatherer societies, but that it is virtually the only form of material exchange that takes place in such societies.

During the course of field research among the north-west Alaskan Eskimos over a period of some twenty-five years I heard many statements about sharing and generosity almost identical to those cited above.[1] But I also heard — in interviews conducted in English — about 'buying' and 'selling', 'stealing', 'borrowing', 'inheriting' and several other ways in which goods were transferred from one person or group to another. When I investigated just how these words were expressed in the native language and what their referents were in terms of actual behavior, it became clear that the social reality of exchange was much more complex than the ideology would lead one to suspect. Not only that, it was evident that there were many contexts in which 'sharing' and 'generosity' had no place at all, even in the ideology. In this chapter I summarize the results of this research.

---

1. The research on which this chapter is based was conducted over the period from 1960 to 1986. It included extensive archival research and fifteen field trips varying in length from one week to ten months. For the past twenty years most of my research has focused on the reconstruction of native life as it was in the nineteenth century. I wish to thank David Damas, June Helm and Lawrence Kaplan for comments on an early draft of this chapter.

The study population

The north-west Alaskan Eskimos live between Bering Strait and the Canadian border; in the early and mid-nineteenth century their eastern boundary was farther west, near the mouth of the Colville river. These boundaries coincide with the Inuit Eskimo language group in Alaska (Woodbury 1984: 56). The ethnography and social history of this region have been summarized by Burch (1980; 1984), Hall (1984), Ray (1984) and Spencer (1984). The present analysis focuses on the 'traditional period', defined as the time from the first direct contact with Europeans in 1816 (or perhaps slightly earlier) to 1881, when a series of disasters precipitated a number of major changes in native life. Many of the specific phenomena described here still exist in north-west Alaska, but they have been altered to varying degrees in the new context, and the contemporary system as a whole differs significantly from the one described here.

The traditional north-west Alaskan Eskimos were organized in terms of twenty-six different social entities of the type referred to by Ray (1967; 1975: 103ff.) as 'tribes', and by Burch (1980) as 'societies'. Informants born prior to about 1885 referred to them in English as 'nations' or 'countries'. The specific societies that existed in north-west Alaska in the early nineteenth century are shown in Map 5.1.

Each society differed from its neighbors with respect to several characteristics. These include at least the following: identification as a separate unit by a societal name; ownership of a discrete territory; an ideology of distinctiveness; a high (80 percent or more) level of endogamy; association with a distinctive subdialect of the Inuit language; and the details of a number of individually minor but cumulatively significant features, such as clothing styles, taboos, annual cycles of movements, and burial customs. Populations ranged between about 175 and 1400 with an average around 450.

North-west Alaskan Eskimo societies were generally similar to one another in their general structure, but they were also adapted to the special circumstances of the different territories. The subsistence base consisted of marine mammals, fish, caribou and a variety of plant products, the precise combination of which varied from one society to another. In general, the people of north-west Alaska were able to exploit a much larger and more diverse set of fish resources than any Eskimo population in Canada and Greenland, and they also had access to a larger and more diverse set of plant resources. These two factors contributed to a higher material standard of living generally than was to be found among the 'typical' Eskimos of the central and eastern Arctic.

North-west Alaskan Eskimo societies were 'segmental' in the sense specified by Service (1970: 70) as being comprised of equal and similar

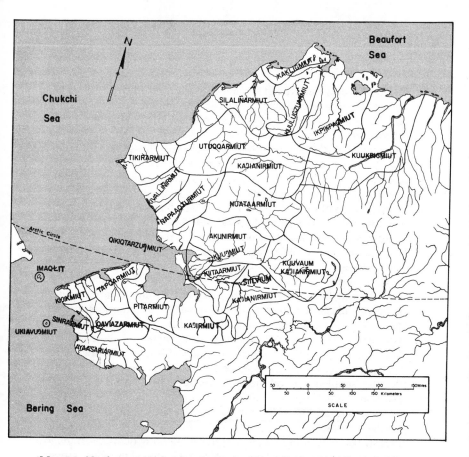

Map 5.1: North-west Alaska showing societal boundaries within the Inuit language area, early nineteenth century.

component groups. The component groups in this case were large extended families, about which more is said below. The several families that comprised a single society were connected to one another through a network of kinship and other ties. There were no offices, or councils or other governmental-type organizations to mediate relations between and among different families.

Types of property

There are many ways to classify property. For present purposes, I find it useful to categorize that of the north-west Alaskan Eskimos according to ownership. Five different types of property may be distinguished on this basis: societal, local family, domestic family, conjugal family and individual.

Societal property

There was only one type of societal property in north-west Alaska, and that was land; specifically, the territories outlined in Map 5.1. The boundaries between territories were precisely defined, and they were known to every adult.

Ownership of a given territory originally may have been usufruct, in the sense of 'ownership which emerges, with the full support of custom, as a result of constant use' by the members of the society concerned (Pearson 1985: 266). But by the beginning of the nineteenth century the criterion of use was no longer relevant. The members of each society owned all of the land within its borders, whether they used it or not. The members of many societies also used land belonging to other societies at certain times of year, and under certain conditions, without asserting any claim of ownership to it.

Recently there has been some discussion (see Cashdan 1983: 49ff.; Hill *et al.* 1983; Rosenberg 1978: 12ff.) about human territoriality in general, and about boundary defense in particular. There seems to be a basic disagreement between, on the one hand, those who insist that perimeters must be actively defended for ownership to be established, and, on the other hand, those who impose less demanding requirements. I include myself among the latter, not for theoretical reasons but because simple empirical observation shows it to be the only tenable position.

A useful model for most north-west Alaskan Eskimo societies is the border between Canada and the United States. Everyone knows, more or less, where it is, despite the fact that it is poorly demarcated in most areas. It is actively defended, if at all, at only a few select crossing points. But there is no doubt that to cross the border without following certain procedures is an offense that, if discovered, is certain to be met with force by the country being entered. And there is no doubt at all that Canada and the United States are separate, territory-owning societies.

Similarly, in north-west Alaska, societal borders were not demarcated at all, although many followed natural boundaries, such as the divide of a range of hills or mountains. They could be crossed peacefully, not at certain places, but at certain times of year or under specific circumstances, following customs that had been worked out over the centuries. To cross them under any other conditions was a threat that, if discovered, was certain to be met with force. The penalty for trespass was harsh: individuals would be killed, often after being tortured, and groups would be attacked by an armed force (see Burch 1974). Like most modern societies, therefore, the north-west Alaskan Eskimos had both rules of accommodation to permit border crossing and sanctions against it when those rules were broken (cf. Lee 1968b: 157). But there was no question about which society owned which land or about what the consequences of trespass were.

Ownership of societal land was, of course, a diffuse quality since there was no government or similar organization to hold it 'in trust' for the people. In practice, this meant that any individual could travel freely about the territory owned by his own society, subject only to some constraints at the local and domestic family levels, which are discussed below. Conversely, a constant watch was kept for foreign trespassers. As Charles Brower (n.d.: 143) discovered in the mid-1880s, 'it was almost impossible to enter a village day or night without someone seeing you'. Strangers were assumed to have hostile intentions unless they could prove otherwise, and they had to do that very quickly or blood would flow.

Local family property

In a previous work (Burch 1975a: 237) I distinguished two different levels of family unit in north-west Alaska, domestic and local. The former was defined as a family whose members occupy a single dwelling, whereas a local family was defined as one whose members occupy more than one dwelling but nevertheless still operate in terms of a single overriding family unit. A local family is what most students of hunter-gatherer peoples (for example, Helm 1965: 375) have called a 'band' or, sometimes more specifically, a 'local band'. In employing the word 'family' instead of 'band' I am not trying to be perverse. It simply seems to me that if such an organization meets a reasonable definition of family, and if investigators in Africa and Asia are likely to use the term 'family' when referring to this type of system, then students of hunters should do likewise — at least if we are attempting to contribute to a science in which broad comparisons are possible.

The local family was the primary 'segment' that made up the segmental societies of north-west Alaska. Domestic and conjugal families could separate from their kinsmen and set out on their own, but very few of them did so except during times of hunger. For most of the people most of the time, the local family was the basic unit of daily life. Indeed, most 'villages' were made up of the members of a single local family involving perhaps a dozen to seventy-five people living in two to seven or eight houses. The men hunted and worked together, the women did likewise, and everyone moved freely among the houses. Dwellings often were linked together by passageways, in which case the entire unit had something of the structure of an apartment house, but one constructed horizontally instead of vertically.

Local families owned very little property outright. One thing they did own was land; specifically, the land on which their houses were built. In contrast to societal land-ownership, this was strictly usufruct;

it was theirs only as long as they used it, at least on a regular seasonal basis. Technically they could not stop another family from building its houses very close by, although if doing so overloaded the local food supply, trouble was likely to follow. If a family failed to return to its previous settlement site in any given year, it lost any claim to it subsequently. There were no family hunting territories or fishing stations in which ownership was considered permanent.

Another type of local family property was the 'community hall', or *qazgi*. This was a building in which men and older boys gathered during the day, when not hunting, to manufacture or repair weapons and tools, to talk, and to eat. Women and children were welcome during festivals, dances, games and story-telling sessions in the evenings. In the smaller settlements, the *qazgi* was simply an ordinary house — the one in which the men gathered during the day.

The third and final type of local family property was food. Here the question of *degree* of ownership becomes especially relevant. Food, in the first instance, belonged to the person who acquired it, but more generally to the domestic and local families of which that person was a member. In the great majority of cases, the food resources of a local family were pooled, usually under the direction of the wife of the family head. All the men and older boys ate together, as did the women and the younger children. Everyone was expected to contribute to the general supply.

Domestic family property

A domestic family was a family whose members occupied a single dwelling. Occasionally a domestic family coincided with a conjugal family. Most of the time, however, domestic families were extended families consisting of at least two, and often three closely-related conjugal families (usually involving some combination of adult siblings or cousins) and perhaps an aged parent or two.

The property of a domestic family consisted primarily of food and the major items of shelter and transportation: houses, tents, large boats (*umiak*), sleds and dogs. Theoretically each of these things could belong to individuals or conjugal families. In practice they always had to be placed at the service of the domestic and local family units, which means that they exercised some ownership rights with respect to them.

Conjugal family property

Conjugal families were pretty well overwhelmed in the framework of north-west Alaskan Eskimo societies by domestic and local families. However, they did own their own bedding and also the hides or pelts of animals killed by any conjugal family member. A supply of skins was absolutely required for clothing, bedding and a few other uses; but beyond that, skins constituted a marketable commodity. Furs, particularly those of species having a restricted distribution within north-west Alaska and of species important in intersocietal trade (discussed in a later section), were a major source of wealth. In practice many couples turned over their surplus furs and hides to the local family head, but this was done in the full expectation that they would receive some benefit from whatever he was able to acquire with them.

Personal property

Personal property consisted of everything not yet discussed: clothing, tools, weapons, hunting boats (*kayak*), utensils, amulets — virtually everything used by individuals during the course of daily life. Clothing was made and maintained by women for other family members, and men made such things as the utensils, but the user was always the owner. Each individual had a personal property mark (Boas 1899; Reynolds 1983a; 1983b) with which most of his possessions — but particularly weapons — were labeled, although the oldest son or daughter (or perhaps a special grandchild) was sometimes given the mark of a parent or grandparent to use as his or her own. When a person died, it was these personally-used goods that were placed with the body on the grave.

One other type of personal property was the song. Some songs were in general use, but others — particularly magic songs — were strictly private property. Some were sung on public occasions and were well known to the other members of one's local family, but could be sung only by the owner. Others were secret, and sung only in private. Both types could be given or sold to someone else, at which point they became the personal property of the recipient.

A final type of personal property consisted of raw or partially modified mineral or plant products that had been picked up or even moved in such a way as to indicate someone's claim to it. For example, if a man found a fine piece of timber on the beach, all he had to do was prop it up in a way that indicated human intervention; then it was his, even if some time passed before he retrieved it. The incision of a property mark would bolster his claim to it, but it was not needed to establish ownership in the first place.

Division of the harvest

Fish and game were owned by individuals and the different kinds of family. However, they attained this status through processes that are sufficiently interesting to justify a separate section on the subject.

The simplest situation was for a single person individually to shoot, trap or catch an animal or fish in isolation, with no witnesses or associates. In that case, the game initially belonged to the person who acquired it. To the extent that it was considered food, it subsequently became the joint property of the domestic and often the local family of which that person was a member, while the pelt or hide became the property of the hunter and spouse.

There were many situations in which a hunter or fisherman was accompanied or assisted or observed by one or more other people, either at the time of the kill or at some subsequent period before the meat and/or skins had been disposed of. There were several possibilities here. One was for an animal taken by one person in the presence of someone else, to belong clearly and solely to the person who killed it. Bears, ringed seals, spotted seals, furbearing animals, birds and fish caught with hook and line or leister were the most common of these. This was known as *ilimikkuaq*, or 'every man for himself'. Some collective hunts were also carried out on this basis. Examples include the major annual belukha hunt carried out by the Kangirmiut people, and caribou drives in which individually owned snares were used to capture and hold the prey. In both instances the animals were herded or driven collectively, but the kill and subsequent ownership of the harvest were strictly individual.

The most common type of division was called *aviktuuzaaq*, which meant a division into equal shares among those in the party, and usually with a share for the *umiak* or net if one was used. Animals divided in this way were caribou, bearded seals, walrus, fish caught by a crew using a seine, and ptarmigan, waterfowl or hares driven into a net. The major belukha hunt at Sisualik, in contrast to the one conducted by the Kangirmiut, was also carried out on an *aviktuuzaaq* basis.

A variation on the theme of *aviktuuzaaq* was known as *pillyuk*, which means 'to take the largest share'. This meant that someone — usually the boat owner or family head — might take a little extra for himself near the end of an otherwise equal division. This was his decision to make, and not everyone appreciated this inequality. Another variation was *umiqtuat*, 'to pick out the best one'. For example, if three men killed three caribou, the senior one, who ordinarily directed the division, might pick the largest or fattest portion for himself.

The second type of division was inherently unequal, and was known as *ningiq*. In the study region this procedure was employed in two different contexts. The first was if a bowhead or gray whale was taken — in which case there was a whole set of rules governing the disposition of the carcass into a series of graded shares (see Worl 1980). The second context was when someone just followed some hunters without actively participating in the hunt, or if someone did not even accompany the hunters but assisted in unloading the sled (or in some similar way); in both cases he would be entitled to a portion of the meat or fish, but not to a full share.

A final form of division was *pikszak*. This occurred when a person was just standing around, perhaps watching someone else divide the fish or else butcher a carcass. The person doing the work might offer some to the observer, although this was a courtesy, not an obligation. This was not the same as an outright gift, however, because the recipient was expected to return the favor at some appropriate time in the future.

Transfers of property

Real estate, including land and buildings, was not subject to transfer from one person or organization to another except by default, such as when a house remained abandoned for some years and was eventually taken over by someone else. But literally everything else, once it became the property of one individual or organization, could be transferred to another, either temporarily or permanently. In English the words 'exchange', 'barter' or 'trade' are normally used to describe these transactions, but the Eskimos had a more complex set of distinctions. These are listed and briefly described below.

Simmiq: direct exchange of similar goods. For example, if one person's parka was a bit too large and another's was a bit too small, they could exchange them. This could happen anywhere, any time, between any two individuals.

Tauqsiq: this is usually translated 'buy'. Nowadays it is what happens in a store. Traditionally, the procedure was for a person to offer goods — usually furs — for sale, and one or more other people would bid (*nallit*) on them. If the seller was not satisfied with the bids, he could withdraw the articles for sale. Otherwise, the top bid (*qazrut*) carried the day. For example, if a person had a poke of seal oil, he could put it up for sale, and other people could bid anything they wanted for it — a boat, caribou skin, three wolverine pelts, a pair of boots — whatever. This type of transaction was on a 'let the buyer beware' basis, usually between people who were not closely related, and certainly not members of the same domestic or local family. Normally *tauqsiq* transactions required immediate payment. However, there was also a well-developed concept of credit, *akiqszuq*, in which payment could be deferred for some time.

Tunilaq: this was was almost the mirror image of *tauqsiq*.[2] In this type of transaction it was the buyer who initiated the transaction. He might want some goods, or some sort of service, such as the aid of a shaman. Here the buyer would state what he wanted, and then would tell what he was willing to pay for it. The 'seller' could accept or reject the offer; in the latter case, the 'buyer' could raise the offer or abandon the proposal. This type of transaction was also usually between people who were not members of the same family.

Niuviq: this type of transaction took place only between people who were in a special, permanent relationship known as *niuviriik*, usually translated as 'trade partners' (Burch 1970; Spencer 1959: 167ff.); usually they were members of entirely different societies. The essence of this relationship was to ask one's partner for some specific thing — a raw material or manufactured good — that one needed, whatever it might be, and for the partner to attempt to satisfy that request. Usually there was a pattern to the exchanges, however. For example, if one person lived far inland, he might be perpetually in need of seal oil, and his partner on the coast regularly might have a difficult time getting, say, muskrat or mink skins. But there was much more to it than that. If a famine struck one country, then the need of the person living there was basic sustenance, which he could request and expect to receive from a partner living in more fortunate circumstances in another region. In traditional times this was the main form of intersocietal alliance. The relevant transactions usually occurred at trade fairs or messenger feasts, about which more is said later.

Atuliq: 'restricted sharing', or 'sharing' with a definite expectation of a return. One type was *aturaksak*, which meant to borrow/loan a good that is dissipated in the process of consumption. Food was the most frequent type of good involved here, but sometimes clothing — especially boots or mittens — were borrowed until they were worn out. The other type was *ataqsi*: borrowing/loaning an item to use, then to be returned intact. Tools, weapons and utensils were the most common goods involved in this type of transaction. Restricted sharing apparently occurred primarily between related local families.

Pigziaq: 'unrestricted sharing'. The borrower could use or consume the good with no expectation of return. This was the sort of sharing that figured so prominently in Eskimo ideology. In practice

2. The *tauqsiq* and *tunilaq* modes governed exchanges with Europeans. The first explorers to reach the region (see, for example, Beechey 1831, I: 391; Kotzebue 1821, I: 10–11) were amazed by the native sophistication in trading and by their elaborate efforts at deception.

it occurred only between relatively close kin — almost always at the local or domestic family levels. It differed from *aiccuq*, which follows, in that ownership of the good involved continued to reside in the lender.

Aiccuq: this is a 'free gift', a transfer of ownership with no expectation of a return. This type of transaction usually involved close relatives. Successful hunters often made free gifts of food to old people or incompetent hunters in other families, however; to the extent that one did so, one acquired prestige in the community at large. Free gifts also figured in the initial stages of partnership formation.

Kinguvaanaqtuq: inheritance. For the most part inheritance involved the passage of domestic family property, such as an *umiak* or a sled, nominally owned by the family head, to his successor. But it could also involve songs or amulets passed on shortly before the donor's death, and the odd item of personal property.

Tiglik: this means 'steal'. Theft was by no means unknown in traditional times. It was one reason why people used property marks, kept as many of their goods as possible inside the stormshed of their house, and staked dogs around any outside caches. In the larger villages, which were occupied by several local families, entrance passages were often booby-trapped to catch or frighten away potential thieves (Simpson 1875: 248).

Trade networks

The various sorts of transaction outlined in the previous section were not hypothetical or ritualized activities, but part of the substance of life in traditional north-west Alaska. Virtually all of the early European explorers to visit the area found that, once their peaceful (and novel) intentions had been explained, the Eskimos became not only eager but sophisticated traders, always on a *tauqsiq* ('buyer beware') basis. Among themselves the Eskimos engaged in some kind of trade whenever members of different families or different societies came together in peaceful circumstances. Two institutions were especially important in the promotion of trade: the trade fair and the messenger feast.

Trade fairs took place annually at Sisualik, on the northern shore of Kotzebue Sound; at Nirliq, in the Colville river delta; and at Point Spencer, just south of Bering Strait. The largest was at Sisualik where, in any given year, as many as 2000 people came together for several weeks of dancing, feasting, athletic competition and trading.

The main focus of the trading at the fairs was *niuviriik*, or partnership. However, once partnership obligations had been taken care of, people were free to engage in any other kind of trade. Apparently the most common was *tauqsiq* trade, in which surplus goods were auctioned off. But *tunilaq* trade could also be initiated, whenever one saw something that he wanted badly enough to bid on. It was primarily through the transactions at the Kotzebue and Point Spencer fairs that goods such as Russian tobacco, metal, Siberian reindeer skins, and glass beads entered the north-west Alaskan economy long before the first direct contact with Europeans (Hickey 1979; V. Smith 1968).

The second major type of event was the messenger feast (*aqpatat*) (see Hawkes 1913; Spencer 1959: 210ff.). This usually took place in late fall or early winter. It involved wealthy *niuviriik* (from two different societies) and the members of the local families they headed. This event resembled the trade fair in that feasting, games, dancing and trading were all involved, but on a much more restricted scale. It has received the English label 'messenger feast' because messengers were sent by the host to his partner (and his family) to issue the invitations to come, to state what the host expected his partner to bring, and to ascertain what was wanted in return. Messenger feasts could not be held as regularly as the summer fairs because particularly successful summer and fall hunts were prerequisites; they did not involve any family every year, or every family in any year. Most of the trade at these events was of the *niuviq* variety, but participants who were not partners could and did engage in both the *tauqsiq* and the *tunilaq* variety as well.

Fairs and messenger feasts were only the major nodes in a network of intersocietal trade that spanned not only north-west Alaska, but all of aboriginal Alaska and beyond. Individuals or families could visit relatives or partners in other societies as long as an active state of war did not exist (see Burch 1976), and some sort of exchange always took place during trips of this kind. As Beechey (1831, I: 408) discovered, 'on meeting with the Esquimaux, after the first salutation is over an exchange of goods invariably ensues, if the party have any thing to sell, which is almost always the case'. Stefansson (1914: 5) estimated that goods could traverse the thousand miles between Bering Strait and Barter Island, near the Canadian border, in little more than a year. Major linguistic and ethnic boundaries were not barriers to the movement of goods across the country (Burch and Correll 1972; Clark 1977).

The accumulation of property

Through a combination of production and exchanges, effectively-led families were able to accumulate physical property in quantities that would be scarcely conceivable to members of most hunter-gatherer societies. An accurate inventory of the holdings of a domestic or local family was never made during the traditional period, but an observation made by the English explorer F.W. Beechey on 6 September 1826 may serve as an indicator of what was possible.

> From two of these [boats] they landed fourteen persons, eight tent poles, forty [caribou] skins, two kyacks, many hundred weight of fish, numerous [storage bags] of oil, earthen jars for cooking, two living foxes, ten large dogs, bundles of lances, harpoons, bows and arrows, a quantity of [baleen], [bags] full of clothing, some immense nets made of hide for taking small whales and porpoises, eight broad planks, masts, sails, paddles, etc., besides [walrus] hides and [tusks], and a variety of nameless articles always to be found among the Esquimaux (Beechey 1831, I: 405).

Beechey also noted that 'the party consisted of two [domestic] families, each of which had its distinct property, tents, baidar [*umiak*], etc.', and that, despite their wealth, they were 'of a much lower condition' than another party he had met shortly before.

As impressive as the quantity of items being transported by these families (clearly the members of a single local family) was the efficiency of their procedures:

> We watched their landing, and were astonished at the rapidity with which they pitched their tents, settled themselves, and transferred to their new habitations the contents of their [boats], which they drew out of the sea and turned bottom upwards. On visiting their abode an hour after they landed, everything was in as complete order as if they had been established there a month, and scarcely any thing was wanting to render their situation comfortable (ibid).

These passages highlight one of the crucial features of property accumulation in north-west Alaska, namely, a means of transporting it. The *umiak* was important in this respect, but sleds were nearly as helpful during the winter months (Burch 1975b).

Through a combination of competent production (both hunting and manufacture), clever trading and wise management of family affairs, it was possible for a north-west Alaskan Eskimo local family head to acquire considerable material wealth and, thereby, influence over his fellows. Such a person was known as an *umialik*, a term which etymologically means 'boat builder', but which is usually translated as 'rich man' or 'chief' by bilingual Eskimos.

No detailed account of the holdings of an *umialik* has come down to us but, again, observations from the nineteenth century indicate the general order of magnitude of one man's holdings. This time the observer is Charles Brower, the time is late winter, 1885, and the settlement is Qikiqtarzuq (Kotzebue):

Kil-yuk-ka-ruk [Kilyagzaq] was the omalik. He was a wealthy man. On his racks he had many bundles of Siberian deer skins, and several bales of Russian tobacco, besides many furs of all kinds. . . . All winter Eskimos came from every section of northern Alaska to buy deer skins and tobacco from Kil-yuk-ka-ruk, trading him their furs in exchange. He had his choice of all that was good, becoming a wealthy man. I think he had more influence with the Eskimos in the [Kotzebue] Sound than At-tung-ow-rah [Atangauzaq] at Tigera [Point Hope]. The omalik at Tigera kept his influence through fear, while the one here at Keg-ic-tow-rak, kept his through his ability to supply his neighbors with things they needed during the winter, extending them credit when they were not in a position to pay. Among his wealth he had many beads which he brought out for my inspection. Some were white. He seemed to value them quite highly. The choicest were the turquoise, of which he had many, arranged in strings and sewn on a background of buckskin, the whole forming a breast ornament with the ends fastened to the shoulders (Brower n.d.: 160–1).

Discussion

The data from north-west Alaska strongly support Gould's (1982: 88) conclusion that sharing is not the only kind of exchange to be found in hunting and gathering societies. It probably occurs to some extent everywhere (in *all* kinds of society) but it does not necessarily exhaust the repertoire of exchanges in any society.

In north-west Alaska sharing, in the sense of generalized reciprocity, was restricted to a very specific social context, namely, the local family (and its constituent parts). However, it could be questioned whether the exchanges that took place within local families involved sharing as much as they did differing degrees of ownership. Oft-repeated formulae such as 'if my brother has a boat *I* have a boat' suggest that family members felt that they had a *right* to use one another's things. The same conclusion is indicated by the vehement reactions of people whose attempts to borrow or consume another family member's goods were challenged. Meeting an obligation to share is not the same thing as being generous. A 'lender' might actually have been recognizing in practice the fact that a kinsman was part owner, even if in lesser degree, of the good concerned.

Well-led families are characterized by informants as having been redistribution networks in which all of the tools, utensils, boats and other goods that were made or acquired by any family member were placed at the disposal of all. There were very few things — amulets, some items of clothing or personal adornment, magic songs — that were exempt from this rule. If one needed something, one took it without even asking. Commodities such as meat and furs were pooled and redistributed as necessary and appropriate by the family head or his wife. It was through hard work, clever trading with outsiders, and effective management of the pooling and redistribution process that some family heads became so much wealthier than others.

Outside the local family context sharing was quite uncommon except in times of great abundance. Indeed, except where partnerships were concerned, exchanges between members of different local families tended to be characterized more by avarice than altruism. As John Simpson (1875: 247) put it, after four years' experience in the region around the middle of the nineteenth century: 'Perhaps it is not too much to say that a free and disinterested gift is totally unknown among them'. Exchange between members of different families was based on a sound knowledge of the law of supply and demand, and exercised in a geographic setting characterized by marked seasonal and regional differences in supply. The goal of buying low and selling high was well understood, and deceit was an integral part of the game.

The north-west Alaskan data also suggest why it is so easy to conclude that sharing was ubiquitous in traditional times. 'Everyone in the village used to share' is a view that is often expressed by native elders today. But of course everyone in most villages used to belong to a single local family, which is the precise context in which generalized reciprocity (or diffused ownership) did occur. It is instructive in this regard to compare single-family villages with multi-family villages such as Point Hope. In the latter the distinction between intrafamily and interfamily relations was clearly drawn, and the generalized reciprocity that one usually associates with the word 'sharing' occurred *only* in the intrafamily context.

This raises the possibility that many, if not most, accounts of generalized sharing among hunters and gatherers have been based on studies of the internal dynamics of single local-family villages. To the extent that this is so, the accounts are not wrong, they simply tell only part of the story. Until this possibility is explored, the view that sharing is the only significant mode of exchange in hunting and gathering societies should be regarded as an assumption requiring investigation, not as a statement of fact.

6. Property, power and conflict among the Batek of Malaysia

Kirk Endicott

Introduction

This chapter is a description and discussion of the ideas and practices of the Batek De' of Malaysia concerning the rights of people over material things.[1] It also explores the political concomitants of Batek views of property. I make limited comparisons with other Semang (Malayan Negrito) groups when they shed light on the Batek material.

The Batek De' are a dialect group of Semang inhabiting the watershed of the Lebir river in the interior of the state of Kelantan in Peninsular Malaysia (see Map 6.1).[2] The Semang are distinguishable from the other populations of the Malay Peninsula in their 'negroid' physical features, which include dark skin, curly hair and broad, flat noses. The language of the Batek De' is in the Mon Khmer family, but it also contains numerous loan words from Malay, an Austronesian language. The Batek population in 1975–6 was about 300, of which roughly 200 were nomadic foragers and traders of forest produce. The nomadic Batek had access to approximately 1870 square kilometers of rain forest, giving them a population density of about one person per 9.3 square kilometers.

The area inhabited by the nomadic Batek until 1976 was almost entirely covered with primary and old secondary rain forest. In recent years, however, the area has been subject to intensive logging, and it is likely that by 1990 little or no primary forest will be left outside the national park (Taman Negara) (Endicott 1982). Before the Second

1. For additional discussion of Batek ideas of rights to land and resources, see K. Endicott and K.L. Endicott (1987).
2. The information on the Batek is based on eighteen months of fieldwork done in three field trips in 1971–2, 1975–6 and 1981. I am grateful to the National Institute of Mental Health (U.S.A.) for financing the first field trip (Predoctoral Fellowship no. 7F01 MH 33054 – 01A2) and to the Australian National University for supporting the second two. I also wish to thank the Jabatan Hal Ehwal Orang Asli for permission to do the research and my wife Karen, who accompanied me in 1975–6, for her help and ideas.

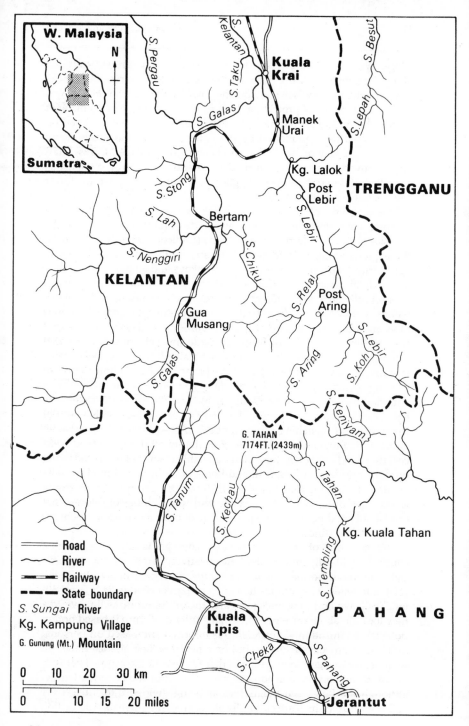

Map 6.1: The Batek area.

World War, there were numerous villages of Malay farmers scattered along the Lebir and Aring rivers, but these people were resettled by the government in 'new villages' on the lower Lebir soon after the war ended, as a means of protecting them from communist insurgents who were based in the deep forest. The departure of the Malays opened up a larger area for exploitation by the Batek and made available many domesticated fruit orchards that had been planted by the Malays, but it also removed a source of cultivated crops and manufactured goods, as the Malay farmers had once supplied such things in return for forest produce or work in their gardens.

The economy of the nomadic Batek is very complex, combining hunting, gathering, the collection and trade of forest products, and the occasional small-scale planting of crops (Endicott 1984). It is based on the exploitation of wild foods, most importantly wild yams (*Dioscorea* spp.), fruit, and small game, such as monkeys and gibbons, which they kill with blowpipes and poisoned darts. But the Batek also engage energetically in trading forest products, such as rattan and fragrant woods, with itinerant Malay traders, for rice, flour, tobacco, cloth, iron tools and other manufactured goods. Before the Malays were removed from the area, the Batek occasionally made small clearings and planted a few crops, using seeds and shoots obtained from the local Malay farmers, and in recent years they have participated from time to time in farming projects sponsored by the Malaysian Department of Aboriginal Affairs (Jabatan Hal Ehwal Orang Asli). The Batek switch frequently between these different types of activity as opportunities change, but the pattern of switching is not random. Aside from fish and game, which they pursue alongside the extraction of all the other food sources, they tend to exploit the various available resources in the following order of priority: (1) wild fruit and honey; (2) purchased food (usually obtained by trading forest products); (3) wild tubers; and (4) self-grown crops. This order seems to correlate with the number of calories that can be obtained per hour of work, the most productive resources being exploited first (Endicott 1984).

The basic unit of Batek society is the conjugal family. Each married couple is politically independent and relatively self-sufficient economically, although normally living in camps consisting of two to fifteen related families. The composition of a camp may change daily, as some families leave and new ones join, and the entire group will move to a new location about once per week. The unity of a camp is based not on political organization — leadership is informal and based on personal influence alone (see below) — but on a moral obligation incumbent on each family to share food with all other families in the camp. There are no enduring corporate groups above the level of the conjugal family, although the Batek see themselves as being divided into three 'river valley groups' (which are culturally almost indistinguishable) according to whether they habitually live in the Aring (a major tributary of the Lebir), upper Lebir or lower Lebir watersheds.

Categories of property

In the Batek De' language, the possessive is formed simply by following the term for the thing possessed by a noun or pronoun indicating the possessor (for example, *belaw ye'*, 'blowpipe me', i.e. 'my blowpipe'). This construction expresses approximately the same range of meanings as the possessive construction in English, thus telling us little about the content of the relationship between the person and the thing. There do not seem to be special terms for different types of 'ownership' in Batek, although the kinds of rights that a person can hold over things vary enormously for different kinds of 'property'.

Land

The idea of exclusive ownership of land is an absurdity to the Batek. They say: 'Only the Batek *hala'* [superhuman beings] can own [Malay: *punya*] the land'. They believe the land was created for all people to use, both Batek and non-Batek, and no one has the right to exclude anyone else from living or working anywhere they wish. The Batek do, however, recognize a special connection between each individual and a certain place or places which they call *pesaka'* (cf. Malay: *pesaka*, 'inheritance'). The *pesaka'*, which is normally indicated by the name of a river or stream, is basically the area in which a person grew up, the primary place of residence of the parents during the person's childhood. The term *pesaka'* can refer to the person's actual place of birth, a whole river valley, or a vaguely-defined region, depending on the context of discussion. It seems never to be conceptualized as a clearly bounded tract of land, however. It is an area to which people have strong sentimental ties, even though they may be living far away from it. All Batek have a right to live in their *pesaka'*, but it is no different from their right to live anywhere else in the forest. There is no sense in which the persons who share a *pesaka'* claim collective rights of ownership or custodianship over it.

The absence of individual or group ownership of land among the Batek contrasts markedly with the situation among the western Semang. Schebesta reports that in the west each 'tribe' (dialect group) owns a clearly defined tract of forest and each family has a limited tract within it. Persons may normally wander over the whole of the tribal area, but only by virtue of their being related by blood or marriage to the owners of its subdivisions (1954: 229–30). Berkeley reports that the Jahai 'are careful to avoid encroaching on the territory of their neighbors, even if their neighbors have ripe jungle fruit and they have none and there is only a little stream dividing them' (quoted in Wilkinson 1926: 12). Most likely the idea of and concern with bounded tracts of land was due to the western Semang groups being hemmed in between the Temiar and the constantly advancing Malays (Schebesta 1954: 232). The horticultural Mendriq on the Nenggiri river also have the idea of bounded territories (called *saka'*) and exclusive ownership of them. They usually live in the *saka'* of the group's headman (Malay: *penghulu*), who is seen as the owner of the land, and he parcels it out to his followers for planting. The Mendriq think of the *saka'* of their headman as theirs even when they are not using it (that is, when it is fallow), and in some cases the Department of Aboriginal Affairs has helped them get legal recognition of their claim. Like the western Semang, the Mendriq are located in a fairly densely settled area and must compete for land with Malay and Temiar farmers. The Batek De' have not been subject to such pressure and in fact have gained land with the resettlement of the upcountry Malays (Endicott 1974: 173–4).

Unharvested resources

The Batek also regard all unharvested naturally-occurring resources as being unownable. All the wild foods, forest produce and raw materials they use are considered freely available to anyone who wants to harvest them, regardless of where they are located or who found them. For example, if a man discovers a *ceh* tree (*Antiaris toxicaria*; Malay: *ipuh*), the sap of which is used to make dart poison, he will freely share with the group the knowledge of where it is to be found and will not attempt to extract any reward for his discovery. There is no need even to ask the discoverer's permission before tapping it. Similarly, the location of a newly discovered wild fruit tree is relayed to the entire group, and it thereafter becomes available to anyone, although occasionally Batek claim they would forbid outsiders, such as Malays, from harvesting it. The orchards that were planted by Malay or Chinese farmers in the past are treated in the same way as naturally occurring fruit trees, and even trees that have been planted by known Batek individuals are considered available to anyone who wants the fruit. Only after resources have been harvested do they become personal property, and then they are subject to certain sharing rules (see below).

Contradicting this general rule, however, there is a vague feeling that the fruit orchards belong to the river valley group on whose river they lie. Batek from the upper Lebir, for example, would be very resentful if Aring Batek utilized orchards on the Lebir without first asking permission — because, it is said, the Aring people have ample fruit trees on their own river. In fact, because the orchards in both rivers are so abundantly productive, such 'poaching' never actually occurs, but it is interesting that the river valley groups assert, at any rate, exclusive rights over certain orchards.

Generally speaking, all Batek have the right to collect rattan and other forest produce in any area, but if two or more camps are collecting in the same vicinity, they may informally agree that each group will harvest the rattan only in the watershed of the stream on which it is camped. This prevents parties from wasting their time searching in areas that have already been harvested by persons from the other camp. These agreements are only temporary and do not compromise the rights of anyone to exploit those areas for food or forest produce at a future time.

Again, the attitude of the Batek De' toward unharvested resources contrasts strongly with that of the western Semang. In the west, both fruit trees and poison trees are owned by the individuals who planted or discovered them. No one may tap the poison trees or climb the fruit trees without first getting the permission of the owner, although any fruit that has fallen is free to all. The trees are inherited by the owner's children or even handed over individually during the owner's lifetime (Schebesta 1954: 230–3). The horticultural Batek Nong of north-central Pahang regard *ipuh* trees as free to all, but consider certain perennial fruit trees to be owned by them as a group, by virtue of their having been planted by the common group of grandfathers (*ta'*). This is a somewhat stronger notion of ownership than that of the Batek De' in that it seems to exclude strangers and other ethnic groups from access to the fruit, although the Batek Nong themselves eat it as a *kongsi*, 'a partnership' or 'society' (the term is Chinese). The Batek Nong have some rubber trees, however, which are owned individually by the persons who planted them or their descendants. With regard to seasonal fruit trees, it would be reasonable to term the Batek Nong custom 'communal' ownership; but the Batek De' system is the lack of any ownership at all. It appears that the Batek De' have such an abundance of fruit and poison trees for their small population — more than they can fully utilize — they have no need for exclusive rights over them (Endicott 1974: 174–5).

Food

Foods become personal property when they have been harvested or purchased. The person who 'extracts' the resource from nature — for example, by digging up a tuber or cutting down a bees' nest — is its owner. If a different person found it, the person who actually procures it would make a special effort to give the finder a share, but this is not an obligation distinguished from the general obligation to share food. In the case of blowpipe hunting, it is technically the owner of the blowpipe, not the hunter, who is the owner of the animal killed, a situation occasionally arising when the hunter borrows someone else's blowpipe (darts are also borrowed, but do not affect ownership of the kill). Yet, in practice, the blowpipe owner would have no reason to assert his right to ownership of the meat, as it must be shared according to strict rules anyway. With a few foods, such as honey, ownership does make a difference, however, because the owner has the option of selling to Malay traders.

The Batek expect people to share any food they obtain with other members of a camp, and they adhere closely to this expectation. The general principle is that they must give shares first to their own children and spouse, then to any parents-in-law or parents present, and finally to all other families in camp. Thus, if they obtain only a small amount of food, it will be consumed within the procurer's conjugal family, but if there is more than the family needs, they will share it with other families. They make no attempt to save food unless everyone in camp already has enough. The portions given out are large enough to make a reasonable contribution to a meal — a plate of tubers, a leg of a monkey, for example. Thus, if a family obtains only a small excess of food, this will normally be shared with a few other families, usually those in adjacent shelters, rather than minute portions being given to all the families in camp. Generally speaking, the amounts of food that are received are roughly the same for each family, regardless of its size. Sometimes a second stage of sharing will then take place, with the smaller families passing on part of what they have received to still other families. The result is that all families end up with some food, though not necessarily the same amount, even on days when very little is brought into camp. Yet even when food is abundant, the sharing goes on according to the same principles, thus taking on a ritualized aspect as each family gives portions of its excess food to other families and receives portions — sometimes of the same kind of food — in turn (see also Schebesta 1954: 231). This apparently unnecessary distribution confirms that sharing of food is a dominant value in Batek culture (cf. Gibson, this volume).

This general sharing principle applies to both vegetable foods and meat, but differences in the actual distribution arise from the different characteristics of the foods and the ways they are obtained. Vegetable foods, especially wild yams, are a reliable food source, and usually anyone who looks for them will get some, although the amount obtained would seldom be more than three times the needs of a single family. Thus, there are usually several sources of vegetable food in the sharing network on any given day, and each source family will supply between one and three other families.

The Batek obtain animals less regularly than vegetable foods and in sizes that vary from less than an ounce to about sixteen pounds. Small animals, such as fish, frogs, birds, bats, bamboo rats, are usually consumed by the family that catches them, unless its members get a large number, while bigger animals are most often shared with the entire camp. The sharing of monkeys and gibbons, the largest animals normally obtained, is a strict obligation, and in a normal sized camp (between five and eight families) the hunter will usually give portions to every family, even when his own family's vegetable food supply is inadequate. Often the hunter will gut and partially roast the kill in the forest, and he and his companions will eat the tail and internal organs, which are the parts that cook fastest. All food collectors eat some of what they find if they get hungry, and no one begrudges them this right. The hunter cuts the rest of the monkey apart at the major joints — with the head, back, and tail forming separate segments — so that it yields about thirteen chunks of meat. If there are more families than that in camp, he may divide it further, or the families who receive the original pieces will share them in turn with other families in a second distribution. If there are fewer families, or several monkeys are brought in on the same day, larger portions or more than one portion will be distributed to each family. Some attempt is made to fit the size of the piece given to the size of the family, and women may be given slightly larger portions than men to compensate them for the prohibition on eating meat which they must observe during their menstrual periods.

Sharing food is an absolute obligation to the Batek, not something the giver has much discretion over. As one hunter said: 'If I didn't take the meat back to camp, everyone would be angry at me'. A person with excess food is expected to share it and if this is not done others do not hesitate to ask for some. And it would be virtually impossible for someone to hoard food in the open shelters of a Batek camp without everyone else knowing about it. Recipients treat the food they are given as a right; no expression of thanks is expected or forthcoming (see also Schebesta 1928: 22), presumably because that would imply that the donor had the right to withhold it. If someone were hoarding food, it would not be considered 'stealing' (*maling*) for others to help themselves to it. The Aring Batek became notorious in the Department of Aboriginal Affairs for stealing food from the medical field staff officers who were stationed at Post Aring, and I had some of my food stolen when I first stayed with the Aring people. Their attitude seems to be that it is more immoral to withhold food from those who need it than to take it without permission. The obligation to give whatever is asked for is reinforced by a belief that to refuse a reasonable request for something can cause harm to the person refused. This is called *pohnen* and is similar to the *punan* of the Semai (Dentan 1968: 55). If a person refuses to give a man food or tobacco (for example) when that man goes to work, he is likely to cut himself or be bitten by a centipede or suffer some other misfortune. Then the victim and the group in general will be angry at the offender, who will come under diffuse social pressure to grant the request. This is related to a general belief that intense emotional upset (*ke'oy*) will cause a person to become sick with fever—perhaps an accurate conception of a type of psychosomatic illness (Endicott 1974: 177–80).

The Batek share purchased or gift foods and nonfood consumables, such as tobacco and kerosene, according to the same principles as wild foods unless they are obtained in unusually large amounts. Quantities of purchased food similar to those obtained by gathering are doled out to the other families in a camp, and any left over will be shared again on following days until it is all gone. I saw no evidence of the purchasers retaining larger shares for themselves, as Howell reports for the Chewong (1983: 70). But sometimes people will buy whole gunny sacks of rice (over 100 lbs each) and other large amounts of food from village shops or Malay traders, either with cash or on credit — given for a promised future delivery of forest produce. The buyer will then resell portions of the food obtained to other Batek at cost, thus becoming, in effect, the purchasing agent for the group as a whole.

The general obligation among the Batek to share food is linked with an expectation that all members of the group will do their best to support themselves. The basic flow of food is from the environment (and traders) to the individual conjugal families, not to the group as a whole to be redistributed among the families. As everyone, except the blind and the very old, has equal access to the resources, it is expected that each family will be basically independent. Because this expectation is generally upheld, the ideal of sharing can be maintained without undue strain on any particular person or family. The Batek themselves explain that they may give food to someone else one day, but on another day they may receive it from the same person, and that this balances out over the long run. Blind and old people are helped by everyone, but especially by their close relatives. Sick persons can also expect assistance from persons outside their conjugal family if needed (Endicott 1974: 181). This system of sharing is obviously open to the possibility of abuse by people who are simply lazy, and there were at least three able-bodied adults among the upper Lebir Batek in 1975–6 who seemed to take more out of the sharing network than they put in. However, the spouses of the two of them who were married (one man and one woman) seemed to make a special effort to contribute, perhaps in compensation for the lazy partner. I once asked why the group did not tell one man, whose laziness was causing some resentment, to leave the group. The horrified answer was: 'Because he is a Batek'. The implication was that they simply could not do such a callous thing to another Batek, whatever his transgressions might be.

Forest produce

The Batek consider forest produce collected for trade to be the property of the person who procures it. That person can dispose of it as he or she sees fit, and anyone who takes it without tacit or expressed permission could be accused of stealing. Trade agreements are normally made between individual Malay traders and individual Batek, not with the group as a whole. If several people work together to collect forest produce, they keep what they get separate, or, if it is joint work, they divide the proceeds according to the amount of work each put in. There is usually no difficulty in arriving at mutually acceptable proportions, and no formal system of calculation is used. If a Batek hires another to perform a particular job, such as building a raft to carry out some rattan, he agrees in advance to pay a fixed wage or share of the profits. It is only after the forest produce has been converted into food or personal possessions that sharing rules may come into play (Endicott 1974: 183).

Personal possessions

Batek own personally anything they make, receive as a gift, or buy with their own money, forest produce or labor. Such personal possessions usually include — for a man — a few clothes, a blowpipe, some musical instruments, some pandanus pouches, a cigarette lighter and possibly a watch or radio-cassette player, and — for a woman — a digging-stick blade, some clothes, baskets, pouches and decorative combs. A couple normally owns jointly some cooking pots, sleeping mats and a bush knife. Ownership of such items is only transferred, except between close relatives, in some sort of immediate or delayed exchange. The partners in such an exchange do not bargain or seek an advantage over each other, but they expect to arrive at a fair equivalence of values regardless of the social relations between them. The only exceptions I know of are that parents and step-parents can claim things their children acquire. If someone has helped a person or given him something in the past, he may lay claim to something that that person acquires much later, if the values are about even. Money is also considered a personal possession, and a person can save it without pressure to share it with anyone else (Endicott 1974: 175–6, 183).

Although ownership is normally transferred only by exchange, personal possessions are very freely loaned and borrowed when not being used by the owners. Among friends or relatives it it not even necessary to ask permission. Thus, things like clothes, tools, and even toothbrushes, may be used by a whole group without their ownership shifting. The continuous circulation of clothes has been a problem for the medical section of the Department of Aboriginal Affairs because it tends to increase the spread of skin diseases (Endicott 1974: 183).

Some durable personal goods may be inherited, although a few of the deceased's tools and ornaments are usually left with the body. Theoretically, inherited things pass first to the spouse, then, when the spouse dies, to the oldest child of either sex. When the oldest child dies, they go to his or her spouse and then their children, but, if no spouse or child exists, to the next oldest child of the original family. In practice, the widow or widower is likely to divide the things up among the children immediately, and few possessions would survive through more than one transfer anyway. Again, the Batek De' contrast with the western Semang, among whom the 'parents bequeath all their moveable and immoveable goods to their children; if there are no children, the siblings inherit, not the wife. If the wife dies, her children and her siblings inherit, not her husband' (Schebesta 1954: 235). The difference may be more apparent than real, however. Since the Batek do not own immovable property and most personal possessions are not suited to the opposite sex (for example, blowpipes, hair combs), the surviving spouse will usually pass them along to a child of the same sex as the deceased, who can use them. The basic tools of living, such as cooking pots and bush knives, are jointly owned and so stay in the hands of the widow or widower (Endicott 1974: 176).

Discussion

The Batek themselves recognize the importance of food-sharing for group survival. They are well aware of the vagaries of the food quest and the ever-present possibility that they might fall ill and be unable to forage for themselves. The Batek system of ownership and distribution ensures that the basic unit of production and consumption, the conjugal family, is relatively independent, yet still has the security of knowing that it can get help when needed. The independence is derived from having free access to all resources in the environment, and the security from the obligation of all Batek to share food with all others whenever there is enough. Thus security is won without a substantial loss of flexibility or of freedom to move and reorganize, unlike the case with communal ownership and a system of redistribution. Obligations to specific relatives only define the pattern of sharing to be followed if such relatives are present; they do not force those relatives to live together (Endicott 1974: 183–4).

The casual attitude of the Batek toward the borrowing and lending of personal possessions is probably related to the general perishability of material things in the tropical rain forest. Things made from natural materials are continually threatened by rot because of the constant dampness. Thus, men must take apart their blowpipes every week or ten days and dry out the tubes, or the weapons will disintegrate.

Manufactured items such as radios soon succumb to the dampness, insects and the battering of the nomadic life. The Batek do not expect things to last forever or even for very long, so they simply enjoy them while they last and throw them away when they get broken. Their attitude is that they can easily make new things (if they are manufactured from natural materials), can buy others (if they are trade goods), and most things are not necessary to their survival anyway (cf. Woodburn 1982a: 444). I was amazed at the relaxed attitude of one man when his two-year-old son began using as a hammer the bamboo flute the man had just made. To my anxious report of what the boy was doing, he responded simply: 'It doesn't matter. I can make another one'.

Property and power

Power — which can be defined very simply as the ability to force others to do one's bidding — is connected with property in two ways. First, a person or group must have power in order to hold exclusive rights over something, that is, the owner must be able to prevent others from taking or using the thing that is owned. Second, people who have exclusive control over a resource necessary for survival gain further power by being in a position selectively to withhold that resource from those who depend on them for it. Not surprisingly, the Batek system of ownership and sharing is associated with a political system in which individuals have very little power, and the power of the group over the individual, while substantial, is clearly circumscribed.

Woodburn, in his article 'Egalitarian societies' (1982a; see also Cashdan 1980), delineates the main reasons why 'immediate-return' foraging societies — societies that do not store food or engage in protracted production processes — are egalitarian, actively suppressing distinctions of wealth, power and status, at least between adult males (relations between the sexes and between different generations vary from one group to another). Political equality, it appears, is due largely to the absence of any basis for individuals exercising power or authority over others. One reason is that these groups are highly nomadic, and this permits people to move away 'at a moment's notice from constraint which others may seek to impose on them' (Woodburn 1982a: 436). Also all men have access to lethal hunting weapons, so anyone subjected to coercive pressure would be able to hurt or kill his would-be oppressor, if not in a face-to-face fight then in an ambush or a sneak attack (ibid.: 436). And finally, in these societies individuals are not dependent upon others for the basic necessities of life.

> Whatever the system of territorial rights, in practice in their own areas and in other areas with which they have ties, people have free and equal access to

wild foods and water; to all the various raw materials they need for making shelters, tools, weapons and ornaments; to whatever wild resources they use, processed or unprocessed, for trade. (ibid.: 437)

Consequently, individuals make most decisions affecting themselves autonomously, and 'there are either no leaders at all or leaders who are very elaborately constrained to prevent them from exercising authority or using their influence to acquire wealth or prestige' (ibid.: 444).

The Batek, who are 'immediate-return' foragers by Woodburn's definition, fit this characterization well. There is nothing to constrain Batek from moving to another camp if someone tries to force them to do something they do not want to do, and movement to avoid potential or real conflict is common. Even the semi-sedentary Mendriq, who have headmen, say that the headman must deal with his followers fairly, or they will desert him.

Although the Batek, like the !Kung and Hadza cited by Woodburn, have ready access to lethal weapons, the Batek attitude toward violence makes it unlikely that potential tyrants would be restrained by a fear of their victims revenging themselves aggressively. Like the nearby Semai (Dentan 1968), the Batek abhor interpersonal violence and have generally fled from their enemies rather than fighting back. I once asked a Batek man why their ancestors had not shot the Malay slave-raiders, who plagued them until the 1920s (Endicott 1983), with poisoned blowpipe darts. His shocked answer was: 'Because it would kill them!' Yet, I would argue that the sheer unacceptability of aggressive behavior suppresses attempted coercion as effectively as the threat of violent retribution, since all Batek know that if they acted belligerently the entire group would abandon them. One notable result of the Batek prohibition of violence is that women as well as men enjoy freedom from the threat of physical coercion.

Batek ideas about rights to resources, their sharing obligations, and the nature of the resources themselves work to prevent any individual or group from establishing a monopoly over some necessity of life and using that monopoly to gain control over other Batek. What Woodburn says about immediate-return foragers in general applies perfectly to the Batek: 'Adults of either sex can readily, if they choose, obtain enough food to feed themselves adequately and are, in spite of the rules of the division of labour, *potentially* autonomous' (emphasis in original, 1982a: 438). The easy accessibility of food to all and the camp-wide sharing network ensure that no adult Batek is dependent upon a particular other individual for food; and even children have rights to food from the general pool and could readily turn to other relatives were their parents to withhold food from them. Thus the threat of withdrawing food or some other essential resource as a means to power simply does not exist.

If the political system is defined in terms of the use of power, then the Batek can hardly be said to have one. Even defined more broadly, as the means by which a people make group decisions and coordinate collective actions, the Batek political system is exceedingly rudimentary. The conjugal family is the only corporate group in Batek society, and the husband and wife together make any decisions concerning the family's activities and movements. They may consult other persons and take account of what others are doing, but their decisions are ultimately independent. A camp is merely a collection of politically autonomous families whose interests have converged enough to cause them to camp in the same place. Group activities, whether involving a few people or more rarely — as in the poisoning of fish — a large number, are coordinated very informally. None requires an elaborate division of labor or careful scheduling, and usually most of the participants know very well what to do. People may well defer to someone who has special knowledge or skills relating to the task at hand, but such acquiescence is strictly voluntary and limited to that particular activity.

Although decisions are ultimately made by individuals or couples, there is often extensive discussion before people make decisions about matters affecting the camp as a whole, such as whether to move. In these discussions, some persons seem to have more influence than others. These persons, who can be termed 'natural leaders', are usually older people, of either sex, who are respected for their intelligence, experience and good judgment. Other Batek often turn to them for advice, and there seems to be a tendency for younger adults to associate themselves with one of these natural leaders, usually, but not always, a fairly close relative. But there is no formal status of leader in Batek society, and many camps do not contain such a person. The ability of natural leaders to influence others depends on the persuasiveness of their arguments; they could not impose their will on others even if they wanted to.

Surprisingly, however, there are a number of Batek men who are called *penghulu*, the Malay term for headman. In fact all current bearers of this title were appointed as such by the Department of Aboriginal Affairs. There is some evidence that this and similar titles were found even before the advent of the Department, but it seems certain that they were always bestowed on Batek individuals by outsiders. It appears that traders and, later, government agencies felt the need to have identifiable leaders among the Batek with whom they could deal and whom they could hold responsible for the people's actions. When officials of the Department of Aboriginal Affairs first designated certain Batek as *penghulu*, they attempted to select what I have termed 'natural leaders' for the positions, and in many, but not all cases, they were successful. The main functions of the *penghulu*, then, are to act as a spokesman for the group in dealings with outsiders and to convey the wishes of the outsiders to the Batek. But whatever influence the *penghulu* has internally depends almost entirely on his qualities as a natural leader. In principle, the *penghulu* should derive some authority from his role as intermediary with government agencies, but since the Batek do not necessarily follow what the government orders them to do, any such derived authority is negligible.

In fact, the only power found in the Batek political system resides in the group and in the superhuman beings. Social pressure is strong in enforcing the behaviors thought crucial to the survival and well-being of the group: the sharing of food, care for the sick and elderly, suppression of violence, and so on. Property rights, such as they are, are enforced by public opinion and social pressure alone. If someone steals a personal possession of another, the group will ostracize the thief until he or she either returns the object or compensates the victim. Outside these areas, however, the behavior of individuals is relatively unconstrained by social pressure. The Batek tolerate a wide degree of individual freedom and eccentricity as long as it does not threaten the well-being of the group.

The most formal rules of proper conduct are the religious prohibitions, termed *lawac* (Endicott 1979). These disallow such acts as incest, mocking certain animals and mixing foods of various categories. People breaking these rules are punished by the thundergod Gobar, who sends a violent thunderstorm to crush the offenders under falling trees, and the earth deity, who sends upwelling floods to drown them. Gobar may also punish offenders by means of diseases or accidents. The power to enforce these rules, then, is projected on to the superhuman beings. It is tempting to view the alleged power of the thundergod and the earth deity as a Durkheimian personification of the power of society over the individual and to suggest that the need for such a mystical means of enforcement lies in the absence of sufficient power in the secular political system.

Conflict over property

Conflict in the traditional system

The traditional Batek system of ownership and sharing works smoothly as a general rule, but there are a few ambiguities in the rules that can lead to disputes, and occasionally someone will break the rules entirely. One source of some strain is the obligation of children-in-law to support their aged parents-in-law. Most Batek share ungrudgingly with their parents and parents-in-law, but a few seem to resent the constant pressure to gather extra food which this obligation imposes. Another occasional cause of conflict is the ambiguity over whether shares of food brought into camp should be saved for camp members who are absent at the time. Because the Batek do not have fixed mealtimes, they will often distribute, cook and eat food as soon as it is brought in, and they may neglect to save any for people who are still away working. There is always an element of randomness in who is given a family's extra food, and it often seems to favor the persons who just happen to be there when the distribution is made. This, too, can occasionally cause hurt feelings. The upper Lebir Batek also believe that they would have arguments with the Aring people if the latter came and camped with them in the Lebir river orchards during the fruit season. Whether this hypothetical conflict would be over the 'ownership' of the fruit or a result of the clash of personalities that can occur in an overly large camp is unclear.

Very occasionally, a person may refuse to share food for some reason. One Aring man who was married to a Lebir woman once left her about eight pounds of rice and instructed her to keep it for herself and their children while he was away working for some Malays. This caused resentment among the other camp members who claimed, correctly, that they had always shared with her. The husband was a man who had developed a reputation for antisocial behavior. He had spent some time working for the Department of Aboriginal Affairs and for Malays, and he seemed to have adopted some of the values of a wage-earner. The stealing of another Batek's forest produce or personal possessions happens very rarely, probably because it would be virtually impossible to conceal the theft.

Conflict due to recent changes

In the mid-1970s, some of the Aring river Batek De' tried to plant good-sized fields of rice and other crops with the help and encouragement of the Department of Aboriginal Affairs. One of the problems they confronted was that the traditional Batek principles of ownership and sharing are inappropriate to agriculture (cf. Woodburn 1982a: 447). The nomadic Batek De' regarded the cultivated food as having exactly the same status as wild food and therefore as being free to anyone who cared to collect it. Consequently, they flocked to the clearings of their industrious kinsmen at the time of the harvest and felt perfectly within their rights eating the crops as long as they harvested them themselves. Those who arrived too late for the harvest simply appealed to the traditional Batek obligation for those who have food to share it with those who do not. One of the farmers said the problem was so serious in 1972 that he finally 'ran away' from his sponging relatives with only a few bags of rice left from the 500 gallons (Malay: *gantang*) of rice heads he had harvested. He moved to Post Lebir, a Department-sponsored settlement on the lower Lebir, and joined the local Batek Teh who had taken up farming a few years before. Of course the Batek who want to take up farming would like to gain the full benefit of their labors, but in order to do so they would have to adopt an idea of privately owned swidden plots and crops and repudiate the obligation to share any food they have that is excess to their immediate needs. Because the foraging and farming ways of life demand opposing principles of ownership and distribution, there is likely to be continuing conflict and misunderstanding between the followers of these two economic systems (Endicott 1974: 176–7).

Another area of potential conflict between Batek arises out of the increasing importance of trade in the Batek economy. In the early 1980s the price of *gaharu* wood, a resinous wood used in incense, rose dramatically because of demand in the Middle East. This led to a proliferation of luxury goods, such as cassette-recorders, in the hands of the young Batek, mostly men, who were able to do the strenuous work of finding and cutting down the trees. Although most Batek benefited from the high price of *gaharu* wood, the benefits were not evenly spread over the population. One man in particular became very well off, by Batek standards, by becoming a middleman in the *gaharu* wood trade. In 1981, he had a large Malay-style house at Post Lebir with elaborate furnishings (such as linoleum on the floor) and two boats, one with an outboard motor. The Batek *gaharu* wood collectors preferred to trade with him, rather than the Malay traders, because he gave them a good price and did not cheat them in weighing the wood. He also continued to fulfil his obligations to share food, and he helped other Batek in their dealings with outsiders. Although at the time there did not seem to be any bad feelings toward him, the potential for jealousy and conflict was there. Yet, in the past, the frequent fluctuations in the prices given for forest produce and the rapid disintegration of things bought have made differences in wealth short-lived. And soon the destruction of the forest will bring both the foraging economy and the trade in forest produce to an end. The Batek will then be forced to live as peasant farmers on the small resettlement projects that have been established by the Department of Aboriginal Affairs, and most likely they will all fall back to a common level of poverty. But perhaps other sources of cash income, such as the salaries of the young Batek men who have recently joined the army, will replace trade as a cause of wealth differentials in the future.

Conclusion

In this chapter I have described the Batek De' ideas and practices relating to property, and the relationship of these to their political system. The traditional Batek notions that all natural resources are unowned until collected and that any food obtained in excess of the needs of the procurer's family must be shared with other families seem well suited to a nomadic foraging life, but wholly unsuited to the peasant farming they are now being forced to adopt. Yet giving up that set of ideas and practices would be psychologically very difficult for them to do, as the obligation to share food is one of the fundamental components of Batek self-identity and one of the main bonds that link Batek families together as a society. This suggests that the transition of a people from hunting and gathering to agriculture presents social and ideological problems that are at least as great a barrier as the technical problems of learning a new way to produce food (see also Woodburn 1982a: 447).

fact is change is forced upon them

Part 2

Equality and domination

7. Teaching social relations to Inuit children

Lee Guemple

Introduction

The purpose of this chapter is to describe and interpret the socialization of Qiqiqtamiut Inuit (Eskimo) children on matters of kinship. The term 'socialization' conventionally refers to situations in which adults teach children how to relate to others in socially established ways. For present purposes I will use the term to refer to three related processes: (1) the manner in which members of a society become familiar with a lexicon of terms for relatedness; (2) the way the meanings embodied in that lexicon are explicated; and (3) the way members contrive to couple labels and meanings with implied actions in order to motivate events in the world. This rather refractory definition points to the three areas I want to focus on descriptively; and it neutralizes the issue of the degree of maturity of both the teacher and the learner in the socialization process. This latter strategy is made necessary by Inuit views on the matter, some of the implications of which will be explored here as well.

The Qiqiqtamiut of the east Hudson Bay area

The Belcher Islands Inuit inhabit an archipelago measuring about 240 by 160 kilometres, located in the south-eastern quadrant of Hudson Bay approximately 160 kilometres westward from the Quebec coast. Estimates from the earliest accounts suggest that the Belchers have sustained a population of approximately 150 members since the first historical contacts in the 1700s. When I studied them in the 1960s, they were organized into four distinct hunting camps, averaging thirty-nine members per camp. The dialect and cultural canons of the Belcher Islanders conform to an areally differentiated subgrouping of Arctic natives usually labelled the East Hudson Bay Inuit; and the conventions and usages described here should be understood to be limited to this group generally and to the Belcher Islanders specifically. Other groups in other areas follow somewhat different usages and practise different techniques of socialization.

Looked at from the inside, the Belcher Islanders call themselves either Qiqiqtamiut, 'Islanders', or Sanikiluarmiut, a term which refers to the administrative town of Sanikiluaq into which the government consolidated the Islands' population in the late 1960s.[1] The Qiqiqtamiut circumscribe the limits of their social world by resort to the Inuktitut root *ila-*, 'relative' (*ilagiit*, 'those who are relatives'). Thus to be *ila-* is to be counted a member of the Qiqiqtamiut community. This category includes all Inuit with whom an individual ordinarily comes into contact on a day-to-day basis and all Inuit who are more or less 'known' to any given reckoner because they have been in contact at one time or another. The concept extends in principle to all who live in the conventional style of the Inuit, even those not known to Islanders. People of mixed pedigree (that is, with one European parent and one Inuit parent) may also become *ila-* should they become known to the reckoner, though the issue of their inclusion is a matter of some complexity.

To fall into any other category — to be anyone else — is to be declared a non-member. Among the categories of non-members are *kadlunat*, 'white men'; *adlat*, which includes 'Indians', 'strangers' and 'enemies'; and *umajasiutiit*, 'animals', which includes all hunted species. Dogs, *qimmit*, occupy a conceptual space intermediate between hunted animals and man and constitute a category unto themselves.

Relatives are not always kinsmen

Up to this point I have assiduously avoided using the term 'kin' or 'kinship' in connection with the concept of *ila-*, preferring instead the rather more generic labels 'relative' and 'relation'. And with good reason. To say that a social connection is a 'kinship' relationship implies that a label and the behaviour which it invokes are based on a genealogical principle of organization — that is, consanguinity and affinity. Neither of these principles is a reliable index of relatedness in Qiqiqtamiut society.

Graburn (1964) has argued that social relatedness among the Ungava coast Inuit is based mostly on co-residential and co-camp membership — that kinship terms take their signification from how people are spatially and cooperatively linked to one another. Graburn's findings are certainly supported by the data on Qiqiqtamiut: space is clearly the

---

1. Prior to consolidation, Qiqiqtamiut were organized into four hunting camps. These were consolidated in the late 1960s into a town site which was called Eskimo Harbour in English map references and Qudlutuq in the local dialect. Sanikiluaq became the official designation for Eskimo Harbour about 1978.

most evident mode through which social relations are expressed in Belcher Islands society. Inuit who co-reside in the same household are *idluqatigiit*, which embodies the notion of 'family'; however such persons may be linked to one another genealogically. The substance of social relations within the household is determined by a traditional division of labour based on relative age and gender. That is, Inuit are more likely to base the choice of relational labels for people on how they act in the household than on how they relate to each other genealogically.

Traditionally, households which were socially closest to each other located their dwellings proximately. Thus if couples or families felt strongly committed to one another they would establish a joint household, *idluqatigiit*, which shared a common living space. In such an arrangement everything, including the sexual and procreative capacities of the adult members of the household, might be shared. If householders felt less solidary they might choose to link their households at the pantry as *tuksuqatigiit*, sharing mainly work and commensality. A number of lesser degrees of interdependence and cooperation, including *paaqatigiit*, 'neighbours', and *nunaqatigiit*, 'landsmen', were also possible. The physical layout of a traditional Qiqiqtamiut hunting camp can be read as a recapitulation of the momentary state of social relations within the community, the distance between sleeping platforms giving a rough estimate of the degree of social solidarity between household and family groupings.

From the vantage point of any given Qiqiqtamiuq all members of the local hunting camp or the regional hunting band are 'relatives' provided that they maintain some kind of regular contact with one another and cooperate according to the traditional rules. The rules, incidentally, enjoin a commitment to generalized exchange, which translates as 'everyone shares whatever they have with everyone'. Beyond the local camp and the regional band is a realm of potential relationships which extend in principle to include all Inuit everywhere.

Damas (1963) has suggested that the Iglulingmiut, to the north-west of Hudson Bay, differentiate between relatives on a qualitative basis, on a kind of 'fade-out' principle, in which primary relatives have greater obligations than secondary relatives, and so on. Qiqiqtamiut deny that they reckon relationships by degrees; and several efforts to elicit some kind of internal differentiation along kinship lines came to nothing.[2]

2. Under the urging of John Roberts of Cornell University, I undertook a number of surveys using 'constant sum ratio' scales while in the field. Assuming that a society having an 'Eskimo' type kinship terminology (Murdock 1949) would be organized on a 'fade-out' principle (in which primary relatives are weighted more heavily as kin than are secondary relatives, secondary more than tertiary relatives, and so on) which was scalable, I employed the surveys in the hope of determining what the step-down and cut-off points for 'important' relatives were. Qiqiqtamiut always insisted on a fifty-fifty weighting in all these attempts, and deftly resisted others in which I tried any kind of forced-choice scaling.

The proximal organization outlined above may well amount to the same thing as a stair-step weighing of relationships, of course. Those who are most proximate interact and cooperate more frequently than those less proximate; and those who do not wish to be socially intimate are free to locate where they choose, either within the local camp or elsewhere within the regional band. But this proximal organization is not, strictly speaking, based on kinship since those who are counted as close relatives may be connected only remotely in strictly kinship terms. In fact, they need not share genealogical connections of any demonstrable kind to be 'relatives'!

So when it is said that this is an examination of how people learn how to relate to one another as relatives, it must be understood that 'relatives' are not, strictly speaking, kinsmen.

Children are not really children

Qiqiqtamiut are inclined to view children as essentially complete social persons in latent form (Guemple 1979a). Children are presumed to be socially whole and complete from shortly after birth and so are believed to require not so much to be taught as to be guided and directed by adults. What Europeans would undertake to invoke in children by 'teaching' Inuit attempt to accomplish by drawing out that which the child is believed already to know. Their learning model is thus closer to Plato than John Dewey.

The Inuit view of a child may best be described ontogenetically. To allow an infant to become a person requires a relatively deliberate act on the part of its parents, for newborn infants are frequently disposed of through infanticide. A decision to allow a child to live must be made prior to its fourth day of life. By that day an animating name spirit, called a *saunik* (lit. 'bone'), is believed to enter the body of the infant; and it becomes necessary to determine who this spirit is. Determining which spirit possesses the body is undertaken by divination, traditionally conducted by a shaman, more recently by someone who 'knows a lot', *qaujimaraaluk*. The process amounts to discovering what spirit, identifiable by name, has been sent from the underworld by the Qiqiqtamiut traditional deity, *nuliakjuq*, to live in the body. This is done by calling out the names which are 'eligible' spirits (see below) till the infant 'recognizes' its name. When the correct identity is discovered, the child will thenceforth bear the name of that spirit as its personal name.

Such spirits are limited in number and recycle over time. At death an individual's spirit remains in the vicinity of the body for four days, then returns to the spirit world where it is held pending 'reassignment' to another body, sometimes, but not necessarily, the first newborn child to come along. Since the ratio of spirits to living Islanders is about one to four, it follows that the child will bear the same name as one or more other living and/or dead members of the Qiqiqtamiut community, so that in some sense to be named at birth is also to share a name with one or more others who also participate in the identity which the name implies. Such sharing is not precisely 'inheritance', since neither the child, nor the bearer, nor even the diviner has any control (at least in theory) over what spirit will inhabit the child. Nevertheless, there is a sense in which the possessor of a name 'gives' it to the child, since the current bearer(s) of a name must in some manner give permission before it may be used by the child. There appear to be two reasons why conferral must be 'approved' by those who possess a name: firstly, because the possession of a common name links the two (or more) possessors by powerful bonds which we will describe in more detail below; and secondly, because the sharing of a name spirit dilutes its efficacy, spiritually weakening its power with each division. Theoretically, it is possible for three people jointly to possess a given name spirit; and almost every name used on the Belcher Islands in the early 1960s had at least two incumbents, often three, in one case four.

All those who bear the same name are considered to be, so to say, the same 'person'; and each addresses and refers to the others as *saunik*, 'bone', an expression which is, incidentally, considered to be a term for a 'relative'. *Saunit* (pl.) are believed to share a common personality, possess the same repertoire of skills, show identical attributes — in brief, all the characteristics which Europeans treat as separable components of individuality. But in Qiqiqtamiut society these attributes are understood to be bundled into unitary identities such that any possessor of a particular bundle receives all its characteristics — all that an individual can ordinarily manifest in a lifetime. Moreover, in European society these elements of character are supposed to be accumulated with age, not (since the Middle Ages, at any rate) by spiritual endowment. To Qiqiqtamiut they are conferred all at once, and complete. From four days after birth a child possesses its entire life potential in capsule form; and the business of socialization becomes one of assisting the new member (who is really an old member) to realize the potential of his or her pre-established identity.

It follows from this that there are no children in the self-formulated world of the Qiqiqtamiut, at least not in the Western 'empty vessel' sense of what it means to be a child. With this understanding of the Qiqiqtamiut outlook on socialization, we can turn to the description of how Belcher Islanders teach their children about social relations.

Qiqiqtamiut socialization

Qiqiqtamiut begin the process of socializing their children *in utero*. If the parents decide not to keep a child no efforts are made to socialize it; but if the decision is positive, even if they intend later to give it out in adoption, the parents begin the process of establishing social relations with the offspring while it is still in the womb.

From the Inuit perspective prenatal 'socialization' has three major aims: developing (protecting) the child's body; protecting it from supernatural attack while *in utero*; and binding it to members of the household and the community at large. A pregnant woman observes a taboo which restricts her diet and limits her activity in prescribed ways from the first sign of pregnancy until the fourth day after parturition. This is said to be done in order that the child may be born well formed. The natal parents and others in the household also talk to the *in utero* child, particularly after quickening, in order to establish rapport with it. These 'conversations' are said to make it feel welcome in the world so that it will want to live and also 'love' (*nadli-*) members of the household.

These activities are carried out discretely within the household. The pregnancy is never discussed outside the household, and no comments about it will be made by other community members, even if they know that the woman is pregnant. After parturition no visitors will come specifically to visit the mother or the child until it has been named; and its arrival is not the subject of comment throughout the community during that time. (If the natal parents plan to give the child away, an adoption will be arranged during this period also.) The reason given is that a foetus is susceptible to the malevolent attacks of evil spirit beings.[3] Silence about the pregnancy is viewed as a means of diverting attention away from the child, affording it some protection against miscarriage, and so on.

By!the fourth day the child is named and thus becomes a person; and thereafter the child and its mother (whether natal or adopting) may be visited in the household and discussed and commented on by the community.

Because of their views on name spirit inheritance, Qiqiqtamiut think of children, even newborn, as having wills of their own. Thus it is said of an infant who is fretful or becomes ill in the early days following birth that the illness was brought about by its 'not wanting to live', or 'not wanting to eat'. In part to help solidify the child's will to live and also to provide it with special protections during its first days after

3. In earlier days Qiqiqtamiut made a practice of disguising the gender of children, always boys, if their health situation and/or behaviour was construed as indicating that they were being supernaturally attacked. In situations of this sort the name was first changed, with the former identity of the child thereafter described as being *tukusimavuk*, 'dead', and the child sometimes raised as a girl — wearing girl's clothing, performing tasks which were part of the female's division of labour, and so on. I recorded a number of children who had undergone name changes in the 1950s, but only one had been given a female identity; he had already resumed a male identity by 1962.

birth, ritual relationships are established on or before the fourth day after birth between the child and members of society who are not of the child's natal or adopting households. We shall have more to say about these ritual relatives presently.

Because children have volition, household and community members' interactions with them take the form more of negotiation than of teaching — in order to promote as external behaviour that which children are believed already to possess inherently on the inside. This outlook manifests itself in a variety of ways. Infants and young children are allowed to explore their environments to the limits of their physical capabilities and with minimal interference from adults. Thus if the child picks up a hazardous object, parents generally leave it to explore the dangers on its own. The child is presumed to know what it is doing even if it is incapable of executing its designs because of physical limitations.

When still small, the behaviour of children is directed by exhortation or by outmanoeuvring them, rather than by issuing orders or attempting to control their behaviour by means of corporal punishment. If a child possesses a complete and unalterable identity shortly after birth, then punishing it would be pointless since, in theory, it cannot become other than what it already is.

Scare tactics are sometimes employed in order to control children. Children are not generally allowed outside alone until after three to four years of age for fear that they might be attacked by dogs which, in the 1960s, outnumbered humans by a ratio of two to one. If very young children persistently press to be taken out or allowed out of the household on their own, parents or others may attempt to dissuade them by invoking a bogey man, sometimes in the form of a dog or polar bear which they suggest may be lurking outside waiting for the opportunity to devour the child. An *adlak* — variously 'Indian', 'stranger', 'enemy' — may also be invoked for this purpose; and one inventive Qiqiqtamiut mother was not above using the resident anthropologist as a frequent stand-in for the 'Indian'. Such warnings can be seen as performing two important purposes: first, they assert the presence of threats from outside the circle of community members and thus imply the importance of maintaining good relations within; second, they underscore the boundaries of the solidary community, the limits to which kin conventions apply, by pointing out that outside there are only 'animals', the traditional prey of Inuit, and 'enemies'. The use of a device of this sort is the only really unambiguous evidence I encountered that adults recognize children to be not only physically immature but also intellectually incomplete, or at any rate gullible. In most other matters they are treated simply as small adults.[4]

---

4. In Repulse Bay I observed several parents with a child who habitually raged

Teaching status terminology

Virtually the entire community is mobilized in socializing children concerning the network of social relations. The 'teaching' of status terminology to children is ritualized in the sense that regular learning sessions take place on an impromptu basis whenever a number of people from the community or elsewhere are present.

A brief description of the generalized form of sessions will be worthwhile. Status-term learning sessions typically take place while a mother, or else another female relative who will be acting as an attendant, carries an infant in the hood of her parka when visiting in another household, something mature women customarily do in the early afternoon while the menfolk are still afield hunting. If a gathering of any sort is encountered in the host household, say a conglomeration of other women, children and older males, an informal session will be convened. The carrying woman will arrange her burden so that the infant is elevated to a position where it can see out over her shoulder. The woman will then turn her head in the direction of the infant, get its attention, then say the term *nauk*, 'where', plus some appropriate relational term, such as *angak*, 'aunt', meaning in this case 'where is your (paternal) aunt?' Very young infants are not immediately responsive to such promptings, of course; but with repetition, and aided in responding 'correctly' by the eye-contact behaviour of the assembled adults, they begin to react appropriately after several months. The use of eye contact as an aid to learning is organized in the following manner: when the carrying woman puts her question to the child, all the assembled adults immediately look directly at the one for whom the 'aunt' term is appropriate while that individual — and that one only — stares directly at the child. Children very quickly learn to scan the assembled group to locate the one who seeks to establish eye contact with them; and when such contact is established, first the named relative and then the assembled group voice a 'cheer' of sorts, laughing and congratulating the child (and perhaps themselves) for having achieved a correct answer. After a few months of such training, a child of less than a year can check off a group of relatives in a moment or two. By twelve months of age identification on the basis of eye contact begins to be replaced by an invitation on the part of the mother to point at the appropriate relative. At this stage, the assembled relatives cease looking only at the named person and increasingly monitor the child's actions so that the 'cheers' become more immediate and, in my experience, more vocal. The end result of these frequent if unscheduled

---

uncontrollably seize it and then use one hand to momentarily 'smother' it till the child ceased to struggle. In every case the child fell silent after the treatment. I never observed this technique among Qiqiqtamiut, and I presume they do not use it.

undertakings is that by fourteen to eighteen months, a child can unerringly identify by an appropriate kinship term everyone in the average hunting camp, which commonly numbered about thirty to thirty-five people in Qiqiqtamiut camps in the 1960s. A few could identify at least some visitors from other camps as well. It is important to emphasize that all of this classical conditioning technique permits passive language acquisition and use on the part of the child.

Passive knowledge of kin terms by infants is reinforced in early childhood when an individual becomes more mobile. Then exhortations to interact with relatives will be frequent and made by almost everyone. These instructions sometimes employ kinship terms. For example, a child will be handed an object of some sort and be told to deliver it to an 'aunt' or 'uncle' located elsewhere in the snow house or tent. The child is aided in making the choice of which participant to deliver the object to by eye-contact and gesture; and, once again, it is praised for a correct response. This practice of reinforcing children's passive knowledge of relationship labels continues until the child becomes articulate and can apply the labels for itself.

Once old enough to use language actively, relational terminology is sometimes verbally invoked in children by means of what E. Goody (1978), following Erwin-Tripp (1970), calls 'prodding for feedback' type questioning. Thus a relative will first attract the attention of a small child by speaking to it, usually by name, and after establishing eye contact, look quickly at some other person present, move his or her head forward and wrinkle the nose in what passes on the Belcher Islands for a 'pointing' gesture. Looking quickly back at the child the interlocutor will ask 'kina' ('who?'). The name of the one designated is acceptable as an answer and children are usually rewarded for it. About as frequently, however, the child will reply with a kinship term. This too is regarded as correct.

By the age of six years children are occasionally 'drilled' on kinship usage, and in particular on those forms which derive from ritual connections such as namesakes. This teaching takes the form of what might almost be called a 'game' in which one or more adults get the child to determine how they — either the adults or the children — are related to other individuals. The game can be played either 'forward' or 'backward': the interlocutor can supply the name of the relative, with the child expected to explain how the term is appropriate. Conversely, the interlocutor can supply the appropriate 'kinship' term for a relative, with the child supplying an appropriate basis. Since, as noted above, the basis for kinship connections is heterogeneous this may require reference to a complex system of connecting principles. By seven or eight years of age most children can supply answers to either form of questioning regardless of the complexity involved.

I believe that the manner in which children are taught the language of relational usage has important implications for understanding how relational networks are formed in the Belcher Islands. Children are taught relational language by rote, by a process which amounts to memorization, at a time in their lives when they are still too young to make much sense of what they are taking in. Lacking an understanding of the basis on which these terms are generated, children first absorb and later apply these terms to relatives as if they were part of a single, coherent system of usage, without much concern for its underlying logic.

There is another important point to emphasize. In the teaching sessions children are taught terms which are extensions of how the assembled adults see themselves as currently connected to one another. There is thus some room for political manoeuvre on the part of the adult participants in the teaching situation. Thus the female attendant may use the teaching session as an opportunity to underscore relations of some particular order with one or more of the assembled 'relatives', to honour them by asserting relations more important than those commonly understood as holding between them. Children come to absorb these subtleties as 'just so'; and they have little reason or occasion to alter the memorized facts later in life. The result is that the relational usages of any given member of Qiqiqtamiut society seem to be tailored just to fit them; they will not necessarily implicate the kinship relations of other members of their own households. So, when informants are queried regarding the derivation of some relational term they not infrequently answer that they were 'told to use that term for that person' or that they 'always used that term for that person'.

Teaching the code for conduct

If the labels which identify and sort out people in social relations are mechanically learned, and approximate genealogical networks in only a very loose way, it does not follow that kinship relationships have no content. The substance of kinship as a culturally enjoined code for conduct (Schneider 1968) is reasonably well formulated in Qiqiqtamiut society, spelled out as a series of clearly defined, abstract prescriptions. But it is not formulated in terms which are relationally specific. That is, with the exception of a very few ritually enjoined 'special' relatives, kinship obligation is on the whole expressed as a series of blanket injunctions to share or exchange. Within the household this is expressed as duties which members of each gender and age category perform for one another. Outside the household the code is expressed as an obligation to 'share everything with everyone'. Concerted efforts to get informants to express these injunctions in terms of genealogical relations were met with utter frustration!

The Qiqiqtamiut code for conduct seems to be encapsulated in three ritual relationships which are established with children shortly after birth; and it is through the enacting of relations between these ritually linked relatives that the more generalized code for conduct governing all social relations is learned. They thus constitute exemplary role models for all social relations. Two of these relationships, the namesake (Guemple 1965) and ritual sponsor (Guemple 1969) roles, are associated with rituals performed for every child. The third, betrothal, is also the subject of a ritual; but it is performed only for some children.

The namesake relationship

As noted previously, an infant receives both the gift of humanity and its social identity through the naming ritual which occurs on the fourth day after birth. A ceremony, known by the term *atiktauvuk*, 'he/she is given a name', is conducted on that day. In the ritual the identity of the spirit inhabiting the child, always expressed as its 'name', is learned through divination. The name the child receives in the ceremony is always that of one or more other members of the Qiqiqtamiut community, whether living or dead. Since the 900 people listed in my genealogies held approximately 240 names, this means that there were frequently three or even four people who shared a common name at any given moment. The conferral of the name upon a child is understood to establish a life-long relationship between the child and the one after whom it was more or less directly named, its *saunik*. This person is summoned following the divination to be the first to greet the child and 'officially' interact with it. Thenceforth, the name-giver and the child and, in a more limited way, all those others who also share its name, *atia?ualugiit* (pl.), have a life-long and continuing relationship of special solidarity. These ritual relatives are in some sense reckoned to be the same 'person' as the newborn. Because of this, all are bound together as joint and mutual 'owners' of their collective material possessions; and all are conceived as one *vis-à-vis* their respective relatives. This unity of identity is expressed in at least four ways. First, as noted previously, the relatives of the bearer of a name are presumed to be the relatives of all those others who bear the name so that, for example, the spouse of any individual is reckoned to be also a 'spouse' of that individual's namesake(s).[5] Second, the property of a namesake may be claimed as one's own, that is, without having to ask permission to

5. I was never able to get informants to give serious consideration to the possibility that namesakes could actually share a spouse in common. Qiqiqtamiut tend to explain by example rather than by reference to abstract principles; and since no one could recall a case where namesakes had actually shared a spouse, all expressed doubt that such a thing could actually happen.

possess it and use it — a facility not available to other relatives. Third, namesakes appear to be linked in what might be called 'spiritual rapport' or 'mystical influence' — such that the actions of one affect the life of the other. Thus actions of adults are sometimes criticized on the grounds that their comportment might have a deleterious effect on that individual's namesake — that the latter might become ill as a result of the adult's indiscretions. Finally, the sharing of a name is acknowledged to be a division of the identity which all participants share. Ideally, the identity should not be divided more than three times in any given generation because it may otherwise make the holders weak. When conferring a name on a child, Qiqiqtamiut claim it is best to choose someone with strength of character, someone who leads a vigorous life.

The rule of mutuality between namesakes is backed by supernatural sanctions, the most notable of which might be described as eternal death: the names of those who habitually violate the canons of traditional comportment are not conferred upon other children for fear that they too will break the 'rules' by participating in an identity which is *piyungittuq*, 'no good'. The names and, in theory, the personalities of those who do not conform are believed instead to ascend into the sky to be embodied in the aurora, barred forever from participation in corporeal existence.

The ritual sponsor relationship

The second rite is called *sanari?atakpuq*, 'he/she takes a *sanari?uk'*. It too is initiated on the fourth day after birth. The natal or adoptive parents of a newborn arrange for some adult member of the community, never one who is a member of the natal or adopting household, to become the *sanaria?unga*, 'one who begins to work', for the newborn. The initial obligation of this relative, whom I have elsewhere (Guemple 1969) termed the 'ritual sponsor' of the child, is to produce (more recently to purchase) the clothing in which the child is dressed for the first time after being named, and to present to it other items which are among those traditionally shared between members of the society as part of the system of generalized exchange: skins, tobacco, tea, and so on. Some of the items given are associated with the traditional division of labour: tools and ammunition to a boy, needles and sewing thread to a girl. A child of either gender is also given as a gift the first item of clothing it appears to take an interest in or seizes with its hands, most frequently an item of outer clothing belonging to the ritual sponsor as he or she dresses the child. In taking and receiving in this way a boy becomes the *angusiak* of the sponsor, a girl the sponsor's *arnaliak*. The parents remunerate the sponsor with similar token offerings on behalf of the child. Thereafter the child and the sponsor are bound for life to a periodic exchange of gifts and a special relationship — second only to that of the namesake — of gift-giving and mutual support.

Inuit periodically celebrate rites of maturation which occur when a child for the first time accomplishes some task associated with its role in the division of labour. Thus, when a boy harpoons and brings home his first seal, the kill is celebrated. Girls' accomplishments are similarly celebrated with a ritual. Such periodic celebrations begin with the handing over of the visible manifestation of the acquired skill to the ritual sponsor whose task it is to dramatize it to the community at large and to praise the child for its success. In the case of the boy's first seal, the sponsor invites everyone in the community to attend and to hear the story of the animal's capture. He or she will also butcher the animal and supervise the consuming of at least a small part of it prior to its division and general distribution to every household in the community. Everyone shares in this largess — all, that is, except the young hunter, who may consume no part of this particular catch. All such firsts are given to the sponsor. The sponsor generally reciprocates the gift of the food (or, in the case of a girl, of the needlework, fish, firewood) soon after with a gift to the sponsored child. In the case of the newly-celebrated seal hunter this commonly takes the form of a rifle case made from the skin of the seal received. Girls generally receive like for like; if they submit sewing to the sponsor they receive a pair of boots or gloves in return. Gifts are not limited to maturation rite celebrations. By 1967 it had become popular practice for the ritual sponsor to give presents to sponsored children on birthdays. The obligation of sponsor and sponsored child to make periodic gifts, each to the other, is life-long, and the child has special obligation to the sponsor to be responsive to his/her needs when the sponsor grows old. The obligations which sponsor and child have to each other are also said to be more efficacious than those owed to the other relatives of either.

My interpretation of the ritual sponsor relationship is that it provides a tangible basis for learning the general obligation incumbent upon relatives to share; the general obligation is expressed through the medium of exemplary acts of sharing with a particular relative whose specific, ritually obligatory role is that of exchange. While Qiqiqtamiut acknowledge that their formula for dealing with relatives is one of generalized reciprocity, to share 'anything with everyone' (*aituivugut sunatuina[ng]mik kinatuina[ng]mut*), the role of ritual sponsor makes it possible to act out that prescription on a regular basis in an everyday life context, and without the necessity of stating the rules as an abstract formula.

Betrothal

There is a third ritual of significance to the issue of teaching (and learning) the substance of social relations which merits description. This one is role-specific, in the sense that it models a relationship of a specific type — marriage. The ritual consists (or at one time consisted) of linking two children together through betrothal. I never witnessed a ritual of this sort because I was told the practice had been discontinued; and I first learned about its former practice through asking questions concerning anomalies I came across while combing through kinship protocols. I suspect that the practice was still current in the Belchers in the 1960s but that Islanders did not care to have others know about it. In any case, I have no term to identify the ritual which forms the basis of betrothal nor do I know anything about its symbolic content. I do know that children are betrothed through a rite of some sort as early as two years of age and that at one time it was considered plausible to betroth them while still *in utero* — though I have no cases of this kind of relationship.

Betrothed children are taught to address and refer to each other as 'potential' spouses, the regular terms for spouses, *arna*, 'wife', and *angutik*, 'husband', to which the modifying suffix *-sak-* is customarily added. Further, betrothal makes it appropriate for each to call the household members of the other by affinal terms. Qiqiqtamiut do not require those betrothed in childhood to actually marry their potential spouses when they reach marriageable age although they may do so. Men and women are free to choose their spouses for themselves at maturity; and in the Belcher Islands they seldom marry the one to whom they are betrothed. However, the terms for 'affines' through betrothal continue to be used into adulthood, even after each member of the betrothed pair has married another partner. The residual use of affinal terms accounts for the fact that some married people in their twenties and thirties have two and occasionally three sets of 'affines' identifiable in their relational protocols. The use of the potential spouse terms between formerly betrothed individuals is dropped after their marriage to others.

What is important for the present discussion is not the details of the betrothal rite or the numbers of 'affines' people possess, but rather the manner in which these relationships are exploited by adults to socialize children. Young children are encouraged to 'play house' with their potential spouses, play that can include going on 'family' expeditions together to fish, making miniature tools associated with domestic life, and so on. They may even engage in the acting out of sexual relations. Thus old women sometimes facetiously enquire whether boys have had sex with their betrothed. The boys always deny it when not too embarrassed to answer.

To come back to the point of the description of the three rituals presented above, each is enacted for children when they are very young, the first two four days after birth, the last by the age of two or so. Each establishes a working relationship between a child and some other member of the community who is not a household member. Each can be seen as a sort of training ground where comportment appropriate to the treatment of relatives is modelled and exemplified. The effect of these relationships is to provide a relatively complete repertoire of role models for the child to practise on. Through them it can learn how to relate to all relatives, learn all the rules which relate to kinship usage. It is important to note that all this can be done concretely, without resort to an elaborate system of abstract rules as guides to action.

Names as alternatives to relational terminology

At this juncture something more should be said about the use of names as alternatives to identification by means of relational terminology. Names are by far the most common means of addressing and referring to everyone in the Island community, even among children; and these are generally taught early and in a manner parallel to that of kinship terminology, except that the names taught are a mixture of proper names and nicknames. Nicknames appear to be generated as a means of differentiating between *saunit* (pl.) who live in a single Qiqiqtamiut hunting camp where, given the 9:2.4 ratio of people to names, noted above, simple identification and differentiation would otherwise be very difficult. By age six to eight or so children have mostly abandoned address and reference to community members by means of status labels — except for namesakes and ritual sponsors, who are referred to by status terms throughout life. Thenceforth either proper names (consisting of Christian first name plus the *saunik*-name) or a single-term nickname, or the *saunik*-name alone are used as identification.

In the light of what has been said above concerning naming and namesake relationships, it is almost as if Qiqiqtamiut conceive of their social world as populated by a cast of characters, each with a unique and already established social identity, with individuals participating in social life as parts of these collective identities. My impression is that it is by means of these collective identities that children and adults conduct much of their everyday life interactions with one another and that these interactions are fostered through concrete interactions between the child and its namesake(s). This is why a child may take whatever it likes from a namesake without asking permission and the namesake too may claim as his/her own any of the child's property. Through transactions of this sort the child is made to acknowledge that other members of society, its relatives, have claims upon its possessions and, indeed, on its very identity as a human being, not merely as a matter of exchange, but rather as a matter of joint possession and ownership.

The description presented so far may have fostered the impression that Qiqiqtamiut social relations are blandly and slavishly equalitarian. Such a conclusion would be erroneous. I have already noted that both the ritual sponsors and namesake relatives are specifically accorded priority status in the matter of giving and receiving and, in the case of the latter, in being. Concerning everyone else who is conceptualized as being a relative, I wish only to underline the fact that choices with respect to preferential treatment are not culturally formulated, or even culturally encouraged. The result is that a decision regarding who within the generalized field of kin relationships is to be treated as 'closer' (as that term is used to differentiate orders of relationships in European society) is a matter to be decided by negotiation through the politics of interpersonal relations.

Summary of the description

It will be best to summarize here what the description above has disclosed. Then we can consider what all this has to do with understanding social life, in Inuit society in particular, and among hunter-gatherers in general.

First, if one takes any protocol of kinship labels elicited from the average Qiqiqtamiut informant and tries to determine the basis on which these terms apply to people, all of whom are acknowledged to be 'relatives' of one sort or another, one finds that only a little more than half of them are linked through a genealogical frame of reference, the remainder being connected by ties which students of kinship systems have commonly designated 'fictive-' or even 'pseudo-kinship'. If one then tries to get an informant to explain the basis for these latter connections one often gets back 'that's the way it is' type answers or simple 'I don't know' explanations. Islanders plainly don't care much how they came to be related to those they call relatives. They know and can explain the source of these designations, some of which apply to everyone and some of which are traceable to the particular life history of the individual concerned; but few people actually care either how relatives are labelled or why they are labelled as they are. Most social reference and address utilizes names, not kinship terms. What seems most important is having some kind of a label for everyone who is a member of the physical community, whether that be a household, hunting camp, the Islands community in general, or someone from outside who is Inuit and acknowledges a pragmatic connection to members of the Islands community.

If one shifts the inquiry from the question of how people are labelled and how they are recruited, to one of determining the 'code for conduct' underlying status terms, one finds that obligations consist mainly of either general statements of the gender-related duties men and women are expected to perform for each other as a part of the division of labour, or iterations of a blanket requirement to 'help everyone with everything' who can be reckoned a relative of any sort. Two categories of relative are acknowledged exceptions to this rule. One is the ritual sponsor who appears to be justifiably entitled to preferential treatment in exchange, the other is the small group of living individuals who share a common name-identity, all of whom are bound together in a system of unqualified mutuality. The interests of everyone else, all other relatives, are subordinate to these, and are theoretically equal. If distinctions are made between them they are made on a basis of proximity — a sorting out which distinguishes between members of the household (whose claims are most pressing), the camp, and the larger Islands community. Beyond these are acknowledged obligations in respect of tentative relations with some mainland families and all Inuit.

The process of socialization, by means of which adults introduce their children to the already established world of the Qiqiqtamiut, can, I believe, be directly linked to the 'structure' of this relational system — if 'system' is the proper term to characterize it. Children are taught the appropriate labels for all or most of the adult members of their society by a technique which looks very much like classical conditioning, and at an age when they are too young to be burdened by the why's and wherefore's of these usages. As a result, when they ultimately reach adulthood, they are inclined to see the system as homogeneous and 'just so' in spite of its heterogeneous origins and pastiche character. The apparent simplicity of the system is supported by the fact that the rules governing how relatives are to be dealt with are simple and general in coverage. Moreover, there is apparently no need to formulate the rules beyond the level of blanket injunctions to be involved in generalized exchange. The concrete exchanges between ritual relatives provide everyday-life models of how to act regarding the larger circle of kin; they train the child in the principles of mutuality and reciprocity without those principles ever having to be formulated intellectually and honed into an explicable, logically coherent philosophy. One may speculate that perhaps this is why these relationships are ritually reinforced. Ritual becomes a substitute not only for the explanation of kinship as such but for an explicit social philosophy.

Qiqiqtamiut kinship and hunter-gatherer societies

Turning now to the question of what all this has to do with hunter-gatherers as a distinctive societal type, three points seem most relevant: first, as regards how one gets to be reckoned a relative, Inuit use a variety of devices to draw people into a network of relatedness, and this network provides that everyone included be accorded equity through their membership regardless of how they managed to get themselves included in the system; second, because of the manner in which children are socialized, this heterogeneous means of linking people together is nevertheless learned and conceptualized as being homogeneous — of a piece; third, the acquisition of ritual relatives (namesakes and ritual sponsors) at a very early age provides a concrete basis for acting out the values which underlie the system as a whole. In the case of the namesake relationship the underlying principle is that which I have labelled 'mutuality'; in the case of the ritual sponsor, it is the principle of generalized exchange.

Sahlins (1974) has suggested that what is unique about band-type societies is their basic strategy. Instead of predicating society on some form of control of the external world, band society results from adapting to the world very much as it comes, adopting a posture of structured exigency, relying on ingenuity and self-limitation to make sure nature yield up its bounty. If we take this perspective to the materials presented above, it should be clear that one way in which Qiqiqtamiut socialization contributes to an exigent lifestyle is by engendering in children a social perspective that is 'just so' when looked at from the inside but highly flexible and malleable when looked at by the anthropologist from the outside. Inuit have a social organization which is like that of most other hunter-gatherer societies: equalitarian rather than hierarchically structured, inclusional (that is, calculated to pull people in) rather than exclusional, organized on proximity (and therefore variable) rather than along genealogical lines (and therefore rigid), and based on a principle of generalized exchange rather than on highly restrained and elaborately structured forms of cooperation.

This loosely organized network is rendered plausible and believable by ritually established relationships which embody the rules of the society and at the same time create special social relations which exemplify how all social relations should be conducted. One logical implication of the belief system created and expressed by the rituals is that the life chances of discrete individuals must be counted as considerably less important to the survival of the society than that of the 'real' social entities — those embodied in names. Because the society is understood to consist of a cast of characters that subsume the identities of discrete individuals, less concern is felt over the life chances of any given individual. Thus an individual's demise, whether that of a child, an adult, or an old person (Guemple 1980), need not be counted as an irrevocable loss since the persona in which that individual participates jointly with others is not lost with his or her death. In the world of the

East Hudson Bay Inuit nobody who lives according to the customary code and thus has a claim to being 'truly' Inuit ever ceases to exist as a personality. This eliminates the risk factor that is involved in choosing to meet nature largely on its own terms.

A second logical implication worth noting is that individuals are free of the kinds of rigidity which kinship as a network of genealogical connections implies. Individual membership in the society is based primarily on participation in an already accredited personality; and that personality is only constrained by the collective definition of who and what its persona already 'is'. Since names are never acquired from primary relatives but are always drawn from the wider social network, the identities of new incoming members are not solely or even mainly dependent on their relationships to parents or siblings. Indeed, 'kinship' relationships, both as a source of personal identity and as a device for securing succession, do not exist in Qiqiqtamiut society. This detachment from family ties makes it possible both to eliminate as yet unnamed children through infanticide, thus keeping community size adjusted to the limits of resources, and to permit a relatively easy flow of personnel between households and hunting camps through adoption (Guemple 1979b). Since children are not fundamentally viewed as belonging to a particular family as such they are not dependent on some particular family for their legitimacy.

The techniques through which the young are taught to relate to others fashion a network of social ties that is pragmatic and concrete in character and this too may be seen as a positive contribution to an exigent lifestyle. Inuit life remains relatively 'unprincipled', dependent largely on an everyday-life world of ongoing relations rather than on any sense of how things ought to be in a highly structured universe of abstract social rules.

8. 'Ideology and domination' in Aboriginal Australia: a Western Desert test case

Robert Tonkinson

In 1979, John Bern published an important analysis of the Australian Aboriginal social formation. From a Marxist perspective, he attempted to 'locate and explain the ideology and relations of domination which constitute its political structure' (1979: 119). Bern addresses problems raised by strikingly divergent anthropological depictions of Aboriginal society, as marked either by 'ordered anarchy and equality' (cf. Meggitt 1966a) or by domination, hierarchy, competition and inequality (Bern 1974; 1979; 1986). In this chapter I examine some of Bern's major contentions in the light of data gathered in the Gibson Desert of Western Australia, among Aborigines for whom I use the collective label 'Mardujarra'.

My focus is on the 'traditional' culture, via the reconstruction of a way of life that existed prior to European invasion of the area. Most of the Aborigines among whom I have worked since the early 1960s were born and raised in the desert proper, away from Whites, and remained strongly tradition-oriented after migrating to settlements; nevertheless, this chapter rests on the same 'shaky empirical foundations' (Hiatt 1984: 1) that underlie all such cultural reconstructions.

Bern claims that Australianists have largely ignored the political structure of religion and have erred in assuming an absence of accumulable wealth; social wealth encompasses both the productive and reproductive capabilities of women and the society's ritual property, which includes secrets held by initiated men and unshared with the rest of society. His major thesis is that inequalities defined within religion establish and articulate the dominance structure of the social formation as a whole. While agreeing with Bern that 'the conditions for domination are evident in the Australian Aboriginal social formation' (1979: 118), I suggest that among the Mardujarra these conditions cannot be realized in any enduring way. Dominance and the monopolization of the means of production by either individuals or a particular local group are inhibited by a combination of ecological, social and religious factors that engender marked interdependence at all levels of

Mardujarra society.

Among the world's hunter-gatherer peoples, Australian Aborigines are often singled out for their high degree of sexual inequality and for their gerontocratic control of valued resources, namely women and the labour of young men (cf. Woodburn 1978; 1982a; K.L. Endicott 1981). Marked differentiation is indeed evident in certain parts of the continent, such as Arnhem Land and western Cape York, but there are clearly major regional differences (Berndt and Berndt 1985). Among the Mardujarra, who are Western Desert people, it is in fact difficult to discern inequalities sufficiently marked to distinguish them from hunter-gatherers elsewhere in the world — especially when one focuses on mundane daily life and on situations undisturbed by crisis. At such times, an egalitarian ethos prevails, and the only visible asymmetries of behaviour are those dictated by kinship. But in two major circumstances — the occurrence of disruptions of a scale demanding sanctions, and in the planning or execution of religious activity of a collective kind — clear status inequalities emerge.

It is argued here that although the potential for inequality is ever-present in Aboriginal societies, among the Mardujarra, at least, this remains submerged most of the time under the considerable weight of an ethos and praxis of mutuality and a notable stress on individual autonomy. Mardujarra society is one in which kinship statuses are rarely normatively overridden by other kinds, and so kinship dominates the structuring of interaction. Major exceptions would be the normal exclusion of young children from the demands of prescribed kin behaviours, and allowances for age difference that are integral to most classificatory kinship systems. Status inequalities are intrinsic to Aboriginal kinship, but its ego-centred networks are such that among adults the total picture is one of balance, with as much deference and respect being owed *by* unequal others as is owed *to* different others (cf. R. Sharp 1958; Tonkinson 1987). In the Mardujarra case, the same system that is invoked to deal with disturbances via a stress on status inequalities, for example when 'older brothers' must chastise or physically punish errant 'young brothers', is also an inhibitor of hierarchy in both mundane and religious affairs. Also, even in relationships that are structurally asymmetrical, as is the case between most adjacent generation members, both parties may appeal to the same imperative, namely nurturance, to assert an equality of responsibility; for example, 'you must feed me, son, because I have reared you' versus 'you must feed me, mother, because you must look after your son'.

In another paper (Tonkinson 1986) I have discussed the importance of ecological considerations and regional variation with respect to the issues presented here, and so will confine myself to a brief summation of major points of relevance. The Western Desert area is one of extreme unreliability and irregularity of rainfall, so in any given region the risk of periodic prolonged drought occurring is ever-present. The dominant cultural logic, which favours permeable boundaries, a decidedly regional world-view and a strong stress on interdependence rather than competition is thus underlain by an ecological imperative: survival may depend on unhindered access to the territories and resources of others, should drought endure in one's own territory. The permeability of boundaries is a major theme of my account of Mardujarra traditional culture (Tonkinson 1978), but the Aborigines' strongly stated spiritual and cultural imperatives can only mask and not obliterate the effect of drought on their survival possibilities. Regional variations are significant in the discussion that follows, for Bern's model is influenced heavily by his research experience in southern Arnhem Land, an ecologically favoured region (cf. Meehan 1982).

Hierarchy and everyday life

The coexistence of egalitarian and hierarchical tendencies is of course universal in human societies, but since in the Australian Aboriginal case the weighting clearly favours egalitarianism, it obliges the observer to discern when, why and for what duration inequalities of status and rights are manifest as a contrary tendency (cf. Hiatt 1986). Age and gender, as the two main hierarchical differentiators in Aboriginal societies, are obvious loci for relations of domination. Among Mardujarra of both sexes, increasing age brings respect, status as a wise person and influence and authority deriving from the possession of unshared knowledge. Mardujarra women clearly have fewer rights and lower status than men, who betroth them as infants, may lend them as sexual partners to 'brothers' or as a means of atonement for serious offence given to others, arrange their remarriages as young widows and generally get the better of them during bouts of domestic violence (cf. I. White 1970).

Adult men and women spend much time apart while engaged in hunting and gathering pursuits, but these subsistence tasks do not usually take up more than a few hours per day. Much time is therefore spent together, in family groups and as parts of multi-family bands whose members camp in close proximity to one another. In these domestic situations, Mardujarra women are not 'dominated' by their menfolk, since the norms of kinship significantly constrain the behaviour of both sexes (cf. C. Berndt 1970). Kinship, as a blueprint for interpersonal behaviour, is sufficiently flexible and comprehensive to obviate the need for additional status differentiation. Given the small size of the Mardujarra band most of the time (probably between fifteen and twenty-five people), it is not difficult for members to make decisions on the basis of informal discussion, with both sexes participating. In cases where there are serious differences of opinion, for instance, as to where or when to move next, members are free to leave one band and join another.

In the event of severe marital upsets, distinct status inequalities emerge. Besides physical abuse, occasioned most often by allegations by men that wives are neglecting domestic responsibilities and/or being adulterous, women are faced with the fact that only men can lawfully initiate a divorce, whereas any unilateral declaration on the part of the wife (for example, via an elopement) would invoke strong sanctions by the husband and his close kin. Since men are considered to be the 'bosses' of their wives, domestic violence rarely leads to major interference by other group members. Whatever a man's particular reputation, as perhaps brutal or excessively jealous, a wife cannot count on the support of the community at large. 'Community', in this sense, includes those many kin beyond the confines of the band, a large number of scattered but periodically interacting people joined in a complex web of kinship, marriage alliance, shared religious responsibility and so on. All are part of a Western Desert society which is notable for its linguistic and cultural homogeneity (cf. R. Berndt 1959).

The roles assumed during the airing of non-marital disputes derive from people's kin ties to the protagonists, and dictate the appropriate action, or inaction, expected of each person present. Should the conflict prove too serious to resolve effectively, normality may well be restored by the departure of one of the protagonists from the band, but the matter will not normally end there. A subsequent attempt at resolution usually occurs when the dispute is aired at a formal dispute-settlement session. These are held at 'big meetings', which are major aggregations of groups from a wide area, and take place prior to commencement of the main ritual business of the gathering. Such meetings normally occur once or twice a year at a prearranged venue, chosen for its reliable water and food resources. They manifest the essence of Mardujarra 'society' and provide a vital focus for its reproduction.

In mundane social process, then, the norms of kinship, in concert with a high degree of self-regulation, normally mask status inequalities beyond those intrinsic to the asymmetries of patterned kin behaviour. When hierarchy is invoked, as for example when husbands assert rights of 'ownership' or dominance over their wives, this generally stems from some disruption. Its aggressive assertion typically lasts only as long as it takes for normality to return, rather than functioning at a behavioural level as intrinsic to the husband–wife dyad. At the level of male ideology, especially when expressed in all-male company, attestations of superior status, knowledge, responsibility and power are frequently made, but their activation into dominating behaviour is contingent and temporary. In the highly important arena of religious activities, however, the potential for generating and maintaining status inequality and hierarchy is great, and it is to this vital dimension of Mardujarra society that attention must be drawn.

Inequality and the religious life

Bern correctly asserts that the key differentiating principles and major ideological representations of Aboriginal society are deeply embedded within the structures of the religious life. The imperatives embodied in the Dreaming are the Law (*yurlubidi*), which situates the origin and ultimate control of power outside human society — that is, as emanating from the withdrawn but interested creative beings of the spiritual realm. These are believed to demand human conformity and the proper performance of ritual as prerequisites for the reproduction of human and physical worlds via the continued release of enabling powers into these domains (Stanner 1964).

Bern presents the main terms of the debate concerning Aboriginal leadership and authority by reference to the opposing views of Meggitt (1962; 1966a) and Strehlow (1947; 1970), who both worked with central Australian groups (the Walbiri and Aranda respectively) but who disagree in their interpretations as to the nature of inequalities within these societies. Bern criticizes both Meggitt and Hiatt (1965) for their alleged failure to show how authority is exercised in the secular arena and in the organization and control of religion. He is in basic agreement with Strehlow that there is a significant carry-over from ritual to secular arenas in the leadership roles of men; and he and Strehlow both oppose Meggitt's kin-centred view of 'government' in Aboriginal Australia.

Bern argues that in the major group-centred cults, which occupy a central place in the ideology of the Aboriginal social formation, the possibility of a concentration of power which overflows into the secular arena is realized. In the case of individual-centred initiation and mortuary rites, however, he asserts that leadership is context-specific. Now, among the Mardujarra, situation-specific leadership is the norm for *all* rituals and not just for those principally associated with rites of passage. During the 'big meetings' of the Mardujarra, different individuals, or more correctly, different small groups, take responsibility for the organization and performance of whichever rituals are chosen. Many middle-aged and older men, because of their high status as *nindibuga*, 'knowledgeable ones', will assume a directive role at some stage in the proceedings of this or subsequent 'big meetings'. Much younger but fully initiated men may also be accorded this role as a result of having travelled to the region of origin of the ritual concerned, and of having had revealed to them the major sites and associated sacred objects 'belonging' to its Dreaming creators. In other words, a large proportion of mature Mardujarra men will assume leadership roles, virtually always in association with other *nindibuga* for that particular ritual.

Part of this diffuseness of ritual leadership roles relates to the high rate and degree of diffusion of rituals throughout the entire Western Desert region. The major initiatory rituals are shared by all groups and are therefore performed everywhere. At any given time, a large number of other rituals are in circulation, handed on from one group to another in circuits that cover thousands of kilometres and may take decades to complete. Each ritual, in each area, must have its local 'bosses' who are responsible for its proper performance and the safe-keeping of its associated paraphernalia. Very strong cultural pressures to exchange rituals (and secret-sacred objects) militate against permanent accretions of prestige or power at particular nodes in the exchange network.

Mardujarra religious life reveals no evidence of a spill-over of authority deriving from ritual pre-eminence into the 'mundane' arena of daily life such that, for instance, kin behavioural rules would be ignored by certain elders in their dealings with other members of the group. With so many rituals, each with a number of 'bosses', leadership roles are not concentrated in the hands of an elderly few. Unquestionably, there is much respect for the knowledge and judgement of older men and women, certain of whom, through strength of personality, may be more noticeable than their fellows in public affairs. Yet this prominence need not coincide with ritual leadership roles and it may not earn them 'leader' status in the eyes of others, especially in a society where any hint of egotism is likely to be contested as *gurndabarni*, 'shameless'. Bern concedes that ritual leaders may not hold sway in everyday life, but claims that this does not preclude interaction between ritual and secular behaviour.

The absence of any clearly discernible conversion of ritual power into secular domination does not mean that the Mardujarra divorce religion from the rest of their culture. Nor can Aboriginal religion be relegated to an apolitical limbo, since there is considerable overlap between these two facets of the culture. Bern notes that in Arnhem Land certain rituals could be used to punish novices whose secular behaviour warranted such sanctions. Many writers have reported this practice in different parts of the continent, and it occurs among the Mardujarra. In their case, however, the verbal onslaught or physical punishment that is meted out is tightly circumscribed by context and kinship rules and is most often highly ritualized (Tonkinson 1978: 78–9).

In the Mardujarra case, strenuous efforts are made to insulate religious activities, and particularly ritual, from unrelated conflicts that occur outside this arena. Thus the obligatory airing and settlement of disputes that are integral to every 'big meeting' is specifically separated from the ritual business that follows. The first formal order of business after the welcoming ceremonies is the adjudication of disputes. The success of these major rituals is held to be dependent partly on correct performance and partly on their being conducted in an atmosphere unmarred by conflict. The watchful beings of the spiritual realm are believed to 'hear' conflicts during rituals and to react by refusing to release enabling life-force or power to those who have flouted the Law in this important respect. During the formal settlement of disputes, the roles adopted by those who take centre stage in each can generally be predicted on the basis of their kinship relationship to the principals. At different levels, the dispute-settlement process involves the entire adult assembly, but it is notable that no one individual or small group of men or women assumes any kind of generalized master of ceremonies or orchestrating role throughout the proceedings.

Bern contends that in order to answer the critical question of where control is situated in the Aboriginal social formation, it is necessary to examine disputes and conflicts of interest, which would lead directly to the structure of religion. This seems true in much of northern Australia, for instance, but among the Mardujarra, where a carry-over of ritual authority does not occur and the kinds of secular leadership roles reported for northern Australia (see Keen 1978; Sutton 1978; Sutton and Rigsby 1982; von Sturmer 1978) are absent, the situation is different. Here, the kinship system is strongly interposed and operates largely as a levelling element. The centrality of kinship is universal in Aboriginal Australia, but some systems appear to permit the generation of enduring inequalities whereas others may inhibit them. Keen (1978; 1982) has demonstrated how kinship facilitates the generation of marked status inequalities in north-east Arnhem Land, and provides strong support for Bern's contentions with respect to the spill-over of ritual authority into secular affairs.

Where such marked inequality has been reported, it is invariably in regions characterized by the presence of clan structures, which have considerable assets, tangible and intangible, and are subject to fluctuating membership and (if in sharp decline) possible absorption through mechanisms of succession (cf. Peterson, Keen and Sansom 1977). The Mardujarra, like other Western Desert peoples, have no clan structures interposed between the family-band grouping and the society at large (cf. Myers 1976). Unlike the Yolngu, few Mardujarra men have more than two wives, despite the fact that the Kariera-type kinship system allows a wide range of choice of spouses through the operation of bilateral cross-cousin marriage rules — and despite polygyny being positively valued. If the structuring of Mardujarra kinship permits a man to amass a large number of wives (one man is said to have had eight), then perhaps the absence of clan structures is a more important differentiating feature than contrasts in kinship systems, as between the Mardujarra and Arnhem Land or Cape York (cf. Tonkinson 1980). I will return to this point below.

In discussing the importance in Aboriginal societies of inequalities between old and young males, Bern notes that the latter are unlikely to develop the kinds of rebellious consciousness that would threaten the dominant older males, given the inevitability of their eventual succession to control of the religious life, plus the effectiveness of the dominant ideology of 'gerontocratic control'. In the Mardujarra case, the control exerted by older men over their younger counterparts is a generalized one. It is based on the older men's monopoly of esoteric knowledge, which will be transmitted only if young men conform to the dictates of the Law, and are willing to hunt meat in continuing reciprocal payment for the major secrets that are progressively being revealed to them. Through the prolonged process of initiation a novice is passively transformed, via his passage through a series of named, ritualized stages, into a social adult. After marriage, he continues to participate in ritual and revelatory episodes in a life-long learning process. Thus he becomes a *nindibuga*, 'knowledgeable one'; yet there is always more to be learned, since the system strains towards but never achieves closure (cf. Stanner 1964) — especially in the Western Desert, where the diffusion of newly-created religious lore is constant.

A key aspect of the acceptance by young Mardujarra men of their subordinate status in religious affairs is the compensatory allocation to them of important responsibilities, almost from the outset of their physical initiation. All initiates are assigned important caretaking roles in connection with the even younger novices, as well as organizational tasks that are integral to ritual performances. Thus, at the same time as they are dominated from above, they are allotted dominating roles over those below them in the male hierarchy. The tenor of these unequal relationships has two distinct elements: an authoritarian tone, often harsh and threatening and calculated to inspire fear and obedience, and a protective and nurturant stance. Again, who plays what role depends on his kin relationship to the unequal other and accords broadly with a major society-wide dual division, that of *garngu* and *jinjanungu*, which is very similar to the ritually important 'endogamous moieties' (more correctly termed 'merged alternate generation level groupings'; cf. Tonkinson 1974; 1978: 58–9).

What the older men are most concerned to impart to the younger in the tense, emotionally-charged ambience of ritual is a strong awareness of the enormous responsibility that is being given them for ensuring the continued well-being of the entire society. What is being indelibly imprinted on the novices is the imperative that they ensure, through conformity and active participation in the religious life, the continued release of power from the realm of the Dreaming into the physical and social world. The inequalities evinced in these ritual situations are palpably great, such is the total control and emotional dominance of the fully initiated men, and there are no situations in mundane life that could even begin to compare. Yet the major message imparted during the disciplinary and revelatory sessions is of a greater authority, outside the human realm, to which all must submit if the legacy of the Dreaming is to be perpetuated. Even the oldest and wisest men are only intermediaries or vehicles for the maintenance of the Law, which is encountered by Aborigines as a fixed and immutable set of spiritual dictates (cf. Tonkinson 1978; 1984).

The ritual hegemony of the initiated men is unassailable as long as the rest of society accepts so utterly the dominant ideology; but even they, too, are prevented from capitalizing on their total control within the frame of the religious life by extending it into secular life, because the Law as received contains no charter for such an arrogation. There are important ritual statuses that differentiate the ranks of initiated men, and of women, as senior and less senior in terms of specific responsibilities — for example, as guardians of the stores of sacred objects, or cooks for major ritual feasts. These, however, do not provide senior incumbents with any charter for asserting their high status outside the domain of the religious life. Fully initiated men regard one another in a generalized sense (beyond the asymmetries intrinsic to kin relationships) as equals, and assert their autonomy — in everyday life the Law is everyone's boss, not other men. This same assertion applies among adult women.

Mardujarra women have their own rituals, some of which are secret-sacred and may partially or totally exclude men. But in volume and social prominence, their religious activities are decidedly more limited than men's, and must be fitted within schedules dictated by the men during 'big meetings', never vice versa. As Bern points out, women are already located in the Aboriginal social formation as antithesis, and neither they nor the men believe that the reproduction of the society at large hinges on women's rituals. Men control the fertility of the natural environment. One of Bern's most important observations is that men even deny women the credit for their major productive input as food gatherers, since the dominant ideology asserts that all such resources are made possible through men's religious practice, the 'work' of ritual. With respect to human physiological reproduction, too, there is in Mardujarra belief a clear element of autonomy in the behaviour of 'spirit-children' as they 'find' and enter their human mothers. It appears that, right across the Western Desert, there is a distinct downplaying, if not denial, of the physiological aspects of both maternity and paternity in the pre-natal phase of the human life cycle (Tonkinson 1984; Mountford 1981).

Intergroup relations and regionalism

In addition to vertical differentiation on the basis of hierarchical principles, Bern discusses what he terms 'segmentary divisions' of the Aboriginal social formation, such as clans, language groups or totemic entities, whose internal structures are repeated in each group of its kind, and within each of which are found members of every category. Bern regards the success of these segmentary groups as dependent on the outcome of competition among mature males for control of valued social resources at the expense of other like groups. His point here is that no matter who prevails, the existing societal structures of 'domination' are reinforced. Among the constituent groups of the Mardujarra, segmentary relationships reveal the dominance of cooperation over competitive tendencies. Throughout their region, and well beyond the Gibson Desert into the Western Desert as a whole, the ramifying and cross-cutting bonds of kinship, social category, language and marriage facilitate an open-ended regional network that transcends local parochial interests and thus diminishes the significance of boundaries.

In accordance with the received truths of the Law, the great ancestral creative beings of the Dreaming epoch left behind different groups, beliefs and customs in different areas, thus laying the foundations for the development of local identities and a concomitant ethnocentrism. But the wanderings of the most prominent beings created meandering *yiwarra* ('paths', 'tracks') criss-crossing most of the Western Desert (cf. R. Berndt 1959; Gould 1969). Since the major creative beings are associated with large cult rituals that are performed throughout the region, the ties thus created by common interest, totemic 'descent', ritual responsibility, and so on, are very strong. These regional bonds link each local group into the much larger geographical and cultural 'community', which extends well beyond the bounds of the large aggregations that occur each year.

Newly-created rituals, 'given' to living Aborigines via dream-spirit beings which act as intermediaries between the spiritual and human realms, constantly enter the circuit of travelling cults. Newly-discovered sacred objects (again, the alleged result of revelations by spirit-beings to humans) and ritual paraphernalia are an integral part of the circulation of wealth among Western Desert groups. All such new knowledge is believed to emanate initially from the spiritual realm, so people therefore cannot and do not claim personal credit for such creativity. Besides, most rituals that are composed from dream-spirit experiences involve more than one person in their creation (Tonkinson 1970). Locally-created rituals, known as *bardunjarrijanu*, 'from the dream-spirit', do not enter the regional circuit immediately, but are a valued resource that is deliberately retained so as to attract other groups to the territory of the composing group.

The hoarding of such rituals by particular groups, however, is viewed by the Mardujarra as akin to someone refusing to share, which is ideologically unthinkable. Groups are therefore under strong pressure to release these rituals, especially if they prove popular, and in so doing they eventually must lose control over them. The rituals and associated paraphernalia are handed on from group to group at larger gatherings and are thus diffused into distant parts of the desert. Rituals must be released in this manner, to leave room for newly-created local rituals and to facilitate the inflow of similar rituals from other areas.

The increase rite (*jabiya*) is possibly the most important category of non-travelling ritual. Of great importance throughout the continent, this ritual is generally a fairly brief and uncomplicated rite performed annually at a particular site. The site is believed to contain within it the spirits of untold numbers of a particular animal or plant species or phenomenon. The performance of the increase rite is thus essential to ensure the release of the species into the physical world. Among the Mardujarra, the scatter of increase sites appears to be such that at least one exists in the territory of every estate-group (cf. Tonkinson 1978: 50–3). There is thus a widespread regional sharing of responsibility for ensuring the continued abundance of vital food resources via the medium of increase rites which are performed at each site by the local elders who have responsibility for it. Each group is thus dependent upon a lot of others, near and far, for the reproduction of the society as a whole.

Recognition of this regional interdependence is evinced by a very interesting Mardujarra practice. If a particular plant or animal species happens not to appear plentifully in an area where it is expected to do well, and there is no obvious reason for its failure to meet local Aboriginal expectations, those who live in the affected area may be sufficiently upset to despatch messengers, who bear a warning to the guardians responsible for the increase centre concerned. A small sacred object, which, significantly, bears the same name as a variety of contract sorcery (*yumbu*), is delivered. It symbolizes both complaint (a tacit allegation of inadequate ritual performance) and admonition.

Mardujarra ritual life demands widespread travel in order for people to acquire essential knowledge. Besides long periods of ritual isolation from the society at large, during which time elders impart much important knowledge, newly subincised young men must spend a year or two in the care of older guardians who take them on an odyssey that retraces the journeys of major creative beings over a wide area. This enables their mentors to teach them the totemic geography and spiritual significance of the sites and territory, by linking these to songlines, rituals and the creative marvels of the Dreaming. Such long journeys also enable the young men to be introduced as adults to all the groups encountered and to enter the secret life of adult men across a wide region.

Most important in this regard is the major ritual known as *mirdayidi*, which is held periodically at estates both far and near to that of the novice. In the secret-sacred feast that is central to this ritual, small groups of novices who have been brought together from neighbouring areas are shown for the first time the content of the estate's storehouse of sacred objects. During this highly dramatic rite, they are fed seed-cakes mixed with the fat which forms a protective coating over the wooden objects. They thus ingest 'country', the very life-essence or ancestral power of the host estate, which is immanent in the objects displayed. Henceforth, every novice has an indisputable right of access to and exploitation of the natural resources of that area. The young men have hunted meat and undergone ordeals to 'pay for' this right, and with each successive *mirdayidi* eaten elsewhere they gain rights of access to more and more territory.

Multiple factors, such as birth, descent, totemic affiliation and initiation link individual Mardujarra to a large number of sites and 'countries' (as well as to other peoples) and thus create a widely overlapping network of territorial anchorages. The religious life, at all levels, seems to anticipate and reflect the realities of an extremely marginal and drought-prone habitat by placing a high valuation on sharing, interdependence and notions of community. These virtues figure prominently in a world-view that encompasses an area well beyond the limits of any particular local group or its range. Nothing in Mardujarra culture fosters the kind of intergroup competition of scarce resources that would generate retaliation of a boundary-closing kind. Kinship, ritual, marriage alliance, shared ideology and a host of other cultural elements stress broader linkages which facilitate access to the territories of many other groups.

The possibilities for the evolution of significant intergroup inequalities in the Western Desert are in any case limited by the relatively even spread of basic ecological resources, as well as by an equality of opportunity with respect to the creation of valued social capital (cf. Chase 1984). All groups are free to compose new rituals, but are equally constrained to release them into the regional network of exchange after a relatively short time. As elsewhere in Aboriginal Australia, Western Desert society is characterized by an elaborate code of host–visitor etiquette in which status inequalities favouring host groups are integral (cf. von Sturmer 1984). In the Mardujarra region, however, uncertainties of rainfall plus the strong convention that 'big meeting' venues will rotate among many estates prevent marked inequalities from developing. Also, while it is true that visitors are initially restricted in their movement and rights when arriving in the territory or camping area of their hosts, this inequality does not endure for the entire visit. The situation is more akin to that described for the G/wi by Silberbauer (1981: 179): 'When short mass visits are made, the politics of the joint

camp are controlled mainly by the host band and the visitor status of
the other band is clearly evident'; but this changes later, such that 'the
distinction between host and visitor is partly obscured'. In the conduct
of Mardujarra 'big meetings', the host–visitor separation largely breaks
down once the business of ritual begins. Major decision-making becomes the concern of a mixed group of mature men, with a good
measure of consultation about the logistics of public activities with a
similarly mixed group of senior women. As with the G/wi, the
host–visitor status distinction is never totally obscured, but it loses its
force as the larger 'community' asserts itself.

The dominant duality during the periodic aggregations that constitute the high point of the Mardujarra social calendar is that of the
merged alternate generation-level division, which figures prominently
in most major rituals. To the extent that the 'endogamous moieties'
compete, they do so as equals, whereas the status inequality that is
maintained between initiated men and the rest of Mardujarra society is
in many respects quite marked. Yet in both cases, ritual competitiveness and the control of the religious life by initiated men are subsumed
within broader and compelling imperatives that demand cooperation
and correct performance if the society is to flourish. Men's and
women's interests are thus conjoined, as are those of the older men and
the younger initiates, leaving little room for the unequal segments
(women and younger men) to develop any enduring counter-ideology
— a point made by Bern in relation to the Aboriginal social formation as
a whole.

Conclusion

At a behavioural level, the dominant ideology deriving from the
Dreaming and manifest in deeply-held values constrains Mardujarra
individuals and groups against sustained attempts to exercise the kinds
of authority and dominance that are successfully attained by some men
in areas such as Arnhem Land and parts of Cape York. In the Western
Desert, the ecological constraint of highly irregular and unreliable
rainfall necessitates that opportunistic adaptive strategies include the
ability of groups to move to and subsist within the territories of others.
Territorial boundaries certainly exist, but they are highly permeable
with respect to subsistence activities, and attempts at closure would
run strongly counter to survival chances in the long term. In the desert,
hegemony has to do battle with the social realities of small groups
scattered in low density across vast spaces.

Bern's account of the Aboriginal social formation appears to assume
that clans are universal features, but this is not the case and the
Western Desert is one large region where they are not found. It may be

that in areas of resource reliability and abundance clan structures provide a major foundation for exclusivity, ethnocentrism and also competitiveness at both individual and group levels. Sutton (in a personal communication) has suggested, however, that the clan, taken alone, is too gross a unit of comparison and that it is therefore necessary to appeal to a set of distinctive features which mark the contexts in which the potential for inequalities may be realized: for example, small agnatically defined kin groups (averaging about thirty people), with shared core-interests in a cluster of mainly adjacent sites. In such groups there is also a statistical likelihood of high linguistic diversity and multilingualism, strong sub-regionalism in cult life, small-region endogamy and probably a relatively small population pool from which spouses can be legitimately drawn (cf. Williams 1982). In the Mardujarra region, the estate group has an agnatic core, but its members are invariably widely scattered and membership criteria are broad, allowing individuals to be actively involved as full members in more than one group (Tonkinson 1978: 50–3).

In resource-rich regions where small patriclans are found and the other conditions suggested by Sutton obtain, the physical and social environment provides a secure economic and social base for men of ambition to devote considerable energy to competitive, prestige-enhancing exploits (cf. Hiatt 1986: 13). Under these conditions, too, conflicts with neighbouring groups can be waged and then factored into the struggle for both individual and group pre-eminence. In such circumstances, the operation of kinship becomes truncated and circumscribed by other considerations favouring local interests over regional solidarity. The conditions favouring inequalities suggested by Sutton are in every respect absent in the Mardujarra case, where interpersonal and intergroup power struggles cannot ensue without threatening people's long-term survival. Here, *contra* Bern, the mature men who constitute the dominant category are fairly equal in their access to resources, and a strongly expressed ethic reinforces this conviction.

The Law, made manifest to individuals principally via kinship and religious belief and activity, operates among the Mardujarra in such a way that the potential for domination that is inherent in the social formation cannot be realized either often or consistently enough to create structures of inequality that could permeate daily life. Here, Bern's contentions concerning power spill-over do not obtain: the religious dominance of groups of mature men is prevented from translating into 'secular' dominance by individual men over other members of the community. As noted above, even in the organization and performance of ritual, the Mardujarra never suspend kinship principles in interpersonal behaviour and in role-allocation. In everyday life the balancing out of kin relations involving status inequality supports an egalitarian ethos that predominates as long as things are running smoothly. Likewise, the persistence of kin statuses within the religious life, when added to the highly situational nature of ritual leadership, inhibits the development of enduring hierarchy there as well. This is as true of adult women as it is of initiated men — but not, of course, across the gender boundary since, as Bern correctly notes, men's hegemonic control of the major reproductive rites and inner secrets is never threatened overtly by women, who accept the secondary status that men accord 'women's business' in their organization of the religious life.

Hamilton, who worked on the eastern side of the Western Desert, has examined sex roles, women's ritual activities, and so on, in the light of Bern's contentions concerning male hegemony. She concludes that in the eastern Western Desert area the structural and ideological dominance of men over women has not become a reality. This accords with my conclusions concerning the Mardujarra case — but for different reasons in the main. Hamilton cites a number of structural features that inhibit the process: 'the existence of unresolved ambiguities in the relation between totemic affiliation and sites, the organisation of women's labour, and the presence of an autonomous religious life for women' (1980: 18). As I have pointed out elsewhere, a number of significant social and cultural differences exist between eastern groups and the Mardujarra, any of which may account for our divergent explanations of why the hegemony of mature men is not realized in the Western Desert. Certainly, Mardujarra women do not seem to be as autonomous in their religious activities as those further east, and the forms and functions of totemic affiliation show some important differences (Tonkinson 1983). In a recent paper, Bern (1986) suggests that totemism is hierarchical and generates important inequalities in Aboriginal society, as do exchange systems. This is not borne out by the Mardujarra case, however, where neither totemism nor exchange systems can possibly be construed as loci for the generation of hierarchy.

9. Meat sharing as a political ritual: forms of transaction versus modes of subsistence

Thomas Gibson

As our knowledge of extant hunting and gathering societies has increased over the past two decades, it has become clear that they do not all possess the same 'ethos'. Some societies, such as Australian Aborigines or North-west Coast Indians, are rather hierarchical in ideology, while others are characterized by what Woodburn has called 'noncompetitive egalitarianism'. In a recent paper Woodburn has set out with admirable clarity the principle on which the latter group of societies is based: *What it above all does is to disengage people from property, from the potentiality in property rights for creating dependency.* I think it is probable that this specialised development can only be realised without impoverishment in societies with a simple hunting and gathering economy . . .' (Woodburn 1982a: 445, emphasis in original). In this chapter,[1] I wish to discuss certain social mechanisms which achieve the same disengagement of people from property among one group of shifting cultivators, the Buid of Mindoro, Philippines (Gibson 1986). The Buid possess a political ideology of ascribed equality every bit as rigorous as that possessed by African and Asian hunter-gatherers. Indeed, in many ways Buid egalitarianism is more consistent and pervasive than that of these hunter-gatherers.

My method will be to examine material transactions in these societies as a guide to their underlying political values. I make a distinction between the form and content of a material transaction.

> . . . technique and ritual, profane and sacred, do not denote *types* of action but *aspects* of almost any kind of action. Technique has economic material consequences which are measurable and predictable; ritual on the other hand is a symbolic statement which 'says' something about the individuals involved in action. Thus from certain points of view a Kachin religious sacrifice may be regarded as a purely technical and economic act (Leach 1954: 13).

1. The writing of this chapter was made possible by a grant from the Harry Frank Guggenheim Foundation.

While the content of material transactions is crucial to a society's mode of subsistence, the forms these transactions take are indicative not of the economic but of the political system. The form taken by the most ritualized transactions is often a key to the dominant political values of a society. In the case of hunters and gatherers, this is usually the sharing of the meat of large game animals. Among the Buid, it is the sharing of sacrificed domesticated animals. The principles observed in animal sacrifice may, however, be found to operate throughout Buid social life.

My chapter falls into three parts. In the first I review and comment on the forms of transaction identified by Polanyi, showing how each form is associated with a certain type of political system and with a certain ideological representation of the social whole. In the second part I provide a number of illustrations of the application of a previously untheorized form of transaction among the Buid. I call this form 'sharing', and show how it is linked to a very different representation of the social whole, and with a thoroughgoing egalitarianism. In the third part I review some of the literature on the forms of material transaction found among the African and Asian hunter-gatherers discussed by Woodburn and consider the implications of my argument for his claim that the disengagement of people from property is 'intrinsic, a necessary component of immediate-return economies which occurs only in such economies' (1982a: 445).

Polanyi's forms of transaction

Polanyi's summary of the three forms of transaction which he identified is worth quoting at length.

> Empirically, we find the main patterns to be reciprocity, redistribution and exchange. Reciprocity denotes movements between correlative points of symmetrical groupings; redistribution designates appropriational movements toward a center and out of it again; exchange refers here to vice-versa movements taking place as between 'hands' under a market system. Reciprocity, then, assumes for a background symmetrically arranged groupings; redistribution is dependent upon the presence of some measure of centricity in the group; exchange in order to produce integration requires a system of price-making markets. It is apparent that the different patterns of integration assume definite institutional supports (1968: 128).

Reciprocity and competitive exchange

To begin, then, with reciprocity. Sahlins, in a classic essay (1965), attempted to develop Polanyi's notions of reciprocity and redistribution, by reducing them to easily discriminable points on a continuum which ranged from 'negative' reciprocity to 'generalized' reciprocity, with 'balanced' reciprocity as a middle term. Under the heading of generalized reciprocity, he included both the mutuality expected among close relatives and the redistribution from a central authority characteristic of chiefdoms. What the two had in common was a certain vagueness in the obligation to repay specific prestations. This elision of fundamental differences between mutuality and redistribution is unfortunate. What is required is an elaborated set of tools for comparison, not an over-simplified set of concepts.

It would probably be best to restrict usage of the term 'reciprocity' to situations in which symmetrical units exchange goods of the same type, so that it is always clear who is the debtor and who the creditor. As the dominant type of transaction, reciprocity in this sense is characteristic of those societies which stress an equality between individuals and groups which must be achieved and maintained, often by strenuous effort. Forge demonstrates this for the New Guinea highlands: 'The principal mechanism by which equality is maintained is equal exchange of things of the same class or of identical things. Basically all presentations of this type are challenges to prove equality. . . . Equal exchange is, in fact, a system of alternating seniority' (Forge 1972: 534–5). Formally speaking, societies which stress competitive feasting are little different from those which stress competitive feuding, the one exchanging pigs, and the other deaths. Indeed, the two are often seen as alternative forms of group interaction within the same society. So long as symmetrical groups are in imbalance with one another, the relationship must continue.

The equivalent to feasting and fighting at the level of kinship is, of course, the direct exchange of women, which is in many ways the prototype of all forms of reciprocity (Lévi-Strauss 1969). The exchange of women is capable of creating long-term credits and debts between groups in a way that other types of good cannot. Thus is the problem of creating a larger social whole out of identical segments resolved in certain societies: by the exchange of identical things between identical units.

A more elaborate form of exchange consists in functionally identical units exchanging qualitatively different things. At the level of kinship this occurs when women are exchanged not for other women but for some form of bridewealth or bride-service. That which is given in return may be of real material value or simply a token of control over women. Now, as Lévi-Strauss points out, such systems are still not forms of organic solidarity: 'If a society with restricted exchange or generalised exchange is envisaged as a whole, each segment fulfils an identical function to each of the other segments. Consequently what we are dealing with is two different forms of mechanical solidarity' (1969: xxxiv). Be that as it may, generalized exchange does represent a crucial step toward organic solidarity: from the perspective of a single segment, there is an exchange of qualitatively different types of good with at least two other segments.

What is more, as soon as goods of fundamentally different type are exchanged, inequality appears, for differences are never neutral but are always ranked according to a hierarchy of values (Parsons, cited in Dumont 1980: 19). Forge, describing the coexistence of this sort of exchange with reciprocity in New Guinea, remarks that, since one can never fully compensate one's affines for the gift of a woman (failing an exchange of sisters), a permanent and irreversible inequality arises between them, providing a respite from the competition which characterizes relations between all other adult men.

> People who are by definition unequal cannot compete; their exchanges, being of different things, cannot be subject to any exact accounting or comparison. . . . In egalitarian societies in which the ideal is of aggressive individualism and in which virtually any man can challenge any other to show what he is made of, in an equal exchange, inequality . . . is a haven of rest from strife (1972: 537).

Redistribution and hierarchical exchange

The first real division of labour, according to Durkheim, occurs when: 'Individuals, instead of subordinating themselves to the group, were subordinated to that which represented it, and as the collective authority, when it was diffuse, was absolute, that of the chief, who is only its organised incarnation, naturally took on the same character. . . . Chiefs are, in fact, the first personalities who emerge from the social mass' (1933: 195).

Normally, that which is given to the center will be seen as inferior to what the center returns to the periphery, but a possible contrary case, in which the chief is perpetually in debt to society, is argued by Clastres (1977). According to Clastres, the 'chief' in lowland Amazonian societies is the only polygynist in the group, and as such stands as inferior wife-taker to the social whole. He is obliged to return food and speech to the group which grants him the privilege of polygyny, but is unable ever to cancel his debt. The specialized functions conferred upon him, that of mediator in disputes and of benefactor in times of famine, do not lead to his acquisition of power and authority over the whole. The chief is, rather, the servant of society, and can be dismissed by it at any time. For Clastres, the basis of all social life is the exchange of words, goods and women. By denying reciprocity in these things with the chief, Amazonians signify their rejection of political power and the state. The executor of those functions defined as political in other societies is symbolically exiled from the interior of society by the unilateral flows of women to him and of goods and speech from him.

The exercise of power is thus placed in the domain of nature, which is the absence of communication, and opposed to culture, which consists in the obligation to give and receive.

Clastres's argument has a certain eccentric appeal, but I think it misses the point. Where there is an exchange of goods and services of qualitatively different type, there is no way to make an exact accounting of credit and debt. The rate of exchange will depend on the values assigned by the culture to the different products exchanged, and on the balance of power between the functionally differentiated units. Clastres is dealing with a situation in which the balance of power is held by the social whole, so that no matter how much the chief returns to society, it will always be defined as never enough.

The difference between powerless chiefs and proper states would lie, then, in a shift of power from the social whole to the specialized unit at its center. Clastres seems to recognize this when later on in his book he states that the difference between the 'Amazonian savage' and the 'Indian of the Inca empire' lies in the fact that the former produces only for his own needs, while the latter works for masters who tell him: 'You must pay what you owe us, you must perpetually repay your debt to us' (1977: 167).

There is a relatively simple symbolic transformation, then, between the chief who works for society and the society which works for the chief. This is scarcely surprising, considering that many of the egalitarian and hierarchical societies of the New World were engaged in a continual dialectic of opposition and transformation. While Clastres deliberately characterizes the anarchism of lowland societies as being directed against the possibility of some future potential state, one must consider the more plausible proposition that it was directed against the actually existing states of the highlands.

We have in the chiefdom the germ of both redistribution and of hierarchy: of a system with a center, and of a part of the whole standing for and representing the whole. The giving of tribute to the center is seen as an obligation, the chiefly counter-prestation being seen as superogatory generosity. 'Goods are in truth *yielded* to powers-that-be, perhaps on call and demand, and likewise goods may have to be *humbly solicited* from them' (Sahlins 1965: 160). In the extreme case, a situation may arise in which the contribution of those holding power in the center is represented as being of such incomparable value that their subjects are in perpetual debt to them. In such a system, a subordinate often has quite specific obligations to give to particular superordinates, while anything given by the latter is considered not as a repayment, but as freely bestowed generosity. It may even be that the latter's contributions are entirely immaterial, consisting of mystical 'grace' or 'fertility'. Such is the logic of tribute and 'divine kingship'.

A similar tendency to mystify the contributions of superior strata to the social whole is observable in more highly differentiated systems, in which there are several functionally specialized units, each making a specific contribution to the whole. The preceding sentence is almost a paraphrase of Dumont's definition of the Indian *jajmani* system: 'Whilst directly religious prestations and "economic" prestations are mingled together, this takes place within the prescribed order, the religious order. The needs of each are conceived to be different, depending on caste, on hierarchy, but this fact should not disguise the entire system's *orientation towards the whole*' (Dumont 1980: 105). In Hindu society, each occupationally specialized group is thought of as producing a qualitatively different kind of good or service for the social whole, each with an intrinsically different value. In such a system, the hierarchy of values attached to goods and services can be mapped onto the occupationally specialized units to produce a thoroughgoing social hierarchy, with priests at the top: 'We shall define hierarchy as the principle by which the elements of a whole are ranked in relation to the whole, it being understood that in the majority of societies it is religion which provides the view of the whole, and that the ranking will thus be religious in nature' (ibid.: 66).

Here power and value have been separated, and the ideology of unequal exchange reaches unsurpassed refinements, so that the intangible mystical benefit acquired from giving to a superior is contingent on the inferior receiving nothing tangible in return. Thus, in some high castes, the ideal type of marriage consists in the free gift of a virgin accompanied by a dowry. One must not so much as eat a meal with one's wife-takers, lest one be viewed as receiving a material return (Parry 1979: 208).

Centralized redistribution and the *jajmani* system can both be seen as variations of what one might call hierarchical complementary exchange. Hierarchical, because of the orientation to the whole on the part of the transactors, and complementary because of the presence of functionally differentiated units.

Exchange and the price-making market

In a market economy, the material characteristics of every type of good and service are reduced to a single abstract form, the commodity. Or, to put it in Marxian terms, the value of a good as an article of use, capable of satisfying definite wants, coexists with its value as an article of exchange. The exchange value of a commodity is determined by the amount of socially necessary labor required to produce it: 'The equalisation of the most different kinds of labour can be the result only of an abstraction from their inequalities, or of reducing them to their denominator, viz., expenditure of human labour-power or human labour in the abstract' (Marx 1954: 78).

In an economic regime where production is primarily for exchange and not for use, and in which value is expressed in terms of a universal medium of exchange, or money, the qualitative differences between goods and between the kinds of labor required to produce them become irrelevant. All commodities are measurable on a single homogeneous monetary scale, all forms of labor are thereby equalized, and hence the notion arises that all laborers are equal. This is the converse of the situation in differentiated but non-monetary societies in which each laborer is differentiated and ranked according to the *kind* of labor he does, and not according to the *amount* of reified social labor he controls in the form of money. In market economies, individuals confront one another in the act of exchange as equivalent, undifferentiated owners of equivalent, undifferentiated exchange-value.

But, Marx points out, the situation becomes more complicated when labor power itself becomes a commodity as a result of the separation of producers from the means of production. The buyer and the seller of labor power confront one another not simply as equals offering in exchange use values that the other requires, but as unequals in which the laborer is required to submit to the will of the owner of the means of production (for a definite period) in exchange for the means of subsistence. The laborer is the political subordinate of the capitalist within the production process, and his equal only in the sphere of exchange. Capitalism is thus built upon two contradictory ideologies: the equality of all men in exchange, and the subordination of the majority to the owners of capital in production.

Capitalism even presents a nice example of Dumontian hierarchy. Production is represented at one level as requiring the combination of two equal 'factors', capital and labor. At another level, however, capital is made to encompass labor, and is represented as a self-sufficient creator of value on its own account. And because the value of labor power is determined by an historically variable level of subsistence, the rate of exchange between capital and labor is in practice defined by the political balance of power between the two classes. Political relations are actually defined, then, within the sphere of production, being fought out in the short term over wages and conditions, and, in the long term, over the control of the production process itself. Social relations as they appear in the sphere of exchange are largely illusory, in that they give rise to feelings of freedom and equality which are contradicted by 'wage slavery' in the sphere of production. This again represents a marked contrast to pre-capitalist systems in which exchange relations serve not to mask political relations, but to express them.

Sharing and ascribed equality

Sharing here is meant to indicate a form of transaction in which both
dyadic indebtedness and hierarchical differentiation are absent. The
individual interacts directly with the group, and not with some other
individual or representative of the group. Before attempting a formal
definition of sharing, it will be useful to give a number of concrete
examples of the operation of this principle in Buid society, where it is
the dominant form of transaction. In order to indicate just how pervasive is sharing within Buid social life, I shall briefly describe how it
applies to transactions of words, labor, spouses and food.

Buid rarely address one another directly, that is, face to face or
otherwise in a way which demands a response. Typically, they sit
facing in the same direction or even with their backs to one another
while conversing. Listeners are at perfect liberty to ignore remarks with
which they disagree. Instead of contradicting a speaker, listeners are
more likely to change the subject entirely or, at least, to make a remark
contradictory to what has come before only by implication. This remark
may of course be ignored by the original speaker. In other words, there
is little dyadic 'exchange of words' between Buid, in which the recipient of speech is under an obligation to reply to (repay) an opening
address. The structural homology between Buid conversational patterns and their sharing of goods is most evident when a large number
of people are gathered, for then one really does address oneself to the
group as a whole, and not to some symmetrical unit within it. Indeed,
Buid prefer to socialize in groups larger than dyads, since there is less
possibility of an unavoidable confrontation arising.

Large groups gather during those parts of the agricultural cycle in
which cooperative labor teams are customary: when the swiddens are
slashed, burned, planted and harvested. Any implication that labor is
exchanged on a reciprocal basis is avoided by recruiting helpers from
the community at large. The community assembles for the purpose of
sorting out which households are going to engage in the above activities at what time, so that clashes can be avoided, and everyone will
have some outside help available. The community squats on the
ground, facing in the same direction, and fixes its eyes on some distant
mountain peak. One by one people address the community in turn,
announcing their intentions. By the time everyone has spoken, it
should have become obvious where the potential clashes are, and
people can adjust their plans accordingly, without anyone having to
directly acknowledge they have allowed another's plan to derange their
own. No two wills are allowed to come into confrontation, for while the
speaker is always an individual, the listener is always a group. The
Buid consistently avoid social interaction between symmetrical units
precisely because of the potential for competition and confrontation it

poses. This potential is even evident in the English expression, 'to have an exchange of words'.

One can never be sure until the last minute just who will turn up for a cooperative labor team, and one can form only a rough estimate of the number of helpers one may expect, since no specific obligation rests on any particular household to provide this labor because of previous labor exchanges with the household sponsoring the collective labor team. Anyone not otherwise engaged will show up for the event. Here we have a case in which the inclusive unit is obliged to give (labor) to one of its component parts. Conversely, the sponsor of the labor team is traditionally not supposed to perform any work on his or her own field, but to spend time preparing a meal for the helpers which is served to them as a collectivity. Just as the sponsor acquires no specific obligations to those who have provided labor on the day, additional to the general obligation which exists to help community members, so none of the helpers acquires a specific obligation to the sponsor, additional to the general obligation to provide food to the undifferentiated community.

Now, if dyadic obligations can be avoided in the public domain through sharing, it is not obvious how they can be avoided in the domestic domain, especially between spouses. Even here, however, Buid strive to limit the claims individuals have on one another. Marriage does not imply long-term rights over the services of one's spouse among the Buid. The most frequent source of quarreling within a marriage is the expression of undue jealousy or possessiveness by one spouse over the extra-marital activities of the other. Such behaviour may in itself constitute grounds for divorce, although the most common motive for initiating a divorce is the desire to marry someone else.

A marriage may be dissolved at any time on condition that the abandoned spouse receives an appropriate amount of compensation from the spouse who initiated the divorce. Formally, the abandoned spouse is allowed to ask for as much compensation as he or she desires. In practice, the amount demanded is usually impossibly high at first but is gradually brought down by a process of collective discussion and negotiation to a more moderate sum, a sum which is in fact standard within an in-marrying region. The payment of compensation is one of the few formal, dyadic transactions in Buid society. It is designed to restore moral equilibrium but, by the same token, it dissolves the relationship. This dyadic transaction negates the bonds of mutuality and the daily sharing of food, labor and sex by which spouses are formally united.

In the collective discussions which precede a divorce, more moral opprobrium is directed against a spouse thought to be too possessive than against the spouse who initiated the proceedings. The existence of higher standard payments in the wealthier down-river regions is sometimes given as a reason for not marrying into them. The unreasonable, even violent, jealousy of spouses from up-river regions is often given as a reason for not marrying there. Buid never contemplate a marriage without considering the possibility of its termination, and tend therefore to marry within a limited region within which the circulation of spouses between households may be expected to occur with minimal friction.

It is impossible to speak of the 'exchange of women' in Buid society, since the typical marriage involves either a husband or a wife divorcing their current partner and remarrying someone else. I have estimated that an average Buid will contract at least five serial marriages in the course of his or her adult life, and often many more. First marriages are not given much attention, and tend to emerge out of adolescent sexual experimentation. Individuals thus tend to be transferred from the domestic group of one spouse to that of another, not from a natal kin group to an affinal one. Children are likely to share a house with a wide range of half- and step-siblings, and step-parents, as they mature, and will spend much of their adult life looking after step-children. The Buid may be said to engage in the sharing of households, spouses and children, in that their system of marriage and residence prevents the emergence of corporate kin groups, ranked internally by age and gender, and externally as 'wife-givers' and 'wife-takers'.

My final example of sharing concerns the sharing of food. Each household is essentially self-sufficient. The members of a household pool their labor and food, but not their property: each spouse maintains a separate swidden from which they contribute to the common larder. Cooked food is divided into two basic categories: *fafa*, or cooked starch staple, and *ufi*, or accompanying side dish. Only *fafa* is necessary for a meal, *ufi* being provided rather sporadically. Any member of the household, man, woman or child, may prepare one of the two daily meals. Household members need not eat simultaneously. Children, in particular, are apt to eat in the household of the friend or neighbour which happens to have the most appetizing side dish on any given day. On the whole staples are not regarded as a scarce resource, are not normally shared with members of other households, unless a visitor from another settlement is present, and are subject to little symbolic elaboration. This attitude contrasts markedly to that displayed toward the most valued kind of side dish, meat. Meat is scarce, is subject to a great deal of symbolic elaboration, and it *must* be shared between households.

Whenever a pig or chicken is killed, its meat must be distributed in exactly equal shares among all the inhabitants of a local community, regardless of their age, sex, or genealogical connection to the owner. the exception of the meals provided to agricultural helpers, mentioned above, domesticated animals are killed only on ritual occasions.

Every household must maintain a stock of animals for such occasions which may arise at any time, perhaps once a month. An individual may expect to receive a share of meat from some other household's ritual activity about once a week. There is thus a continual flow of meat through the community, constituting the most frequent form of material transaction between households.

Households perform most rituals in response to some misfortune occurring within them, such as the illness or death of a member. The sharing of meat draws the rest of the community into the household's misfortune. Because of the link between sacrifice and misfortune, a household which is obliged to perform many sacrifices does not gain any prestige by doing so, but becomes rather an object of pity. The same rule of sharing applies also to the meat of any captured wild animal.

In sharing, the rule is that a sub-unit engages in exchange only with a larger unit which includes it. That is, each unit is obliged to give only to the whole of which it is a part, and is entitled to receive only from that whole, or as an undifferentiated part of it. Recipients do not become indebted to the sponsor of the moment: their obligation is only to the group as a whole. Rights and duties are formulated only between individuals and the inclusive group, not between particular individuals. It is a mistake to view sponsors of events in which sharing occurs as 'investing' a 'surplus' by indebting other individuals who will be obliged to repay them in future. One 'invests' only in the sense that by following the rule of giving to the group, one retains one's membership in it, and one's entitlement to the distributions of others.

Another example of the whole giving to the part would be an obligation for all members of the community to contribute to the funeral expenses of one of its members. Again, there need not be any direct accounting of credit and debt between specific units within the whole. In neither instance is dyadic indebtedness the integrating principle of the group, but rather a deliberate disproportion between giver and recipient. Individuals are required only to acknowledge dependence on, and subordination to, the group. They construct a sort of egalitarianism far removed from the tenuous equality constructed between symmetrical units in reciprocal exchange, and from the instituted hierarchy at the core of redistributive systems.

There are, then, at least four types of relationship between giver, recipient and the social whole, any one of which may predominate in a given society and serve as the principal form of transaction. I summarize them again below:

Reciprocity. Symmetry between giver and recipient, generating a 'mechanical' social whole, made up of the sum of dyadic relationships.

Redistribution. Asymmetry between giver and recipient, generating an organic whole with hierarchical parts.

Exchange. Symmetry between giver and recipient, generating a statistical whole.

Sharing. Asymmetry between giver and recipient, one of which is the whole and the other a part of it.

African and Asian hunter-gatherers

And so we come to the forms of transaction found among African and Asian hunter-gatherers. In the following discussion, I propose to limit myself to the six societies recently discussed by Woodburn as possessing 'immediate-return' economies, and an ideology of non-competitive egalitarianism: the !Kung, Mbuti and Hadza of Africa, and the Batek, Paliyan and Pandaram of Asia (Woodburn 1982a). In all these cases, the distribution of meat is the most formalized transaction, and used to symbolize the most highly valued social and political relationships.

Among the !Kung, the meat of large game animals is manipulated in a number of ways before being finally consumed. Although the accounts of Lee and Marshall are somewhat obscure, it seems to be the case that:

(1) the 'owner' of the animal is defined as the one whose arrow first penetrates it, and 'ownership' in the !Kung context consists primarily of the right to distribute the meat formally (Lee 1979: 247);

(2) there is much borrowing and lending of arrows, so that hunters often kill an animal with another man's arrow, giving the latter the right to make the initial distribution of the animal's meat;

(3) a man's primary obligation is to his wife's parents, but he is also obliged to give to his own parents, spouse and offspring;

(4) the first wave of sharing is followed by a second wave in which the same kin categories are marked out;

(5) visitors, 'name relatives' (namesakes or the kin of such) and friends are included in further waves; and

(6) 'It ends in everybody getting some meat' (Marshall 1961: 238–9; cf. Lee 1979: 247).

Thus, while meat transactions are used to mark out ties between primary kinsmen, particularly between affines, this marking is essentially symbolic and is not used to establish domination over recipients. A !Kung man is expected to perform bride-service for three to ten years, hunting meat for his parents-in-law. But since these in-laws do not seem to actually consume any more of his meat than anyone else in the camp, what this rule really amounts to is not an obligation to give food or labor to one's parents-in-law, but to share a camp with them, so that they will get a share of any meat one brings in (Lee 1979: 247). Meat distributions are also used to mark gender roles: 'The !Kung believe that the women must never eat the men's part of the animals or hunting success will drop to zero' (ibid.).

Among the Mbuti, there appear to be several competing sets of 'rules' governing meat distributions, which generally mark out the statuses of elders, children, women and men by assigning them different parts of the animal's body, and which also give special consideration to the owner of the dog, net or spear which captured the animal. But these 'rules' again seem primarily to provide an opportunity to make statements concerning the interdependence of genders and generations, for no one hesitates 'to override them in order to bring about the recognized goal — equitable division of the spoils' (Turnbull 1965: 158). Another political function of meat distributions is to provide an opportunity for 'personal grievances, however far out of context, to be aired and expressed in terms of sharing rights' (ibid.). But no one is made to feel indebted to, or dependent on, any other specific individual.

Among the Hadza, the distribution of meat is again used as an opportunity to mark off symbolically the role of initiated man from that of woman and child: certain portions are reserved for initiates and must be eaten by them as a group. 'If a woman or child approaches close to the men when they are eating the sacred meat, then the men may decide to take action against the offender: mass rape is said to be a possibility' (Woodburn 1979: 254). The rest of the meat is distributed first to those who walk out to a carcass to carry it back to camp. The shares are said to 'belong' to those who carry them, but they redistribute their shares once they reach camp, and as the meat is cooked it is redistributed once again. There is a rather vague obligation for a man to 'make sure his wife and mother-in-law do from time to time obtain meat killed by himself or others' (ibid.: 255n). In the end, however, everyone, including temporary visitors to a camp, shares freely and equally, consuming all the meat in a camp as it is cooked.

Among the Pandaram, 'any game captured is shared among all members of the encampment. This applies not only to larger game animals . . . but also to any small creatures found' (Morris 1982: 103). Men tend to get the choicest morsels, while children may get only leftovers, but there is no indication of discrimination among recipients according to their past contributions or their specific kinship ties to the hunters.

As for the Batek, Endicott says only that 'food, especially meat, is always shared with as many people as possible, whether it is needed or not' (1979: 11). Gardner reports for the Paliyan only that 'group-hunted game is dissected into tiny pieces, then apportioned out into piles which contain equal amounts of each part of the animal' (1972: 415).

Indeed, while food production is usually discussed in great detail, there is often a frustrating lack of data in the ethnography when it comes to food transactions. I think this is due in part to the tendency to view such transactions entirely in economic terms. Since they have little bearing on people's actual rates of consumption, the details of who gives to whom, and in what order, are left out. In fact, however, highly significant political statements are made in each wave of distribution. In the act of meat distribution, most of these hunting and gathering societies represent the social whole as being internally differentiated according to gender and generation. But it is significant that these are relationships between social categories, not between specific individuals. In this respect, the model of the whole which can be derived from formalized material transactions among immediate-return hunter-gatherers is similar, but not identical, to that found among the Buid.

The most important difference between the Buid, on the one hand, and the Hadza and !Kung, on the other, is that among the latter 'the bridegroom does take on various long-term economic obligations to his affines' (Woodburn 1980: 111). Woodburn sees 'the intensification of control by men of rights over women who are to be given in marriage' as one of the chief means by which non-competitive egalitarianism may be transformed into a system in which subordination and dependency are present. Having noted this, however, it is important also to emphasize that marriage is in practice a freely terminable contract between individuals in all six societies discussed by Woodburn, not an alliance between groups. Everywhere husbands have little authority over their wives, marriage is defined by co-residence, and there are few social repercussions to divorce (see Endicott 1979: 10; Turnbull 1965: 274–5; Woodburn 1968: 107; Marshall 1959: 358; Gardner 1972: 419; Morris 1982: 111).

The point is that hunters and gatherers seem to be able to tolerate a greater degree of incipient social differentiation (into genders and generations) and of interpersonal dependency (between affines) than the Buid, without compromising their egalitarianism. I have argued elsewhere that the Buid rigorously confine recognition of the relevance of differences of age and sex to the sphere of child-bearing and rearing, and stress the absolute equality of all adult men and women in all other spheres (Gibson 1985). In conclusion, I want to agree that there is an 'elective affinity' between an immediate-return, hunting and gathering way of life, and the sort of non-competitive, ascribed egalitarianism described by Woodburn. Indeed, it is this very affinity which allows such societies to tolerate social distinctions and dependencies which might prove fatal to the principle of equality in a society like the Buid whose economy is, of course, a delayed-return one. And it is because there is a certain tension between economy and polity among the Buid that the principles of sharing and individual autonomy from kin, spouse, and creditor receive such a clear and definite formulation. Paradoxically, it may be that an agricultural society provides a key to a deeper understanding of hunter-gatherer societies, in that the Buid have formulated a set of principles which are also operative, if rather less consistently and clearly, among the hunters and gatherers of Africa and Asia.

Part 3

Symbols and representations

10. Dry meat and gender: the absence of Chipewyan ritual for the regulation of hunting and animal numbers

Henry S. Sharp

The northern hunting cultures of the boreal forest of Canada provide a special and significant case for the development and testing of theories about hunting and gathering societies. From east of Hudson Bay to the Alaska border, a distance of several thousand kilometers, these cultures form a continuous belt of hunter-gatherers that are still the almost exclusive residents of their traditional subsistence areas and which have extensive, sometimes exclusive, access to the subsistence resources. These cultures have long been in contact with the larger Canadian society and have had an even longer intermittent commercial interaction with its predecessors; there has been adroit adaptation to and exploitation of opportunities provided by the technology and social systems of Western culture, leading to often dramatic change. Yet in spite of this contact and change, the cultures have proven remarkably resistant to subordination by, and incorporation within, the larger society (Tanner 1979). Even if the underlying factor in their resilience should prove to be nothing beyond the lack of massive face-to-face co-residential contact, stemming from the unsuitability of their land for agricultural or extractive operations requiring large residential labor pools, their current situation approximates the pre-agricultural condition of exclusive control of productive land and resources by hunter-gatherer peoples better than anywhere else in the contemporary world.

In the literature on the westernmost of these groups, the northern Athapaskans, there is a curious tendency to characterize societies by identifying their absent features — a tendency recognized and commented upon by area specialists. As Koolage (1975) notably observes, this is certainly the case for the Chipewyan, the easternmost of the northern Athapaskans; but all the same, it remains as a feature of contemporary ethnographic representations. It would be easy to dismiss this pattern of representation as reflecting lacunae of knowledge

183

due to the acculturative changes of the contact era coupled with the late
onset of ethnographic research in the region (Rogers 1981: 19–29;
McClellan 1981: 35–42; Davis 1981: 43–8), but I wish to sugget that it is
worthwhile to consider these 'absent features' as fairly systematic
expressions of the manner in which these cultures violate anthropological expectations about the nature, composition and operation of hunting and gathering societies. In this chapter I intend to address some
aspects of ritual, one of the apparently 'absent features' among the
Chipewyan. I confirm that such ritual is absent and then explore how
Chipewyan society operates without it.

VanStone has noted that the Chipewyan pay scant attention to ritual:
'The absence among the Chipewyan of elements associated with the
placation of game animals is noteworthy. In general, Athapaskans
appear to have attached less significance to the relationship between
ritual and the successful pursuit of game than did Algonquin speakers'
(1985: 42). This comment, from VanStone's analysis of the William
Duncan Strong Collection (Field Museum of Natural History), raises an
interesting problem. Given our contemporary understanding of
hunter-gatherers and given, too, the rather lengthy debates about the
role of uncertainty and stress in generating ritual, it is not surprising
that Algonquian speakers should pay attention to the ritual regulation
of hunting game animals. But why should the northern Athapaskans in
general and Chipewyan in particular apparently pay little or no attention to it?

First of all, the problem is a real one. VanStone's characterization of
Athapaskan societies, including Chipewyan society, is not to be taken
lightly, but if his was an isolated view it might be suspect. However,
serious consideration of, and information on, ritual activity is lacking in
the works of all contemporary ethnographers (see, for example,
Jarvenpa 1976; 1977; Irimoto 1981; J.G.E. Smith 1970; 1975; 1976; 1978;
see a'so my own works), save the limited treatment given the topic by
David M. Smith (1982). My sense of the literature after 1900 is that the
Chipewyan pay almost no ritual attention to the primary game animal,
the barren ground caribou, *Rangifer tarandus groenlandicus* (Banfield
1961), and not much ritual attention to anything else.

The term 'ritual' has been used in so many contexts from theology to
ethology that it is difficult to see it having any consistent meaning. But
collective ceremony on public occasions — which is how I and, I think,
VanStone understand the term — is clearly lacking among the Chipewyan. Interestingly, the earliest useful account of the Chipewyan,
Hearne's journal of life in the 1770s (1971), gives ample evidence of
ritual, though not about hunting or the regulation of animal numbers;
so it cannot be assumed that the recent situation is to be projected

backwards indefinitely. Change has plainly occurred between 1770 and now, and I assume that the loss of 'traditional' practices is heavily related to the Roman Catholic Church's missionary efforts in the nineteenth century and the subsequent Chipewyan adsorption of Catholicism — but I fear that the delineation of those changes is forever beyond our reach. However, even if a major transformation of Chipewyan culture occurred just beyond the memory and experience of living Chipewyan, there is still a period, from the early part of this century up to the present, in which Chipewyan life is marked by an almost total absence of ritual activity beyond that organized by the Roman Catholic missionaries. That a people could be a functional population throughout the twentieth century, maintaining their territory and language and creating a great deal of political autonomy in the face of progressively stronger social pressure from Canadian culture, without strongly marked ritual activity, is in itself worthy of consideration.

Given the nature of Chipewyan culture and the ubiquitous notion of guardian spirits in northern North America, Lévi-Strauss's characterization of totemism as 'relations, posed ideologically, between two series, one *natural*, the other *cultural*' (1962: 16) provides the key point of departure for examining the relationship between the regulation of animal numbers, hunting, and the absence of ritual among the Chipewyan. But his delineation of 'individual' totemism among the North American Indians (ibid.: 17) faces immediate difficulty, for his 'natural' series, comprising a distinction between Category and Particular, is not valid. In Chipewyan culture animal species cannot be treated through the Western concepts of number or the particular,[1] though there is a clear mechanism through which analogous relationships can occur.

Inkoze, a term my informants insist refers to the killing of humans by magical means (Sharp 1987), has been used by myself, David M. Smith (1973; 1982; 1985) and Jarvenpa (1977) to signify an entire Chipewyan complex of supernatural power — though our emerging knowledge indicates that it is no longer safe to assume that the complex is identical for each local group (D.M. Smith n.d.). *Inkoze* is essentially an order of causality partially and imperfectly revealed to humans through dreams of supranatural beings. In this system of thought, knowledge has as one of its aspects the ability to manipulate the universe to achieve determined ends. Relevant to our problem is that through this system men enter into relationships with game animals so that they may prey successfully upon them.

1. Some Chipewyan have special relationships with species, fitting Lévi-Strauss's 'Category', but they also enter into relationships with other 'supernatural' entities in animal form that have indeterminate aspects of both 'Category' and 'Particular'.

A game animal cannot be killed without its consent and it is through the domain of *inkoze* that this consensual process takes place. Killing prey is, then, an interaction between two parties standing in a particular relationship to each other. Execution of this interaction depends upon the individual Chipewyan being in a state such that the animal will allow itself to die for the hunter. The immediate and measured interaction between man and prey animal within the field of *inkoze* is as real when the prey escapes as when it consents to die. Chipewyan often explain, in English, the willingness of animals to die by saying of a specific hunter that, 'they like him'.[2] Another mode of explanation is through the concept of 'pity', sometimes expressed as saying the animal 'felt sorry' for the hunter (D.M. Smith 1982).

Achieving a state such that a game animal will consent to its death involves more than just the degree of *inkoze* the hunter possesses. Even Chipewyan most knowledgeable about *inkoze* — those whom D.M. Smith calls 'adepts' (1973: 8–10; 1982: 37–9) — can find themselves reduced to impotence via pollution (Sharp 1981; 1988). Among the Chipewyan I studied, *inkoze* has become something that only men can possess — in marked contrast both to the situation at Fort Resolution (D.M. Smith 1973; 1982: 38) and to the stories and myths my own group tells of its past. Pollution beliefs are diffuse but center upon females and in particular menstruation. During their periods women can negatively influence the behaviour of game animals — either directly by such acts as stepping over a carcass, especially its head, or through contagion, pollution readily spreading to the hunter's implements (for example, weapons), as well as to his person.

Prey animals are able to do more than just refuse their individual consent to be killed; others of their species respond to the treatment of their dead fellows. Animal abuse, as regards manner of killing, treatment of the carcass, wastage of the prey animal, and (in the past) allowing dogs to feed improperly upon an animal's parts, can result in the entire species taking offense, all the animals refusing to die for a specific hunter and even being so outraged as to abandon whole areas for a time, perhaps longer than a generation.

These basic aspects of the Chipewyan conceptualization of the relationship between themselves and animals roughly outline a paradigmatic solution to VanStone's observation. Animals are part of a systemic framework, simultaneously natural and supernatural, embedded in the causal mechanisms of the traditional universe. They are self-renewing, becoming young again each spring.[3] They are in com-

---

2. 'Like' here must be understood as referring to a notion combining the individual animal, its conspecifics and any supernatural form capable of acting for them.

3. See D.M. Smith (1985). The general principle sometimes results in curious classificatory determinations as individuals try to cope with conflicting empirical evidence. One informant, who had just killed an obviously old black bear, decided that the principle was true but that it did not apply to bears and dogs.

munication with others of their species as well as with other species. The relationships among them transcend individual being, as shown by their noting, and responding to, the manner of death and subsequent treatment of the remains of their fellows. The upshot is the delineation of a universe of being beyond the natural whose history is only imperfectly known through dreams, supernatural encounters, and observation.

According to the Chipewyan, the *contemporary* universe of material causality is a creation of the white man, the power for this creation won from God by trickery. Contemporary Chipewyan regard themselves as having been an integral part of the other universe of being until the white man's priests came among them (Sharp 1979). In this myth the revelation of Roman Catholicism led to the appearance of the Chipewyan language and the initiation of a progressive sundering of ties between the realm of *inkoze* and the material realm of the whites. The Chipewyan lost the use of the common tongue of the other universe of being, communication with this other universe thus becoming restricted to the single bridge provided by *inkoze*.

In common with most humans, the symbolic forms of Chipewyan culture are concerned with the relationships between eating, reproduction and gender. In particular, this concern manifests itself in deep semantic distinctions between scavenging and hunting (obtaining one's own food/being fed) (Carter 1974; Sharp 1976). Hunting (primarily caribou and secondarily any significant prey species[4]), as the means by which food is provided, assumes a mediating role between the secular world within which the Chipewyan now find themselves and this other world of universal being from which they see themselves as having so recently emerged. As *Dene* ('people'), they depend upon the willingness of prey species to yield their own physical existence on behalf of the maintenance of human physical existence. Hunting, as a primary bridge between the non-physical aspects of the human and non-human worlds, takes on a sacrificial character, in a manner somewhat alien to classical Western conceptualizations (Robertson Smith 1901; Hubert and Mauss 1964: 1–13; Evans-Pritchard 1956: 272–86; de Heusch 1985: 22–5). Animals sacrifice themselves to *Dene* not just to maintain *Dene* physical existence but also to hold the people in contact with that other, and older, realm of being from which the circumstances of contemporary *Dene* life threaten to remove them entirely.

Within this framework, the lack of public ritual for the regulation of hunting and the maintenance of self-renewing animal populations is

---

4. These include obvious candidates such as bear and moose but also some less obvious ones such as loon and swans.

explicable. Public ritual is superfluous in a system where every encounter between a man and a prey animal has so many characteristics
of a sacrificial event.

Chipewyan recount the events of the hunt to other members of their
residential groups. This is done without drama or a specific rhetorical
format, but obviously involves a fairly consistent manner of representation. The particular characteristics of hunting show most clearly when
the encounter is such that the hunter has the time and opportunity to
engage in the deliberate pursuit of a specific animal. The determined
nature of these encounters provides ample opportunity for the hunter's
knowledge of the forms of *inkoze* to enter his own internal representa-
tional processes, as well as his knowledge relating to the recounting of
other hunts. Anticipation of future recountings of the unfolding events
becomes an active factor in his perception of the situation and a
delimiting factor in the decisions he makes. The events of 'now', the
perception of 'now', are inescapably merged with past and future
recounting, taking each hunting episode a step beyond linear time
into a non-linear continuity (Sharp 1988). Taking a routine activity
necessary for the support of life, namely the conversion of living
animals to raw meat, and inserting it into a unified framework of
causality creates a ritualized — if not ritual — activity system that is
dispersed throughout the social system. Each hunt, individual or
cooperative, locates the activities of men within the field of *inkoze*.
Through recounting, the values and relationships centering on
hunting are shared between men and their co-resident others, per-
meating past, present, and future.

The gender specificity of this explanation leaves unresolved a major
issue. Women, because of their exclusion from possessing *inkoze*,
appear in this solution in only a negative and passive manner — as a
source of pollution negating the effectiveness of *inkoze*. Aspects of the
ethnographic situation support this view, for just as the local group
under study seems atypical among Chipewyan in excluding women
from the possession of *inkoze*, it also seems atypical among northern
Athapaskans in the stringency of its exclusion of women from killing
large game. Not to consider the women's participation within this
apparently overwhelming symbolic bias towards males, in a culture
with a strong reputation for the 'oppression' of women (Sharp 1981;
Oswalt 1967; Hearne 1971), is implicitly to consent in the routinization
of a 'terror' model of social organization for half of adult society.

For years during my fieldwork a woman in her fifties liked to
intersperse our conversations at bush camps with stories she had heard
about the old days. The stories she chose to tell had a common pattern,
always beginning with how some past and unnamed group of people
were successfully making vast quantities of caribou dry meat. She

would enlarge fondly upon the abundance of prime meat and how it was processed into dry meat and then stored. She never finished these stories. Occasionally she would get so far as to tell how the people would have to move away and abandon their dry meat, but she never went beyond this point. It was the making, in and of itself, that she valued. The product itself was always abandoned and the circumstances forcing abandonment were only rarely worth mention.

These tales are indicative of another way in which both Chipewyan experience and practice conflict with contemporary ethnographic understandings of hunter-gatherers. The preponderant role of African bush and rain-forest cultures in the development of such understandings has conditioned ethnology into thinking of hunter-gatherer social organization in terms of the distribution of small kills of game or of the rapid distribution of a single large kill. Indeed, most discussion about primitive communism in hunter-gatherer societies and about uneven (asymmetric) availabilities of resources to individuals in these societies is predicated upon the near universal occurrence of these conditions. The circumstances of Chipewyan life, less certainly the life of all northern Canadian hunter-gatherer societies, belie these assumptions. Resource symmetry is an inherent part of Chipewyan life. The basis of their egalitarianism and of their control over the proliferation of hierarchy must be sought via other conditions — and so it must be for other hunter-gatherer cultures as well. I have discussed Chipewyan social ecology elsewhere (Sharp 1977; 1978; 1981), but the salient point is that the sheer volume of resources available to the Chipewyan collapses any meaningful consideration of primitive communism among them. At the leading edge of the fall caribou migrations, contemporary groups of no more than twenty people containing only three or four active hunters kill, and preserve, upwards of 200 caribou in six to eight weeks.[5] There is every indication that contemporary groups are substantially less able to kill large numbers of caribou than were their ancestors who used traditional methods of pounds and drives. Now, anthropological assumptions of distribution, control and reciprocity in hunter-gatherer society and their concomitant extrapolation into the structuring of social systems simply make no sense when per-capita yearly meat resources come to be measured in tons.

The pleasure and satisfaction my informant took from the stories reflects the deep and fundamental values adult Chipewyan women hold towards the idea of making dry meat.[6] Why this particular aspect

5. Barren ground caribou are large animals and the preference is always for the fattest animals. To be conservative I am assuming a live weight of about 250 pounds. Throughout the rest of the year there are caribou, moose, birds, fish and small game. I have no figures for the yearly yield but judging from my field experience, the Chipewyan substantially exceed the volume of prey reported by Tanner (1979) as being secured by the Mistassini Cree.

6. These values are undergoing change as the younger generations adjust to the new village-oriented lifestyle.

of women's activities has been chosen above other aspects is beyond my ken. The work itself is difficult and often not avidly sought or thoroughly pursued, but this does not detract from its importance as a symbol of gender and social role. As with material culture, people 'attach themselves to it, but also build up their relationships through it and see them in terms of it' (Evans-Pritchard 1940: 89). This one activity, far more important both in the Chipewyan past and in their current ideas about that past, is a key point of articulation between women's and men's separate self-conceptualizations and activities and their shared ideas of *Dene* as an entity rooted in an alternative order of being.

Woodburn's caution not 'to reduce social organization in hunter-gatherer or other societies to no more than a mere epiphenomenon of technology, the work process and the rules governing the control of assets' (1982a: 434) and Ingold's point about native categories (1983: 569) are relevant to the issue because the Chipewyan do not conceptualize 'the hunting system' (Irimoto 1981) in terms of its product (food), but as a process. The distinction which Carter (1974) and I found, through very different methods, between obtaining food and depending upon others for food, is a deep and pervasive one, but it is embedded in unconscious perceptions and processes far from Chipewyan awareness. In terms of the relationships and modes of thought of which people are consciously aware, there is a gender-based dichotomy of perception incorporating sublime ignorance of, and indifference to, the mode of conceptualization employed by the other gender. Men think in terms of *inkoze* in their pursuit of their routine subsistence activities. Women are well aware of *inkoze* but think of it mostly in terms of healing and sorcery. They do not conceptualize their routine subsistence activities in terms of it and are little aware of, or impressed by, the application of this framework of causality to male subsistence activities.

As the application of *inkoze* to particular aspects of male hunting leads to a subtle but competitive process of ranking that has implications for social and political relations beyond the household, so the valuation women apply to the basic processes of converting raw meat into food has similar implications (Sharp 1977; 1981; 1988). In a society little utilizing what Foucault (1979: 135–94) calls 'discipline', the separation of the sexual division of labor in food production between two different ideologies establishes alternate frameworks for the expression and exercise of power in interpersonal relationships, centering in each case upon the role of food in the establishment and maintenance of relations between both individuals and groups. For each gender the appropriate framework provides mechanisms of individuation, ranking and self-definition. Between each gender this dual framework, individualized, ritualized but shareable for men, individualized, non-ritualized but even more shareable for women (Sharp 1981; 1988), exists concomitantly with and in dependence upon a mutual ignorance that enables a dialogue over the production and distribution of food. It is basal to the formation not only of gender but also of social and family organization, to ecological functioning, and to political relations, adequately ordering the expression and transmission of values, and substituting a dialogue of gender and subsistence for public ritual performances.

11. Animals in Bushman thought, myth and art

Mathias Guenther

The Bushmen's letters are in their bodies. They speak, they move, they make the Bushmen's bodies move. . . . He feels a tapping at his ribs; he says to the children: 'The springbok seem to be coming, for I feel the springbok sensation'. For I am wont to feel thus, I feel a sensation in the calves of my legs when the springbok's blood is going to run down them. For I always feel blood, when I am about to kill springbok. For I sit feeling a sensation behind my back, which the blood is wont to run down, when I am carrying springbok. The springbok hair lies behind my back.

Therefore we are wont to lie quietly, when the sensation is like this, when we are feeling the things come. . . . We have a sensation in our feet, as we feel the rustling feet of the springbok with which the springbok come, making the bushes rustle. . . . We have a sensation in our heads, when we are about to chop the springbok's horns. We have a sensation in our face, on account of the blackness of the stripe on the face of the springbok; we feel a sensation in our eyes, on account of the black marks on the eyes of the springbok. . . .

We are used to feel this when the things are walking (//Kabbo, a /Xam Bushman, 1873, cited in Bleek and Lloyd 1911: 331–5).

Introduction

Bushman (and, more generally, hunter-gatherer) expressive culture abounds with animals. In art and mythology, the preponderance of animals, depicted naturalistically or anthropomorphically, suggests an intense and abiding interest. I seek to explain this interest in terms of aesthetic, cognitive and symbolic factors, as well as in terms of the ontological condition of animals in relation to man. This latter aspect of the relationship between man (both as hunter and as artist) and animal receives special attention, for I hold it to be the main cause of mankind's preoccupation with animalkind and the root cause of man's 'longing for other bloods' (as C.S. Lewis termed man's universal fascination with animals). I also show that the contemplation of the ontological condition of animals gives rise to two distinct cognitive patterns. The adaptive significance of these thought patterns about fauna is examined: they are seen to enhance the short-term exploitation and long-term conservation of the hunters' game resources.

The prominence of animals in Bushman thought and lore

Along with a trickster figure (himself animalian in his favourite guises), animal characters dominate the mythological landscape of all Bushman groups of southern Africa. In the myths animals almost completely eclipse humans, while in art humans constitute only about half of all representations in one genre (painting) and are almost completely absent in another (engraving). In contrast to art, which for the most part depicts animals naturalistically, Bushman myths and tales depict animal protagonists and principals as therianthropical beings, persistently and pervasively merging faunal and human traits.

The key creation myth, and the exemplar of Bushman cosmology, is the myth of double creation. In the variant of the Nharo Bushmen of Botswana, it pronounces the present order of existence to be a reversal of primal time — an earlier time when animals were humans and humans animals. In the present order, man and beast carry within themselves residual traces of their previous state, such that some Bushman groups (for example the /Xam of the Cape) have forbidden the eating of portions of a slain prey animal, the meat being held to contain concentrations of this primal humanity (Bleek and Lloyd 1911: 60–1). According to the Nharo, women, more extensively than men, especially carry primalcy, as well as animality, for they have not been fully reversed from earier times. The principal characters of the Bushman myths and tales comprise virtually all the animal beings of the first order of existence — of primal time. These animal beings are featured as enigmatic blends of human and animal. They each contain distinctive animalian traits, for example the ostrich has her wings, the aardwolf lives in a burrow, baboons live in the rock up which they climb. Yet they are also human: they are bipedal, tool- and language-using social beings that lead lives very similar to those of the Bushmen of today. Their imposing presence in the myths suggests that animals are appreciated as more than objects of nature providing an aesthetic backdrop for the doings of humans or humanoid spirit beings. Animality was an intrinsic component of the ontological condition of the beings of the 'first race', the forebears of Bushman society and culture.

Man-animal representations are also found on the rock surfaces that served as canvases for the Bushman artists of southern Africa. As Lewis-Williams (1981a; 1983b) has compellingly suggested, they depict the transformation experiences that some Bushman trance dancers (or medicine men) believed, and today still believe, themselves to undergo. The most common animal motif of Bushman art is not therianthropic, however, but consists of straightforward, naturalistic animals, painted either as simple monochromes or as lavish, detailed bi- or polychromes. These paintings primarily depict antelope or other large animals such as elephant or giraffe, as well as felines, ostriches and, in later paintings, cattle. In the art complexes in various regions of southern Africa (for example, Drakensberg, western Cape, Brandberg in Namibia), one animal species is usually predominant, being depicted with far greater frequency and with more detail and colour than all the others. In the Drakensberg complex this is the eland (Vinnicombe 1976; Lewis-Williams 1981a); in the western Cape, the elephant (Maggs and Sealy 1983). In the Brandberg the statistical breakdown of motifs is not yet complete and in the mid-1980s three animal species are vying for the preponderant position: the gemsbok, the springbok and the giraffe (Jacobson 1975; Guenther 1984: 35–51, 55). The extent to which naturalistically depicted animal scenes are simply a 'menu or checklist' (Vinnicombe 1976), that is, straightforward scale-model representations of the hunters' prey animals, or else are informed with symbolic, religious as well as socio-economic significance, is the subject of fierce debate amongst contemporary students of southern African rock art (Lewis-Williams 1981a; 1982; 1983a; 1984; Nettleton 1984; Willcox 1984).

Pondering the question why animals hold so pre-eminent a position within Bushman imagination and expressive culture, one is moved, given the pre-eminent ecological paradigm in Bushman research, to consider that Bushman myth and art reflect gastronomic, subsistence concerns. The plausibility of this suggestion is specious, however. For one thing, the animals painted with the greatest care are not the ones most frequently hunted. The Bushmen typically hunt various types of small antelope and such humble creatures as hyrax, hare, springhare or porcupine — all species which die within a few hours of being shot with a poison arrow and which do not need to be tracked for days with the constant risk of being lost to such competing predators and scavengers as lions or vultures. In the art, what is depicted with greatest frequency, detail and elaboration are the 'big' species which, while being quintessential, 'centre-fold' game animals, tend, for practical reasons, not to be hunted very often. Also, plants, gathered by the women and constituting between 60 and 80 per cent of the Kalahari Bushman diet, are conspicuous through their absence from the rock panels. Clearly, non-economic, non-gastronomic factors motivated the painters; Bushman art is no more 'wildlife art' than are the scenes in nativity paintings depicting the ox, ass and sheep (not to mention the therianthropic angels up in the rafters.).

One of the non-economic factors motivating Bushman painting is aesthetic salience. The animals painted with the greatest care, the game animals *par excellence*, are all of striking appearance: towering height, massive size, unique shape, striking markings, strange appurtenances. They spring to the eye, presumably any eye, irrespective of cultural conditioning. They command a high degree of aesthetic and cognitive impact, in contrast to the more generalized (and more hunted) ante-lopes, such as steenbok, duiker or reebok, which are somewhat drab, with their unremarkable basic buck-shape. However, it should be noted that the latter animals do appear on the rock surfaces; but they tend to be painted with little embellishment, in monochrome — and monotone — fashion and in small format. Moreover, their 'positional' placement on the rock panel, though symbolically guided (Lewis-Williams 1981a: 10–13), seems to be more haphazard. The central beasts — eland, elephant, giraffe, gemsbok — appear classically *bon à penser*: these vitally important goods are 'good to think', and thus to draw and to feature in myth and lore. Moreover, as Vinnicombe (1976) and Lewis-Williams (1981a) have shown, animals such as these — and most especially, the eland — are also of deep religious significance, specifi-cally in their role as dominant symbols. Here they represent either group identity or, more especially, trance, the central preoccupation of Bushman ritual, and in particular initiation ritual wherein the animal assumes the stature and status of an *animal de passage* (Lewis-Williams 1981a).

By considering the aesthetic, cognitive and religious salience of animals in order to explain their pre-eminent position in Bushman culture, we have gone some way beyond simple ecological-economic explanatory notions. However, to appreciate the subtleties of the cognitive manner by which Bushmen relate to animals, and the vari-ations in this manner within either economic or expressive contexts, we must consider not only the animal's functional, aesthetic and cognitive qualities, but also its ontological status. Hunter-gatherers, living in cheek-by-jowl proximity to animals, have, since time immemorial, doubtless probed the fundamental problematic surrounding this issue, capturing it in such basic questions as: What are animals, in relation to man? What are 'we', what are 'they'? What are the differences, what the similarities, between beast and man?

The answer to these questions, as given by the Bushmen and, likely, all hunter-gatherers (if not all mankind) is an ambiguous one: animals are both the same as man and they are other than man (cf. Lévi-Strauss 1962: 96–102; Willis 1974: 127–9; Shepard 1978; Fernandez 1974: 120–4). Their otherness derives from their distinctive anatomies, their poly-typic heterogeneity, their lack of sapience, symboling and language, and their innocence of the incest taboo and its resultant social patterns.

Yet they are also like man, in their basic anatomical plan, their basic behavioural repertoire (eating, sleeping, mating, fleeing or attacking) and their shared basic patterns of sentience. 'Same as' and 'other than' man, 'within' and 'without', 'kindred' and 'alien': such are the fundamental structural oppositions that become both defined and obliterated, mediated and confounded, as mankind contemplates animalkind. Such contemplation is done with an interest that is as compelling as it is abiding — an interest mentally aroused by the dimensions of ambiguity and disjuncture.

Otherness titillates aesthetically, and variety and richness of form get noted: this is what happens in the scanning of the multiplicity of discretely defined, distinctive (animal) beings, each sporting its own striking shape, colour, markings, horns, appurtenances. In contrast to man, a somewhat bland, monotypic homogeneous species, one of God's — N!eri's — less inspired, creative efforts, all such beings are striking in their exotic otherness, their distinctiveness. Yet, these 'other' objects are also fellow-subjects; connectedness, affinity, sympathy, kindredness — *participation mystique* — are the affective links between 'them and us', filling man with wonder, and also a touch of numinous dread. Cosmologies and ritual in tribal societies often formalize this aspect of the man–animal relationship and work it out in mythopoeic charters which formally include animals within man's moral community. (Examples of such charters are the Bushman myth of double creation, or totemic rituals of one kind or another which ascribe some form of ancestor-status to an animal species.) Moreover, Bushman expressive culture further confounds the ontological binary pair of sameness and otherness, defined by the man–animal duality, by conjuring up, in myth, art and ritual, therianthropes and man-animal transformation. Such conflations bring to a pitch the ambiguity and disjuncture within the animal's being, and thus the interest of man — Bushman — in animals. Man's affective and mental interaction becomes an elaborate and effusive commentary on the opposed and confounded dual qualities, not only in his capacity as expressive performer but also as hunter. Of the two, myth and art give emphasis principally to the theme of the animal's sameness; in contrast, the hunt places emphasis on otherness.

Bushman art and myth abound with anthropomorphic and therianthropic motifs. Man and beast forever change shape and assume one another's forms, such that no clear conceptual boundaries separate the two life forms. A good many of the animal representations are symbolically linked to man, through metaphors or positional placement in the composition — for example, by being placed within a scene depicting a ritual event. Or else they are animal–human conflations, some of them, as in the Drakensberg complex, flying or floating figures, referred to by one researcher as 'trance bucks' (Lewis-Williams 1981a: 84–100). The blending of human and animal ontological qualities, within the 'early race' of mythological time and also in contemporary beings (human as well as animal) is the cosmological theme of the basic Bushman creation myth, and the leitmotif of Bushman mythology. The myths imbue animals with an abiding human, moral, sentient and spiritual quality. In categorizing animals, the Nharo apply the designation '/wa' ('little child'). They attribute them with soul, speech, reason and volition, as well as personality, customs and human-cast social patterns (such as band- and multi-band aggregation, territoriality, marriage, siblingship, parenthood, but not, as I have mentioned, kin categories or the incest taboo) (Barnard 1980b; Silberbauer 1981: 63–77; Guenther 1983).

Like some men, particularly trance dancers, some animals (such as the giraffe or eland) also possess 'potency', a spiritual, supernatural power employed by trancers for curing (Lewis-Williams 1981a: 83–4; Thackeray 1983: 42). Bushman ritual, like mythology, is informed with the themes of animal simulation and transformation, notably in the trance dance and the passage ritual, the two ritual patterns of Bushman society (Lewis-Williams 1981a; 1982; 1983b). Among the /Xam some medicine men were believed to have certain powers over specific animals. They were believed capable of 'possessing' them, that is, taking on their guise and thereby becoming capable of influencing the success of the hunt of 'their' species. In addition to 'springbok shamans' (reminiscent of the Shoshone, whose 'antelope shamans' led the pronghorn hunts), there were medicine men with powers over lion, ostrich and locusts (D. Bleek 1935; 1936; Lewis-Williams 1981a: 95–7; Hewitt 1986: 297).

The therianthropic element that pervades Bushman myth, art, dance and ritual thus reflects an entrenched sense of sympathy, affinity and kinship between man and animal. Yet, on the other hand, *qua* hunters Bushmen view the animal principally as a food object, which will be killed, butchered, divided out and eaten. To such tasks they bring, soberly and carefully, a rich body of zoological knowledge and an efficient and ingenious complex of hunting technology and techniques, including remarkable tracking skills that have been described as 'uncanny' by one Western observer (Lee 1979: 212). But in neither of these two forms of man–animal relationship is the opposite ontological dimension ever fully bracketed out, whether it be in the expressive or the economic mode.

Thus, the myths and the art, while predominantly 'same'-oriented, do not lose sight of the 'other'-dimension. When the artist paints a lone buck, or a herd in the veld, or men hunting an animal as quarry, then he paints the animal as other. It is the same when, delighting in the animal's distinctiveness, he paints its markings with lavish detail, especially the head, horns and back line, the part of the animal that Bushman artists most develop — these are the parts the animal will most likely present to the hunter, for its lower parts will be covered by the Kalahari veld's tall grass and shrubs. The myth-narrator, too, dwells on the animals' otherness, telling of the animal protagonists of primal time skinning a buck they had hunted or trying to milk a dumb and wild cow they had happened across in the veld one day (and doing it unsuccessfully, one might add, for lack of cultural polish was one of the flaws of the 'early race'). So it is that animals are appreciated as alien and autonomous beings of nature, living beastly lives out in the veld. In fact, I suggest that the showing in a number of paintings of 'wild' animals and hunting scenes is probably amenable to the currently out-of-favour 'sympathetic' theory of (hunting) magic.

Despite the primary focus on the animal's sameness, then, the Bushman expressive performer is not blind to the animal's otherness. This is the focus the hunt embellishes. The fact that artists, myth-tellers and trance dancers (who, of course, are hunters as well) *are* aware of the otherness of animals prevents the Bushmen's mind experiencing schizoid guilt about killing and eating their (animal) 'brothers'. Such guilt racks the conscience of so many Western animal lovers who, try as they may, cannot reconcile this love with the love of a steak, as they concentrate in heart and mind, on the animal's 'sameness' quality. For the Bushmen, perceiving the animal as a kindred being is held in balance by perceiving it as 'other', with this latter focus foremost in the hunter's mind. This balanced appraisal of the animal's ontological being precludes the establishment, in the hunter's mind, of a Western-style, Beatrix Potteresque or Richard Adamsesque, notion of the animal as a surrogate human. It allows the hunter to proceed with his bloody business without any qualms about committing some act of cannibalism.

Yet hunting, for all of its sobriety and *Zweckrationalität*, does not *obliterate* the perception of affinity vis-à-vis the animal quarry. Each hunt is a renewed encounter with a fellow-creature. Activated in each hunt is a feeling of sympathy, and the implicit recognition that the animal is a moral and sentient kindred being, to be treated with decorum. This latter notion is not merely carried vaguely in the back of the hunter's mind, but is something 'operationalized': it is brought to bear on the hunt, complementing the empirical, pragmatic, control- and exploitation-oriented component of the hunting enterprise.

In his account of /Gwi hunting, Silberbauer (1981: 63–77) precisely emphasizes the anthropomorphic overlay of the event, which casts animals as sentient beings to whom the hunter responds with sympathy. In my own work, among the linguistically-related and geographically-close Ghanzi farm Bushmen (predominantly the Nharo) I was not able to observe hunting nearly as closely (Silberbauer worked in the remote Central Kalahari Game Reserve). The few hunts I did observe impressed on me the affective and affectionate manner by which the hunters related to the game animals, especially when describing the hunt afterwards and dwelling on the actions of the animals encountered. The Nharo also appear to have the notion that certain hunters are especially skilled at hunting particular species of animal because of a moral or spiritual affinity the hunter has for that species.

The clearest evidence for the sympathy-bond between hunter and hunted comes from the /Xam Bushmen of the nineteenth-century Cape (Hewitt 1986: 124–5). Here the hunt was accompanied by a number of mystical techniques (called *n!anna-se* by the /Xam) which had the effect of riveting the hunter's attention, emotionally and spiritually, on the animal he was hunting, so that the hunt became an ongoing process of intersubjectivity, the hunter projecting himself into the animal and viewing himself as the object, through the antelope's eyes (akin to D.H. Lawrence's experience, as described in his poem 'A Doe in the Morning': 'I looked at her,/ and felt her watching;/ I became a strange being'). Throughout the hunt the hunter would monitor his every thought, emotion and action, in order to sustain the bond of connectedness with the animal by which he felt he could steer the hunt towards an auspicious conclusion. For example, he would refrain from drinking water, and in addition observe a variety of food taboos, lest the animal gain strength through his succour; he would walk with a limp to slow the animal down, and he would attempt to avoid contact with any animal whose attributes — for example, speed or nocturnal travel — might be to the dying animal's benefit (supposing it had been wounded with the slow-working poison arrow). The bond of sympathy was something set up during the hours or days preceding the hunt, when the hunters would attune themselves spiritually to one animal species or another and, in the process, attempt to gather whatever presentiments they could about the impending hunt: the animals they might encounter, the direction they could come from, the likely dangers, the duration of the hunt. These presentiments, as well as the experiences of sympathy throughout the hunt, the /Xam called 'tappings' (or, as explained by the /Xam informant to his European interrogator, 'Bushman letters'). They activated the hunter's entire body; they were felt at his ribs, his back, his calves, his face and eyes. His body would be astir with the 'antelope sensation', at places on his body corresponding with those on the antelope's (Bleek and Lloyd 1911: 33–5).

Animal cognition and adaptation

The perception of animals in the dual mode of 'other than' and 'same as' man engenders a double cognitive approach towards animals. Each cognitive approach has its special adaptive significance.

The respective patterns of thought may be grasped through the familiar rational-mystical dichotomy, which I label 'knowledge' versus 'understanding' (this parallels such other contrasts as 'scientific' versus 'religious', 'instrumental' versus 'expressive', 'cerebral' versus 'visceral', 'hard' versus 'soft'). As regards animals, knowledge is the epistemological mode appropriate to the ontological quality of 'otherness', while understanding is the mode in tune with 'sameness'. In the knowledge mode, the animal is wont to be treated as an object — to be studied and analyzed, and controlled and used. Understanding, on the other hand, connotes intuition and empathy and the treatment of the animal as a subject — to be appreciated through the processes of sympathy and intersubjectivity. The course and direction of knowledge are unilateral, one-way, dominating; of understanding reflexive, two-way, reciprocal. The *modus operandi* of the former is control, of the latter, encounter; their goals respectively self-preservation and self-knowledge. Thus knowledge is the cognitive mode appropriate to the hunter, as he stalks his quarry, bent on killing it and butchering and distributing its carcass. Understanding is the cognitive mode of both the artist and narrative performer, as they encounter the animals of the natural or mythological landscape, with a view to recreating them by means of icons or myths. The hunt feeds primarily the stomach, the expressive performance primarily the soul.

Yet, as was seen, the two epistemological modes of relating to animals, and the two ontological qualities upon which they are focused, are never polarized. Both knowledge and understanding are applied to animals in both economic and artistic contexts, and animals are at all times perceived as simultaneously 'other than' and 'same as' man. Thus the perceptual aspect of the Bushmen's exploitative relationship with animals is not solely 'symbolic work', with people's cognitive appreciation simply an augmentation of hunting tools and techniques (Ridington 1982). This point is illustrated rather poignantly by the !Kung hunter who gets so engrossed in some beguiling trait or action observed in the stalked animal that he forgets about the task at hand — until indeed it is too late and the animal is out of range (Blurton Jones and Konner 1976: 334). On the other hand, an extreme situation such as this is not frequent; the hunter is rarely interrupted, and the hunt aborted, through mystical interference or fallout of this kind. For, to repeat: in neither the hunt nor in art and myth is the man–animal relationship a matter solely of 'mystical participation'. Were such to be the case, the consequence could easily be the hunters' befuddlement. An exclusive notion of mystical solidarity might soon prove counter-productive to a people whose livelihood depends in some measure upon the killing, butchering and eating of creatures defined culturally as kinsfolk. Instead, symbolic work and mystic participation are combined, with the effect both of galvanizing the attention which animals command in man, and of balancing both the artistic and economic relationships of man with animals.

'Knowledge' of an animal, wherein it is held to be an alien other, or a wild food object, provides the hunter-gatherer with the mental attitude to hunt and consume it. 'Knowledge' also generates the requisite information, of an empirical and pragmatic kind, to conduct the business of hunting (such knowledge is extensive among the Bushmen, paralleling the women's superb botanical knowledge). On the other hand, sympathetic identification with the animal contributes towards the embedding of the animal within the hunter's consciousness, which allows for intense and persistent inner concentration on the quarry, as its 'letters' are read, before and throughout the hunt, both in the visible presence of the animals and in their absence. The other adaptive effect of this 'understanding' mode is that, by virtue of its portrayal of the game animal as a fellow-creature which deep-down is human, a type of moral attitude is engendered in hunters militating against over-hunting and abuse. Thus, 'knowledge' of a creature perceived as 'other' aids and abets its exploitation; 'understanding', its preservation. The two mental approaches towards the environment are vital for efficient and long-term adaptation. The obvious contrast is with the West, where there has been a consistent selection of one approach — knowledge and exploitation — at the expense of the other, with the one-sidedness of this choice lying at the root of the Western ecological crisis (L. White 1967; Suzuki 1984). The Bushmen, like hunter-gatherers generally, have held both approaches in balance and, as a rule, managed to live in harmony with their environment for centuries, if not millennia.

Conclusion

This chapter has been concerned to explore certain aspects of the symbolic and expressive dimension of animals in a non-totemic society, that is, a society entirely without clans, moieties and other classes of relatives. It has been primarily in the context of totemic societies that the supra-ecological, symbolic role of animals has been explored, by such masters as Boas, Goldenweiser, van Gennep, Malinowski, Radcliffe-Brown and Lévi-Strauss. These writers' focus has typically been to establish the relationship between the animal species singled out by members of a society for aesthetic and mystical attention, and the social classes or categories which obtain in that society, the latter thus being given a high degree of affective or cognitive salience. Usually such studies make only passing references to societies which lack descent groups, clans or moieties, treating them as relatively residual, inchoate and anomalous. This chapter, showing the extensive expressive and symbolic involvement of members of these sorts of societies with the many animal species that share the natural environment, suggests that man's mental elaboration of animals is a process occurring independently of a segmentary, unilineal social context. Man's beguilement by animals is strong and lasting, even when there is an absence of an equivalent, homologous social system of classes and categories providing a matrix within which the classification of the animals can play itself out analogously and metaphorically.

In sum, I suggest that animals are beguiling and interesting to man prima facie, in and of themselves, without any mediation through social structure. The interest and beguilement derive from the relationship, one-to-one, between the hunter-gatherer and the animal he or she comes across every day in the veld and in the myths. This relationship intrigues relentlessly, because of the readily appreciated other–same ambiguity that attaches to the animals.

12. 'People of the eland': an archaeo-linguistic crux

J.D. Lewis-Williams

As long ago as 1908, Werner (1908: 393) observed the large number of painted eland in southern San rock art and suggested that this antelope had been 'in some sense . . . a sacred animal'. Later Battiss (1948: 61) similarly wondered if there were some religious significance in the fact that San artists painted so many eland. Much evidence for a more sophisticated version of this explanation was eventually adduced by Vinnicombe (1975; 1976) in her study of rock paintings in the southern Drakensberg. In the first place, her inventory of 8478 paintings showed that 35 per cent of all identifiable wild animals were eland; she thus confirmed and gave greater accuracy to the earlier writers' impressions. Then she went on to show, again numerically, that the artists lavished greater care on their depictions of eland than on any other paintings: more eland are painted in the complex shaded polychrome technique and, further, they are portrayed in a variety of postures which must have been a challenge to the artists' draughtsmanship.

To explain this numerical and technical emphasis, Vinnicombe rightly turned to San ethnography and demonstrated that the eland held multiple meanings for the artists. One was its association with /Kaggen (the Mantis), the southern San trickster-deity. Vinnicombe also argued for social symbolism: the eland may have symbolized the San camp, or band, for eland herds amalgamate annually as do most San camps. She summed up these and other associations in the title of her book *People of the eland*.

She derived this apposite phrase from an indigenous account of San rock painting obtained by Marion Walsham How in 1930 (How 1962: 26–42). Unfortunately the phrase, as used by How's informant, is more evocative than communicative. In exactly what sense were the San 'of' the eland? Does the phrase mean, as Vinnicombe argues, that the San identified themselves with the eland? Or that the eland was some sort of totem? Or, perhaps, that, like /Kaggen, it was divine and they were under its protection? The phrase permits of various glosses.

Because there are so few direct comments on rock art obtained from San informants or from those closely associated with the San, every remark, no matter how puzzling, must, as Vinnicombe (1976: 314) herself has urged, be subjected to the closest scrutiny. This is especially true of How's account because it is, as far as I am aware, the nearest we can come to an explicit, authentic statement on why the south-eastern San painted so many eland. Indeed, I argue that, despite its seeming ambiguities, it also identifies the social and cognitive context of San rock art.[1]

My argument begins with an account of the circumstances under which the statement was obtained. In 1930 How invited Mapote, a son of the Phuti chief Moorosi, to visit her at Qacha's Nek in what is now Lesotho. Mapote's mother, a Pondomise, had been an inferior wife of Moorosi, but he had half-San step-brothers and had learned to paint with San in their caves. In 1930 Mapote was about seventy-four years old, and How realized that it was imperative to learn all she could from him. Her interest was restricted principally to the preparation of paint and its application to the rock surface, and she provides a most valuable account of at least one artist's painting technique. As Mapote painted, the years seemed to fall away, and, starting from the animal's chest, he moved 'his brush along smoothly without the slightest hesitation' (How 1962: 38). Unfortunately, How was less interested in the meaning of the art and appears not to have questioned Mapote on this point. She, like so many writers both before and after her, accepted the meaning as self-evident. Mapote, however, volunteered the crucial remark, saying 'he would paint an eland, as the Bushmen of that part of the country were of the eland' (ibid.: 38).

It appears that the language used in this interview was Sesotho and that How was not in need of an interpreter. San concepts were thus first expressed in Sesotho and then translated, by How herself, into English. As with so much ethnography recorded under similarly unsatisfactory circumstances, difficulties arose from, among other things, translating foreign idioms which express concepts unfamiliar to Westerners. Unintelligible passages in the English version of such ethnography often result from a literal rendering of metaphors and idiomatic phrases. Certainly, 'of the eland' is by no means clear as it stands in English.

One way to sort out this problem is to see if the phrase is a literal translation of a San idiom, the meaning of which we can ascertain independently. This task is less easy than one might suppose because the language of the Maluti San has not been preserved, but the few

1. I am grateful for useful comments on this chapter made by numerous colleagues: T.N. Huffman, C. Campbell, T.A. Dowson, Z.E. Kingdon. The research was funded by the University of the Witwatersrand and the Human Sciences Research Council. The illustrations were drawn by T.A. Dowson. Mrs M.-C. Clarke typed the manuscript.

fragments that do exist suggest it was closely related to the /Xam language which was spoken by San farther to the west. Moreover, the Orpen (1874) collection shows that the Maluti San shared a great many important concepts and rituals with the /Xam (Lewis-Williams 1980; 1981a). Though the /Xam language and people are also extinct, we can at least turn to the Bleek collection (Lewis-Williams 1981a: 25–34). In the 1870s the Bleek family recorded approximately 12,000 pages of verbatim /Xam texts in an orthography developed by Wilhelm Bleek himself. These texts are, for the most part, accompanied by literal English translations, and Dorothea Bleek, Wilhelm's daughter, prepared a /Xam–English dictionary which derives from the translations prepared by her father and her aunt, Lucy Lloyd. We are thus able to identify phrases and idioms in the original language and, by comparing the various contexts in which the informants used them, arrive at some idea of their meaning. One such phrase is the key to what Mapote was really telling How.

/Xam informants spoke of medicine people who had an association with various things such as springbok, rain, locusts and mantises. Medicine men who, for instance, were associated with game in general were *Opwaiten-ka !gi:ten* (D. Bleek 1935: 35). More specifically, a woman who was associated with springbok was *wai-ta !gi:xa* (ibid.: 47). In such phrases, *!gi:xa* (plural *!gi:ten*) means medicine person, and the suffix -*ga*, -*ta* or -*ka* forms the possessive case. The Bleeks usually give these phrases as 'the game's medicine people' or 'the springboks' medicine people', but the phrases can also be translated 'medicine people of the game' or ' . . . of springbok', whatever the case may be. Sometimes, and this is the important point, the /Xam phrase is slightly different: informants spoke merely of 'a rain's man' (*!kwa-ka !kwe*, D. Bleek 1933: 306) or 'the rain's people' (*!kwa:ga !k?e*, ibid.: 375; W.H.I. Bleek 1866–77: B.27.2543; L.VIII.I. 6063–8). In these expressions it was understood that the 'man' or 'people' were in fact medicine people because only medicine people had this type of relationship with game, rain, and so forth.

We can now begin to understand Mapote's expression 'the Bushmen . . . were of the eland'. He was saying that he would paint an eland because medicine people were associated with eland. In How's translation the phrase is obscure, but in his own language it was a common expression with a precise meaning.

To appreciate this meaning more fully and thus the importance of Mapote's remark for a proper understanding of San rock art we examine the nature of the relationship between medicine people and the things with which they were associated. A /Xam word which expresses this association is /*ki*. Bleek and Lloyd give /*ki* as 'possess' or simply 'have' in literal, 'secular' contexts, such as owning an arrow, but it is the idiomatic contexts in which we are interested. Both /*ki* and the use of the possessive case appear in a phrase like '!gvrriten-dé was a springbok sorcerer (*wai-ta !gi:xa*), he had (*/ki*) springbok' (D. Bleek 1936: 144). Here the possessive (*-ta*) and */ki* are equivalent. The informant added the second part of the statement to explain what he meant by *wai-ta !gixa*. The relationship which both */ki* and *wai-ta* express is one of those multifaceted concepts which have no exact English equivalent. One facet is suggested by the phrase *!gi:xa a /ki //xi* which Lloyd translated as 'a medicine man who brings illness' (D. Bleek 1935: 29). Certain medicine people, only vaguely identified, were thought to have the ability to shoot 'arrows of sickness' into people (ibid.: 5). They were thus able to control, not merely possess, sickness and deploy it at will. Other people were able to */ki* rain (Lewis-Williams 1981a: 103–16). They were the 'medicine people of the rain' (D. Bleek 1933: 306, 376, 379, 386) who captured and killed a 'rain animal' in order to make rain. They controlled rain. Medicine people exercised these powers while in trance (for accounts of the San trance dance, see L. Marshall 1969; Lee 1967; 1968a; Biesele 1975; 1978; Katz 1982; Guenther 1975).

These instances enlarge our understanding of */ki* and prepare for its use in connection with animals. Because the techniques medicine people employed in exercising their relationships with animals have an important bearing on the art, I examine them in some detail. Four distinct techniques have been recorded. This variety accords with San religious belief which is markedly idiosyncratic though contained within certain parameters.

Finding animals is, of course, a major component in hunting, and San are expert trackers. But the supernatural also played a part. According to an early report, some San medicine men believed that God revealed the whereabouts of herds to them while they were in trance (J. Campbell 1822, II: 33; see also Lee 1967: 34). Antelope were also decoyed into the hunters' ambush by two further techniques. A /Xam medicine woman spoke of a cap with antelope ears. Springbok were said to follow the wearer of such a cap into the ambush (D. Bleek 1935: 46; 1936: 144). Eared caps are sometimes depicted in the paintings (Figure 12.1; see also Lewis-Williams 1981a: Fig. 21; 1983a: Figs. 16, 22, 23, 100). Another informant claimed to possess (*/ki*) a 'castrated' springbok which she could send among the antelope and which would lead the herd to the hunters (D. Bleek 1935: 44–46). Although she did not say this was done in trance, her use of */ki* and the bizarre nature of the method suggests hallucination rather than reality; actually training a springbok to perform this function seems highly improbable.

In what is perhaps the simplest method of ensuring good hunting, and one still used today, a medicine man enters trance and then places his hands on a hunter who has enjoyed no success and draws the debilitating sickness out of him before expelling it through a 'hole' in the nape of his neck, the *n//au* spot. The hunter is then believed to achieve better success. This curing process is depicted in some paintings (see, for example, Summers 1959: P1. 91; Lewis-Williams 1981a: Fig. 18).

These, then, are the recorded techniques and trance experiences associated with the concept of /ki. The Bleek collection, however, records another use of /ki which does not seem to imply 'control' but a relationship of a different though associated kind. Using both /ki and the possessive, a /Xam informant said: 'My father-in-law //Khabbó had (/ki) Mantises, he was a Mantis's man (/kaggen-ka !kwi)' (D. Bleek 1936: 143). Because mantises were not a part of San diet, as, say, locusts were and which medicine people also controlled (D. Bleek 1933: 388; 1935: 10–11), it seems that this informant was referring to his father-in-law's source of power (!gi or //ken). Medicine songs, which are sung as part of the activation of power, are named after a variety of 'powerful' things. Mantises were evidently considered powerful, but antelope were and still are the most prominent symbols of power. As Biesele (1978: 931) remarks, animals become 'metaphors with the strength to bridge worlds'. Medicine people are said to possess medicine songs many of which are named after powerful animals. A man may, for instance, be said to possess eland and giraffe medicine. The !Kung, in fact, consider eland to be the most potent of all creatures, and the eland medicine song is considered especially efficacious (Lewis-Williams and Biesele 1978). The southern San also believed the eland to contain a great deal of power (D. Bleek 1932: 237; Lewis-Williams 1981b: 6). Thus another implication of Mapote's statement is that the medicine people of that area derived much of their power from eland in addition to being able to control their movements.

Some of this eland-power seems to have been transferred to the paintings because Mapote required eland blood for the manufacture of his paint (How 1962: 37). This implication was recently confirmed by a very old woman who is the last surviving descendant of a San family who lived with a Pondomise chief as rain-makers. She independently confirmed the use of eland blood and added that the paintings themselves contained power. As the people danced, she said, they turned to face the paintings when they wished to increase their power. Power could also be obtained by placing a hand on one of the painted eland (Jolly 1986; Lewis-Williams 1986).

The link between medicine people and the creatures they controlled was further explained by a /Xam informant who was asked to comment on a copy of a painting depicting therianthropes. He said the therianthropes were medicine people and that they 'have (/ki) things whose bodies they own (/ki). These things enable them to appear to see. So it happens that when these things have seen anything which the sorcerer does not know, he perceives by his magic what is happening' (D. Bleek 1935: 15; W.H.I. Bleek 1866–77: L.V.25.6008–13). In other words, a medicine man of the eland would see what the eland saw and thus

Figure 12.1: Rock painting of a San medicine man of the game wearing an eared cap (Natal, Drakensberg).

know their whereabouts (see also ibid.: 24). Such knowledge implies an identity between a shaman and the animal whose potency he harnessed. He could, as it were, slip from one persona to the other. An informant described in equivocal terms a shaman who had this sort of relationship with jackals: 'A jackal who is a sorcerer . . . he turns himself into a jackal' (ibid.: 15, 17, 25). The animal is a man, and the man is an animal; man and the possessed creature become one.

The implications of this dual identity are far-reaching for an under-standing of the art. That painted therianthropes (e.g. Figure 11.1B), which share a variety of features with medicine men, express the duality is readily acceptable (Lewis-Williams 1981a: 75–101). But the identity also implies that some of the painted animals may be medicine men in the form of the creatures they possess. Realistic representation is no guarantee that real creatures are depicted. Some of the 'real' animals may portray the trance experience of people in their zoo-morphic personae: in other words, the dual nature of the medicine

Scale in centimetres

Figure 12.2: Rock painting of a therianthrope with
eland head and horns (north-eastern Cape).
Colours: red and white.

man. This is clearly so in the case of many painted felines which are
depicted along with trance and hallucinatory elements (see, for
example, Lewis-Williams 1981a: Fig. 31; 1981b: Fig. 3; 1985). Medicine
men were and still are believed to turn themselves into felines. One
man said he could 'mix with' a pride of lions while in his feline form
(Heinz 1975: 29), and others describe entering trance to drive off
medicine men who threaten them in the form of lions (Katz 1982: 115,
227). Such 'lions' can be seen only by other medicine men (ibid.: 227).

Mapote's statement that 'the Bushmen of that part of the country
were of the eland' thus probably had three closely related meanings:
medicine people in that area possessed eland power; they used this
power to control eland; and they could become eland. In saying that he

would paint an eland *because* the San were 'of the eland', Mapote established an explicit connection between rock paintings and animal potency and thus pointed to the social and cognitive context of rock painting — shamanism. At a fairly simple level, he was saying that the most frequently depicted animal in many regions of southern Africa related directly to potency. The unequivocal establishment of this link alone shows that a substantial proportion of southern African rock art was shamanistic. Whatever else he may have painted, this was the principal association in his mind: because the medicine people were especially linked to eland, it was appropriate for him to begin with that antelope.

All this was most important to the old man despite the unfamiliar circumstances of his painting — on a piece of rock in a magistrate's garden rather than with the San in their caves as was his former experience. Although How's interest was confined to technique and Mapote could reasonably have been expected to respond to her interest only, he did not, probably could not, divorce technique from belief. His call for the blood of a freshly killed eland is further evidence of that. The act of painting was indissolubly bound up with a set of beliefs.

Thus far I have confined my discussion to the relationship between medicine people and eland because that is the origin and chief meaning of the phrase 'of the eland'. There is, however, evidence of an extension of the relationship. The !Kung San of Namibia and Botswana never define themselves by race or by their foraging economy. Instead they call themselves the owners of *n/um*, the !Kung word for potency. More specifically they say they are 'the owners of Giraffe Music' (J. Marshall and Ritchie 1984: 2); the Giraffe Medicine song is currently very popular. In other words, they all share in some way in the potency their medicine people possess and activate to cure and care for them all. The panoply of animal power, though controlled by medicine people, protects everyone. It is therefore possible that Mapote may also have been expressing an extension from medicine people, the real controllers of potency, to all people.

A deeper and perhaps fainter implication is that, because the act of painting recalled to him, first and foremost, a relationship with animal potency, painting was, along with curing, controlling animals and rainmaking, another of the medicine people's tasks — a suggestion supported by depictions which are clearly hallucinatory. If some people who were not medicine people but were, by extension, also 'of the eland' added to the accumulation of paintings in the rock shelters, they drew, as Mapote did, on the vocabulary of shamanistic images. (Apparently historic scenes may seem to count against this; but see C. Campbell 1986; 1987.) Ordinary people, if they painted at all, may have painted the apparently realistic depictions of medicine dances, eland and so forth, while the medicine people themselves painted these and also the hallucinatory elements.

This is a conservative position because the old San woman to whom I have referred insisted that the paintings were done by medicine people only. The authorship of the art may, of course, have varied through time and from place to place, but research increasingly shows that, whoever the authors were, the art was essentially shamanistic throughout southern Africa (Lewis-Williams 1981a, 1983a; Maggs and Sealy 1983; Huffman 1983; Yates *et al.* 1985). Trance experience and symbols of shamanistic power are its chief concerns.

Part 4

Power and ideology

13. The unending ceremony and a warm house: representation of a patriarchal ideal and the silent complementarity in Okiek blessings

Corinne A. Kratz

Introduction

Like greeting, prayer is a virtually universal communicative function, though the formal characteristics, contexts and modes of performance of its culturally specific forms vary tremendously. Within particular cultures, prayer can take several forms and serve several purposes: silent or spoken; private or public; addressing gods, ancestors or other forces directly or indirectly; or performed as invocation, consecration, blessing, a specific request, praise or as an affirmation of faith.

Blessings are the primary form of prayer in the verbal repertoire of Okiek in Kenya: a brief but pervasive genre. Okiek bless during ceremonies, to begin and end formal meetings where disputes are arbitrated, to begin and end marriage talks, to defuse the potentially deadly effects of a close relative's curse, or simply to give spontaneous expression of satisfaction or gratitude. Blessings are also a standard prescription to help resolve unexpected and unfamiliar problems in social relations. The corpus for analysis here consists of blessings recorded (on tape) in all these contexts,[1] along with observations recorded on the performances and circumstances of each. I also draw on interviews and discussions with Okiek about blessings and related genres. My research with Okiek has been centred with Kipchorn-

1. The blessings analyzed were drawn from five different initiation ceremonies (eighteen blessings), four shaving ceremonies (twenty-two blessings), two occasions of marriage discussions (seventeen blessings), one wedding (two blessings), three meetings (ten blessings), and three occasions to neutralize arguments or curses (twelve blessings). Simon ole Nchoe worked on some of the Maa transcriptions and Fredrick Kilagui Salimu assisted with some Okiek transcriptions. O.S. Sarone advised on some of the translation from Maa. Thanks are due to all of them, and especially to Kopot Teloti, Kirutari, and Kaina for their patient assistance in my own transcribing and checking of texts. Thanks are also due to Chet Creider and David McMurray for perceptive comments, though I was not able to respond to them all in revisions and, finally, to Basil Sansom for a helpful citation.

wonek and Kaplelach Okiek in Narok District,[2] the southernmost of Okiek local groups living on the western Mau escarpment.

Traditionally, Okiek made their basic living by hunting game and collecting honey from hives and trees in the highland forests of Kenya. Most Okiek now also keep domestic animals and cultivate domestic crops on a small scale. The earliest ethnographic descriptions of Okiek life were written by G.W.B. Huntingford about Kapchepkendi and Kamelilo Okiek living north of Nakuru, near Nandi (1929; 1942; 1954; 1955). He used the more commonly known name 'Dorobo', derived from the Maasai *il Torrobo* meaning people without cattle. 'Dorobo' was also the name used in earlier references to Okiek in travelers' accounts. After Huntingford's papers, scholarly research and writing about Okiek life picked up again with Blackburn's work in the late 1960s (1971; 1973; 1974; 1976) and my own research beginning in 1974.

Okiek usually live as neighbors to numerically larger ethnic groups who are herders or mixed farmers. They have formed friendships, sometimes married, and traded honey and other forest products with their neighbors for generations. Maasai have been among the most important and influential neighbors to Kaplelach and Kipchornwonek for over a century; many Okiek there are bilingual in Maa as well as Okiek. Their other important neighbors are Kipsigis, with whom they share a Kalenjin home language. Kipsigis became increasingly influential neighbors as they drew nearer to Okiek and as Okiek diversified their economic base, especially among the Kipchornwonek (see Kratz 1986c).

Kipchornwonek and Kaplelach, then, are part of a regional network of ethnic identity and interaction which is expressed in a number of ways in Okiek communicative patterns, such as code-switching, lexical borrowing, and overlapping song and story repertoires. Okiek blessings also portray their history with various neighbors; there are three blessing styles — Okiek, Maasai, and Kipsigis — though not all elders are comfortable and able to perform blessings in all three.

One purpose of this chapter is descriptive: to discuss what constitutes blessings as a genre of Okiek speech and to elaborate their performative variations. In the course of description, I hope to illuminate several theoretical questions about ritual uses of language, relations between different communicative channels in ceremony, and

2. My intial research with Kaplelach and Kipchornwonek Okiek was done in 1974–5 with assistance from the Anthropology Department, Wesleyan University. Further research during 1982–6 was supported by the National Science Foundation (BNS 8112153), the Joint Committee on Africa of the Social Science Research Council and the American Council of Learned Societies, the Fulbright-Hayes program (022AH20034), the Wenner Gren Foundation, the Institute for Intercultural Studies, and the University of Texas at Austin. I thank all of these institutions for their support and I am also grateful to the Sociology Department, University of Nairobi, for affiliating me as Research Associate, and to the Office of the President, Government of Kenya, for approving my research project in Kenya.

the ways in which communicative patterns create and express important aspects of social structure and relations.

The many uses of language in ceremonies are intricate and complex. I concentrate here on a particular genre in Okiek ceremonies so that its other performative contexts and formal and performative variations are brought into focus. In this way, the meanings and implications of its form and performance in ceremonial context become clearer. In addition, the question of the relation between ceremony and 'everyday life' can be considered with respect to specific expressive forms, providing cases from which general formulations might be made and which must be accommodated by them.

I will discuss in turn several aspects of Okiek blessings which are united in actual performance: selected parameters of performance; verbal form and content; and material objects and substances used in blessing. Chords common to them all sound a counterpoint which resonates around four mutually reinforcing values. Together these define the ideal state that those who give blessings would wish on their recipients: continuity, fecundity, prosperity and cooperation. The representations of the values, in actors and stages, verbal themes and images, and material form, differ, but at the same time overlap and converge. In each case, they are predicated on a model in which elder men are the center of power and authority. Blessings are themselves one of the means by which this model of society is realized and perpetuated. The complementarity of male and female roles is also recognized and included, albeit largely in symbolic associations which are part of conventional blessing form rather than in ways more prominent socially and ideologically.

Different aspects of the model of Okiek society are emphasized or underplayed in different communicative channels. Thus the priority of elder men is emphasized and legitimized in the definition of appropriate performance, while a slightly more balanced view comes through in verbal expression. Material representations of the four thematic values also emphasize general notions of Okiek identity, often inflected for sexual differences. Okiek blessings, then, have a unified overall message, but different communicative channels carry it in different forms and with different ideological evaluations and emphases. The question of how more generally these channels are combined and related in ceremonies can be approached by looking at their relations in specific ritual events included in ceremonies.

Blessings are a good example of the way communicative patterns help create and perpetuate patterns of social organization and interaction. Okiek blessings are foremost in a trio of genres of power — along with curses and oaths.[3] Genres of power are communicative genres

3. Several sources of power are involved in these genres. This chapter, concentrating on

which have a hierarchy, or imbalance of influence, inherent in their pragmatic definition. The blesser, curser, and rightful oath-taker all affect others by their act. The performance of the genre can be culturally defined so that its inherent pragmatic power or authority reinforces the definition of authority and control in other social, political or economic domains. It might be concentrated in ritual specialists or political leaders, for instance, or be exercised in more fleeting manner by members of a general social category. In the Okiek case, the cultural definition of who are the most appropriate verbal blessers helps to establish and reinforce authority exercised by male elders in consequential matters such as marriage and dispute cases. At the same time, the rationale offered for their appropriateness draws on that same authority and on fundamental assumptions about social roles which are its basis.

Parameters of performance: dimensions of power and a concentration of the auspicious

Blessings are prayers. Blessings are prayers, however, in which a kind of power is thought to reside in those who say them, for they pray on behalf of others. Pragmatically, they are requests, entreaties or consecrations; a favorable outcome is hoped for but uncertain. These two aspects of blessings — that blessers pray *for* others and that the success of the prayer is uncertain — are important factors in defining the appropriate performance of Okiek blessings. In combination they create a situation in which a difference of ritual power and authority, though slight and fleetingly exercised, helps to create and legitimate similar relations in other aspects of life. This section will discuss three parameters of performance: actors, setttings, and types of blessing as marked by the use of different substances.

Actors

Okiek blessings are usually performed by a pair or quartet of adult men, usually senior elders. In general, members of the oldest age-set present are called on to bless. Women bless in public, by spitting honey wine and calling out a blessing, on only one occasion, in the evening of a ceremony for shaving and naming a child (*suumeek*); at that time, the quartet of blessers consists of two men and two women. The women

---

Okiek blessings, is the first step in comparative analysis of the three genres which spells out the nature of the power and imbalance involved more explicitly. Its sequel, 'Genres of power: a comparative analysis of Okiek blessings, curses and oaths' (Kratz 1986b), was presented in Philadelphia at the Annual Meetings of the American Anthropological Association in December 1986.

often laugh and disclaim knowledge of how to say a blessing. In fact, their blessings are often very short, and done quickly and laughingly. Other women, however, especially older ones, bless with no hesitation or self-consciousness. At other ceremonies, the mother of the child smears a dab of fat on the foreheads of participants before male elders bless the proceedings and participants. The mother's anointing in this way is also regarded as a kind of blessing; note that she blesses silently, by act alone.

Blessings require some attention and also response from others present, as evidenced in prefatory comments such as 'Be quiet, now' and 'Listen to the blessing', a pause and new beginning when people fail to listen, and admonitions during opening lines such as 'Quiet, you're not listening' and 'Respond, then'. The response is in unison with a word at the end of each blessing line: *nai, sere, Enkai (ai), aya* (*kiyan*, to agree, to respond, for example when called, in song, in blessings). People might answer with different words, except when the line itself specifies their response, as in Kipsigis blessings.

There are three important dimensions to consider in the definition of the Okiek role of blesser: sex, age, and number of performers. Why are Okiek spoken blessings performed primarily by men, primarily by elders, and almost always by a pair of actors? The following two commentaries summarize Okiek ideas about male and female roles and will help explain why men are the ones considered in a position to speak on behalf of others.[4]

In ceremonies, you can't bless without spitting honey wine. . . . Women don't spit honey wine like that. They don't bless; it's not good. But in a girls' ceremony, once they are at their place of seclusion, then a woman blesses things. On the first day men bless, but then women take over (in seclusion). (But why is it bad for women to bless?) Women are small/young people; she is like a child. If you tell a woman something she goes to tell another woman. You don't let a woman lead if a man is there. Even if she has become old, she is still called a child. Women are like children because they care for them, cook for them. And she eats all the time like a child because she is the one cooking . . . also, if you send a child to do something, a good child will go and run. Like women who go for water and for firewood without even being told. Haven't you heard [people greeting say] '*Camgei laakokcu*' (greetings, you children)? We combine women and children. . . .

When you hear someone say *piik ap kaai* (people of this house), it means the woman of the house. You say *piik* (people) because she is always together with children. But *ciit ap kaai* (person of this house) is the man of the house, because you meet him when he is alone. . . . Women are also called *eemeet ap*

4. The first is from an interview about ceremonies and blessings. The second is from one pair of texts which I elicited to compare Okiek speaking Okiek and Kipsigis by asking various men to give speeches as if they were in a meeting; no suggestions were made about the content of the orations.

kaa (the home country) because they are always at home. They are the ones who are always at home, while men are out roaming about.

. . . [We need to find chiefs and leaders so that people will follow laws and accomplish something.] It's like, now, if there are women without leaders who speak to them. Those ones are like children, they can't. — There's nothing that they can do by themselves. If there is no leader, then that speaks to them and says, 'You stop that because we don't want a mess.' Because they can even argue, whether its them or the children, they can argue. They're children themselves, they can't even send out an alarm cry. Because they're like dogs, women. (Like dogs?) Women. Women are like dogs. They can't.— There's nothing that they know. Because if they aren't watched, they just go themselves . . . and meet another and can fight there, and there are no people who send out an alarm. So now if you go about looking at men, you see that it is usually men that make people get along. Because otherwise . . . if there were no more men to speak to the other ones then people could have finished each other. Even if (for example) it's thought so-and-so is a bad person. When he goes and meets people (men) and he is talked to, because he is a man he can listen and say, 'People (men) have talked to me.' And the person can stop making trouble and follow what people have said.

Okiek think women are like children not simply because they care for them and are constantly with them: they are seen similarly as unrestrained in eating and in keeping their own counsel, and as speaking their minds and doing what they please. As the saying goes, 'A woman can neither lead nor follow'.[5] Because of this, women need to be directed and organized, or they would fall into chaotic quarreling.

Men, on the other hand, can not only speak in a reasoned way; they also listen and respond to the reason of consensus expressed by their peers and elders. In this way, direction and organization emerge and peace is created and maintained. Because Okiek consider men to be the only ones capable of such reason, of making decisions and abiding by them, only men attend meetings where cases are heard, disputes settled and issues discussed. Even if a case involves a woman, she is represented by her husband, brothers or sons.

Blessings are an important organizational feature in each type of occasion when they are regularly performed. As those who hold the monopoly on the invocation of blessings, Okiek men are, indeed, organizers of these occasions. Blessings are a framing device in meetings and marriage talks, a way of calling the gathering to order and of terminating official discussion. When blessing counteracts anger or a curse, its performance is the central reason for brewing liquor and gathering people. Blessings are one essential constitutive act of ceremonial occasions. Without blessing and the men who do it, these occasions cannot take place.

The reasoning here, however, is both circular and self-perpetuating.

5. *Makiindoincin cepyosa amakiletuncin.*

Women are unable to organize things, to have reasonable discussions and to agree. They are therefore barred from saying blessings and from meetings, and thus prevented from learning and practicing both blessing and the oratorical style of men's meetings. When called upon occasionally to bless or speak publicly, as at shaving ceremonies or marriage talks, they are uncomfortable and generally not adept. The notion that women cannot bless and the assumptions on which it is based are thereby reinforced. When people respond to a blessing by answering its lines, they do more than agree to the wishes expressed and add their prayer. By their participation, they also agree that the men who pray are suitable spokesmen. They accept and affirm both the role of blesser as primarily a male prerogative and the general structure of male authority on which it is based.

Okiek women acknowledge the view that prevents them from being important blessers, but do not seem to recognize it as a form of control. In fact, they offer additional rationalizations for male prominence in public ceremonies, for example that women's blessings are not as effective, or that men should bless because ceremonies are held by their families. Nevertheless, women do bless during their own secret ceremonies, and also bless with acts and objects in ways which show their complementary importance within the patriarchal organization. Similarly, women can exercise influence in matters such as marriage negotiations by informal lobbying and discussion with those involved.

The actual role of Okiek women, then, is not quite as powerless as portrayed in the ideological version that emphasizes male authority. In fact, the texts quoted above hint at that. What is represented as childish inability to listen to orders and heedless pursuit of their own desires could be seen in another light, as women's own strength of decision and alternative ideas of how things should be done. Significantly, a woman's strength, control and influence are expressed at the level of individual action; in particular cases women do not unite as a group to discuss, agree and present an alternative (cf. Llewelyn-Davis 1978).

There is yet another side to the perceived inappropriateness of women as blessers that derives from their role as child-bearers and -carers. Those who bless should be holy or auspicious people (*esinya*), that is, one whose first born has survived, who has never killed a person, who is kind and gets along well with people, who has no physical defects. *Esinya* people should bless so that the blessing will carry and that those blessed will be *esinya* like them. Women of child-bearing age are thought to carry a kind of dirt and pollution (*kereek*), especially those who gave birth recently. Though the pollution of child-bearing is not a permanent physical or characterological defect, it is, none the less, a temporary handicap to that most auspicious of states which blessers should represent. Though blessed with children, mothers are joined to their young ones in their polluted state. When

food handled by child-bearing women can transmit *kereek* and be a
health hazard, could a blessing of wine and words direct from their
mouths be exempt from that danger?

Why, then, do women bless the child's new name during shaving
ceremonies? Shavings are considered women's ceremonies, minor
celebrations. 'It's not (really) a ceremony. But it's the day the child is
shaved, a day for women. So then [the child] will be initiated. It's just
for women.' 'When a child is shaved, that is a small ceremony, for
women especially. . . . It's just a slight ceremony, so they can give
women a chance to bless since it's their ceremony.' In the eyes of men,
it is just a day for eating and drinking — of little import. Women alone
do the ritual work in the early morning. Naming the child in the
evening, however, involves the child's father as well as the mother; at
that point, men become involved in deciding the procedure for naming
and blessing.

Whatever its ideological status, the shaving ceremony is necessary to
the progression of life-cycle ceremonies, and women are necessary to
do it and help bestow a new name on the child. Women participate in
other ceremonies, but then their public roles are mainly a matter of act
and song, involving little speaking. Since men consider themselves the
dominant organizers the women's part requires no comment or justification. A more cynical interpretation might point out the ideological
importance of women having one chance to bless in shavings, so that
the dominant view can be reinforced.

The first dimension in the Okiek role of blesser, then, defines a kind
of power by exclusion with respect to women. It is based on assumptions about the nature and abilities of women which delimit the ways in
which Okiek women participate in legal and political forums as well as
in ceremonies. The linking of ceremonial and juridical spheres through
blessings further reinforces these assumptions with the sanctions of
religion and tradition in a way that helps make their acceptance and
perpetuation unquestioned.

The second dimension, age, defines authority by social rank. Virtually all adult men can or will eventually be blessers. Young men are not
excluded from the role, like women, but are educated and incorporated
into it as they become older and more experienced. As men are
designated the more appropriate, knowledgeable, and auspicious
spokesmen vis-à-vis women, elders are similarly designated vis-à-vis
young men. Again, there are both ritual and sociopolitical aspects
involved, their expression combined in the notion of respect (*kaany'it*).

At initiation, boys become members of a particular age-set. Men of
the next alternate senior age-set act as general ritual sponsors, called
fire-stick elders (as with Maasai[6]), and initiates are taught by a pair of

---

6. Cf. Maasai: 'The making of fire establishes a very special relationship between the two

men senior to them.[7] During seclusion, one important lesson impressed on initiates is the proper way to relate to older men, that is, to listen to them and follow their advice and direction with honour and respect. Older men thus initiate boys into the ritual secrets and demeanor of manhood and at the same time secure the ideal and dominance of their own authority.

The other side of respect is impressed on young men with reference to the cooperation needed in governance and group decisions and the young men's dependence on their elders in marriage. Leaders emerge from age-sets who show themselves to be articulate, persuasive and wise as they gain experience and hear of precedents in meetings and discussion. All men should be heard, but older men should be heeded; they have the presence to speak and carry decisions and also the weight of experience. Wives come from elders (from their fathers) and are brought to a man by elders of his own family — who conduct marriage talks on his behalf and help to find property for marriage payments. Respect is a way to acknowledge an interdependence, which for younger men is more of a dependence, and to facilitate the cooperation and help needed.

Elders are seen as more appropriate spokesmen, then, because of their experience, and are also respected because of their authority and influence in decisions about the exchange of women. Once again, to understand the priority of age in the role of blesser, the notion of auspiciousness (*esinya*) is relevant. As mentioned above, one who is *esinya* has a surviving first-born child. Accordingly, young men who have not married or whose families are still beginning have not yet proven to be *esinya*. Similarly, young men may still be rather hotheaded — hardly the *esinya* ideal of the good-natured and kind man blessed with children. They might yet kill someone in anger or drunkenness. In contrast, elders have passed their youth and lived with people long enough for their character, offspring and history to be known. Senior elders are likely to have initiated grandchildren, not simply their own first-borns. The continuity of their line and unblemished personal history are well-established facts.

The final dimension of the role of blesser to be discussed is that of number: why are blessings said by two or four elders? This is also explained in part by the Okiek notion of *esinya*. Repetitions in two and four proliferate in Okiek blessings, and in Okiek ceremonies in general, because they are auspicious numbers. Not only are the blessers and blessings in pairs, the honey wine used to bless is sprayed two or four

age-sets, with the senior set being considered the "fathers" of the junior set, with the power of blessing and cursing' (Galaty and Lembuya 1984: 15).

7. The alternate age-set relation does not always hold for the role of ritual leaders/ teachers (*matireenik*); in many cases, the pair of ritual leaders for a group of initiates are of the next senior age-set, not the next alternate one.

times, and paired blessings are themselves done at four different times over the course of initiation ceremonies. A pair of paired blessings brackets discussion and debate at men's meetings and marriage discussions. Two and four are associated with males in ceremonies — in contrast to the association of three with females.

Auspiciousness (*esinya*) has figured in each aspect of Okiek blessers; maleness, relative age and number of performers. In each case, a hierarchy of relative *esinya*ness has been noted. People considered most suitable to bless maximize the *esinya* in their person, character and history. This concentration of the auspicious can be related to the pragmatic characteristic of blessings as prayers, noted at the beginning of this section, namely, as requests the outcome of blessings is uncertain. Though the granting of the prayer cannot be controlled, the most favorable conditions for it can be created. Elders are the most appropriate spokesmen in other domains and relatively the most auspicious; they thus become the ones most likely to be heard when entreaties are made in prayer — the ones with power to bless and pray on behalf of others. Elders organize their juniors and children in prayer and ceremony, as well as in marriage, disputes and political matters. At the same time, a kind of ritual power derives from their intercession and faculty to bless (and its converse, the power to curse) which reinforces and legitimates their authority in those spheres.

Settings

Okiek sex roles, as discussed above, are relevant to understanding the settings for blessings, but other associations which figure in spoken blessings are also important. Ceremonial settings offer the most elaborated representation here, and so will be discussed in more detail than the others. During ceremonies, blessings are said either at the *mabwaita* shrine built outside the host house or else inside the house near the hearth. The *mabwaita* is ceremonial center-stage, the place where most ritual events take place.[8] As such, it is itself a sign of blessing, and a sign, too, of the values ceremonies epitomize: fecundity, since ceremonies are performed for one's children; prosperity, since the host can afford the ceremony and entertain guests; cooperation, since the prevailing tone of ceremonies is ideally convivial and celebratory; and continuity, since the children carry on the family line, and the *mabwaita* and ceremony continue Okiek cultural tradition through performance.

The *mabwaita* has a foundation of four stout poles bound at the base with vines. Filled out with leafy branches, the structure as a whole resembles a tree. The species used are of note here; both the properties which make them appropriate for use and their other contexts of use

8. See Kratz (1986a) for further discussion of the *mabwaita*.

contribute to the significance and associations of Okiek blessings. Three species are essential: *olerienit* poles; *korosik* saplings; and *sinenteet* vines. *Tanguriot* grass, sometimes added at the base of the *mabwaita*, is also widely and consistently used in ceremonies and blessings, bringing the regular ritual species to an *esinya* four.[9] All the species have in common hardness of wood, slowness to dry (or long-lasting greenness), abundance, and apparent immunity to being struck by lightning. These properties represent the similar attributes wished for by their users; long life, strength, fertility, health and freedom from adversity. The essential *mabwaita* species become metaphors in blessing texts, their generally favored nature intensified by further ceremonial associations.

Olerienit and *sinenteet* are both used in the ritual structure which during initiations is also built inside, at the household hearth. *Olerienit* is a hard wood, dries slowly, and is excellent firewood since it catches easily and burns long and slowly. A blazing bundle of *olerienit* sticks is used to smoke out especially fierce bees. Ceremonial fires always use *olerienit* wood, for example when initiates come out of seclusion. Some families use *olerienit* leaves to close calabashes of liquor which are used for blessing or carried by the host of a ceremony. *Olerienit* is also a home for bees, a home for the honey guide bird (which leads to bees and honey), yields some honey from its flowers, and has its leaves consumed by all domestic livestock. All told, it is a tree which brings to mind warmth, strength, food, home and the sweetness of honey and wine. Its associations are predominantly male ones: bees, gathering honey, elders, and fathers.

Sinenteet, a flexible, long-lasting forest vine, binds together *olerienit* sticks in ritual structures, and women wear *sinenteet* wreaths in some ceremonies. A special ceremonial pot of liquor for maternal relatives is tied with *sinenteet*. A ewe of all one color (another sense of *esinya*), with *sinenteet* round her neck, is brought with her lamb for the mother of a bride before the girl is taken away. Also in weddings, the bride's waist is tied with *sinenteet* at her father's home and untied by her mother-in-law on reaching her new home. *Sinenteet*, with its milky white sap, clearly draws in associations with women, marriage, fertility and peace along with the general values of all plants used in the *mabwaita*.

Korosik saplings fill out the basic *mabwaita* structure, to make it full, bushy and healthy looking (*sarur*), and are brought from the forest in an opening procession by young people and children. Each initiate also holds his or her own *korosiot* sapling throughout the ceremony; it is brought to the initiate's mother after circumcision to show success in

9. *Olerienit*: Olea africana mill.; *sinenteet*: Periploca linearifolia Dill. & Rich; *tanguriot*: Stipa dregeana Steud. var. elongata (nees) Stapf. *Tanguriot* will be discussed below in the section on materials used in blessings. Thanks to the East African Herbarium for identification of botanical specimens collected.

the trial. Compared to *sinenteet* and *olerienit*, the saplings have a much sparser aura of associations. Yet this third species adds to the combined female and male emphases of the other species the counterpart of offspring — to complete the botanical imagery of fertility and blessing carried in the very structure of the *mabwaita*.

The hearth, for its part, is the centre of the intimate side of the house where the bed is. In some situations, those to be blessed sit on the bed. Associations with fecundity and lineal reproduction are obvious; the area within the hearth stones (*koiik ap maat*) and the long slow-burning log (*supeneet*) which projects out of the hearth and keeps the fire alive are associated with female and male principles. Continuity is symbolized as well in the fire itself, which should never die; during blessings its embers are fanned into flame. Prosperity and cooperation are not obviously and distinctly represented in the hearth. Rather, the overall image of a well-built home, stocked with ample firewood for cooking, brewing honey wine, and heating evokes both the idea of family cooperation in providing the household and also a sense of the warmth and comfort of a harmonious home. 'There is no food or warmth without fire. You want [those blessed] to have food, not to be cold, so you light the fire when blessing. It is for every house. Fire is where you cook and where you warm yourself; there is nothing without it to eat.' Finally, both *mabwaita* and hearth are places not only of blessing, but also of libation to ancestor spirits, adding yet a further dimension to the extent of lineal and temporal continuity there represented.

Each of these home places of blessing, then, carries within its physical structure an image of sexual complementarity and reproductive unity as well as a representation of ideal values. Taken together, they also represent a complementary pair of ritual spaces with different sexual and symbolic associations. The *mabwaita* is the male place, outside, while the hearth is in the women's domain, inside. Remembering the quotation, cited earlier, about the need to direct women, it is of note that the *olerienit* and *sinenteet* used near the hearth are brought first to the *mabwaita* to be blessed. Similarly, the shaving ceremony, which is considered a women's ceremony, involves no *mabwaita*, only blessings performed inside near the hearth.

The setting for blessings on other occasions requires less elaborate analysis. None the less, the symbolic layering of ceremonial settings provides the basis for interpreting other locations as well. Representations of the cultural framework and assumptions about social categories and relations are not in the foreground, as in ceremonies, but they are implicit in use. Men's meetings (*kiiruaaket*, from *kiruaac*, 'to debate', or 'discuss') are not held at anybody's home, but usually convened in an open field under a large shade tree. A male forum for collective decision-making, they are held in no man's land, in the male domain of outside/away from home. Men lounge in the shade while the speaker stands in front, pacing and emphasizing points with a thwack of his long walking stick on the ground. Blessings are said from the same position. Elders who bless are the first speakers at a meeting, each person following his prayer with news of his area before discussion starts. As noted earlier, representatives of the oldest age present bless meetings. As the opening orators who convene discussion, they can set its initial course, taking and reinforcing the authority and priority which age gives them. Since they are at no one's home, blessings are said with words alone. At the end of a meeting, however, all adjourn to the home of the disputants to drink liquor that has been brewed.

Marriage talks (*kaayta*) are held at night in the home of the girl's parents.[10] As at meetings, blessings here are a way to convene formal discussion. If it is crowded, some of the girl's male relatives move to the fire side of the house, but usually men sit in the outer part of the house. Whether near the hearth or near the door, blessers speak from their seats. There is a protocol of arrival and of receiving the marriage liquor before discussion (amplifying symbolism which has already been eluci- dated), but the blessings themselves are straightforward. When people are settled and ready to talk, the opening blessing is called for; when discussion is finished, even if people continue to drink, a blessing concludes formal talks. The thing of note here is that all blessings are done inside the house, the innermost realm, associated with women and children; this befits the nature and topic of the discussions.

Finally, when blessings neutralize anger or a curse, the family of the person in danger brews liquor and calls the one who is angered to come and bless at their home. The person blessed sits inside, on the bed. Not simply a single life, but the entire family is endangered, so the blessing is performed at the most intimate place in the house, the centre of family reproduction.

Types of blessing

Okiek blessings have several performance variations, some using words alone and some using various substances in conjunction with spoken prayer. These distinctions show some of the differences among both occasions and reasons for blessings. A fuller discussion of the substances used to bless will be presented below; here I only point out major differences as they mark blessing types.

There should always be beer to drink when there is a blessing; elders cannot be called for nothing. The beer, however, is not always used in the blessing. At men's meetings and marriage talks, blessings use words alone. At initiation ceremonies, the father and blessing elder

10. There is another tradition of marriage dicussion which is now being followed by Kipchornwonek Okiek. The one I describe here is that which they used to follow and which Kaplelach still do.

each carry a calabash of honey wine. On those occasions, liquor is sprayed on both ritual items and the people present before a blessing is said. The spray concretizes the desired effect of the words, settling on all. It is a way, in effect, to broadcast and extend the benefit and blessing of the most potent substance of benediction, the saliva of the elders (*ng'uleek*).

When danger to health and life is averted with blessing, the person who was angry and gave this danger spits on the ones blessed. They receive the saliva with outstretched hands and rub it down their faces and chests. That day, they should not wander far from home and must sleep in no house but their own, so that they 'don't leave the saliva they were blessed with in any other place'. The blessing should not be diluted or weakened spatially, but concentrated and localized in the blessed ones' own home and bed, where they received it. Blessing with undiluted saliva is the strongest and most serious blessing; when people fight and spill blood, the blessing combines saliva along with the tying of *sinenteet* on the ones who fought.

Blessings sprayed at ceremonies are to make people fruitful. In contrast, the blessings in the house are to wash away a misfortune and keep bad things from happening again. Marriage talks are important and difficult; blessings there help prevent people from shouting or arguing, as well as ask favor for all present. Similarly, meetings are an arena of controlled disagreement and debate; such difficult matters are best initiated by blessing, to enjoin people to peaceful discussion.

There are, then, three communicative functions combined in Okiek blessings: the obvious one of prayer, as well as two metacommunicative ones, namely to define the frame of occasions, and to define the key appropriate to them. Ceremony blessings are in some ways quintessential, with all three functions important and balanced. Blessings help constitute the ceremonial frame, remind people that the occasion celebrated calls for peace at the risk of harming the initiates, and wish similar good fortune on all present. The general prayer is broadcast, in words and beer, by the most auspicious members of society, in places resonant with the symbols of these members' auspiciousness and authority.

When a curse is being counteracted, the framing function of blessing is less prominent because it is itself the central act of the occasion. Prayer and re-establishment of a harmonious key are not simply important, but essential for survival. A concentrated substance for blessing, saliva, is thus most appropriate and necessary. This most potent of blessings, from the most suitable spokesmen, is also most critical; it attempts to avert misfortune, not simply seek good fortune. Being under the control of elders, as usual, the importance of the blessing further boosts the basis of their ritual power and authority.

At men's meetings and marriage discussions, the functions of framing and key definition take priority. The final blessing is 'goodbye'; closure of frame is the main purpose. The blessing asks for prosperity and peace, but usually also makes specific reference to the situation. It thus makes explicit the cordial and cooperative key which should be maintained to facilitate discussion. Still a prayer, of course, it is turned to other primary purposes, indirectly stating the metacommunicative requirements for success. Words alone are sufficient when the prayerful purpose of blessing is thus subordinated.

This section has discussed the actors, settings and occasions of Okiek blessings and outlined assumptions basic to understanding the performance, pragmatics and cultural significance of the genre. The attributes of appropriate and capable Okiek blessers were seen to be at once based on and helping to define and reinforce the Okiek elders' position of precedence and authority in ritual matters, as well as other social and political spheres. Just as in their person elders concentrate the claim to be heard as honorable and holy spokesmen, the settings for ceremonial blessings embody the ideal values that are prayed for within their physical structure. All these values are based on the same assumptions about relations between men and women and between ages.

Finally, three types of spoken blessing were seen to differ, according to the use of liquor, saliva, or words alone. They were seen to correspond to different emphases in the threefold combination of communicative functions identified in Okiek blessings. Honey wine and words carry male associations, in part by virtue of their role in blessings. Saliva is a concentrated and potent symbol of life in general.[11] Coming from the mouths of elders, it carries a particularly *esinya* essence, also imparted to the wine and to words as they issue forth.[12] Again, the potency and auspiciousness of the substances themselves carries a vital part of the blessing, and at the same time reinforces these substances' power and appropriateness for such uses. It strengthens, as well, the definition of male dominion over the use and performance of blessings.

Verbal form and themes: images of the ideal and blessed life

This section will discuss the verbal form, themes and images of blessings. I cannot discuss sociolinguistic dimensions of the three styles and languages of Okiek blessing in this chapter due to space limitations. The overall generic structure — call lines which alternate with a re-

11. This is the case in many cultures, not just Okiek, from neighboring Kalenjin and Maasai to other Nilotic-speaking peoples (Evans-Pritchard 1956: 171), Berber-speakers in Morocco (Westermarck 1926:93ff.) and Fang in West Africa (Fernandez 1982: 218), to cite only other African examples.

12. This can be contrasted to pouring libation (*kipieesta*), which is done by both men and women, can make use of honey water or milk, as well as honey wine, and is poured from a calabash, basket or horn, rather than coming from the mouth.

sponding chorus of agreement — is common to all three, and the thematic groupings of call lines presented here also holds good for all. It is worth noting, however, that the lines in Kipsigis-style blessings are drawn from a more clearly delimited set of line structures and are generally less elaborated descriptively. Discussion here of the grammatical form of blessing lines is very brief and general; it applies mainly to Okiek blessings in their own language and in Maa.

Formal structure of blessings

Blessers often draw attention before their prayer with a remark such as 'Listen now', or simply 'eeee'; sometimes others make the remark, telling the speaker to start his prayer. Such a remark is needed at times, if the blessing is to be heard above the general hubbub of people talking and drinking; at other times, it is chiefly a framing device — a means to get into the prayer. As already noted, blessings are said in auspicious multiples of two. The second blesser usually begins with a link to the first with the line, 'May God agree to what the first has said.' The end of a blessing is also often marked with a comment by the blesser or others, such as 'Well, that's done', 'That's enough now' or just *'Bas'* ('OK', 'enough'). A closing line in Maa is also used in some blessings in Okiek as well as in many Maasai ones: *(orrik) toiki ol-ari oleng*. Paralinguistic features such as a decrease in volume, speed or pitch can also mark the end of the prayer; when these alone are used, the blessing trails off into the noise of other discussions.

Blessings vary a great deal in length, from just a few lines to over ninety. Most are between fifteen and fifty lines long. Contiguous lines within a blessing show three patterns of formal and semantic relations. Lines can occur singly, that is, stand independent of adjacent lines. Some lines are repeated more or less exactly two or more times in a row (see Table 13.1 lines 21–2; 23–4) or form groups based on parallel structure (2–3; 6–9; 13–20). Others are linked by continuation of content (26–27/8; 31–3). These relations beween lines are also combined in various ways (e.g. repetition and continuation, 30–3; repetition and parallel structure, 21–4) and also link non-adjacent lines into larger groupings within the texts. A full analysis of the texture and structure of blessings is not possible here, though consideration of which lines and themes are linked, which repeated, the location of repetitions in the texts, and thematic progressions in portions of the texts would be of interest.

The lines of blessings also vary in length from two or three syllables to occasional rapid-fire ones of over forty, with the majority under ten syllables long. Lines are usually delivered forcefully, loudly, and at a higher pitch than ordinary speech, with a narrower range of pitch variation. This difference of pitch and loudness is especially noticeable

Table 13.1: Blessing 7B.

1. ileincin-a osiruait ink'ap kietnyan	
2. ot opwan inke orropil	(sere)
3. ot opwan iyet ng'omdut	(sere)
4. ot piak iyet myaceen	(sere)
5. ot omiakiitu ak okwek	(sere/Enkai)
6. piak Tororet tuuka	(sere)
7. piak Tororet laakok	(sere)
8. piak Tororet oloshoit	(sere/Enkai)
9. piak Tororet amtit	(sere)
10. ot pieci ak ecek cu	(sere)
11. piak Tororet embokishiit	(sere/Enkai)
12. kopieci ak ecek cu	(sere/Enkai)
13. ot camak Tororet	(sere/Enkai)
14. ot camak asiista	(sere/Enkai)
15. ot camak araaweet	(sere/Enkai)
16. ot camak oloshoit	(sere/Enkai)
17. ot camak Purko	(sere)
18. ot camak Cumpeek	(sere)
19. ot camak Uas Nkishu	(sere/nai)
20. ot camak Kosopeek	(sere/nai)
21. ot oeku saruuni	(nai/Enkai)
22. ot oeku saruuni	(nai/sere)
23. ot oeku eipoturi	(nai/Enkai)
24. ot oeku eipoturi	(nai/Enkai)
25. ot orropil-aa	(sere/nai)
26. ot orropil-aa	(Enkai/sere)
27. ko yu sogoomik	(sere)
28. ko yu esong'ounait	(sere)
29. nk'ap teeta	(sere)
30. piak Tororet laakok	(sere)
31. piak Tororet laakok	(sere)
32. inko inten meenceet	(sere/Enkai)
33. ak inko osic en kaau	(sere/Enkai)
34. ot yaatwok Tororet	(sere)
35. ot yaatwok oloshoit	(sere)
36. ot yaatwok oloshoit	(sere)
(Basi . . .)	

1. tell the ceremony of our country
2. may you come from a fragrant place
3. may you come from a fragrant place
4. may he give you a good place
5. may you become well

yourselves also
6. God give you cows
7. God give you children
8. God give you a neighborhood/section
9. God give you food
10. may he give us these things as well

continued

[Table 13.1: *continued*]

11. God give you a home	24. may you become one who is always called
12. and give us these things as well	
13. may God like you	25. may you be fragrant
14. may the sun like you	26. may you be fragrant
15. may the moon like you	27. like sweet grass necklaces
16. may the neighborhood like you	28. like the odour of roast meat
17. may Purko like you	29. of a cow
18. may the government/Europeans like you	30. God give you children
19. may Uas Nkishu like you	31. God give you children
20. may Kipsigis like you	32. that are in the seclusion hut
21. may you become one who helps others	33. and that you bear at home
22. may you become one who helps others	34. may God open (agree) for you
23. may you become one who is always called	35. may the neighborhood open for you
	36. may the neighborhood open for you

as a contrast to the answering responses, which are said in a more or less normal voice. Loudness, pitch and force of delivery are all greatest at the beginning of a line. Within an overall falling pitch contour, some lines break into two falling patterns with the second high in the middle of the line lower than the initial pitch at the start. The speed of delivery, on the other hand, is greatest in the middle for longer lines; the first and last words may be a bit drawn out.

This general style of delivery is most exaggerated in ceremonial blessings, and also in blessings said in Maa. Blessings in Okiek are usually said a bit more slowly than those in Maa, and in a tone that can only be characterized as warm or affectionate. Delivery also distinguishes women's blessings at shaving ceremonies from those of men; women bless with less force and loudness, at lower pitch and speed than men. They seem to speak blessings rather than to call them.

Grammatically, lines are chiefly verb phrases in the subjunctive (e.g. lines 2–5) or imperative (e.g. 6–9), descriptive continuations that modify such lines (e.g. 27–9), or statements that enumerate the consensus wishing the blessing on those present (e.g. *etejo il yangusi; etejo eseuri;* those of *yangusi* age-set said so; those of *eseuri* age-set said so). The imperative verbs are more exhortative wishes than commands, since verbs such as be, become, have, and give birth, as used in the texts, are not felicitous in commands. The grammatical form of the lines is in keeping with the nature of blessings as wishes or requests. It is also appropriate for the metacommunicative function of blessings as defining the ideal key of an occasion as harmonious. The creation and maintenance of such an atmosphere is a matter of cooperation and mutual respect and consideration by those present, something to be suggested or urged rather than demanded.

Themes of blessing

The themes of Okiek blessings center around four main values: continuity, fecundity, prosperity and cooperation. In addition, one group of lines combines these under general rubrics such as *sopondo* (good life), *en-kishonit* (life, < Maa), sweet fragrance, and the help of God, nature and the world. Some themes are contextually specific, others are elaborated on different occasions (for example, ceremonial roles are mentioned in ceremonial blessings), and the litany of dangers to be bypassed is usually more developed in a blessing to remove a curse. Context-specific themes and elaborations are one aspect of the metacommunicative function of blessings that defines the frame of an occasion. Specific themes are mixed in with other lines to present the four-way picture of a happy and blessed life. Brief discussion, with examples of blessing lines centering on each of these values, will clarify what the values mean in the context of Okiek life and relate their expression to assumptions described above. The following shows examples of lines grouped by theme.

Table 13.2: Themes in Okiek blessing lines[1].

Continuity

the rock of Koipasoyet (14D)
be the hill of Olekorei (17B)
(be) a star (7A)
may you rise like the sun
may (he) give you good birth fluids that never end any time (7E)
may you join (children) together like a chain (12A)
may the father's sons inherit themselves and no other person inherit (13H)
may God give you always a ceremony that never ends (12A)
may we come evening and morning, my child, coming to eat a ceremony in
    your home (22F)
il yangusi (age) says, here is a name (12B)
may il talala (age) agree (22C)
may those in the ground agree
may those living agree (13H)
may you have a long life (22B)

Prosperity

may you mix both boys and girls (22B)
have cows (2B)

[Table 13.2: *continued*]

may he give you bees with which to bless children doing ceremonies (11A)
there are sheep that are coming with lambs (22B)
don't be sick, my child (22A)
may leopards not eat you (22A)
may you be one who is always called (13B)
I say (be one) of cows
   that come bellowing happily
   that come from the soda lick (6)
he who spoils this ceremony today,
   may he lack a ceremony (of his own) (12A)
may you excel in all countries (10B)
I give you success (22B)
   take the bow
   take the thing to kill with, then
   until you bring us a special elders' meat
   from an elephant
   or from a buffalo
may you rise like the sun (18B)
a burning fire (23E)
   that harms no child
   that harms nothing
   that consumes only the firewood given
prosper (9A)
a warm house
   of children
   a warm house
   of cows (22B)

Fecundity

have children as in the past (11D)
God give you children (7B)
may God help the fertile women (5D)
may God give you your birth fluids
   that are not painful (14F)
may you intermarry, then
   Kaplelach (Okiek)
   Maresionik (Okiek)
   Maasai (7E)
you are given a life of children . . .
   of cows
   of sheep
   that come with calves
   that come with lambs (21B)
be locusts (15D)
be many (17B)
may there be a ceremony
   that stays in this home today
   and tomorrow (3)

Cooperation

may God give us a section/group (16C)
may those in the ground agree to you
  may the living agree to you (13H)
we pray to all those past elders
if it's Lekookoo
  if it's Lekuruon (21B)
do things together (21B)
get along together well, then (23E)
may the section/group like you
  may Purko (Maasai) like you
  may officials/Europeans like you
  may Uas Nkishu (Maasai) like you
  may Kipsigis like you (7B)
may God give you a ceremony always
  that doesn't end
  to which the ages come
  eseuri (age)
  il yangusi (age) (12A)
may he have milk in the mouth (21A)
  may he have honey in the mouth
God give you harmony (16A)
may you become one that gathers
people to him (16C)

General (*sopondo*)

may you be sweet-smelling (3)
may God like you (11D)
God give us *sopondo* (10B)
may you become a *sapoitit* tree (10B)
become *sinenteet* (21B)
may (God) help you (5D)
may the wind help you (11A)

1. Numbers after lines refer to blessing texts.

Continuity. Continuity is expressed in the blessings with natural and human themes, though both are intended to apply to the people blessed. It means a long and happy life, now and in its extension forward and backward in time, through the perpetuation of one's lineage with offspring and through the remembrance of ancestor spirits.

'Be like a rock.' 'Be like a mountain.' Mention of such enduring natural features was explained to me as follows: 'A hill is never lost any time. It's hard/strong. People are born and grow old and die, and more are born and grow old and die, and still you see that that hill is still there and goes nowhere.' Similarly, the moon and stars are mentioned,

always present and continuing, just as would be hoped for on behalf of
a long-lived patriarch and his family. The natural theme used most
frequently in this respect carries a sense of prosperity as well: 'May you
rise like the sun.' The time and direction of sunrise define dimensions
of the auspicious in performance of Okiek ceremonies.

The human expression of continuity overlaps with themes of fecundity and cooperation. Some lines simply wish for children; continuity is more explicit in the wish for births night and day, a chain of
children that does not break, and inheritance by one's own sons. The
recurrent wish for unending ceremonies combines all of the ideal
values at once. The fire kept always alive in the hearth is another image
of perseverance mentioned in blessings.

Continuity is also expressed in the invocation of age-set names.
Elders' age-sets are usually named, including age-sets with no more
living members. Younger age-sets are included at times, joining them
into the male chain. The continuity of particular lineages is specified in
blessings as well, by deceased family elders being addressed by name.
The authority of age and men is thus called on and incorporated into
the prayers; elders are those who can agree to and ask for the prayers of
others. This position is further strengthened and legitimated by linking
the lines which name ages with parallel lines invoking ancestor spirits
and God.

Fecundity. Praying for fecundity means praying for one thing: a multitude of children. However, these lines do not all simply ask for
children, boys or girls; they also draw on a number of synecdochal
associations. Blessings often refer to women as *solootwek,* the term for
child-bearing women. Lines also ask for *ol masi* (the hair grown by a
woman with a new child), *enkipa* (the slime of birth), and *kereek* (the
uncleanness of women with infants). The associations appropriately
highlight the link of women with their children, but also emphasize
their non-*esinya* state. One wish in the blessings recognizes a difficulty
of this unrelenting reproduction for women; the phrase 'without pain'
sometimes modifies the exhortation to bear unceasingly, day and
night.

Other lines asking for prolific increase focus on numbers and on
swelling the size and strength of the family — to be as many as the
locusts or grains of millet. The wish for sons to inherit is another way to
pray for a long and large family line.

Finally, fecundity and prosperity are merged in lines which pray not
simply for cows and sheep, but for animals with their calves and lambs.
The association with human offspring here is not whimsical; children
are called calves in a number of contexts, for example in ceremonial
songs, marriage talks and affectionate address.

Prosperity. The prosperity prayed for has several dimensions. Some lines ask for animal property, especially cows, but also sheep. Women and children, focus of the prayer of fecundity, are also a kind of property in the view of Okiek men who control their circulation. The means to care for them are also requested in wishes for abundant foods, from luck in the hunt and finding honey, to maize and food in general. Prayers for honey are usually related to its ceremonial use as honey wine. Again, the prayer for unending ceremonies is also a prayer for prosperity in children and in food to call guests in celebration.

Health and safety are also part of a prosperous family. Lines which focus on these chiefly list dangers to be avoided: illness, leopards, spears (i.e. enemies), predatory birds, flies, snakes, worms (which would eat anyone who died), ants which weaken the structure of a house, general badness. Some blessings include a short curse as protection against anyone jealous of the blessed, who might harm them.

The final touch to the picture of prosperity is the prayer that the man of the family will be regarded by others with respect and esteem so that people come to ask advice and invite him to ceremonies. He wins, succeeds, prospers and has a warm and comfortable home full of property, food and the women and children to care for and populate it.

The prosperity portrayed in blessings is one of a patriarchal ideal. The blessed family is populous, propertied and presided over by a wise and articulate man. He has sons to continue his line, hold his property and perpetuate the patriarchal organization. The women who maintain the home, produce the offspring and care for the property remain in the background in blessing themes, except as the source of children. Concerns or wishes specific to women are not expressed. One could imagine lines that would focus on women's roles and activities paralleling those that do occur in blessings, e.g. Have good men; May your source of water be nearby, sweet and clear; May the ax (of firewood) never harm you.[13]

Of course, women share the wish for healthy children, prosperity and a happy home. The point of these imaginary lines is simply to illustrate the dominance of men ideologically in defining Okiek interests, desires and goals. Women are not ignored; in fact, they are necessary to even conceive of the blessed life. The complementarity of male and female roles is expressed to some extent in the birth-dominated imagery of lines centered on fecundity, and in the general wishes that men and women alike share. The expression of the ideal, though, for both men and women is in terms of male-oriented social institutions, such as age-sets and lineages, and male-dominated prerogatives such as inheritance. Similarly, in another verbal genre,

---

13. To correspond to actual lines such as: 'Have bearing women'; 'May you have a success with the bow'; 'May you escape spears/leopards'.

women praise themselves and each other in song by singing about their links to male relatives, husbands and children, while men sing praise about their own hunting success, hives, cows, beauty or bravery (Kratz 1981a).

Cooperation. Fecundity and prosperity are blessings wished on each individual and family. Continuity perpetuates not only a man's family but swells and carries on his whole lineage. Blessing lines which stress cooperation address a more inclusive level of social structure as well, praying for harmony and peace within a neighborhood, between lineages and between ethnic groups. Lines pray for understanding, cooperation and general agreement, and for intermarriage, mutual invitations and amity between named ethnic groups and sections. Lines which name age-sets and ask the living and dead all to agree also add to the image of consensus and harmony.

Agreement is prayed for, it being said that all should follow one mouth, that there should be only sweet things like honey, milk or honey water in the mouth, not bitterness and disagreement. As before, the prayer for ceremonies contributes to this theme as well. If the ceremony is unending, so too should be its ideal conviviality.

Lines which focus on cooperation and peace may also contribute to the metacommunicative role of blessings in defining a harmonious key on particular occasions. The ideal painted can serve as a model and reminder to those present to help create that respectful atmosphere that very day.

The image of sopondo. Examples of lines which pray for general luck and blessing were given before the four thematic line groupings were discussed. A good life, luck, blessing and good fortune — all of these are summarized and carried by the word *sopondo* (<*-sap*, to live). The thematic groups described are, in essence, descriptions and elaborations of what *sopondo* means and how it would be realized in its fullest sense. This last section mentions lines which carry the general sense of blessed in botanical form, and briefly recapitulates the general image the verbal themes portray together.

The fire of the home hearth, one place of blessing, appears in the imagery of spoken blessings. The other place of blessing, the *mabwaita*, is rarely mentioned in any of the texts considered. It is present only by implication, in the frequent lines which pray for unending ceremonies. The *mabwaita* is also represented in blessing texts, however, by its constituent plants. Five kinds of trees or vines were mentioned in the corpus of blessings analyzed: *olerienit* (*ol-oirien* in Maa), *sinenteet*, *koroseek* (and their Maasai equivalent *ol-timi*), *oloinini*, and *sapoitit* (*reteti* in Maa). The first three are the basic building blocks of the *mabwaita*, with associations which I have already discussed. *Olerienit* is also mentioned in blessings because it is fragrant (*ng'omdut*), with leaves as abundant as one's children should be (12B:25). *Oloinini*, too, is used in ceremonies, tied on the *toloocik* structure built by the hearth. It is hard and slow to break (14E:2). All of these botanical themes, then, index the settings for blessings and the symbolic associations they carry.

Finally, *sapoitit* is a tree with milky sap. The basis for including it in blessings is a well-known story in which *sapoitit* moves in with *cedar* 'temporarily' and eventually takes over entirely. The wish expressed, then, is that the blessed ones should stay long and well, as *sapoitit* did (10B:5).

What image of a blessed life is portrayed by the blessings, then? One blessed with fecundity and prosperity, and who cooperates with relatives and neighbors, has a home which reflects his general state of well-being. Blessing lines describe it as a warm house, full of children who are happy, well-fed and playing. They run to meet their father when he comes home from his journey, which has itself been lucky and well-favored; either the man comes from the forest with meat and a bag full of honey or from a visit where he was well received. The fire in the house never goes out. Ceremonies are constantly celebrated there, the house ever full of guests. Even the cows in this homestead play and low happily. Such is the home of one with *sopondo*. Again, the woman of the house is relatively invisible in this picture, although she shares the general good fortune and is undoubtedly the one bearing the children, caring for them, making the food and beer for the ceremony, cutting and carrying the wood for the fire that never goes out, and milking those happy cows. The ritual prominence and organizational priority of elders is represented and reinforced again and again in the verbal expression of Okiek blessings.

Materials of blessing: concretizing and dispersing the auspicious

The preceding sections have already touched on material objects and substances used in Okiek blessings; the significance and associations of different aspects of blessings resonate, repeat and reinforce each other. This section will focus on three kinds of things used in blessings: the substances with which they are performed, the substances' containers, and the plants which stop the containers. As noted already, blessings are said with words alone at meetings and at marriage discussions. This discussion, then, refers chiefly to a subset of Okiek blessings.[14]

In general, the materials of blessing are concrete vehicles for the themes and associations of blessings that I have already elaborated;

14. Much of what will be said is also relevant to marriage discussions, since similar materials are used but not associated specifically with spoken blessings at that time.

they also amplify the blessings with their own associations, contexts of use and symbolic contrasts. The substances of blessing are all dispersable; they provide a material means to represent and broadcast the auspiciousness of the blessers and the good fortune they pray for to all concerned. In some cases, for example curse-removal, the dissemination is limited and, as mentioned before, the substance of blessing remains concentrated and powerful. Okiek see all blessing substances as things to be received and to be welcomed (*-taac*) as a sign that the blessing has touched them.

The stopped containers are indices of the role of blesser. Blessing elders concentrate the auspicious in their person, and the objects they hold are signs of their role and all it implies. The substances they use similarly concentrate two key items in Okiek tradition, history and identity: meat and honey.

Substances of blessing

Honey wine and saliva are the main substances combined with words in blessing. Two other ritual substances of prayer and dispersal, honey water and fat, should be considered in conjunction with them; their containers will also be discussed. The central occasions for blessing with honey wine and saliva have been discussed, namely ceremonies and rescue from accursed danger. Honey water is used to pour libations[15] to ancestor spirits (*aiik*) in the absence of honey wine. If no honey products are available and a bit of milk is, then that can be diluted for a libation. At times, a mixture of honey water and milk is also used.

Fat is used to bless, by anointment, on two occasions: during initiation ceremonies and during weddings. Both times, the anointing is done by the mother of the initiate (or bride) before elders bless with a shower of honey wine. The substances are similarly dispersed in both cases. At ceremonies, everyone present gets a dab of fat on the forehead, just as all are sprayed with wine. At weddings, it is the wedding procession whose heads are anointed and whose feet and legs are sprayed before elders pray. This women's blessing is necessary to the

---

15. Pouring libations (*-pieesta*) could, if space allowed, be related to blessing as a genre of prayer. Addressed to ancestor spirits rather than to Tororet (God), libations are poured and said by men and women equally. They are poured at the places of blessing, *mabwaita* and hearth, and the same objects are used as containers. Honey wine is usually the preferred substance of libation. It is frequently replaced by other things, though, because libations are often poured with little advance planning, as an immediate measure to help cure the sick or avert misfortune. Liquid is poured directly from container to the ground, not dispersed from the mouth as blessings are. Verbally, libations are less formal, more conversational in tone. No response from others present is necessary. Thematically they consist chiefly of statements addressed to ancestor spirits, sometimes named, telling them that the libation is food meant for them, apologizing for wrongs and asking them to stop causing trouble and go away.

rites, complementary to the elders' spray, but silent within the encompassing jurisdiction and organization of their spoken prayers.

Fat is also used to anoint in forgiveness. In initiation ceremonies, adults anoint initiates as a sign of goodwill after they have confessed their wrongs. In peace ceremonies, anointing helps reconcile lineages estranged by homicide. Again, blessings follow anointing in both cases.

In more secular contexts, fat is associated on the one hand with women and children and on the other with general prosperity and health. The birth of a baby calls for the slaughter of a sheep or goat so that the mother can drink fat and soup to recuperate. Among neighboring Maasai, a special piece of fatty meat, called *e-naikuti*, is cut from the sheep and eaten by women in a post-partum celebration; in Okiek, this word has a more general sense of ceremony, used as a synonym for a child's shaving ceremony. New-born babies are also fed small amounts of fat throughout the first year of life, and rubbed regularly with it so that they will grow well.

These associations help to make fat a most appropriate substance for women to use in blessing. Fat thus also picks up a sense of the theme of fecundity, and is a sign of peaceful and cooperative relations as well. It also calls forth images related to the other themes, particularly prosperity, and so becomes a substance which is generally well suited for blessing, not only by women, although perhaps particularly by them.

Sleek, fat, well-fed livestock show the wealth of their owner; a man who can slaughter such a beast for family or for guests to eat gives further evidence of this. Okiek prize fatty meat as particularly tasty. The most delicious meat treat, *munono*, can only be prepared from a fatty animal. Fat is also used medicinally for serious illness. If possible, a sheep is slaughtered, for the invalid to have nourishing meat and broth as well.

Finally, fat is also a sign of prosperity in its cosmetic uses. Gleaming, well-oiled skin is not only attractive, but shows a well-cared-for household, prosperous enough to have a supply of fat for cosmetic purposes. People going to a ceremony rub on fat to get spruced up for the occasion, and fat is ideally given to women at shaving ceremonies to rub on to show they have been celebrating a child. Initiates coming out of seclusion are well anointed, and decorated too, for their first public appearance, youthful good looks being thus epitomized. In part a sign of ceremonies, then, fat also carries associations of the various occasions which I have already described, combining the four values thematic to blessings.

Galaty (1977: 176ff.) analyzes symbolic contrasts and relations among food products with respect to Maasai cultural identity and stereotypes of Torrobo (Okiek). In his scheme, fat — a special and concentrated product refined from meat or milk — corresponds to honey wine, similar as it is in relative scarcity and in its transformation from its natural state through brewing. The link between fat and honey wine is also clear in their use by the Okiek, but the relation can be extended to include a sense of sexual complementarity as well. Fat, the blessing substance associated with women's silent blessings, can be contrasted with honey wine, the most male of honey products, used in elders' spoken prayers. Okiek comments suggest such a link and so invite a brief consideration of honey products.

The finest and most prized of honeys, deliciously sweet and white, are likened to fat in color, consistency and sweetness. Such honey is considered the best for small children and also for the first gift in marriage negotiations which is brought for women of the bride's family to eat. Honey is not given to new-born children, but it replaces fat in their diet after about the first year.

Honey is provided by men, but once brought home is said to be eaten by women and children especially. Men eat it too, of course, but say that they prefer to consume honey as wine. Honey wine is also made by men in leather bags like those they use to gather honey. Okiek say that formerly honey wine was not consumed by women or by young men. Its use in blessings, then, draws on and adds to these associations and helps define it as an adult form of honey, the beverage of older men.

Honey water lies between honey and honey wine in its associations. Part of the diet of children, like honey, honey diluted with water is also the first stage in preparing honey wine. Weak or unripe wine is also referred to as honey water. A friendly and affectionate phrase of farewell is 'Honey water and milk' or '(Follow) the path of honey water', similar to the goodnight of 'Sleep in the way of honey' (Sweet dreams).

A mediating substance, honey water can be used in libations when a timely performance of the act is the important thing and there is not enough honey to brew wine. Libations recognize ancestor spirits and so are a way that these may be kept included in ordinary family life. Wine might be preferred by the ancestor spirits, as it is by the living, but a gift of whatever appropriate food is available will not be refused.

Containers of blessing and plants of consecration

The containers which hold substances of blessing are three: calabash, *paleito* basket, and horn. In blessings or libations, leaves from an auspicious plant are put in the mouth of the container. Each container is used especially in certain circumstances and has particular associations, though substitutions are sometimes made. Calabashes are usual in ceremonial blessings. For libations, a *paleito* is the container sought. A small black horn holds fat for anointing, with sprigs of *tanguriot* grass in the mouth.

When elders bless with honey wine, they use a calabash of liquor set aside for that purpose. During ceremonies, the blessing elder continues to carry the leaf-plugged calabash, blessing as needed and taking and offering sips from it. Though other ethnic groups use calabashes to hold many things, most Okiek ones are for honey wine; when a ceremony begins, the collection of wine-filled calabashes stored away for guests is impressive. Okiek with cattle may also have a few milk gourds now, but certainly not the large, differentiated array of their neighbors.

The primary association of gourds, then, is with honey wine, men, ceremonies and blessing. They are plugged with *tanguriot* grass or leaves from trees such as *olerienit* or *lepeekwet*; the type of leaves can indicate the lineage of those holding the ceremony. The associations of most of these ritual plants have been discussed. In addition, the plants are signs marking occasions as ceremonial and the objects in which they are placed as ritual objects in use for purposes other than their usual daily ones. The containers and the substances within are marked for prayerful use, consecrated for a ceremonial role by putting plants of invocation in their mouths.

The *paleito* basket is a traditional and distinctive Okiek household object. A honey container, it is a tightly woven, rounded grass basket, made by women. *Paleiyuek* (pl.) come in all sizes. Those right for libations are small, like a child's honey basket, and nicely decorated with beads or cowrie shells on their leather tops or straps. In ceremonies, *paleiyuek* hold the honey ritually fed to a child during shaving, to an initiate coming out of seclusion, or to a bride and groom at marriage. Associated with honey, honey water, milk, women, children and traditional life, *paleiyuek* are admired and regarded with a kind of reminiscent affection, in some cases almost like a teddy bear in American culture.

These are the objects for communication with ancestor spirits, holding the honey water or milk given to the spirits while they are called upon and placated. Libations have a less formal tone and key than blessings, more like an apologetic, coaxing conversation than a formal invocation. The agents addressed are conceived of more personally, and the request posed in the more concrete and specific form of a particular situation being in need of remedy. Yet libation, too, is a prayer and request for the four values epitomized in blessings. The *paleito* basket of libation is an affectively charged container which contrasts with the calabash of elders' blessing in a way similar to the contrast between the genres of prayer.

The green in the mouth of a *paleito* in libations is almost invariably *tanguriot* grass. The use of *tanguriot* is also resonant with tradition and distinctly Okiek. The iconic basis for using *tanguriot* is the same as that for other ritual plants; it is abundant, green, and resilient even in the worst drought in the manner that those using it would wish to be fruitful, long-lived and healthy. In addition, *tanguriot* has a strong association with the forest, where it grows, which is the particular ecological domain of Okiek identity and history. Only blades unmarred by rips or tears, uprooted whole rather than cut at the base, are selected for libations or blessings. *Tanguriot* is placed in the horn of fat at initiations and weddings, in calabashes of liquor brought for marriage discussions, and on the foreheads of those in a wedding procession. A bit of *tanguriot* grass in a *paleito* basket is a particularly Okiek diacritic in a ceremonial system that shares a number of elements with various neighbors.

The final container to be considered is the horn, which holds fat for anointing. A large horn is sometimes used by men to drink liquor, but the horn for ritual use is small and black, the tip of a larger horn in many cases. Ideally from a buffalo, it could be from an *esinya* cow, that is, from a cow slaughtered, not killed by sickness or misfortune. Buffalo and elephant are the two large animals commemorated in hunting songs; men remember and recount buffalo hunts much as young men recall cattle raids. Buffalo horn brings to ritual a sign of men's bravery in hunting and also a sign of meat, the traditional complement to honey in Okiek diet. It holds a concentrated essence of meat — fat — for blessing, just as *paleito* and calabash hold honey products. The two key products of Okiek traditional life, meat and honey, thus become ritual material — as containers as well as blessing substances. With *tanguriot* grass stuck in the fat-filled horn, meat and honey's forest source is added to this material condensation of Okiek identity used in ritual.

This section has considered blessing materials, the way the substances used and the objects which hold them concretize the values and auspiciousness of blessing and spread them in material form to those blessed. A wider set of genres and occasions was brought into account by including honey water and fat (for libations and anointing), which are linked to spoken blessings both in their associations and as other types of prayer. Usually excluded from the spoken genre as blessers, women reappear in a complementary role as silent anointers who convey their blessing within the framework of the general prayer. A complementarity of men and women in ritual roles becomes evident, though ideologically under male management and organization, for economic roles are under male authority despite the indispensible contribution of women. The four primary values of Okiek blessings were once again traced in associations and uses of blessing substances. A more general sense of Okiek identity and tradition was also signified by the representation of meat, honey and the forest in various material forms and combinations.

Benediction and benefactors: perpetuating priority through prayer

This chapter has described and analyzed blessings as a verbal genre essential to the enactment of a number of important occasions in Okiek life. The very nature of blessings as a genre of prayer, together with the cultural definition of who can most appropriately and auspiciously bless on these occasions, was seen to define a kind of hierarchy of authority. A temporary priority of ritual rank carried by persons of a general social category, this heirarchy is enacted by representative individual elders. The definition and justification of the latters' appropriateness to the blessing role was based on assumptions about the natural roles and abilities of men and women.

The fleeting ritual authority exercised by elders was also seen to correspond with their organizational priority on other social and political occasions, so that religious and social rank reinforce and legitimate one another. Thus understood as those most suitable to pray and intercede on behalf of others, Okiek elders, by blessing, appear to favor and help their women, juniors and each other. That such help is given cannot be gainsaid, yet at the same time the elders are helping themselves by legitimating and perpetuating their own position of auspicious and organizational priority and authority.

Turning to the blessing texts, the Okiek image of the ideal life was seen to center around four values: continuity, fecundity, prosperity and cooperation. The representation of these values in terms of a patriarchally-oriented social organization corresponds with the authority and precedence defined by their enactment. The complementary importance of women does receive some expression, as it also does in the symbolism of ceremonial settings for blessings.

In general, the representation of Okiek sex roles by material means and in ceremonial roles portrays the complementarity of men and women. Verbally, however, when attitudes and assumptions about the roles of men and women are more self-consciously articulated, a male dominance emerges in themes and ways of expression. Male dominance is thus made ideologically salient, yet it is not strictly true in ordinary social relations. Women can make their influence felt in ways that work around an overtly male-controlled social organization.

Analysis of the materials used in blessings also shows a picture of complementarity, but their significance at the same time includes a more general sense of Okiek identity. Blessings are not unique to Okiek in the regional network of ethnic interaction. Indeed, they are an important common link, and way of relating ceremonial practices, throughout East Africa in general — specifically with Maasai and Kalenjin neighbors in the case of Kipchornwonek and Kaplelach Okiek. Language, particular themes, and styles of blessing show obvious ethnic differences. Materials used, however, are often in part shared.

The material channel is suitable, then, for the appearance of signs of ethnic identity and specificity in a genre that occurs throughout the region. Considered within the context of a particular culture and a particular understanding of blessing, the specific diacritics of ethnic identity become clear.

By focusing on a particular verbal genre central to Okiek ceremonies, I was able to bring in other performance contexts and variations and so illuminate the relation between ceremony and daily life. Within the genre itself, the three communicative functions of blessing were seen to be differentially relevant in different contexts, with ceremonial performance presenting the most balanced functional combination. The section on blessing materials suggested that comparison with related genres (for example, libation) would be fruitful, but that is beyond the scope of this chapter.

Throughout the description and analysis, I relied heavily on cross-contextual associations based on iconic and indexical links, to fill out, clarify and investigate the performance, themes and materials of blessings, and Okiek comments about them. In some instances, ceremonial context may be shown to offer a key to understanding other occasions, as is the case with ceremonial settings of blessings. In ceremonies the significance of certain signs is foregrounded and made explicit by the concentration of relevant contrasts and associations drawn from many contexts. In other cases, the concentration is only partial. Thus, materials used in ceremonial blessings carry a rich symbolic load, but still more layers of significance are added by associations with other materials more typical of other contexts and genres. Still, the path to these associations is present in the ceremonial signs, contributing to the signs' affective aura, though in a more inconspicuous way.

It must be emphasized, however, that the elaborate and concentrated associations of some signs in ceremonial context are drawn from more dispersed and less emotionally charged and contextually marked uses on other occasions. In other words, when ceremonial signs are unpacked, their baggage is full of the old laundry of daily life. The relation between ceremonial contexts and other contexts is not a simple one, then. Ceremonial signs pull together many associations and contexts and help make explicit the relations between them. Their use and sequence in ceremonies also gives them an affective charge which then can often be traced in the contexts which contribute to their significance. In ceremonies, certain objects, acts and relations from daily life become material for sign vehicles, and receive an additional cognitive and emotional significance. This is not true of all ceremonial signs, of course; some are specific to ceremonies alone.

The question of relations between, and specializations of, different communicative channels has been addressed, in part, in the summary of the blessing analysis with which I began this section. While the basic image of a blessed life and the ideal values which encapsulate it are represented in all the channels discussed, different channels have different emphases, tones and valuations.

The formal and functional nature of the language of ritual has long been a regular topic of scholarly investigation (Malinowski 1934; Crawley 1929; Samarin 1976; Tambiah 1968; 1979). The present analysis of Okiek blessings has not focused on this question alone, but contributes a case study to the discussion. The language of ritual contexts has been characterized as being reduced in the use of the formal and semantic possibilities of ordinary speech (Bloch 1986). Delimitation of some set of formal linguistic means is one way in which distinctive speech styles more generally are constituted and recognizable (Urban 1986). Formal restrictions do not eliminate the creative potential of performers, but set parameters within which they play, and in some cases give an overall pragmatic meaning to the speech style.

Okiek blessings were seen to draw on a limited range of semantic fields, though there is room for variety and creativity in the expression of the themes identified. Formally, blessings are characterized by a specific intonational contour, manner of delivery, and set of grammatical and syntactic forms. The length of blessings and blessing lines varies considerably, though still within a definable range. A great creative potential is available in the way a limited set of relations can create semantic and formal patterns linking lines and groups of lines throughout the texts. Okiek blessings, then, fall stylistically somewhere between the more open choice in the combination of linguistic means typical of daily conversation and the more radically limited combination of ritual genres present in some cultures which are memorized and repeated verbatim, with little semantic or formal variability.

Discussion of the pragmatic aspects of ritual has at times prefigured and later drawn explicitly on speech-act theory (see, for example, Ravenhill 1976). Ritual language is often taken up within the question of the nature of ritual in general, as 'events that combine the properties of statements and actions' (Bloch 1986: 181). Since I have concentrated here on blessings as a genre, and not simply on their ceremonial performance, the pragmatic aspects that have emerged from the analysis relate to the varied balance of communicative functions in different contexts, and to the nature of blessings as one of the Okiek genres of power. Still, the metacommunicative functions of blessings which I have outlined might be seen as helping to establish the conditions, and to define the occasion, for the work of cultural transformation which ceremonies accomplish. Future study will consider verbal genres combined in Okiek ceremonial enactments as a whole, and will relate more specifically to the pragmatic analysis of ritual and language in ceremonies.

The existence of blessings and other genres of power in the Okiek communicative repertoire might seem to contradict the usual characterization of hunter-gatherer societies as egalitarian and unranked, and raises the comparative question with respect to other hunter-gatherers. While spoken prayer and prayer songs are mentioned in ethnographic sources on San and Pygmy groups, published sources both on these African hunter-gatherers and on Hadza make no mention of blessing as a genre of prayer. Prayers noted are typically either in praise of God, the moon, the sun or other beings, or else simply outright requests for food, luck in the hunt, rain, health, and safety, which may include reasons why the prayer should be granted. Evans-Pritchard notes a basic difference between blessings and other Nuer prayers, characterizing the former as 'benedictory prayers'. Blessings 'are thought to be effective only because God makes them so' (1956: 172), but are bestowed or invoked by persons. The difference here revolves around precisely the power and authority constituent of blessings and other genres of power. The definition of unequal rank and power is what is missing in the prayers of other African hunter-gatherer groups; as described, their prayers are all direct requests, with no human intermediary praying for others.

This apparent difference in the genres of prayer used by African hunter-gatherers brings to mind the distinction drawn by Woodburn (1988) between socioeconomic organizations oriented towards 'delayed return' and 'immediate return'; the contrast between the Okiek and other hunter-gatherers (above) replicates this division. Hunter-gatherers in Australia also have delayed-return systems, by Woodburn's definition, because of their elaboration of clans and clan land rights, and because of the way they organize marriage and the exchange of women.

Blessings do not seem prominent in Australia, but there is no reason to expect Okiek and Australian cultural manifestations of ritual, rank or authority to be the same. In Australia, it is all a matter of knowledge and control of sacred paintings, songs, dances and places, defined not only by sex and age, but also by clan (see, for example, Morphy 1984: 113–15). Blessings are inherently genres of power; though comparatively widespread, they may not occur universally. The Australian material is a reminder that there are also culturally specific genres of power. These genres' pragmatic authority is created by the definition of who can know them and perform them, and in what contexts, as with some Australian genres of ritual song.

The point here, however, is that in both Okiek and Australian cases, 'delayed-return' hunter-gatherer societies, an obvious and relatively prominent expression of ritual power and authority exists in the communicative repertoire. More detailed descriptions of the communicative resources and patterns of 'immediate-return' groups would answer some of the questions raised by this observation.

14. Maintaining cosmic unity: ideology and the reproduction of Yolngu clans

Howard Morphy

Introduction

The purpose of this chapter is an investigation of apparently contradictory features of the relationship between cosmology and society over time, among the Yolngu people of north-east Arnhem Land.[1] I will be focusing on the system of clan designs: designs that are associated with social groups and which are a major component of Yolngu art and ceremonial objects and constructions. From a synchronic perspective the system of clan designs seems to be characterized by an overarching and systematic order, from a diachronic perspective it can appear chaotic. I will be concerned with the interpenetration of order and chaos or, to paraphrase Stanner (1963), with how cosmos and society are *made* correlative. I will argue that the contradiction between synchronic order and diachronic chaos is resolved when it is realized that the former is an imposed order created through political process but shaped by the constraints of a relatively autonomous system of cosmological relations.

One view from within: overarching order

On the surface the Yolngu system of clan designs appears to be a Durkheimian ideal-type in which there is a fairly precise covariation between design form and social group. Each group has a set of designs each of which varies morphologically from the design of any other group, although in some cases morphological differences are minimal. The set of designs is held jointly by all members of a group, and the rights to hold the designs are traced back to the Ancestral past (the

1. The research upon which this chapter is based was carried out between 1974 and 1980, funded by the Australian National University and the Australian Institute of Aboriginal Studies. I would like to thank Frances Morphy, Anthony Forge, Nicolas Peterson and Ian Keen for providing intellectual input into the analysis presented here. The drawings are by Joan Goodrum and the chapter was typed by Marion Cobbold.

Dreamtime) when they were entrusted to the founding human ancestors of the group. They are thus part of that group's sacred inheritance (*mardayin*), which is handed on from one generation of its members to the next. The designs are sources of Ancestral power (*maar*), and as components of paintings are used in ritual to direct that power to particular purposes.

Clan designs are themselves manifestations of Ancestral beings (*wangarr*) and have their origin in the Ancestral past. Stories exist which explain the origin of each design in some mythological event. For example the 🐚 design of the Manggalili clan was first formed on the body of an Ancestral fisherman by the mark of the tide as it washed across his drowned body where it lay stranded on the beach. The diamond design of the Mardarrpa clan is the pattern burnt into the back of the Ancestral crocodile as his body was scorched in the fire of his burning bark hut. Elements of the myth of origin are encoded in details of the design. For example, the Mardarrpa diamond pattern has segments of the different colours, red, white and black, which represent respectively the flames, ash and burnt wood from the fire. The design is thus a sign of a particular Ancestral being and of an event that occurred on his journeys in the Ancestral past — an event through which the design is linked with a particular area of land. The Mardarrpa design is most closely associated with Gunmurrutjpi on Blue Mud Bay where the crocodile was burnt, but by extension it is also associated with all areas of Mardarrpa land where the crocodile travelled. The word *likan*, when applied to clan designs, refers to their connection to the Ancestral beings.

Likan has a number of meanings, some with ceremonial and some with mundane references. What all the meanings share in common is the idea of connection. In a secular context, *likan* refers variously to the elbow, a bay between two promontories and the fork where the branch of a tree joins its trunk. In the ritual sphere it refers to a variety of extensions of the Ancestral past into the present, to clan designs, to power names and to certain songs. Clan designs and power names are both in a sense components of the clan's sacred objects (*rangga*), which are the most powerful and restricted manifestation of the Ancestral beings. The clan designs are painted or engraved on the *rangga* and the power names are names of the *rangga*.

Clan designs are also referred to as *ngaraka* (bones), *ngaraka wangarr* (bones of the Ancestral being), *ngaraka ngilimurru* (our bones) and *ngaraka baapurru* (bones of the clan). The design as a whole is said to refer to bones in a general and metaphorical sense, that is, as a manifestation of the bones of an Ancestral being, but it may also refer to bones at a more specific level. Thus the design in the centre of the snakes in Plate 14.1 signifies the backbone of a *wangarr* snake. The pointed oval design in Plate 14.2 refers to the same snake, *mikarran*. In

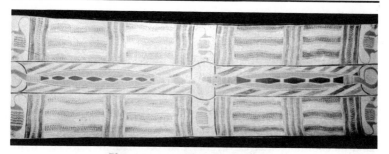

Plate 14.1: A painting by Banapana
Maymuru of the Manggalili clan. The
painting represents an Ancestral snake
during the wet season emerging from
a hole in the ground to hunt mice.
The pattern in the centre of the snake
represents the snake's ribs.

Plate 14.2: A painting by Yanggarriny of the
Dharlwangu clan. The painting represents two adjacent
areas of country belonging to different clans. The
long-necked fresh-water turtle is associated with the
Dharlwangu clan as is the clan design. The left hand
panel represents Mardarrpa clan country. The
oval-shaped sign represents the snake's ribs
transformed into an Ancestral fish trap.

this case the design signifies the snake's ribs transformed into the stakes of a *wangarr* fish trap.

As well as stories which explain the Ancestral origin of the designs, there are also stories which detail the transmission of those designs from the *wangarr* to the founding ancestors of particular clans. Elsewhere I have referred to these stories as myths of inheritance (Morphy 1977). These are of a fairly standard form and are additional to the myths of origin. A typical myth would go: 'An Ancestral being X then gave the designs, songs and sacred objects that originated through the land-transforming *wangarr* events that occurred in place Y, to the founding human ancestors of group Z. And he said that no one else should use the designs without permission and that the designs and land would belong to the group Z forever as long as they continued to perform the ceremonies as they had been shown'.

Clan designs thus encode a triadic relationship between a particular social group, an Ancestral being or set of Ancestral beings, and a particular area of land. The relationship between the people and the land is one of ownership, that between Ancestral beings and the land one of creation, and that between the Ancestral beings and the social group one of authorization or designation. Today paintings are referred to both as title deeds for the land and as copyright (Morphy 1983). From the perspective of this ideal model, the system of clan designs creates a landscape of an almost tartan-like pattern occupied by people who are stamped with the designs of their respective countries and who maintain rights in that country over time by virtue of patrilineal descent.

What we have so far is essentially a synchronic model of the system of clan designs; it is a model that is concerned with the ideological essence of the system, not a model of the system in operation over time. It is not the only model that can be constructed from Yolngu exegesis and it is one that must to an extent be contradicted by experience. From an etic perspective it is quite clear that, given the average size of Yolngu clans, the relationship between people, Ancestral beings and land must be full of discontinuities over time. The average Yolngu clan (cf. Warner 1958; Peterson 1972) numbers around fifty people, and clans range in size between one and around 250 members (Keen 1982). Demographic factors alone would suggest that every decade or so some clan becomes extinct while others split to form new clans. This is especially so as the marriage system and political structure tend to favour large clans over small ones, a point I will return to later (cf. Keen 1982). From the Yolngu perspective, evidence of this process of the decline and fall, or the fission and fusion, of clans abounds. There are always one or two clans on the point of extinction; there is invariably a hole somewhere in the tartan where the thread of continuity between social group and the Ancestral past has been temporarily broken and no one has yet repaired the gap. Much Yolngu politics, indeed, is concerned with taking over the land and the ceremonies and designs of an extinct clan, and well-defined rules exist on which such claims may be based (Morphy 1978; Peterson, Keen and Sansom 1977; Williams 1983). However, although Yolngu have clearly defined procedures for succession — for the recognized transfer of rights in a set of designs and an area of land from one group of people to another — it is rare to find a land-owning group that acknowledges its ownership to be the result of a recent transaction rather than an Ancestral event. The transaction appears to be rapidly forgotten and replaced by a myth of inheritance that re-establishes continuity between the present and the Ancestral past. So although there are well defined procedures for adjusting the relationships between people, Ancestors and land, it appears that the ideal model is rapidly reinstituted. A detailed analysis of the system of clan designs shows clearly that it reflects such historical processes and that it is able to accommodate future changes.

Clan designs

The dynamics of clan designs

Yolngu society, together with natural species and the universe, is divided into two patrilineal moieties, Dhuwa and Yirritja. Each clan belongs to either the Dhuwa or the Yirritja moiety and the land is likewise classified as belonging to one or the other; the clans themselves are exogamous groups with an ideology of patrilineal descent.

According to Yolngu ideology, a clan's paintings are jointly owned by the members of the clan, and the ownership of designs reflects this pattern (on the surface at least). However, I will show that designs have the potential to distinguish between groups at a lower level than that of the clan. Designs are not associated with the clan's territory as a whole; each design is associated with a particular part of the clan's territory. This means that the system has the potential to reflect changing social and demographic realities by encoding new relationships between people, places and Ancestral beings.

Furthermore, clan designs signify particular social groups not in isolation, but in the context of a network of relationships of similarity and difference with other groups at the same level of organization. The designs always have dual reference: they refer to a particular Ancestral being or group of such beings, and to a social group which is associated with it. Clan designs show similarities with other designs belonging to the same Ancestral track, and with designs deriving from the actions of the same Ancestral being. At this level, then, designs refer to the system of mythologically defined relationships between groups.

Similar designs belonging to a number of different groups linked by the same mythological track will be termed 'Ancestral design sets'. Similarity does not imply identity: each clan's design differs by at least one feature from those of other clans who own a design belonging to the same set. There is no overlap in the design sets of clans belonging to opposite moieties, since the *wangarr* beings are moiety-specific. Figures 14.1 and 14.2 include a number of clan designs belonging to clans of the two moieties. Although the designs within each moiety show considerable variation, it is possible to suggest ways in which Yirritja moiety designs, as a set, differ from Dhuwa moiety designs. Thus Yirritja moiety designs (Figure 14.1) can be divided into two main types: diamond designs and open diamonds. A further design type, pointed ovals, is used by three of the southern Yirritja clans. This differs from the other designs in that it does not always occur in linked chains. Other Yirritija designs are sets of linked triangles and zigzags. Diamond designs are always drawn as a series of separate strings of diamonds linked top to bottom. They may or may not touch the chains at either side, depending upon which clan the design belongs to. Within a section of a painting, Yirritja clan designs are not broken up by changing the orientation of the geometric element employed: strings of elements all follow the same orientation.

Dhuwa moiety clan designs consist, in the majority of cases, of combinations of squares, curved and straight parallel lines, and circles. In several cases, differences between clan designs are due to variations in the orientation of the elements employed (see Figure 14.2).

Yirritja moiety clan designs

I will examine in detail only those designs which belong to the clans of the Yirritja moiety. The analysis and the conclusions drawn apply equally to Dhuwa moiety clan designs, since the system operates in the same way for both moieties.

Figure 14.1 lists the basic series of Ancestral design sets that I have identified for Yirritja moiety clans, and the clans that own them. The design owned by each clan is a variant on the basic design type illustrated. In all cases clans sharing a design of the same set are believed to be connected by the journeys of Ancestral beings. In some cases the designs belonging to a set are primarily associated with a single Ancestral being (although other Ancestral beings will also be associated with the design in the territories of particular clans). For example the triangle pattern is always associated with the whale *wuy-mirri*. In other cases, designs are linked to a constellation of Ancestral beings, the particular ones emphasized varying from clan to clan.

The basic diamond pattern is associated with at least three major Yirritja moiety Ancestors: sugar bag (*birrkurda*), fire (*gurtha*) and yellow ochre (see also Berndt and Berndt 1949: 320). In the case of the Mun-

Figure 14.1: Main Yirritja moiety design types, and owning clans.

Design type	Clans owning variant of design type
 diamond	Dharlwangu, Gumatj 1, Gumatj 2, Gumatj 3, Mardarrpa, Munyuku, (Gupapuyngu-Daygurrgurr), (Gupapuyngu-Birrkili), (Ritharrngu)
 open diamond	Mardarrpa, Manggalili, Munyuku, Wan.guri, (Guyamirrilili), (Gorlpa), (Ritharrngu), (Wuwulkara)
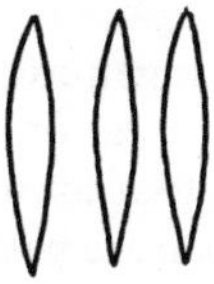 pointed oval	Dharlwangu, Mardarrpa, Munyuku
 triangle	Gumatj 1, Gumatj 2, Munyuku, Waramirri, (Gupapuyngu-Birrkili), (Lamamirri), (Mildjingi), (Gorlpa)
 zigzag	Dharlwangu, Manggalili, Munyuku, Wan.guri, (Gupapuyngu), (Ritharrngu)

Note: Clans enclosed in parentheses are not resident at Yirrkala. Information on the designs was obtained from paintings in the Donald Thomson collection and from Groger-Wurm (1973), in addition to my own field data.

Figure 14.2: Dhuwa moiety clan design types.

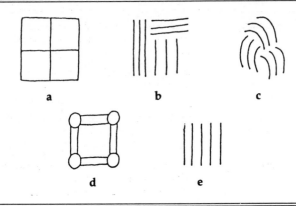

yuku and Dharlwangu clans the primary referent for it is sugar bag, and in the case of the Mardarrpa and Gumatj clans it is fire. However, fire also travelled through Dharlwangu and Munyuku country, and sugar bag through Gumatj country. Fire and sugar bag are best seen as a constellation of Ancestors that share an overlapping route, with different clans whose territories lie on those routes emphasizing one or the other. The yellow ochre Ancestor is centered on the ochre quarry at Gurrurunga which is primarily owned by the Yarrwirdi (Gumatj 3) clan.

Although clans sharing members of the same Ancestral design set are all linked by the journey of one or more Ancestral beings, each clan has one or more distinct myths which refer to the origin of its own clan designs. Myths referring to the origin of the diamond pattern of different clans are summarized in Table 14.1. Myth 2 is shared in some form by all the clans owning the sugar bag Ancestor. The myths at one level confirm the distinctiveness of the events that took place in each locality. Thus although there are basic similarities between the designs, they belong to different clans and are associated with different Ancestral events. This distinctiveness is contradicted at other levels, however. Myths 3 and 5 refer to the origin of the diamond design with respect to the fire Ancestor. The same fire is acknowledged to be involved in both cases. It is also believed to have travelled in a particular direction from Baaniyala in Mardarrpa country to Yarrwirdi Gumatj country in Caledon Bay. Although the main events of myth 3 took place at Baaniyala, the fire was carried from there to Caledon Bay by the crocodile. Thus the myth belongs both to Mardarrpa and Yarrwirdi Gumatj, and provides a link between these two clans which is not shared with other

Table 14.1: Summary of myths concerning the origin of diamond clan designs.

Myth 1	Dharlwangu	The design represents the marks of water-weed on the back of the freshwater turtle.
Myth 2	Munyuku Dharlwangu Gupapuyngu	The design represents the honeycomb of the *wangarr* sugar bag.
Myth 3	Mardarrpa Gumatj 3	The design was formed on the back of the *wangarr* crocodile (*baaru*) by the burning stringy-bark hut which stuck to his back.
Myth 4	Gumatj 3	The design represents the pattern made in the yellow ochre quarry at Gurrurunga by the *wangarr* goanna as he dug the ochre with his stick.
Myth 5	Gumatj 1 Gumatj 2	The design originated from the marks burnt into a wooden clapstick as the fire burnt through a ceremonial ground.
Myth 6	Gumatj 1 Gumatj 2	The design was made by the marks left on the sheets of paper-bark that a *wangarr* sugar-bag hunter stripped from a tree and folded as he searched for honey.

clans at Yirrkala which own diamond designs. A further myth (myth 5) describes how fire was carried from where the clapstick was burnt, in Gumatj 2 country in Caledon Bay, to other more northern Yirritja clans by the quail (*djirrikitj*). This myth concerns events that took place in Gumatj 2 country, and is not connected with Mardarrpa crocodile except through being an event at a later stage in the journey of the fire. Along their length, mythological tracks are typically characterized by such discontinuous but overlapping sequences of events, which provide a series of potential links between the groups that they connect.

Connections between different mythological tracks may be stated in terms of paintings: elements of different myths may be encoded in the same painting. Plate 14.3 illustrates a painting by Liyawulumu of the yellow ochre quarry at Gurrurunga. The painting encodes elements associated with the fire myth and the ochre quarry. The yellow diamonds signify the ochre dug away by the Ancestral goanna, and the red diamonds signify the flames of the fire as it passed through the area. Plate 14.4 illustrates a similar phenomenon in a Munyuku painting. At one level the barred diamond design represents sugar bag, the outline representing the honey comb, the bar representing sticks inside the hive and the cross-hatching representing bees. The pattern is also said to represent fire, specifically the fire caused by Laanydjung, an Ancestral being, who threw paper-bark brands around the country as he tried to drive the bees from their hive. In this case the cross-hatching represents smoke, and the design as a whole represents paper-bark brands rolled around a wooden core.

Like the closed diamond, the open diamond pattern is also linked with a number of Ancestors, and can occur on paintings referring to several Ancestral beings. The set of Ancestors linked with it does not overlap with the Ancestors associated with closed diamond patterns, although individual clans may possess the right to produce designs belonging to both sets. The open design is shared by all the clans belonging to what Warner (1958: 34) terms the Manjikay phratry. The clans sharing variants of this design are listed in Figure 14.1. These clans are linked by one of two major Ancestral beings, *gardawark* (mangrove tree) or *dukurrurru* (giant boulder), the majority of the clans having rights in both. In the case of the mangrove tree, one meaning for the design that is shared by all clans is related to the mangrove worm (*tereda* sp.). The mangrove tree travelled through saltwater and freshwater places. Some clans own sacred objects representing it in its freshwater aspect (for example the Wan.guri) and others own objects representing it in its saltwater aspect (for example Manggalili). The mangrove worms are said to be alive when the mangrove tree is in saltwater places and dead when it is in freshwater places. In paintings referring to freshwater places, the open diamond design signifies the calcareous tube of the worm. In the case of paintings associated with the boulder Ancestor the design is said to represent a species of fresh-water plant, the species varying according to the clan and the place represented. In Manggalili paintings it represents the leaves of the *yoku*, a freshwater lily. The *yoku* occurs in rivers that were made by the *dukurrurru* boulder as it came downstream from Burrwanydji in Ritharrngu country. *Yoku* leaves are carried downstream by the wet season floodwaters and taken far out to sea. This is given as a reason why *yoku* is a meaning for the open diamond design in both fresh- and saltwater places.

The fact that a number of clans share common designs belonging to the same set does not necessarily mean that they form a ceremonial group which comes together as a unit to perform ceremonies associated with the particular Ancestral being. Such a set of clans simply represents the maximum extension at any one point in time of clans acknowledged to have an interest in a particular Ancestor or set of Ancestors. The sharing of designs represents a potential ideological basis for the joint performance of ceremonies, but it does not entail such a relationship. However, the fact that Ancestral beings link countries of different clans is exploited in ritual and is indeed a key struc-

Plate 14.3: A painting by Liyawulumu of the Gumatj
clan. The painting represents an area of coastal land at
Caledon Bay. The bottom left panel represents the ochre
quarries at Gururunga associated with the Ancestral
goanna. Sea birds are shown walking along the beach
beneath the cliffs. The Yirritja crocodile brought fire to
Caledon Bay from where it was carried by the quail
(*djirrikitj*). The lighter diamonds (yellow) represent yellow
ochre pits and the darker diamonds (red) fire.

Plate 14.4: A painting by Dula of the
Munyuku clan. The painting represents a view of
the wild honey-fire complex at Mandjawuy inland
from Blue Mud Bay.

tural component of the ceremonial system (Morphy 1984).

Design differentiation

Figure 14.3 illustrates the diamond patterns owned by the Yirritja moiety clans at Yirrkala. They are drawn according to peoples' specifications of significant features which distinguish their clan designs from those of other clans. Every informant agreed on where these differences lay. The differences are essentially relational: a Munyuku diamond should be larger than a Dharlwangu diamond, and a Gumatj one should be elongated relative to both. Open diamond patterns are differentiated from one another in a similar way. In this case the main parameters along which designs vary are length and width of each diamond, and whether the basic pattern is outlined by a single line or multiple lines.

Designs vary from one another in ways other than their shape. Two other features may serve to differentiate them: the details of the infill design and, in the context of whole paintings, the way in which they are combined with other geometric elements including other clan designs. Munyuku and Dharlwangu diamonds, for example, sometimes have a bar drawn down their centre. Manggalili open diamonds are often outlined with a dotted line in two or more colours. Dotted line infill is a general characteristic of Manggalili paintings which differentiates them from all others.

Dharlwangu diamonds are not only smaller than Munyuku ones, but can also combine with other elements in a different way. Plate 14.5 illustrates a Dharlwangu painting in which the chain of diamonds is broken up by the inclusion of a pointed oval, and the design is bordered by a multiple zigzag pattern. This particular combination of elements occurs only in Dharlwangu paintings. The open diamond design in Munyuku paintings also occurs with variations in Manggalili paintings. In Munyuku paintings it can only occur as a single chain enclosed within another component, whereas in Manggalili paintings the design may be repeated any number of times.

Particular variants of a clan design, and variation in the way in which it is combined with other elements in a painting, can signify different parts of a clan's territory associated with the same Ancestral complex, or different events that took place along the same mythological track. Thus the Dharlwangu design is associated with inland parts of the clan's territory around Gaarngarn. The pointed ovals signify waterholes, and the zigzag design represents streamers of water weed. The presence of dots representing air bubbles in the water indicates that the painting represents freshwater country around the river (Figure 14.4). Absence of dots signifies that the painting represents dry country at a distance from the river.

Figure 14.3: Variants of the diamond design type.

Clan design	Owning clan	Description
	Dharlwangu	Equilateral diamond, smaller than the Munyuku one.
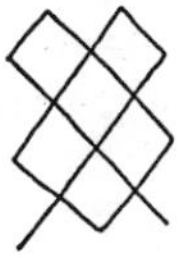	Munyuku	Equilateral diamond, larger than the Dharlwangu one.
	Gumatj 1 Gumatj 2	Elongated diamond, shorter than the Gumatj 3 one.
	Gumatj 3	Elongated diamond, longer than the Gumatj 1 and Gumatj 2 one.
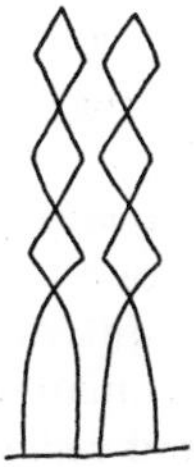	Mardarrpa	Separate strings of elongated diamonds, ending in ∩∧

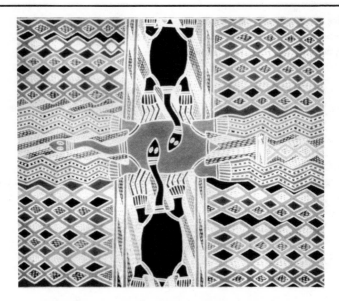

Plate 14.5: A painting by Yanggarriny of the Dharlwangu
clan representing the long-necked fresh-water tortoise at
Garngarn emerging with streamers of water weed
attached to his limbs.

Differences in the colour of infill may also signify different topographical referents of the design. The main difference between the
Dhuwa moiety Rirratjingu clan designs for Nhulunbuy and those for
Bremmer Island is that the former include black cross-hatching as infill
for elements of the design, whereas the latter do not.

The set of paintings owned by a clan

Yolngu clans generally hold rights of ownership in a number of different areas of land, each of which may be associated with a different
Ancestral being or set of Ancestral beings, and each of which may be
associated with different clan designs. Thus whereas Ancestral design
sets link a number of clans along the same mythological track, each clan
owns a unique constellation of designs, the majority of which relate to
different tracks. Thus clan designs, rather than being associated with a
clan's territory as a whole, refer to parts of it only. The set of designs
belonging to a particular clan will be referred to as a 'clan's design set'.
   Figure 14.5 illustrates the clan designs owned by the Munyuku clan,
and shows the main *wangarr* beings and the main area of the clan's
territory with which each design is associated. Each design is more

Figure 14.4: Dharlwangu clan design variants.

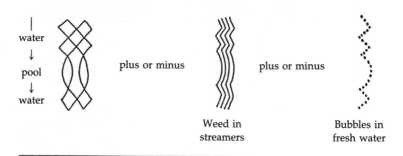

closely associated with one particular Munyuku subgroup than it is with the others. However, the clan members publicly acknowledge joint ownership of all the designs and the associated areas of land.

Figure 14.6 shows the way in which Munyuku clan designs are linked to the designs of other clans at Yirrkala. The zigzag design is linked with two places, Yarrinya and Mayawunydji, which are on separate Ancestral tracks. A variant of the design is also owned by the Manggalili clan. In the Manggalili case, the design is said to be an outside one (that is, one used in publicly displayed paintings) for paintings connected with saltwater places. In the Munyuku case it is also a design representing saltwater. Yarrinya is on the coast, and Mayawunydji is on estuarine swamplands which are partly inundated by the high tides.

The Munyuku diamond pattern is linked with the Gupapuyngu, Dharlwangu, Mardarrpa, and the three Gumatj clans: that is, the clans which share the *birrkurda* (sugar bag) and *gurtha* (fire) Ancestors. The linked triangles are shared with the Gumatj clans and with the Warramiri and Gorlpa. In all cases they are associated with the whale Ancestor, and in three cases (Gumatj 2, Warramiri and Gorlpa) with the crayfish. The pointed oval is shared with the Mardarrpa and the Dharlwangu. In all cases it is linked with *mikarran*, the yellow snake. *Mikarran* is an Ancestral being for all the Yirritja moiety clans. The oval design refers to the connection between Mardarrpa, Dharlwangu and Munyuku with respect to an Ancestral fish trap created by the snake at the north of Blue Mud Bay. The open diamond pattern links the Munyuku to the Manggalili and Wan.guri clans.

Figure 14.5: Designs owned by the Munyuku clan.

Design	Place	*Wangarr* being
	Mandjawuy	*Birrkurda* (wild honey)
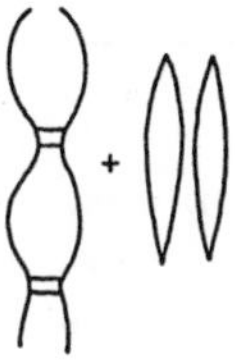	Mayawunydji	*Mundukul* (yellow snake)
	Mayawunydji and Yarrinya	Salt water design
	Yarrinya	*Wuymirri* (whale) and *Maardi* (crayfish)

Clan designs and social process

The artifice of unity and the creation of clans

The Durkheimian model of Australian totemism and its subsequent developments share with the Yolngu model of the Ancestral origin of clans the assumption that the existence of the clan is unproblematic. It has rightly been taken as significant for some time now that any particular set of clans is a temporally based structure of groups that are often ill-defined around the edges. Although some clans may appear to be firmly in view, just as many appear imminent or on·the point of vanishing. It has also been demonstrated that societies with clans have

Figure 14.6: Designs shared by the Munyuku with other clans at Yirrkala.

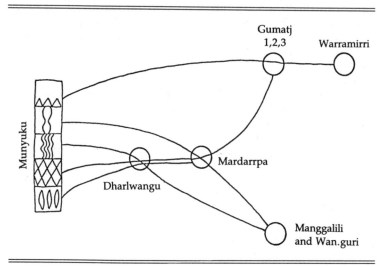

procedures for dealing with demographic contingencies and that many
have practices that create such contingencies. The vanishing of clans is
often the result of consequential and indeed intentional action. The
realization that clans are often temporary artefacts, created by the
analyst and by the consensus of members of the society, made it
fashionable for a while to relegate the clan to the status of an anthropological fiction, a faulty synchronic description. The 'real' social processes were to be found elsewhere. The debates phrased in terms of
alliance versus descent, lineal versus filiational, and institutional versus
transactional, were all to an extent preliminaries to the debate over the
relationship between structure and action which has become the central topic of current sociological theory (cf. Giddens 1979). In analyzing
Yolngu society I see no reason to reduce the clan to the status of a fig-
leaf, the removal of which will reveal an underlying reality. From many
different perspectives clans have been shown to be central components
of Yolngu social organization and of the way Yolngu talk about and act
in the world (Keen 1978; 1982; Morphy 1977; 1984; Williams 1983; 1985).
Certainly, individual clans have no permanence and their existence is
only conditional; nevertheless I will argue that the creation of clans is a
central feature of the Yolngu system, and that the reproduction of
Yolngu society involves the dynamics of the reproduction of clans.

My analysis of the system of clan designs has shown that formal
variations in design type both coincide with and cross-cut the system of

clan segmentation, depending on the perspective adopted and level of difference taken to be significant. Thus each clan owns a unique set of designs and each of those designs differs from those belonging to any other clan. From another perspective, however, the system of clan designs can be seen to be quite independent of clans, with Ancestral design sets linking places which cross-cut clan affiliation and separating places which belong to the same clan. To the extent that the system coincides with existing social divisions, it does so because it is made to. The diamond pattern is adjusted to differentiate it from that of neighbouring clans, and the myth of inheritance is created that links the different designs belonging to the group into the same clan set. The system is thus compatible with a model that sees new relationships between people, Ancestral beings and place being continually created as a consequence of demographic and political process. A clan would be that set of people that exercises collective rights of ownership in a set of designs (songs, sacred objects, and so on) and a set of countries associated with those designs (Williams 1983: 99). In the remainder of this section I will discuss some examples that suggest that this may indeed be the case.

Clan growth and the fiction of unity

Although all Yolngu clans claim to hold rights in sacred property and land jointly, it is mostly the case that in practice members exercise certain rights differentially. Clans generally own two or more distinct countries associated with different Ancestral beings and usually one section of the clan is more closely associated with one country than it is with the others. In the case of clans which contain more than one lineage, normally each lineage is most closely associated with a distinct area of land. The close association may take the form of living in or close to one area of the clan's land or of using the songs, dances and paintings from that country more than those from any of the other areas of the clan's land. In cases of clans with many separate countries and few lineages (or other subdivisions), then one or more of the countries may in effect be left vacant or unattached (cf. Keen 1982: 631). When asked, people will play down the significance of such divisions, putting them down to individual choice and personal responsibility, asserting that in fact all members have equal rights in and equal access to clan lands and ceremonies. However, the division of attachment is significant in a number of respects. It provides a focal point for the development of subgroups within a clan. It provides the basis for creating separate identities which may result in the subgroups acquiring separate names, usually names associated with the place of their primary association. It provides the potential point of fission into separate clans should the clan's size grow too large or should relations within it reach breaking point. There are several examples of clan fission having occurred in north-east Arnhem Land. In such cases the segments of the clan claim separate ownership of and rights in land that they previously held jointly, become known by separate names, and establish separate marriage relationships with other clans. Keen (1982) has shown how the Yolngu system of marriage tends to favour the growth of large clans and the subsequent fission of those clans into smaller units. Clans expand at the expense of other clans of the same moiety. Senior members of large groups are able to manipulate the marriage system so that they deny members of competing clans access to women and can rapidly engineer the extinction or decline of the smaller clans.

The extinction of clans and the consequences of take-over

When a clan nears extinction, manoeuvrings begin among clans of the same moiety to take over the land and its ceremonies.To simplify a little, clans have a good basis for making a claim if they stand in a relation of (sister's) daughter's child to the dying clan, if they are acknowledged holders of its sacred law, if they have the blessing of its last members and if they are numerically strong.This last is not so much a principle of succession as an observation of practice. Large clans are likely to win out over small clans with equally good claims. A successful take-over may take place over a considerable period of time. In one case I recorded, forty years after the death of the last member of a Yirritja moiety clan at least three clans maintained a claim over the same area of its country. All three clans advertised their claim by producing paintings belonging to the land, in each case with minor variations, and one clan had established its outstation on the estate. The rival claims showed no sign of being resolved, perhaps because of the equivalent size of two of the clans, and this occasionally resulted in open disputes between members of the respective groups. In a second case, however, the take-over was progressing very smoothly. In this case there was one acknowledged claimant, a large clan which had itself been created by the fission of a still larger unit. The new 'owner' had taken over the songs and paintings that had been used by the previous group and had begun to use them in ceremonies.

The principles of succession used by the Yolngu mean that in taking over an area of land belonging to another clan, the previous relationship between Ancestral beings and the land is maintained. No new clan designs need be created and no new myths of origin introduced — indeed knowledge of the existing ones and acceptance of responsibility for maintaining them are both conditions of legitimate take-over. What is created, however, is a new clan's set of designs and a new myth of inheritance. The second case above, for example, concerned a clan that was the product of clan fission taking over the country of an extinct clan. When the original clan split the new clan took half of the countries associated with the previous clan together with the respective ceremonial law (the designs, and so on) belonging to them. The other countries and their associated ceremonial law went to the second clan created by the division. When the first clan took over the land of the extinct clan, the countries and ceremonial law of the latter became part of the overall set owned jointly by the new clan. Over time it is likely that a new myth of inheritance will be developed which links those countries into a single clan set, whereas previously they belonged to different sets, and which projects the agreement into the Ancestral past (Morphy 1977: 96 gives an example of such a myth).

Clan fusion and the politics of unity

Another way in which the triadic relationship between Ancestors, people and land is readjusted is through the fusion of previously separate groups or the incorporation of smaller groups into larger ones. The former may enable weak clans to survive in the face of the expansion of larger ones and the latter is a means of ensuring succession in advance of extinction. The main sign of clan fusion is when groups that had previously asserted separate ownership of ceremonial law and land claim joint ownership over it. The best example I have of this process is in fact an atypical one, concerning the temporary fusion of three groups in the context of land-claim proceedings, in order to simplify the situation for European understanding. The case concerns three clans that share the same name. These three clans temporarily united to form a single clan in the late 1960s. Prior to this one of the clans owned a unique set of paintings characterized by different clan designs from the other two. The latter two clans were in fact in the process of dividing and were in a sense Siamese twins, having separate countries but with overlapping Ancestral law. The respective countries were in any case on the same Ancestral track and hence would continue to have closely related sets of songs, dances, clan designs, and so on, even after the separation was complete. In 1974 I frequently saw members of the respective clans producing what were in effect the other's paintings. When I questioned this I was informed that, at the time of the Gove Land Rights case, the clans concerned were told that it would complicate their case if there were a number of clans with the same name. The senior members of the clans therefore decided to become one group, jointly owning their land and sacred law. A sign of this was that they could produce each others' paintings without asking permission.

Whether or not the explanation I was given was the correct one, the important point is that the fusion of clans entails the decision to exercise joint rights in land and sacred law. There is evidence that today the situation is reversed, with the groups asserting their separate rights to land and sacra.

A second example of clan fusion involves a failed attempt. A man X and his son Y were the last surviving members of their clan (A). X was a man of considerable ritual knowledge and had, moreover, been entrusted with the ceremonial law of a second clan (B). Clan A and clan B had sets of paintings belonging to different Ancestral design sets, and clan A's law was closely linked to that of a third and larger clan (C). X, however, strongly asserted that his clan owned a different set of paintings from clan C and that they were associated with different countries. He refused to live at clan C's settlement and preferred to live at the settlement where the last senior member of clan B lived. Clan B, like clan A, consisted of few members. X intended to establish a settlement jointly with the members of clan B and intended that eventually the two groups should unite to form a single clan by combining the sacred law in a single set and owning land jointly. He taught his own clan's and clan B's paintings to the senior man of that clan. Other groups were hostile to his objective and he received little community support. He died while still trying to maintain his group's independence.

A year after X's death his son Y was effectively incorporated into clan C. At a Djungguwan ceremony (Keen 1978; Morphy 1977) Y had a painting of clan C placed on his chest in the seclusion of the men's ground. While the painting was being produced, leaders of other clans of the same moiety told him that it was his painting and that he belonged to clan C. They said he should forget what his father had told him and that his father had been too concerned with the paintings of other clans to teach him his own paintings (those of clan C). Instead of a new clan being created through a process of fusion, X's clan became incorporated within clan C.

The consequence of both clan fusion and incorporation is the creation of a new clan's design sets. The new clan combines the territories or parts of the territories of two previous clans. It is quite conceivable that such processes may involve parts of clans rather than whole clans, for example, one lineage of a clan being incorporated in a second clan while the remainder of the clan maintains its separate identity. Such a process would result in two new clans' design sets being formed.

Conclusion: reslicing the cake

We are now in a position to draw the separate threads of the analysis together and present an overall model of the relationship between Ancestors, land and social group. Over time some clans grow and divide, others combine and still others disappear. Thus the relationship between clans as actual groups of people and the land which such groups own is discontinuous. However the groups that take over the land and that combine countries into new sets do not necessarily alter the relationship between Ancestors and the land. The designs, songs and sacred objects are maintained in their relationship with the land at least beyond the change in ownership of the land, though there may be some minor alterations in the form of the ceremonial law, for example in the shape of the design. There are a number of reasons for this continuity. First, in order successfully to claim an area of land, the new group has to show knowledge of its Ancestral relationships, and it is entrusted with the responsibility of ensuring that such knowledge does not die out and that the ceremonies are maintained. Second, the tracks of the respective Ancestral beings cross over the lands of many different clans. Other groups will always have an interest in maintaining the continuity of Ancestral law along the length of that track and in maintaining linkages across clan boundaries. Third, rights in Ancestral law extend beyond the boundaries of a clan, and other people will see it as their responsibility to continue existing relationships between the Ancestral beings and the land, even if the new owners should want to change them (Morphy 1978; Williams 1985). Although Ancestral law clearly does change over time and although the change of ownership of land is one factor that may increase the rate of change in a particular case, the take-over of an area of land by another group does not result in the rupture of existing ceremonial law. In a sense the group taking over is made to slot into an existing system. The relationship between Ancestors and land is thus relatively continuous. The tartan on the landscape remains, and though it may fade a little in places the knowledge exists to restore it to its former glory with a similar pattern to the one it had before.

What of the relationship between Ancestral beings and people? At first this, too, would seem discontinuous, as is the case between people and the land: an old group dies out and a new group takes over. But here the individual relationship may not be the most important one. The group that takes over must don the same spiritual clothes as the old one, and in a sense the donning of clothes creates the spiritual relationship which is in continuity with the one enacted by the previous group. The contract between human beings and the Ancestral past is maintained as one set of people replace another in a continuing relationship. I have also argued elsewhere that succession by a (sister's) daughter's child's clan (one of the main principles of succession) means that a Yolngu group is succeeded by the clan of its own moiety that contains its closest living blood relatives (Morphy 1978: 219). The (sister's) daughter's child's clan is also one of the main clans with rights in its mother's mother's (brother's) clan's designs and land while that clan is still strong. These factors taken together suggest that the discontinuity between people and Ancestors is not great when one clan takes over from another.

Over time what changes most are the sets of countries that are linked together as members of the same clan's set. Each time an adjustment is made to the relationship between people, Ancestors and land it involves, if I may be permitted to switch metaphors, a new slice being cut out of the cake. However, when the slice is replaced and the cake is fitted together again it remains the same cake. And it is this latter fact that resolves the contradiction between the myths of the perpetual clan stretching from the Ancestral past to the present, and the reality of continuous flux as, over time, the cake is continually cut in different ways.

15. Yolngu religious property

Ian Keen

The application of property concepts to Aboriginal social life

An invitation to contribute to the session on 'Property' in the Fourth International Conference on Hunting and Gathering Societies led me to enquire into whether the concept of property is appropriate for thinking about the relation of the Yolngu to ritual and land. Williams (1986) deals in detail with Yolngu rights in land; this paper focuses on ritual, but relates land and ritual as inalienable property within an economy of gift-exchange.

European concepts of property have a number of dimensions, including the notion of possession, the right to use and enjoy, the right to exclude others from use and enjoyment, and the right to dispose of an object. These elements occur in varying combinations in discussions of law and of rights, and in anthropological definitions. Some scholars highlight use (Proudhon, n.d; Bentham 1931; Macpherson 1978: 104), while others give possession a central place (Green 1858; Sen Gupta 1962; Diamond 1935). Exclusion is the key element for some (Cohen 1927; Noyes 1936; Hoebel 1954); disposal plays a role in the opinion of others (Gluckman 1955; Goldschmidt 1967: 23). As J. Goody remarks (1962: 290), apart from the broad categories of use and control, property rights are subject to much variation. In my view the notion of 'control' is implied by all these elements.

The terms 'property' and 'ownership' have been used by many students of Aboriginal social life to denote rights in land, ritual and other entities, but there has been much disagreement over which rights and relations constitute 'ownership'. A shift has recently taken place away from an emphasis on some kind of patrilineal group as the 'owner' of land and associated ritual (Radcliffe-Brown 1951; Hiatt 1965) and towards a model in which a more broadly defined network of people share complementary rights (Meggitt 1962; Maddock 1981; Verdon and Jorion 1981). Some writers have described individual 'ownership' of ritual objects and songs (Meggitt 1966b: 39; Moyle 1979: 59–61). More broadly, in a model of Aboriginal social order in which gender relations are treated as class relations, Bern (1979) argues that, contrary to Meggitt, there was accumulable wealth in Aboriginal society in the form of religious property and of rights in women's productive and reproductive powers.

As for the Yolngu, Warner ascribes the ownership of land to clans and moieties, and of 'totems' and 'minute variations of the ritual' to clans (1937: 147). The ownership of land does not entail the right to exclusive use, and no songs, designs or 'magics' were owned by individuals or groups. Totems and rituals 'are not so much properties in an economic sense as integral parts of the structure of the clans', and the same is true of land to a great degree, yet 'the effect of their being part of the clan and moiety configuration has many of the attributes of our concept of property' (ibid.). Peterson (1972) writes of Yolngu (and Warlpiri) clan 'ownership' of estates. Morphy, however, distinguishes three sorts of rights to Yolngu 'sacred law': rights of ownership, vested in members of a clan; managerial rights, vested in children of women of a clan; and rights as guardians, also vested in a clan, and which can in certain circumstances be converted to ownership (1984: 29). Like Hiatt (1965), Morphy thus uses 'ownership' as a member of a set of terms to denote a certain part of a set of complementary, if ranked, rights and relations. Similarly, Williams (1986) describes as the 'land-owning group' a unit whose members are joint holders of title to land and own sacred objects and non-corporeal property. A person also has rights of responsibility in his or her mother's land and ritual. Williams describes rights in the mother's mother's land, ritual, and so on, as 'steward-ship', which entails the duty to protect the mother's mother's group and its ritual property. Only members of the patrilineal land-owning group are the 'full owners' in Williams's view (ibid.: 54).

But are the terms 'owner' and 'property' applicable at all to Aboriginal rights in land and ritual? The Judge in the renowned Gove case did not think so (*Millirrpum* v *Nabalco Pty. Ltd. and The Commonwealth of Australia* 1971). Yolngu people of the Gove Peninsula sought to prevent bauxite mining on their lands, excised from the Arnhem Land Reserve by the Commonwealth government. Judge Blackburn found that the relation between a Yolngu clan and its land was not a proprietorial one. Property rights in English and Australian law entail the right to enjoy, the right to exclude others and the right to alienate. However, clan members did not have exclusive use of their lands and they could not alienate the land (Maddock 1983: 11ff.).

In spite of findings in the Gove case, intuitively there do seem to be elements in common between Yolngu rights in ritual and land, and ownership in European culture — elements which have led anthropologists and others to use the language of property. One common element is, as I implied above, a very general power to exercise a greater degree of control over the object by an 'owner' than by others.

There are also linguistic usages in common, especially the use of the possessive case, and the idioms 'holding' or 'keeping' (*ngayathama*), and 'looking after' (*djaga*). Property concepts in European cultures, however, are related to an economy in which goods, services, land and labour are commodities. In commodity exchange the right to alienate is focal, so that the findings in the Gove case are consistent with property as a commodity. Discussion of Yolngu rights in land and ritual, on the other hand, requires a concept of property which does not entail the attributes of commodities.

Gift exchange and commodity exchange

Sansom (1982) contrasts Aboriginal concepts of 'ownership' with the Western emphasis on property as the prime object of possession. The Aboriginal economy is a service economy rather than a market economy. People own 'slices of action' such as business (an affair, a concern), trouble, a problem, or a ceremony; and they offer services. In relation to ceremony Sansom says that Aborigines own 'a warranty that licenses an order of performance and/or the thing that symbolizes the socially acknowledged capacity'. Ownership entails a capacity to generate and regenerate debt, and such debts are balanced in an overall accounting (ibid.: 134).

The goal of maximizing the number of debtors is an aspect of what Gregory (1982) defines as a 'gift economy'. Drawing on Marx and the classical economists, Mauss, and Lévi-Strauss, Gregory describes polar types of exchange and economy. Commodity exchange in a 'class-based' economy is 'an exchange of alienable objects between people who are in a state of reciprocal independence that establishes a quantitative relationship between the objects exchanged . . . [T]he principles governing the production and exchange of things as commodities are to be explained with reference to control over productive labour'. Gift exchange is 'an exchange of inalienable objects between people who are in a state of reciprocal dependence that establishes a qualitative relationship between the transactors . . . [T]he principles governing the production and exchange of things as gifts are to be explained with reference to control over births, marriages and deaths' (ibid.: 100–1).

In a class-based economy, where there is private property, a person has alienable rights over the things that he owns. This requires a sharp distinction between a thing and its owner, so that commodities are objectified or 'fetishized'. In simple commodity exchange the alienability of objects brings about a complete transfer of ownership (ibid.: 47). In a 'clan'-based economy, where there is no private property, people do not have alienable rights over things, and the objects are anthropomorphized, or in Mauss's words, 'never completely separable from the men who exchange them' (Mauss 1954: 46; Gregory 1982: 18, 41). The gift economy is a debt economy. The aim of the transactor is to acquire as many gift-debtors as possible, and not to maximize profit (Gregory 1982: 19). The personification of objects of exchange is a consequence of the inalienable relation between a gift and its producer (ibid.: 45).

More recently Weiner (1985) explores Maori 'inalienable wealth' in a Maussian framework. She is concerned with the problem of how people avoid giving things away, in order to secure social identity, and relates this question to social hierarchy. In Papua New Guinea, where political power is diffuse, stones or the bones of ancestors are believed to anchor a clan or lineage to a particular locality, securing its identity and ancestral rights. Where a society keeps some things out of circulation permanently, these things take on a heightened quality of sacredness (ibid: 211). In cases as varied as Egyptian rulers, the Trobrianders and the Australian Aborigines, things kept to oneself 'carry the affective qualities of sacredness that constitute the social self in relation to a past and future that, out of all the myriad possibilities, create a totality of ancestral identities' (ibid.: 212).

Yolngu ritual elements and land are embedded as 'inalienable property' in an economy that Gregory typifies as 'clan-based' (by contrast with class-based) — an economy in which gift-exchange is the predominant transaction, even since the introduction of money on a large scale in the 1960s.

The Yolngu exchange economy

The term 'Yolngu' refers to the Aboriginal population of north-east Arnhem Land, and includes most of those groups whom Warner called the 'Murngin'. The population of about 3500 lives in three settlements (former missions) of between 700 and over 1000, two smaller mission settlements, and numerous small 'outstations' situated on the residents' traditional lands.[1]

Yolngu property relations conform in general to Gregory's model of gift-exchange in that there is little in the way of private property, and until the introduction of money into the settlement economy in the 1960s there was no universal medium of exchange. Each adult is at the node of a nexus of exchange with every category of close relative and with some more distantly related exchange partners among whom gifts of food and artefacts (*girri*) as well as services are exchanged — this

1. The data in this paper derive from fieldwork at Milingimbi mission and nearby outstations from 1974 to 1976, and in 1980. I thank the many Yolngu people of Milingimbi and nearby communities for helping me to understand something of their culture. I thank also Chris Gregory, Basil Sansom and Richard Lee for comments, suggestions, and encouragement.

formerly linking regions of specialized artefact manufacture (Warner 1937; Thomson 1949). Men's productive labour was exchanged for rights in women as wives through bride-service to the wife's parents. *Milmarra* gifts or payments were and are made to the wife's kin throughout the duration of a marriage, and a man owes services and goods to his wife's brother on demand. As well, payments were and are made for particular specialist services such as canoe-building and ritual (Thomson 1949).

Religious elements and land (and waters) partake in the exchange system in various ways. Women's labour funded men's secret ceremonies in the past, through the provision of food. Novices gain religious knowledge in return for gifts or payments to the ritual leaders, and ritual specialists are paid for their labours. People, especially those in a relation of *ma:ri–gutharra* (MM/MMB–wDC/ZDC[2]) and *ngapipi–waku* (MB–wC/ZC), make gifts of ritual artefacts such as tassles, bracelets, bark paintings, message strings and dilly-bags. Much more rarely, one group may make a gift of the right to make or perform ritual elements. The *Marradjirri* ceremony is itself an item of exchange. A performance is commissioned from the owners who make a gift of a ceremonial pole and string in return for a gift such as a boat (Borsboom 1978; Wild 1986).

As Thomson (1949) notes, however, the Yolngu make a distinction between ritual or 'sanctified' (*maḏayinbuy*) artefacts, and 'ordinary' (*wakinngu*) artefacts. The exchange of the former is restricted to men. Furthermore, men can consecrate an ordinary artefact such as a paddle or spear, and, more recently, an electric stove, by invoking the names of Ancestral Spirit Beings over it, or by painting on an Ancestral design. This consecration has two effects. First, it enables the holder to maintain a greater degree of control over the object because of the restricted rights in clan designs and names. Second, consumption restrictions apply to food caught or processed with the aid of the object, and these become subject to the control of male leaders of the clan whose design or names are used, or of other males with rights in the design or names, such as a *waku* (wC) of the clan (see below).[3] Ritual artefacts given in exchange are inalienably bound to the original donor as tokens of types instituted by the Ancestral Spirit Being of the clan, and a sign of clan identity.

The temporary right to use land and waters that are not one's own is exchanged for gifts or payments, and part of the product of such use should be given to the 'owners'. Also, rights of ownership of small

2. This chapter uses standard anthropological abbreviations for more complex kinship relationship: M = mother; F = father; B = brother; Z = sister; S = Son; D = daughter; C = child; W = wife; H = husband; w = woman; m = man. Thus ZDC = sister's daughter's child.

3. The difference between 'ordinary' and ritual items parallels the Maori distinction between *taonga*, which possess *hau*, and objects that do not (Weiner 1985: 215).

areas within a clan estate may have been granted at some time in the past, while the 'root title' remains with the clan of the encapsulating estate. The right may be granted to members of another clan to 'look after' an estate. (Most clans have two or three distinct estates, often some distance from one another.) Land/waters and ritual holdings are somewhat insulated from the exchange network, however. Land is held by members of a clan and certain of their uterine descendants as a group, so that an individual has rights in land through filiation, and to a lesser extent, spiritual conception. Ritual elements are tied to land and waters, and are in general acquired in the same way as land.

There is, none the less, a strong connection between land and ritual holdings, and the exchange nexus. The products of land use are exchanged for rights in reproductive powers: hence the capacity to reproduce the networks which hold land and ritual. Men sometimes bestow a daughter or sister's daughter as a wife in return for religious knowledge, but there is a more fundamental structural connection between religious practice and marriage. Ritual holdings are the currency in an economy of religious knowledge, which is the foundation of the authority of older men and women. This authority is fundamental to the institution of polygynous promised marriage. Gift-exchange is the transactional form which articulates use-rights in land, production and distribution, marriage bestowal and the control of reproduction, and religious knowledge.[4]

As 'inalienable property' Yolngu rights in ritual elements and land have the following features. Rights are shared in principle (as Williams 1986 points out with respect to land), even where a person has rights on the strength of an individual relationship. The basis for rights is believed to be a causal connection between the creator of the land (an Ancestral Spirit Being), the ceremony, design or sacred object, and the clan members. The property cannot be alienated, although rights can be shared with people who did not previously have them. But a gift does not extinguish the rights of the original owner, and the gift is not necessarily transferable to the descendants of the recipient. In the case of ceremony, ownership implies the right to perform the ceremony, as well as other abilities.

There is some individual private property, however. Individuals or families have exclusive possession (if not exclusive use-rights) of objects such as houses, spears, dogs and cassette-players. Nevertheless, a person has to take steps to guard against others demanding an object as a gift, such as making sure that he or she has only sufficient for personal use, or by hiding the object. The most readily transferable

---

4. I think it is not unreasonable to include feuding, motivated largely by competition among men for bestowals, as a mode of exchange, for it was informed by the same goal of reciprocity, and payments could be made to end a dispute.

items are food, money and everyday artefacts. In the case of these items I do not think that chains of debt are created by the connection of the original donor to an object that has passed from hand to hand, as in Gregory's model. Nevertheless Thomson's (1949) informant Rraywala did speak of the obligation to send objects along 'roads' or 'paths' (*dhukarr*) in the proper direction, and of the obligation to make return gifts. Religious property and rights in land, on the other hand, conform closely to Gregory's ideal type.

We can thus place different kinds of object, or rather rights in different kinds of object (and also in persons), along a continuum of alienability. At the most readily alienable end of the continuum are food and everyday objects; next come ritual artefacts which are publicly accessible — and perhaps use-rights in land are of a similar order; then come esoteric ritual artefacts, or artefacts which bear esoteric designs or names; and finally religious ceremonies as types, and also land. Different kinds of object circulate among distinct categories of people along age, gender and kin-relational lines.

Yolngu ritual

Just as the Yolngu have no general terms for 'owner' or 'property', nor any specialized property law, there is no specialized system of government or of law. Instead, customary laws or jural rules are encoded in a regime which conforms rather closely to Weber's (1947) ideal type of gerontocratic traditional authority. Laws or jural rules are believed to have been laid down by Ancestral Spirit Beings. The religious 'law' (*rom*) is seen as a received and unchanging tradition which the older people hand down to younger people. The authority of older men in particular derives from their apparent access to supernatural powers, as well as from their control of secret religious knowledge, to which men are gradually admitted, and from which women are largely excluded.

The Yolngu refer to the body of beliefs, norms and practices associated with Ancestral Spirit Beings (*wangarr*) as *rom*, or, in English, 'law' or 'culture'. Myths describe events involving one or more Spirit Beings, often with the names and attributes of non-human species, or entities such as water or a hollow log. The Beings travelled, foraged, camped, defecated or menstruated, copulated, fought other Beings. The land and waters are full of the signs of these activities and of transformed substance of the Beings in the form of rocks, gullies, creeks and hills, trees and waterholes, bodies of ochre, and so on. Some Beings are believed to live in deep waters, others to be moving with the tide. Some Beings created human groups and instituted the songs and ceremonies which 'follow' their precedent. The powers of the Beings are also thought to be present in associated designs and (I believe) names, as well as places. Thus each song, design and dance is related to a specific Being, the place or places where the respective event occurred, and the clan which possesses that country. Mythical journeys link the estates of several clans of the same moiety, which have similar ceremonies and ceremony elements apparently as a consequence of the mythical events. Religious practices both describe and 'follow' the activities of the *wangarr*, and the objects and places associated with them, or which they created.

Yolngu ceremonies form three implicit sets which I have labelled public, regional, and the *Nga:rra* revelatory ceremony (Keen 1978). Due to limitations on length, this chapter focuses on public ceremonies, and within that genre, rights in songs. A ceremony is a complete event with a programme, possessing either a descriptive name such as 'hollow log', or a proper name such as Djalumbu (which is the proper name of a specific hollow log coffin). Elements of ceremonies which may be recombined to form many different programmes include designs, objects, song types and dances.

The word *madayin* refers to a set of ceremonies, designs, songs, objects and entities associated with one or more *wangarr* or to any member of the set. I shall gloss the word as 'sacra' here. The religious law of each exogamus patrilineal moiety (Dhuwa and Yirritja) is discrete in its definition and primary affiliation, although Spirit Beings cross the estates of clans of the opposite moiety in myth, and interact with Beings of the opposite moiety. Elements of the ritual complexes are 'held' and 'looked after' by individuals and groups. The network of holders of each distinct complex centres on a clan, although it extends beyond the clan, so that a person of one moiety 'holds' and performs the ceremonies of both moieties.

Clans and kin networks

Rights in religious elements and land are held by clans, sets of clans (clans-aggregate), and networks of kin related through uterine links to clans.

Yolngu clans are patrifilial kin groups (Scheffler 1978) of between one and 230 members (mean 42.3 in 1976). Although members of some clans are descended from a common ancestor, many clans consist of several distinct patrilineages of up to five generations' depth, whose ancestors' genealogical relations are not known. Most clans hold several estates, often separated by distances of up to sixty kilometres, as well as small areas embedded in the estates of other clans; they also hold the associated rituals, sacred objects, songs and designs.

Clan members have an unqualified right of access to any one of the clan estates, and jointly hold and perform the clan songs and dances.

Some clans are divided into discrete land-holding units, each referred to as the 'people of X place' (X-*wuy mala* = X-*wuy*) group, among which the lineages are divided. The land-holding units of the same clan may make somewhat different designs and hold some different sacred objects, but they assert their unity and hold joint rights in land, and the members join together to perform their whole corpus of rituals (see Morphy 1977: 51).

The suffix -*watangu* denotes the primary relationship between persons, land and sacra, and can be glossed 'holder of'.[5] According to the Gupapuyngu dictionary (Lowe n.d.) the suffix denotes 'ownership'. In relation to clan land, clan members are individually and severally *wa:nga-watangu* (land-*watangu*). In relation to the clan sacra they are *madayin-watangu*. The suffix -*watangu* applies also to a person's relationship with the land and sacra of his or her mother's, mother's mother's and MMM's clans:

wa:nga-watangu	members of the clan in question
ngandi-watangu (mother-*watangu*) or *ngamini-watangu* (breast-*watangu*) or *waku-mala* (wC-group)	people whose mothers are or were of the clan in question
ma:ri-watangu (MM-*watangu*) or *gutharra-mala* (wDC-group)	people whose mother's mothers are or were of the clan in question
waku-watangu (MMM-watangu) or *ngandi/ngapipi mala* (wDDC-group)	people whose mother's mother's mothers are or were of the clan in question

---

5. That -*watangu* has the sense 'holder of' is supported by linguistic evidence. The form -*ngu* is a nominalizing suffix (Schebeck 1968: 31). The following appear to be cognates of the first syllable (Lowe n.d.):

bat	an interjection or particle associated with the verb *ngayathama*, 'hold'
gat-thun (*gat* + verbalizer)	caught, stuck in the throat
watthun	stick up
watthu-watthun	stick out, poke out
gatthun	caught, stuck in the throat
gatmarama	catch
gattjarrarra'yun	slide (*djarrarra'yun* = 'slide', 'drift', hence 'hold-slide')
gattjarrkthun	slide (*djarrkthun* = 'scrape', hence 'hold/catch-scrape')

The sounds *w*, *b*, *g* and *k* are allophones. On this evidence the suffix-*watangu* has the sense 'holder,' or perhaps 'one who stands in relation to' or 'one who catches hold of'.

I shall gloss these terms and relations 'land-holders', 'mother-holders', 'MM-holders' and 'MMM-holders', in preference to 'owners', 'guardians', and so on, since the latter terms have misleading connotations.

Individuals and clans in a MM–wDC (*ma:ri-gutharra*) relation are of the same patri-moiety, whereas people and clans in a relation of M–wC, or MMM–wDDC are in opposite moieties. Since clans, land and sacra are divided between the two moieties, a transfer of rights from one clan to another can only occur within the moiety, usually between individuals and their mother's mother's (*ma:ri*) clan. The land-holders comprise a social group, a clan, but the set of mother-holders and the MMM-holders comprise networks of people, usually members of several clans, having mothers in the same clan. The MM-holders form a similar network, although according to Morphy (1984) the *ma:ri-gutharra* (MM/MMB–wDC) relation between clans as wholes is important in ceremonies in the eastern region of north-east Arnhem Land.

The above terms apply to people by virtue of their clan membership or their individual kin relationship to a clan other than their own. Some rights in a clan's land and sacra are also held by members of other clans of the same clan-aggregate — a named set of clans of the same patri-moiety. A clan-aggregate is distinct from a clan in that it is divisible into its constituent clans. Moreover, the rights of members of one clan in the land and sacra of another clan of the same clan-aggregate differ from their rights in their own land and sacra.

Yolngu religious practice divides people into age and gender categories which cut across the categories of 'holders'. The young are gradually admitted to religious competence and knowledge through participation and revelation. Men and women have distinct dance styles; only men may paint certain designs and sing *manikay* and *bilma* songs, while women sing mourning songs. Only men take the role of *djirrikaymirri* (Dhuwa moiety) or *dalkarramirri* (Yirritja moiety) to lead ceremonies and invoke the names of Spirit Beings, and only men are admitted to esoteric aspects of ceremonies and to esoteric meanings of songs and designs. The one exception is the Gunapipi ceremony in which women conduct an aspect to which adult men are not admitted. Furthermore, men may recognize that an older woman is very knowledgeable of the religious law, and the oldest woman of a clan may 'hold' and 'look after' sacred objects such as a ritual digging stick or dilly-bag. Thus it is within the network of holders that powers to control bodies of religious knowledge and practice are differentiated on the bases of age and gender.

I turn now to examine rights in the public genre of ceremonies in some detail.

Public ceremonies

Public (*garma*) ceremonies have a variety of purposes including circumcision initiation of males, disposal of the dead, purification, exchange, greetings and partings, dispute settlement, and simple entertainment. They are composed from named series of *manikay* songs, performed with clapping-stick and dronepipe accompaniment, and related dances, painted designs, sand sculptures and objects. The song-series are classified topographically as forest, plains, saltwater, freshwater, swamp, beach and other series (Warner 1937; R.M.Berndt 1948; Keen 1978; Clunies-Ross and Hiatt 1977; Borsboom 1978; Morphy 1984). These elements are distinct for each moiety, every clan possessing several series, each of which it shares with several other clans of the same moiety. Clans also combine to possess the public ceremonies with proper names — the Exchange ceremonies and the Hollow Log reinterment ceremonies.

Public ceremonies have flexible programmes. Each performance is made up from a large repertoire of songs, dances, designs, and so on, which can be varied and elaborated in an infinite number of ways. The performance of *manikay* songs is at the core of the public ceremonies.

A song-series with its related myths, objects, dances and designs forms a complex which is possessed as a unit by clans, clans-aggregate and individuals as members of clans. With each complex related to a topographical category such as forest, swamp or sea, every clan possesses several complexes appropriate to the topography of its country. The songs are (at one level) about some of the contents of such an environment, and refer to particular places on a clan's estate. At another level they are about the activities of *wangarr* Ancestral Spirit Beings.

The Yolngu represent each song-series as a journey made by the Ghost or *wangarr* through the country, and as a passage of time from sunrise to sunset. Myths account for the relation of a song to a place and to a Spirit Being, and many songs have myths associated with them. The man who explained the songs to me would say, 'There is a story for this song', and then relate it.

Both musical and semantic dimensions of song are important in matters of ownership. The Yolngu differentiate tunes (*mayali, rirrakay*) and clapstick rhythms (*bilma*), and assign tunes, rhythms, songs and song-series to clans. Each of a clan's song-series has its own particular tune or tunes, although singers may use other clans' tunes for some songs. So in possessing or using several song-series, one clan may use several tunes. But each tune is used by several clans, and so clans are related by having 'the same tune'. Clans of the same moiety share women's and men's dances where they share the same song, for the dances are performed to the songs. Each clan is related to several sets of clans (clans-aggregate) in having the same song-series, or set of related series, and the same-named Hollow Log and Exchange ceremonies.

A clan may use complexes not strictly its own. Daygurrgurr clan men, for example, say that the forest songs which they use are properly Wora clan songs, and are their own *ma:ri* (MM/MMB). Their own true songs are Birrkili clan Sea songs about the Ghost at their island estate. Daygurrgurr and Birrkili are unified as Gupapuyngu clan-aggregate, 'Up-country People', and have a common tongue of that name.

A clan-centred view of Yolngu social organization is not adequate, for clans-aggregate are highly relevant to the control and performance of public ceremonies. Such categorical relationships are manifested in various kinds and degrees of cooperation in the performance of rituals. Clans with the same song and tune are able to sit together and sing, and members of one may take the place of members of the other in a ceremony.

Thus *manikay* songs and other elements make connections within and between clans. However, particular features, as well as the total configuration, mark a clan's identity, and such differentiating features are jealously guarded. A clan's song-series is slightly different from others in the same set, and each clan's total constellation of songs is unique. Whereas clans may share many topics in common, and songs about these *madayin*, each represents the topic in a rather different way — as a dance, as a message string, as its major Ancestral Being, and so on. Similarly, Morphy (1977; 1984) shows how certain infill patterns of painted designs are particular to each clan, whereas other forms are shared among sets of clans with the same Ancestral Spirit Being. Minor differences among sacred objects with the same general form perform that same function. The following myth illustrates the way in which such differences may be guarded, while at the same time connections are made:

> Murayana Ghost went from Wora clan country to the Ritharrngu clan estate, and found the Ritharrngu men making the Djalumbu Hollow Log coffin and the Stringybark Exchange ceremony pole. They called him over to see, but he cried, 'My pole is pointed but yours is blunt. Cut it!' Murayana was covered with pointed designs of flowers and plants, and he said, 'I will carry all the designs to Djiliwirri [Daygurrgurr clan estate]; thus we have the same ceremony'. He went off, laughing.

Another version of the myth tells how Murayana was jealous and angry at the men using the pointed pole. He told them to cut it, and called out his clan names.

Each clan or more cohesive clan-aggregate performs an identifying men's dance at public ceremonies. For example Gupapuyngu clan-aggregate men dance Emu, Ganalbingu men dance Magpie Goose,

Dambugawumirr men dance Djang'kawu Sisters and Djambarrpungu dance Shark or King Brown snake.

Roles in public ceremonies are organized on the bases of sex, age, competence and kin relation to the focal clan. Men can sing their own and *ma:ri* songs, and people can perform dances of their own, their mother's, their mother's mother's, and their MMM's clans. As Williams (1986) points out, people have the right to be consulted with reference to their mother's and mother's mother's clan ritual, and a man has the duty to make and decorate his mother's clan's sacred objects. Men paint or make sand-sculptures of the designs of their own, their mother's and mother's mother's clans. I have heard two leaders of a large and powerful clan sing songs with tunes belonging to clans of the same moiety, in each case not their actual MM/MMB's clan, but a clan of the same clan-aggregate. In one case the men of the clan were said not to be knowledgeable of their own songs. Within these categories of people with rights to perform, roles are defined by age and competence, with older men, for example, taking the roles of *djirrikaymirr* and *dalkarramirri*, calling out the names of ancestral beings in the invocation.

Rights in the other two genres differ somewhat from one another, and from the public ceremonies.

Regional and *Nga:rra* ceremonies

Myths about the Wa:gilak sisters explain the origin of Regional ceremonies, and inform the various acts of the ceremonies. Most northeast Arnhem Land people agree that the sisters travelled to Mirarrmina, a Liyagalaumirr clan mainland estate, where they were swallowed by a giant Snake, although Dhuwa moiety clans map their own King Brown Snake or Olive Python Spirit Ancestor on to the myth. People say that the ceremonies are Liyagalawumirr clan ceremonies, but that they are 'for everyone', Dhuwa and Yirritja. Rights also extend to other Dhuwa clans whose estates are on the Wa:gilak myth track, and/or who possess Spirit Beings and associated artefacts central to the ceremonies: a drone pipe and poles. Those possessing other sacra related to the myth and the ceremony, such as Cabbage Palm and Fishtrap, also have interests. Body designs are assigned to subsections as well as clans.

The *waku* (wC) and *gutharra* (wDC) of these clans have the same kind of rights as they do in public ceremonies of the same clans. But the *waku* also have the right to initiate and organize the ceremonies, and they have a very distinctive role in the performance of the regional ceremonies as the 'helpers'.

In the regional ceremonies moiety and subsection affiliation determine what individuals can sing and dance, as well as the roles of 'helper', 'worker' and 'manager' in Gunapipi. The *waku* take part in leading the singing and dancing, and control the manufacture of the artefacts (trenches, pits and poles). The Dhuwa moiety 'holders' may not make the artefacts. Other roles are determined by gender, age and competence, as in the other genres. Those who have rights through their own clan, their mother's, mother's mother's and MMM's clans are the main participants. Leaders among the first two of these categories can initiate a performance, but the cooperation of 'land-owners' and *waku* is required.

Ownership of the Dhuwa *Nga:rra* ceremony follows from the journey of the Djang'kawu sisters passing through a clan's estate, although Dhuwa men outside the Yolngu region attribute the creation of the ceremony to other beings (Elkin 1961: 86). Clans whose main estates do not lie on the track have small places embedded in the estates of clans on the Djang'kawu track, so giving them rights in the ceremony. The Yirritja *Nga:rra* ceremony relates to several different Ancestral Spirit Beings, however, depending on the clans involved. According to Daygurrgurr men, Quail and Honeybee made the first ceremony, but Dingo is central in the Mildjingi clan ceremony (Thomson 1939b), and the creator of several Yirritja moiety clans of the hinterland is Snake-necked Tortoise. Rights in elements of the ceremony are also variously distributed among clans — yellow ochre and white clay body paint, the Digging Stick sacred object, the use of ironwood to make sacred objects, the *bilma* genre of songs (which uses no dronepipe accompaniment), and choruses which accompany the invocation of names of the Spirit Beings (*bundurr* or *likan* names) in the public ceremonies and the Nga:rra. Despite the sharing of some elements, each clan possesses a distinct set of *rangga* sacred objects which make connections and differences in the same way as the distribution of *manikay* songs, although the sets and relations do not coincide. Similarly, clans raise different sacred objects to diacritical status.

Rights to perform the *Nga:rra* ceremony are a little more complex than in the public ceremonies. In one performance I observed, men of the *Dambugawumirr* clan planned and organized the ceremony. At the performance their leader was joined by the Guyula clan leader, and both men directed the proceedings at the climax. Older women of the two clans also took leading roles during the final days' dancing. The two clans share the Djang'kawu as Ancestral Being, and have adjacent estates. Male *waku* (wC) of the organizing clan observed and also made certain calls during esoteric dances, looked after novices, played the dronepipe at the daily public dance, and collected money and food one night ostensibly to feed visiting deceased ancestors. They also helped to organize women's body painting and led the chorus during the invocation. Three women *waku* took leading roles in organizing the women's dances on the final two days.

These were the main organizing roles, but members of eleven

Dhuwa moiety and three Yirritja moiety clans participated, the Dhuwa participants painting their bodies and dancing. But the Djambarrpuyngu clan, wDC to the Dambugawumirr clan, was the most strongly represented among the non-organizers. The participating Dhuwa moiety clans, for the most part, had estates on the myth track of the Djang'kawu sisters.

To sum up, in all three genres people have rights to perform ceremonies of their own, their mothers, mother's mother's and MMM's clans, as well as clans of the same clan-aggregate, qualified by criteria of age, gender and knowledge.

Alienating the inalienable

The preceding section describes formal 'ownership' and roles, but ownership is not sufficient for the exercise of control. The Yolngu express the difference between formal ownership and powers or abilities in terms of 'knowledge' and 'ignorance' (*marnggi* = knowledgeable; *dhunga* = ignorant, unable) and 'looking after' (*djaga, djaka;* cf. Myers 1980). If one asks people for information about a ceremony in which they do not possess holding rights, or the prerogatives of age, they are quite likely to say, *'Yaka ngarra marnggi'*, 'I am not knowledgeable', or 'I am not competent'.

I said above that members of some clans do not have control of their own ceremonies, but that *ma:ri-watangu* ('MM/MMB-holders') have control on the basis of greater age and superior knowledge, and 'look after' the sacra of their *ma:ri* clan. This relationship may extend to more distantly related clans. Thus leadership is not confined to the clan, for one clan and its leader or leaders may dominate the religious affairs of another. Morphy writes in relation to clan paintings that 'if there are younger members of the owning clan, then it is the responsibility of the man possessing knowledge of the clan's paintings to pass it on to them, when they attain the right age' (1978: 210). Some evidence suggests, however, that those who control the ritual may sustain control by maintaining the ignorance of the 'land-holders'. The following case study shows how the large Daygurrgurr clan, whose leader was styled 'the headman' of the Mission by the missionaries, dominated the religious life of another Yirritja moiety clan.

Case 1

The Daygurrgurr and Birrkili clans comprise the Gupapuyngu clan-aggregate, and are in a relation of *ma:ri-gutharra*. Each has a distinct Ancestral Spirit Being, but they share many songs, public ceremonies and *rangga*. Some evidence suggests that the Birrkili clan was independent and possibly even the stronger of the two before mid-century (Warner 1937: 44; Webb 1933: 409; Thomson, unpublished field notes).

By the mid-1970s the relative position of the two clans was asymmetrical. The Birrkili clan conducted no ceremonies of their own. To my knowledge they had only one song-man, and no *ḏalkarramirri*. The one male singer, Peter, used to sing with Daygurrgurr men, and did not sing his own clan's songs. Thus members at Milingimbi Mission were largely dependent on the Daygurrgurr clan to conduct their ceremonies, although they did paint their own clan designs, for example as bark-paintings. Birrkili men explained to me that their fathers had died young without teaching them the songs. The Daygurrgurr clan leader Dh—— (actually, the nominal leader) was also their leader. Their clan estate was his estate 'of the water', that is, his country of spirit conception. If they wanted a Birrkili sand-sculpture or ceremony they had to ask the Daygurrgurr leader, who was the boss of their country, and he customarily agreed.

The Birrkili clan had two leaders; the older man lived at Elcho Island, and reputedly did not know the clan songs, while the younger man, a man of about thirty-eight who lived at the Mission, was something of an outsider, partly because of his relative youth, but also because he had been closely involved with the missionaries, and had contracted a Christian marriage. His outsider status is shown by the fact that he spent many months of the year in Darwin, and was accused of sorcery by the Djambarrpuyngu clan men after a death. The one singer was of a different lineage to the majority, and his own particular estate was distinct from those of the leader.

The Birrkili clan was not entirely dependent upon the Daygurrgurr leaders. One Birrkili man and his young Daygurrgurr clan *ma:ri* (MMB) asked the Dhaḻwangu clan of a remote outstation to perform a circumcision ceremony for their sons. Members of three other Yirritja clans (Wan.gurri, Warramiri, and Gumatj) joined with the Dhaḻwangu to perform the Sea songs and dances, which the Birrkili also possess but do not sing. Daygurrgurr clan members joined in for the invocation and chorus. The Birrkili men danced with the Dhaḻwangu, whereas they usually danced with Daygurrgurr men at the Mission.

The *de facto* Daygurrgurr clan leader was Dj——, the second oldest man of the clan (Dh—— was the nominal leader, but rather senile). Dj—— and other male members of the clan asserted that only he and two of his brothers were knowledgeable of the Birrkili Sea songs, which are 'truly' Gupapuyngu clan-aggregate songs. (The Forest series they used was attributed to the Wora clan). Dj—— told me that they never performed them because the young people did not know them. I witnessed only one performance of the Sea songs, and that was by the leader of the Garrawarrpa lineage of the Daygurrgurr clan at Ngangalala outstation, where no Birrkili clan members lived.

This was the situation in 1976. Ten years later, however, Peter was a *yindi yolngu* ('big man'), that is, a man with grey hair (and in his case, beard), and an active singer with the Daygurrgurr. He had the right to perform the Wora clan songs which the Daygurrgurr clan usually performed because they were his *ma:ri* (MM/MMB) clan songs. Significantly, one of his sons was now in his early twenties, and a confident and vigorous singer. The competence of this branch of the clan may be on the road to recovery through the rights of one man in his *ma:ri* clan songs, and the transmission of his competence to his sons.

It seems likely that the Daygurrgurr clan leaders temporarily ensured the continued incompetence of most Birrkili clan males by not performing the songs regularly and in their presence. Yolngu people learn by participating in performances over a long period, gradually taking a more and more prominent role as they get older, and as older people become less active or die. Most of the young Birrkili men and women were denied access to this learning process. The case also illustrates the importance of the father–son relationship in the transmission of knowledge.

The Daygurrgurr clan men dominated the Wobulkarra clan in a similar way.

Case 2
Wobulkarra men were not able to sing their own songs, ostensibly because the previous generation of men had died too young to teach them. At a circumcision ceremony for Daygurrgurr and Wobulkarra clan boys Dj—— sang mainly Daygurrgurr songs, and a few Wobulkarra songs. He admitted to me that he never sang many of these songs.

Dj—— had rights in Wobulkarra and Birrkili clan public ceremonies partly because the first was his actual mother's mother's clan, and the other was also in a *ma:ri* relation to him. This relationship, as well as his status as leading *dalkarramirri*, gave him a specialist role in the public ceremonies of several Yirritja moiety clans, such as the Walamangu, but because Wobulkarra clan had no knowledgeable old men, he had control of that clan's public ceremonies. Had he and his clan been less powerful it seems likely that they might have retained the nominal ownership of the invocation and *Nga:rra* ceremony, at least for a while, but not effective control. This was precisely the position of the Liyagalawumirr clan in respect of the Regional ceremonies. In 1980, after the death of Dj——, a performance of the Wobulkarra clan *Nga:rra* ceremony was the occasion of tense competition between men of the Wan.gurri clan, which is of the same clan-aggregate as the Wobulkarra, and Daygurrgurr men.

Men also compete for control of ritual within a clan, and for succession to leadership. For example, during 1976 the leader of the Waltji-mirri sublineage of the Daygurrgurr clan was anxiously awaiting the death of Dj——, his older half-brother of the Garrawarrpa sublineage of the same lineage, so that he would be leader. Dj——, the clan leader, refused to consent to the performance of a *Nga:rra* ceremony on the grounds of the other man's overt ambition.

Let me now relate these processes in the exercise of control to formal rights. Being a holder implies the right to control ritual 'property', subject to the condition that the holder is knowledgeable, both by virtue of age and also in having learned the rituals and acquired other religious knowledge. Differential powers to perform or make certain ritual elements, on the basis of differences in age and knowledge, are found within and among different categories of -*waṯangu* of the same moiety. However the arena within which control is exercised is not closed, for in the absence of a land-holder or close MM-holder, people with a more remote relation to the estate and body of sacra in question, either more distant MM-holders or those with the same *maḏayin* (that is, of the same clan-aggregate), may assert control. There may, of course, be competition among such people for control.

I should add a note on the powers of mother-holders here. Whereas MM-holders may become land-holders of the *ma:ri* country and rituals when there are no more males in the clan, mother-holders may not, for people cannot change moiety, or take the ritual roles of the opposite moiety. Mother-holders do have the power to control the performance of ritual to some extent, however, for their cooperation is required, for example in making the sand-sculpture for a purification ceremony, or the artefacts and ceremony-ground for a regional ceremony.

The above cases illustrate at least the short-term domination of one clan's religious life by another, but the ability of one clan to exercise long-term dominance over the religious life of another clan is limited by a number of structural features. First, a dominant clan is itself subject to demographic vicissitudes, as well as those of clans on whom the men are dependent for wives. Second, larger clans tend to split into competing factions along lineage lines. Third, the cross-cutting links between clans, and the existence of several routes for individual rights and ritual knowledge, give clans opportunities to recover from incompetence. And fourth, through the same links, clans and individuals provide 'checks and balances' on the ambitions of others (Myers 1980; Williams 1986).

Nevertheless, competition between the men of different clans suggests that men of one clan may sometimes hasten the demise of another, or at least limit its growth. Furthermore, there is a connection between competition over land, reproductive powers of men and women, and the control of ritual. The Yolngu are highly polygynous, with some older men married to ten or eleven wives, and men in general marrying late. Success in marriage on the part of men, in the sense that they acquire wives and father children, is a condition for clan growth. Indeed one can posit a feedback process in which the larger the clan, the more likely its men are to be successful in acquiring wives. This is at the expense of the men of smaller and politically weaker clans, for men of larger clans are more able to press their marriage claims than the men of smaller ones, and to elope successfully (Keen 1982). Clan growth is limited by the process of fission, although the maximum viable size of a clan probably depends on the demographic and social conditions, for clans in the mid-1970s (a period of strong demographic growth in the Aboriginal population as a whole) were larger on average than in the 1920s.

Not only can men of larger clans deprive men of smaller clans of the same moiety of potential wives (in former times sometimes killing such men and taking their wives), it is also the case that the larger clans tend to dominate the religious lives of the smaller clans of the same moiety, as we have seen. Men of larger clans can affiliate their children to the estates of smaller clans through spirit conception beliefs, take over estates of their deceased *ma:ri* clans, and perhaps claim women as wives who would formerly have been wives of men of the *ma:ri* clan. Control of the designs and *rangga* sacred objects associated with an estate implies control of the land, and residence rights for those in control and their close kin. In this way, subject to the kinds of checks already outlined, members of demographically and religiously successful clans can legitimately take over the land of declining or deceased clans of the same moiety, although control of the ritual life of clans other than one's own is no doubt a goal in itself for some men.

Concluding remarks

Let us return to the notion of inalienable property. I agree with Warner both that ritual elements are an integral part of the structure of the clans, and that the effect of ritual elements and land 'being part of the clan and moiety configuration has many of the attributes of our concept of property' (1937: 147). The concept of property is appropriate to elements of Yolngu ritual practice and land tenure in several respects. They are possessed or 'held'. Possession entails the right to use and to perform, subject to other conditions. The rights are to a degree exclusive, for non-holders do not have the right to perform ceremonies, and are expected to ask permission to visit or exploit the resources of an estate, and to make recompense for such use. However, rights are potentially extensible, as Verdon and Jorion (1981) argue, with no clear boundaries to the bases of claims. Weaker bases will be invoked in the absence of claimants with stronger rights.

Despite these common elements, there remain crucial differences between property in the Yolngu gift-exchange economy and property in a system of commodity exchange. Let me comment on two areas of difference.

First, in so far as ritual elements are disposed of, these are, with few exceptions, gifts. But it is important to distinguish here the gift (or sale) of tokens and of types (Wollheim 1968). It is one thing to give a song, or the right to make a sacred object, which is the gift of a type, or programme. Such a gift does not extinguish the rights of the donor, and so it follows that, far from alienating the object from the holder, the gift creates a new relationship between donor and recipient, or re-inforces an existing relationship — just as, for example, the exchange of names does. It is quite another thing to make a gift of an object which is the token of a type, such as a cassette tape of a song, a bark-painting or a feather string. The gift or sale of bark paintings and other artefacts does not extend rights to make or perform. Where types have been exchanged I suspect that differences in the types have been instituted to maintain the distinctiveness of each clan involved.

A second area of difference lies in what Gregory refers to as the 'personification' of property. I suggested that one attribute of Yolngu inalienable property was that the connection between the thing and the holder was regarded as a causal one. The causal nexus that entitles a holder to religious property is the creation of persons, powers, places and ceremonies by the Ancestral Spirit Beings, and the chains of filiation that link the living to the *wangarr*. In short, the personification of Yolngu property relations renders them in the idiom of kinship, which contrasts with the commodification of personal relations in a class society. Furthermore, an individual closely identifies his or her own being with ritual and land. A person is identified with the Ances-tral Spirit Being whence the spirit of conception came, and identifies with the *wangarr* during the performance of rituals. Representation of the *wangarr* in the form of mimetic dances, designs and sacred objects is not conceived of as mere iconic *signs* of the Beings, but as having a causal relation to them, so imbued with their powers. Where rights in ritual property and land are transferred, those causal links must be maintained intact through spiritual conception, through the conversion of the *ma:ri-waṯangu* relation to a *wa:nga-waṯangu* relation, and through the rearrangement of myths to legitimize the new relationships. It is these causal links between persons and property that render the rights relatively inalienable except through a relation that can at least be construed as descent.

References

Altman, J.C. 1984. 'Hunter-gatherer subsistence production in Arnhem Land: the original affluence hypothesis re-examined', *Mankind*, *14*, 179–90.

—— 1985. 'Gambling as a mode of redistributing and accumulating cash among Aborigines: a case study from Arnhem Land', in G. Caldwell, M. Dickerson, B. Haig and L. Sylvan (eds.), *Gambling in Australia*, Sydney: Croom Helm.

—— 1987. *Hunter-gatherers today: an Aboriginal economy in North Australia*, Canberra: Australian Institute of Aboriginal Studies.

Asch, M. 1984. *Home and native land: aboriginal rights and the Canadian constitution*, Toronto: Methuen.

Banfield, A. 1961. *A revision of the reindeer and caribou, genus* Rangifer, Ottawa: National Museums of Canada.

Barnard, A. 1978. 'The kin terminology system of the Nharo Bushmen', *Cahiers d'Etudes Africaines*, *18*, 607–29.

—— 1980a. 'Sex roles among the Nharo Bushmen of Botswana', *Africa*, *50*, 115–24.

—— 1980b. 'Kinship and social organization in Nharo cosmology', paper presented at the Second International Conference on Hunting and Gathering Societies, Quebec.

—— 1983. 'Contemporary hunter-gatherers: current theoretical issues in ecology and social organization', *Annual Review of Anthropology*, *12*, 193–214.

Battiss, W. 1948. *The artists of the rocks*, Pretoria: Red Fawn Press.

Beechey, F.W. 1831. *Narrative of a voyage to the Pacific and Bering's Strait, to co-operate with the polar expeditions: performed in His Majesty's ship 'Blossom'. . . in the years 1825, 26, 27, 28*, London: Colburn and Bently.

Bentham, J. 1931. 'Principles of the civil code', in C.K. Ogden (ed.), *The theory of legislation*, London: Routledge and Kegan Paul.

Bern, J. 1974. 'Blackfella Business, Whitefella Law: political struggle and competition in a south-east Arnhem Land Aboriginal community', PhD dissertation, Macquarie University.

—— 1979. 'Ideology and domination: toward a reconstruction of Australian Aboriginal social formation', *Oceania*, *50*, 118–32.

—— 1986. 'Inequality and Australian Aboriginal Societies', paper delivered at AIAS Biennial Conference, Canberra.

Berndt, C.H. 1970. 'Digging-sticks and spears, or, the two-sex model', in F. Gale (ed.), *Woman's role in Aboriginal society*, Canberra: Australian Institute of Aboriginal Studies.

Berndt, R.M. 1948. 'A Wonguri-Maridzikai song-cycle of the moon-bone', *Oceania*, *19*, 16–50.

—— 1959. 'The concept of "the tribe" in the Western Desert of Australia', *Oceania, 30,* 81–107.

Berndt, R.M. and C.H. Berndt 1949. 'Secular figures of north-eastern Arnhem Land', *American Anthropologist, 51,* 213–22.

—— 1985. *The world of the first Australians* (revised edition). Sydney: Ure Smith.

Biesele, M. 1975. 'Folklore and ritual of !Kung hunter-gatherers', PhD dissertation, Harvard University.

—— 1978. 'Sapience and scarce resources: communication systems of the !Kung and other foragers', *Social Science Information, 17,* 921–47.

Blackburn, R. 1971. 'Honey in Okiek personality, culture and society', PhD dissertation, Michigan State University.

—— 1973. 'Okiek ceramics', *Azania, 8,* 55–70.

—— 1974. 'The Okiek and their history', *Azania 9,* 139–57.

—— 1976. 'Okiek history', in B. Ogot (ed.), *Kenya before 1900,* Nairobi: East African Publishing House.

Bleek, D. 1932. 'Customs and beliefs of the /Xam Bushmen', *Bantu Studies, 6,* 233–49.

—— 1933. 'Beliefs and customs of the /Xam Bushmen', *Bantu Studies, 7,* 297–312, 375–92.

—— 1935. 'Beliefs and customs of the /Xam Bushmen', *Bantu Studies, 9,* 1–47.

—— 1936. 'Beliefs and customs of the /Xam Bushmen', *Bantu Studies, 10,* 131–62.

Bleek, W. and L. Lloyd 1911. *Specimens of Bushman folklore,* London: G. Allen & Unwin.

Bleek W.H.I. 1866–77. Unpublished manuscripts. J.W. Jagger Library, University of Cape Town.

Bloch, M. 1986. *From blessing to violence: history and ideology in the circumcision ritual of the Merina of Madagascar,* Cambridge: Cambridge University Press.

Blurton Jones, N. and M. Konner 1976. '!Kung knowledge of animal behaviour (or: the proper study of mankind is animals)', in R. Lee and I. DeVore (eds.), *Kalahari hunter-gatherers,* Cambridge, MA: Harvard University Press.

Boas, F. 1899. 'Property marks of Alaskan Eskimo', *American Anthropologist, 1,* 601–13.

Borsboom, A. 1978. 'Maradjiri: a modern ritual complex in Arnhem Land, north Australia', PhD dissertation, Katholieke Universiteit Nijmegen.

Brower, C. n.d. 'The northernmost American: an autobiography', unpublished manuscript, Stefansson Collection, Dartmouth College Library.

Burch, E.S. 1970. 'The Eskimo trading partnership in north Alaska: a study in "balanced reciprocity"', *Anthropological Papers of the University of Alaska, 15,* 49–80.

—— 1974. 'Eskimo warfare in northwest Alaska', *Anthropological Papers of the University of Alaska, 16,* 1–14.

—— 1975a. *Eskimo kinsmen. Changing family relationships in northwest Alaska.* St Paul, MN: West Publishing Company.

—— 1975b. 'Inter-regional transportation in traditional northwest Alaska', *Anthropological Papers of the University of Alaska, 17,* 1–11.

—— 1976. 'Overland travel routes in northwest Alaska', *Anthropological Papers of the University of Alaska, 18,* 1–10.

—— 1980. 'Traditional Eskimo societies in northwest Alaska', in Y. Kotani and W. Workman (eds.), *Alaska native culture and history,* Suita, Osaka, Japan:

National Museum of Ethnology.
—— 1984. 'Kotzebue Sound Eskimo', in D. Damas (ed.), *Handbook of North American Indians, Volume 5*, Washington, DC: Smithsonian Institution.
Burch, E.S. and T. Correll 1972. 'Alliance and conflict: inter-regional relations in north Alaska', in D.L. Guemple (ed.), *Alliance in Eskimo society*, Seattle: University of Washington Press.
Campbell, C. 1986. 'Images of war: a problem in San rock art research', *World Archaeology*, 18, 255–68.
—— 1987. 'Art in crisis: contact period rock art of the south-eastern mountains', MSc dissertation, Witwatersrand University.
Campbell, J. 1822. *Travels in South Africa*, London: Westley.
Canada 1975. *James Bay and Northern Quebec Agreement*, Quebec: Editeur officiel du Québec.
—— n.d. Department of Indian Affairs and Northern Development Files, RG-10 Series. Public Archives of Canada.
Carter, R. 1974. 'Chipewyan semantics: form and meaning in the language and culture of an Athapaskan-speaking people of Canada', PhD dissertation, Duke University.
Cashdan, E. 1980. 'Egalitarianism among hunters and gatherers', *American Anthropologist*, 82, 116–20.
—— 1983. 'Territoriality among human foragers: ecological models and an application to four Bushman groups', *Current Anthropology*, 24, 47–66.
Chase, A. 1984. 'Belonging to country: territory, identity and environment in Cape York Peninsula, northern Australia', *Oceania Monograph*, 27, 104–22.
Clark, A. McF. 1977. 'Trade at the cross roads', in J. Helmer, S. Van Dyke and F. Kense (eds.), *Problems in the prehistory of the North American Subarctic: the Athapaskan question*, Calgary: University of Calgary Archaeological Association.
Clastres, P. 1977. *Society against the state*, Oxford: Blackwell.
Clunies-Ross, M. and L.R. Hiatt 1977. 'Sand-sculptures at a Gidjingali burial rite', in P.J. Ucko (ed.), *Form in indigenous art*, Canberra: Australian Institute of Aboriginal Studies.
Cohen, M. 1927. 'Property and sovereignty', *Cornell Law Quarterly*, 13(8).
Cooper, J. 1939. 'Is the Algonkian family hunting ground system pre-Columbian?', *American Anthropologist*, 41, 66–90.
Crawley, E. 1929. 'The oath, the curse and the blessing', in T. Besterman (ed.), *Studies of savages and sex*, London: Methuen (reprinted 1969).
Damas, D. 1963. *Igluligmiut kinship and local groupings: a structural approach*, Ottawa: National Museums of Canada.
Davis, N. 1981. 'History of research in subarctic Alaska', in J. Helm (ed.), *Handbook of North American Indians, Volume 6*, Washington, DC: Smithsonian Institution.
Dawson, J. 1881. *Australian Aborigines: the language and customs of several tribes of Aborigines in the Western Desert of Victoria, Australia*, Melbourne: George Robertson.
de Heusch, L. 1981. *Why marry her? Society and symbolic structures*, Cambridge: Cambridge University Press.
—— 1985. *Sacrifice in Africa*, Bloomington: Indiana University Press.
Dentan, R. 1968. *The Semai: a nonviolent people of Malaya*, New York: Holt,

Rinehart and Winston.

Diamond, A. 1935. *Primitive law*, London: Longmans, Green.

Dowling, J. 1968. 'Individual ownership and the sharing of game in hunting societies', *American Anthropologist*, 70, 502–7.

Dumont, L. 1980. *Homo hierarchicus*, Chicago: University of Chicago Press.

Durkheim, E. 1933. *Division of labour in society*, London: Macmillan.

Elkin, A.P. 1961. 'Maraian at Mainoru', *Oceania*, 32, 1–15.

Endicott, K. 1974. 'Batek Negrito economy and social organization', PhD dissertation, Harvard University.

—— 1979. *Batek Negrito religion*, Oxford: Clarendon Press.

—— 1982. 'The effects of logging on the Batek of Malaysia', *Cultural Survival Quarterly*, 6, 19–20.

—— 1983. 'The effects of slave raiding on the aborigines of the Malay Peninsula', in A. Reid (ed.), *Slavery, bondage and dependency in Southeast Asia*, Brisbane: University of Queensland Press.

—— 1984. 'The economy of the Batek of Malaysia: annual and historical perspectives', *Research in Economic Anthropology*, 6, 29–52.

Endicott, K. and K.L. Endicott 1987. 'The question of hunter-gatherer territoriality: the case of the Batek of Malaysia', in M. Biesele (ed.), *Past and future of !Kung ethnography: critical reflections and symbolic perspectives*, Hamburg: Helmut Büske Verlag.

Endicott, K.L. 1981. 'The conditions of egalitarian male–female relationships in foraging societies', *Canberra Anthropology*, 4, 1–10.

Erwin-Tripp, S. 1970. 'Discourse agreement: how children answer questions', in J. Haynes (ed.), *Cognition and development of language*, New York: Harper and Row.

Evans-Pritchard, E. 1940. *The Nuer*, London: Oxford University Press.

—— 1956. *Nuer religion*, London: Oxford University Press.

Feit, H. 1978. 'Waswanipi realities and adaptations: resource management and cognitive structure', PhD dissertation, McGill University.

—— 1979. 'Political articulation of hunters to the state: means of resisting threats to subsistence production in the James Bay and Northern Quebec Agreement', *Inuit Studies*, 3, 37–52.

—— 1980. 'Negotiating recognition of aboriginal rights: history, strategies and reactions to the James Bay and Northern Quebec Agreement', *Canadian Journal of Anthropology*, 1, 159–72.

—— 1982. 'The future of hunters within nation-states: anthropology and the James Bay Cree', in E. Leacock and R. Lee (eds.), *Politics and history in band societies*, Cambridge: Cambridge University Press.

—— 1983. 'Decision-making and management of wildlife resources: contemporary and historical perspectives on Waswanipi Cree hunting', paper presented at the Eleventh International Congress of Anthropological and Ethnological Sciences, Quebec.

—— 1984. 'Conflict areas in the management of renewable resources in the Canadian north: perspectives based on conflicts and responses in James Bay Quebec', in *National and regional interests in the north: third national workshop on people, resources and the environment north of 60 degrees*, Ottawa: Canadian Arctic Resources Committee.

—— 1986. 'Anthropologists and the state: the relationship between social policy advocacy and academic practice in the history of the Algonquian hunting territory debate, 1910–1950', paper presented at the Fourth International Conference on Hunting and Gathering Societies, London.

Fernandez, J. 1974. 'The mission of metaphor in expressive culture', *Current Anthropology*, 15, 119–45.

—— 1982. *Bwiti: an ethnography of the religious imagination in Africa*, Princeton, NJ: Princeton University Press.

Forge, A. 1972. 'The golden fleece', *Man*, 7, 527–40.

Foucault, M. 1979. *Discipline and punish*, New York: Vintage Books.

Francis, D. and T. Morantz 1983. *Partners in furs: a history of the fur trade in eastern James Bay 1600–1870*, Montreal: McGill-Queen's University Press.

Galaty, J. 1977. 'In the pastoral image: dialectics of Maasai identity', PhD dissertation, University of Chicago.

Galaty, J. and P. Lembuya 1984. 'The white dance: a descriptive account of the 1983 Ilkeekonyokie Maasai Enkipaata ceremony to inaugurate a new age-set', unpublished manuscript.

Gardner, P. 1972. 'The Paliyans', in M. Bicchieri (ed.), *Hunters and gatherers today*, New York: Holt, Rinehart and Winston.

Gibson, T. 1985. 'The sharing of substance versus the sharing of activity among the Buid', *Man*, 20, 391–411.

—— 1986. *Sacrifice and sharing in the Philippine highlands*, London: Athlone Press.

Giddens, A. 1979. *Central problems in social theory: action, structure and contradiction in social analysis*, Berkeley: University of California Press.

Gluckman, M. 1955. *The judicial process among the Barotse of Northern Rhodesia*, Manchester: Manchester University Press.

—— 1965. *Politics, law and ritual in tribal society*, Oxford: Blackwell.

Goldschmidt, W. 1967. *Sebei law*, Berkeley: University of California Press.

Goody, E. 1978. 'Towards a theory of questions', in E. Goody (ed.), *Questions and politeness: strategies in social interaction*, Cambridge: Cambridge University Press.

Goody, J. 1962. *Death, property and the ancestors*, London: Tavistock.

Gould, R. 1969. *Yiwara: foragers of the Australian desert*, New York: Scribner.

—— 1982. 'To have and have not: the ecology of sharing among hunter-gatherers', in N. Williams and E. Hunn (eds.), *Resource managers: North American and Australian hunter-gatherers*, Boulder, CO: Westview Press.

Graburn, N. 1964. *Taqamiut Eskimo kinship terminology*, Ottawa: Northern Coordination and Research Centre.

Green, T. 1858. 'Lectures on the principles of political obligation', in T. Green, *Works, Volume 2*, London: Longmans, Green.

Gregory, C. 1982. *Gifts and commodities*, London: Academic Press.

Grey, T. 1980. 'The disintegration of property', *Nomos*, 24, 69–85.

Groger-Wurm, H. 1973. *Australian Aboriginal bark paintings and their mythological interpretations*, Canberra: Australian Institute of Aboriginal Studies.

Guemple, D.L. 1965. 'Saunik: name sharing as a factor governing Eskimo kinship terms', *Ethnology*, 4, 323–35.

—— 1969. 'The Eskimo ritual sponsor: a problem in the fusion of semantic domains', *Ethnology*, 8, 468–83.

—— 1979a. 'Inuit socialization: a study of children as social actors in an Eskimo community', in K. Ishwaran (ed.), *Childhood and adolescence in Canada*, Toronto:

McGraw-Hill Ryerson Ltd.

—— 1979b. *Inuit adoption*, Ottawa: National Museums of Canada.

—— 1980. 'Growing old in Inuit society', in V. Marshall (ed.), *Aging in Canada: social perspectives*, Don Mills, Ont.: Fitzhenry and Whiteside.

Guenther, M. 1975. 'The trance dancer as an agent of social change among the farm Bushmen of the Ghanzi district', *Botswana Notes and Records*, 7, 161–6.

—— 1983. 'Die Nharo Buschmänner', in K. Müller (ed.), *Menschenbilder früher Gesellschaften*, Frankfurt: Campus Verlag.

—— 1984. *The rock art of the Brandberg of Namibia: an interpretive analysis*, Wilfred Laurier University: Research Paper Series.

—— 1986. *The Nharo Bushmen of Botswana*, Hamburg: Helmut Buske Verlag.

Hall, E.S., Jr. 1984. 'Interior north Alaska Eskimo', in D. Damas (ed.), *Handbook of North American Indians, Volume 5*, Washington, DC: Smithsonian Institution.

Hamilton, A. 1980. 'Dual social systems: technology, labour and women's secret rites in the eastern Western Desert of Australia', *Oceania*, 51, 4–19.

Hansen, K. and L. Hansen 1977. *Pintupi-Loritja dictionary*, Alice Springs: Institute for Aboriginal Development.

Hawkes, E. 1913. *The 'inviting-in' feast of the Alaskan Eskimo*, Ottawa: Government Printing Bureau.

Hearne, S. 1971. *A journey from Prince of Wales' Fort in Hudson Bay to the Northern Ocean*, Edmonton: Hurtig.

Heinz, H.-J. 1975. 'Elements of !Ko Bushman religious beliefs', *Anthropos*, 70, 17–41.

Helm, J. 1965. 'Bilaterality in the socio-territorial organization of the Arctic drainage Dene', *Ethnology*, 4, 361–85.

Hewitt, R. 1986. *Structure, meaning and ritual in the narratives of the Southern San* (Quellen zur Khoisan Forschung, Vol. 2), Hamburg: Helmut Buske Verlag.

Hiatt, L. 1965. *Kinship and conflict: a study of an Aboriginal community in northern Arnhem Land*, Canberra: Australian National University Press.

—— 1971. 'Secret pseudo-procreation rites among the Australian Aborigines', in L. Hiatt and C. Jayawardena (eds.), *Anthropology in Oceania*, Sydney: Angus and Robertson.

—— 1982. 'Traditional attitudes to land resources', in R.M. Berndt (ed.), *Aboriginal sites, rights and resource development*, Perth: University of Western Australia Press.

—— 1984. 'Introduction', in L. Hiatt (ed.), *Aboriginal landowners*, Sydney: Oceania Monograph 27.

—— 1986. *Aboriginal political life* (Australian Institute of Aboriginal Studies Wentworth Lecture), Canberra: Australian Institute of Aboriginal Studies.

Hickey, C. 1979. 'The historic Beringian trade network: its nature and origins', in A. McCartney (ed.), *Thule Eskimo culture: an anthropological retrospective*, Ottawa: National Museum of Man.

Hill, K., B. King and E. Cashdan 1983. 'On territoriality in hunter-gatherers', *Current Anthropology*, 24, 534–37.

Hoebel, E.A. 1954. *The law of primitive man*, Cambridge, MA: Harvard University Press.

How, M. 1962. *The mountain Bushmen of Basutoland*, Pretoria: J. van Schaik.

Howell, S. 1983. 'Chewong women in transition: the effects of monetization on a hunter-gatherer society in Malaysia', in *Women and development in South-East*

Asia 1, Centre of South-East Asian Studies, Occasional Paper 1, Canterbury: University of Kent.

Hubert, H. and M. Mauss 1964. *Sacrifice: its nature and function*, Chicago: University of Chicago Press.

Huffman, T. 1983. 'The trance hypothesis and the rock art of Zimbabwe', *South African Archaeological Society Goodwin Series*, 4, 49–53.

Huntingford, G. 1929. 'Modern hunters', *Journal of the Royal Anthropological Institute*, 59, 333–78.

—— 1942. 'Social organization of the Dorobo', *Anthropos*, 46, 1–48.

—— 1954. 'The political organization of the Dorobo', *Anthropos*, 49, 123–48.

—— 1955. 'The economic life of the Dorobo', *Anthropos*, 50, 602–34.

Hutchins, P. 1987. 'The law applying to trapping of furbearing animals by aboriginal peoples: a case of double jeopardy', in M. Novak and J. Baker (eds.), *Wildlife furbearer management and conservation in North America*.

Ingold, T. 1980a. *Hunters, pastoralists and ranchers*, Cambridge: Cambridge University Press.

—— 1980b. 'The principle of individual autonomy and the collective appropriation of nature', paper presented at the Second International Conference on Hunting and Gathering Societies, Quebec.

—— 1983. 'The significance of storage in hunting societies', *Man*, 18, 553–71.

—— 1986. *The appropriation of nature: essays on human ecology and social relations*, Manchester: Manchester University Press.

Irimoto, T. 1981. *Chipeweyan ecology*. Senri Ethnological Studies 8, Osaka, Japan: National Museum of Ethnology.

Jacobson, L. 1975. 'The Gemsbok creation myth and Brandberg rock art', *South African Journal of Science*, 7, 314.

Jarvenpa, R. 1976. 'Spatial and ecological factors in the annual economic cycle of the English River band of Chipewyan', *Arctic Anthropology*, 13, 43–69.

—— 1977. 'The ubiquitous Bushman: Chipewyan–White trapper relations of the 1930s', in J. Helmer, S. Van Dyke and F. Kense (eds.), *Problems in the prehistory of the North American Subarctic: the Athapaskan question*, Calgary: The Archaeological Association of the University of Calgary.

Jolly, P. 1986. 'A first generation descendant of the Transkei San', *South African Archaeological Bulletin*, 41, 6–9.

Katz, R. 1982. *Boiling energy: community healing among the Kalahari !Kung*, Cambridge, MA: Harvard University Press.

Keen, I. 1978. 'One ceremony, one song: an economy of religious knowledge among the Yolngu of northeast Arnhem Land', PhD dissertation, Australian National University.

—— 1982. 'How some Murngin marry ten wives: the marital implications of matrilateral cross-cousin structures', *Man*, 17, 620–42.

Koolage, W. 1975. 'Conceptual negativism in Chipewyan ethnology', *Anthropologica*, 17, 45–60.

Kotzebue, O. von 1821. *A voyage of discovery into the South Sea and Bering's Straits, 1815–18*. London: Longman, Hurst, Rees, Orme and Brown.

Kratz, C. 1977. 'The liquors of forest and garden: drinking in Okiek life', MA dissertation, Wesleyan University.

—— 1981a. 'Identity and context in Okiek song', paper presented at the annual meeting of the American Folklore Society, San Antonio, TX.

—— 1981b. 'Are the Okiek really Maasai? or Kipsigis? or Kikuyu?', *Cahiers d'Etudes Africaines*, 79, 355–68.

—— 1986a. 'Chords of tradition, lens of analogy: iconic signs in Okiek ceremonies', *Journal of Ritual Studies*, 1, 75–97.

—— 1986b. 'Genres of power: a comparative analysis of Okiek blessings, curses and oaths', paper presented at the Annual Meeting of the American Anthropological Association, Philadelphia.

—— 1986c. 'Ethnic interaction, economic diversification and language use: a report on research with Kaplelach and Kipchornwonek Okiek', in F. Rottland and R. Vossen (eds.), *Proceedings of international symposium on African hunter-gatherers, SUGIA*, 7, 189–226.

LaRusic, I. 1979. *Negotiating a way of life: initial Cree experience with the administrative structure arising from the James Bay Agreement*, Montreal: SSDCC.

Leach, E. 1954. *Political systems of Highland Burma*, London: Athlone.

Leacock, E. 1954. *The Montagnais hunting territory and the fur trade*, Washington, DC: American Anthropological Association.

Leacock, E. and R. Lee (eds.) 1982. *Politics and history in band societies*, Cambridge: Cambridge University Press.

Lee, R. 1967. 'Trance cure of the !Kung Bushmen', *Natural History*, 76, 31–7.

—— 1968a. 'The sociology of !Kung Bushman trance performance', in R. Prince (ed.), *Trance and possession states*, Montreal: R.M. Bucke Memorial Society.

—— 1968b. 'Territorial boundaries (discussion)', in R. Lee and I. DeVore (eds.), *Man the hunter*, Chicago: Aldine.

—— 1979. *The !Kung San. Men, women and work in a foraging society*, Cambridge: Cambridge University Press.

—— 1984. *The Dobe !Kung*, New York: Holt, Rinehart and Winston.

Lee, R. and I. DeVore 1968. 'Problems in the study of hunter-gatherers', in R. Lee and I. DeVore (eds.), *Man the hunter*, Chicago: Aldine.

Lévi-Strauss, C. 1962. *Totemism* (trans. R. Needham), London: Merlin Press.

—— 1966. *The savage mind*, Chicago: University of Chicago Press.

—— 1969. *Elementary structures of kinship*, London: Eyre and Spottiswoode.

Lewis-Williams, J.D. 1980. 'Ethnography and iconography: aspects of southern San thought and art', *Man*, 15, 467–82.

—— 1981a. *Believing and seeing: symbolic meanings in southern San rock art*, London: Academic.

—— 1981b. 'The thin red line: southern San notions and rock paintings of supernatural potency', *South African Archaeological Bulletin*, 36, 5–13.

—— 1982. 'The economic and social context of southern San rock art', *Current Anthropology*, 23, 429–49.

—— 1983a. *The rock art of southern Africa*, Cambridge: Cambridge University Press.

—— (ed.) 1983b. *New approaches to southern African rock art*, South African Archaeological Society, Goodwin Series, 4.

—— 1984. 'The empirical impasse in southern African rock art studies', *The South African Archaeological Bulletin*, 39, 58–66.

—— 1985. 'Testing the trance explanation of southern African rock art: depictions of felines', *Bollettino: World Journal of Rock Art Studies*, 22, 47–62.

—— 1986. 'The last testament of the southern San', *South African Archaeological Bulletin*, 41, 10–11.

Lewis-Williams, J.D. and M. Biesele 1978. 'Eland hunting rituals among northern and southern San groups: striking similarities', *Africa*, *48*, 117–34.

Lips, J. 1947. 'Naskapi law', *Transactions of the American Philosophical Society*, *37*, 379–492.

Llewelyn-Davis, M. 1978. 'Two contexts of solidarity', in P. Caplan and J. Bujra (eds.), *Women united, women divided*, London: Tavistock.

Lowe, B. n.d. 'Gupapuyngu dictionary', typescript.

Lowie, R. 1928. 'Incorporeal property in primitive society', *Yale Law Journal*, *37*, 551–63.

McClellan, C. 1981. 'History of research in the subarctic cordillera', in J. Helm (ed.), *Handbook of North American Indians, Volume 6*, Washington, DC: Smithsonian Institution.

Macpherson, C. (ed.) 1978. *Property: mainstream and critical positions*, Buffalo, NY: University of Toronto Press.

Maddock, K. 1981. *Anthropology, law, and the definition of Australian Aboriginal rights to land*, Nijmegen: Catholic University Faculty of Law.

—— 1983. *Your land is our land*, Ringwood, Vic.: Penguin.

Maggs, T. and J. Sealy 1983. 'Elephants in boxes', *South African Archaeological Society*, Goodwin Series, *4*, 44–8.

Malinowski, B. 1934. *Coral gardens and their magic, Volume 1*, New York: Dover.

Marshall, J. and C. Ritchie 1984. *Where are the Ju/wasi of Nyae Nyae?*, Cape Town: Centre for African Studies, University of Cape Town.

Marshall, L. 1959. 'Marriage among !Kung Bushmen', *Africa*, *29*, 335–65.

—— 1961. 'Sharing, talking and giving: relief of social tensions among !Kung Bushmen', *Africa*, *31*, 231–49.

—— 1969. 'The medicine dance of the !Kung Bushmen', *Africa*, *39*, 347–81.

—— 1976. *The !Kung of Nyae Nyae*, Cambridge, MA: Harvard University Press.

Marx, K. 1954. *Capital*, London: Lawrence and Wishart.

Mauss, M. 1954. *The gift*, London: Cohen and West.

—— 1979. *Seasonal variations of the Eskimo*, London: Routledge and Kegan Paul.

Meehan, B. 1982. *Shell bed to shell midden*, Canberra: Australian Institute of Aboriginal Studies.

Meggitt, M. 1962. *Desert people: a study of the Walbiri Aborigines of central Australia*, Sydney: Angus and Robertson.

—— 1966a. 'Indigenous forms of government among the Australian Aborigines', in I. Hogbin and L. Hiatt (eds.), *Readings in Australian and Pacific anthropology*, Melbourne: Melbourne University Press.

—— 1966b. 'Gadjari among the Walbiri Aborigines of central Australia', *Oceania Monograph*, *14*.

Meillassoux, C. 1973. 'On the mode of production of the hunting band', in P. Alexandre (ed.), *French perspectives in African studies*, London: Oxford University Press.

Morgan, L.H. 1877. *Ancient society*. New York: World Publishing.

Morphy, H. 1977. 'Too many meanings', PhD dissertation, Australian National University.

—— 1978. 'Rights in paintings and rights in women: a consideration of the basic problems posed by the asymmetry of the "Murngin" system', *Mankind*, *11*, 208–19.

—— 1983. ' "Now you understand": an analysis of the way Yolngu have used sacred knowledge to retain their autonomy', in N. Peterson and M. Langton (eds.), *Aborigines, land and landrights*, Canberra: Australian Institute of Aboriginal Studies.

—— 1984. *Journey to the crocodile's nest*, Canberra: Australian Institute of Aboriginal Studies.

Morris, B. 1982. *Forest traders*, London: Athlone.

Mountford, C. 1981. *Aboriginal conception beliefs*, Melbourne: Hyland House.

Moyle, R. 1979. *Songs of the Pintubi*, Canberra: Australian Institute of Aboriginal Studies.

Munn, N. 1970. 'The transformation of subjects into objects in Walbiri and Pitjantjatjara myth', in R.M. Berndt (ed.), *Australian Aboriginal anthropology*, Nedlands: University of Western Australia Press.

Murdock, G.P. 1949. *Social structure*, London: Macmillan.

Murphy, R. and J. Steward 1956. 'Tappers and trappers: parallel processes in acculturation', *Economic Development and Cultural Change*, 4, 335–55.

Myers, F. 1976. 'To have and to hold: a study of persistence and change in Pintupi social life', PhD dissertation, Bryn Mawr College.

—— 1979. 'Emotions and the self', *Ethos*, 7, 343–70.

—— 1980. 'The cultural basis of politics in Pintupi social life', *Mankind*, 12, 197–214.

—— 1982. 'Always ask: resource use and landownership among Pintupi Aborigines', in N. Williams and E. Hunn (eds.), *Resource managers. North American and Australian hunter-gatherers*, Boulder, CO: Westview Press.

—— 1986. *Pintupi country, Pintupi self: sentiment, place and politics among Western Desert Aborigines*, Washington, DC: Smithsonian Institution.

Nettleton, A. 1984. 'San rock art: image, function and meaning: a reply to A.R. Wilcox', *The South African Archaeological Bulletin*, 39, 67–8.

Noyes, G. 1936. *The institution of property*, New York: Longmans, Green.

Orpen, J.M. 1874. 'A glimpse into the mythology of the Maluti Bushmen', *Cape Monthly Magazine*, 9, 1–13.

Oswalt, W. 1967. *This land was theirs*, San Francisco: Chandler.

Parry, J. 1979. *Caste and kinship in Kangra*, London: Routledge and Kegan Paul.

—— 1986. ' *The gift*, the Indian gift and the "Indian gift" ', *Man*, 21, 453–73.

Partridge, E. 1983. *Origins: a short etymological dictionary of modern English*, New York: Greenwich House.

Pearson, R. 1985. *Anthropological glossary*, Malabar: Robert E. Krieger Publishing Company.

Peterson, N. 1972. 'Totemism yesterday: sentiment and local organization among the Australian Aborigines', *Man*, 7, 12–32.

Peterson, N., I. Keen and B. Sansom 1977. 'Succession to land: primary and secondary rights to Aboriginal estates', in *Hansard of the Joint Select Committee on Aboriginal Land Rights in the Northern Territory*, Canberra: Government Printer.

Polanyi, K. 1968. 'The economy as instituted process', in E. LeClair and H. Schneider (eds.), *Economic anthropology*, New York: Holt, Rinehart and Winston.

Price, J. 1975. 'Sharing: the integration of intimate economies', *Anthropologica*, 17, 3–27.

Proudhon, P., n.d. *What is property? An inquiry into the principle of right and of government* (trans. B. Tucker), London: William Reeves, first published in 1841.

Radcliffe-Brown, A. 1951. 'Murngin social organization', *American Anthropologist*, 53, 37–55.

Ravenhill, P. 1976. 'Religious utterances and the theory of speech acts', in W. Samarin (ed.), *Language in religious practice*, Rowley, MA: Newbury House.

Ray, D.J. 1967. 'Land tenure and polity of the Bering Strait Eskimos', *Journal of the West*, 6, 371–94.

—— 1975. *The Eskimos of Bering Strait, 1650–1898*, Seattle: University of Washington Press.

—— 1984. 'Bering Strait Eskimo', in D. Damas (ed.), *Handbook of North American Indians, Volume 5*, Washington, DC: Smithsonian Institution.

Reynolds, G. 1983a. 'Ownership marks and social relationships in northwestern Alaska', paper presented at the annual meeting of the Alaska Anthropological Association.

—— 1983b. 'Ownership marks', Unpublished manuscript.

Riches, D. 1982. *Northern nomadic hunter-gatherers: a humanistic approach*, London: Academic.

Ridington, R. 1982. 'Technology, world view and adaptive strategy in a northern hunting society', *Canadian Review of Sociology and Anthropology*, 19, 469–81.

Robertson Smith, W. 1901. *The religion of the Semites*, London: Black.

Rogers, E. 1963. *The hunting group – hunting territory complex among the Mistassini Indians*, Ottawa: National Museums of Canada.

—— 1981. 'History of ethnological research in the Subarctic shield and Mackenzie Valley', in J. Helm (ed.), *Handbook of North American Indians, Vol. 6*, Washington, DC: Smithsonian Institution.

Rosenberg, M. 1978. 'Ownership and population pressure: an evaluation of hunter-gatherer territoriality and the role of ownership in the development of systematic food production', MA dissertation, University of Pennsylvania.

Sahlins, M. 1965. 'On the sociology of primitive exchange', in M. Banton (ed.), *The relevance of models for social anthropology*, London: Tavistock.

—— 1968. 'Notes on the original affluent society', in R. Lee and I. DeVore (eds.), *Man the hunter*, Chicago: Aldine.

—— 1974. *Stone age economics*, London: Tavistock.

Salisbury, R. 1986. *A homeland for the Cree: regional development in James Bay 1971–1981*, Montreal: McGill-Queen's University Press.

Samarin, W. (ed.), 1976. *Language in religious practice*, Rowley, MA: Newbury House.

Sansom, B. 1980. *The camp at Wallaby Cross*, Canberra: Australian Institute of Aboriginal Studies.

—— 1982. 'The Aboriginal commonality', in R.M. Berndt (ed.), *Aboriginal sites, rites and resources*, Nedlands: University of Western Australia Press.

Schebeck, B. 1968. 'Dialect and social groupings in northeast Arnhem Land', typescript, Australian Institute of Aboriginal Studies.

Schebesta, P. 1928. *Among the forest dwarfs of Malaya* (transl. A. Chambers), London: Hutchinson.

—— 1954. *Die Negrito Asiens: Wirtschaft und Soziologie* (Studia Instituti Anthropos, Vol. 12), Vienna-Mödling: St. Gabriel-Verlag.

Scheffler, H. 1978. *Australian kin classification*, Cambridge: Cambridge University Press.

Schneider, D. 1968. *American kinship: a cultural account*, Chicago: University of

Chicago Press.

Scott, C. 1979. *Modes of production and guaranteed annual income in James Bay Cree society*, Montreal: McGill University, Programme in the Anthropology of Development.

—— 1983a. 'The semiotics of material life among Wemindji Cree hunters', PhD dissertation, McGill University.

—— 1983b. 'Reciprocity with the White Man: the ideology of James Bay Crees' relations with the state', paper presented at the Eleventh International Congress of Anthropological and Ethnological Sciences, Quebec.

—— 1984. 'Between "original affluence" and consumer affluence: domestic production and guaranteed income for James Bay Cree hunters', in R. Salisbury and E. Tooker (eds.), *Affluence and cultural survival* (Proceedings of the Spring Meeting of the American Ethnological Society, 1981), Washington, DC: American Ethnological Society.

—— 1986. 'Hunting territories and their uses in Wemindji Cree goose hunting', *Anthropologica*.

Scott, C., T. Morantz and J. Morrison. 1986. 'Quebec Cree land rights west of the Ontario–Quebec border: report of the Ontario claim research project, phase II', Contract Study, Grand Council of the Crees of Quebec, Val d'Or.

Sen Gupta, N. 1962. *The evolution of law*, Calcutta: K.L. Mukhapadhyay.

Service, E. 1970. *Origins of the state and civilization. The process of cultural evolution*, New York: W. Norton.

—— 1979. *The hunters*, Englewood Cliffs, NJ: Prentice Hall.

Sharp, H.S. 1975. 'Introducing the sororate to a Northern Saskatchewan Chipewyan village', *Ethnology*, 14, 71–82.

—— 1976. 'Man: Wolf:: Woman: Dog', *Arctic Anthropology*, 13, 25–34.

—— 1977. 'The Chipewyan hunting unit', *American Ethnologist*, 4, 376–93.

—— 1978. 'Comparative ethnology of the wolf and the Chipewyan', in J. Hall and H.S. Sharp (eds.), *Wolf and man: evolution in parallel*, New York: Academic Press.

—— 1979. *Chipewyan marriage*, Ottawa: National Museums of Canada.

—— 1981. 'The null case: the Chipewyan', in F. Dahlberg (ed.), *Woman the gatherer*, New Haven, CT: Yale University Press.

—— 1987. 'Giant fish, giant otters and dinosaurs: apparently irrational beliefs in a Chipewyan community', *American Ethnologist*, 14, 226–35.

—— 1988. *The transformation of Bigfoot: maleness, power and belief among the Chipewyan*, Washington, DC: Smithsonian Institution.

Sharp, L. 1958. 'People without politics', in V. Ray (ed.), *Systems of political control and bureaucracy in human societies*, Seattle: University of Washington Press.

Shepard, P. 1978. *Thinking animals. Animals and the development of human intelligence*. New York: The Viking Press.

Sieciechowicz, K. 1983. 'We are all related here: the social relations of land utilization in Wunnummin Lake, northwestern Ontario', PhD dissertation, University of Toronto.

Silberbauer, G. 1981. *Hunter and habitat in the Central Kalahari*, Cambridge: Cambridge University Press.

Simpson, J. 1875. 'The western Eskimo', in *A selection of papers on Arctic geography and ethnology, reprinted and presented to the Arctic expedition of 1875*, London:

Royal Geographical Society.

Smith, D. 1973. *Inkoze: magico-religious beliefs of contact-traditional Chipewyan trading at Fort Resolution, NWT, Canada*, Ottawa: National Museums of Canada.

—— 1983. *Moose-Deer Island House people: a history of the native people of Fort Resolution*, Ottawa: National Museums of Canada.

—— 1985. 'Big stone foundations: manifest meaning in Chipewyan myths', *Journal of American Culture*, 8, 73–7.

—— n.d. 'The Chipewyan medicine-fight in cultural and ecological context', unpublished manuscript.

Smith, J.G.E. 1970. 'The Chipewyan hunting group in a village context', *Western Canadian Journal of Anthropology*, 2, 60–6.

—— 1975. 'The ecological basis of Chipewyan socio-territorial organization', in A.M. Clark (ed.), *Proceedings of the Northern Athapaskan conference, 1971*, Ottawa: National Museums of Canada.

—— 1976. 'Local band organization of the Caribou-Eater Chipewyan', *Arctic Anthropology*, 13, 12–24.

—— 1978. 'The emergence of the micro-urban village among the Caribou-Eater Chipewyan', *Human Organization*, 37, 38–49.

Smith, V. 1968. 'Intercontinental aboriginal trade in the Bering Straits area', paper presented at the International Congress of Anthropological and Ethnological Sciences, Tokyo.

Speck, F. 1915. 'The family hunting band as the basis of Algonkian social organization', *American Anthropologist*, 17, 289–305.

—— 1923. 'Mistassini hunting territories in the Labrador Peninsula', *American Anthropologist*, 25, 452–71.

Speck, F. and L. Eiseley 1939. 'The significance of hunting territory systems of the Algonkian in social theory', *American Anthropologist*, 41, 269–80.

Spencer, R. 1959. *The North Alaskan Eskimo. A study in ecology and society*, Washington, DC: Bureau of American Ethnology.

—— 1984. 'North Alaska Coast Eskimo', in D. Damas (ed.), *Handbook of North American Indians, Volume 5*, Washington, DC: Smithsonian Institution.

Stanner, W. 1963. 'On Aboriginal religion: cosmos and society made correlative', *Oceania*, 33, 239–73.

—— 1964. *On Aboriginal religion*, Sydney: *Oceania* Monograph 11.

Stefansson, V. 1914. 'Prehistoric and present commerce among the Arctic Coast Eskimo', *Geological Survey of Canada Museum Bulletin*, 6.

Strehlow, T. 1947. *Aranda traditions*, Melbourne: Melbourne University Press.

—— 1970. 'Geography and the totemic landscape in central Australia', in R.M. Berndt (ed.), *Australian Aboriginal anthropology*, Perth: University of Western Australia Press.

Summers, R. (ed.) 1959. *Prehistoric rock art of the Federation of Rhodesia and Nyasaland*, Salisbury: National Publication Trust.

Sutton, P. 1978. 'Wik: Aboriginal society, territory and language at Cape Keerweer, Cape York Peninsula, Australia', PhD dissertation, University of Queensland.

Sutton, P. and B. Rigsby 1982. 'People with "politicks": management of land and personnel on Australia's Cape York Peninsula', in N. Williams and E. Hunn (eds.), *Resource managers: North American and Australian hunter-gatherers*,

Boulder, CO: Westview Press.

Suzuki, D. 1984. 'A planet for the taking', *Canadian Forum*, 64, 87–99.

Tambiah, S.J. 1968. 'The magical power of words', *Man*, 3, 175–208.

—— 1979. 'A performative approach to ritual', *Proceedings of the British Academy*, 65, 113–66.

Tanner, A. 1979. *Bringing home animals: religious ideology and mode of production of the Mistassini Cree hunters*, London: Hurst.

—— 1986. 'A child's introduction to the post-classical hunting territory debate', *Anthropologica*.

Thackeray, J. 1983. 'Disguises, animal behaviour and concepts of control in relation to the rock art of southern Africa', in J.D. Lewis-Williams (1983b).

Thomson, D. 1939a. 'Notes on the smoking pipes of north Queensland and the Northern Territory of Australia', *Man* (old series), 39, 81–91.

—— 1939b. 'Proof of Indonesian influence upon the Aborigines of north Australia: the remarkable dog Ngarra of the Mildjingi clan', *Illustrated London News*, 12 August, 271–9.

—— 1949. *Economic structure and the ceremonial exchange cycle in Arnhem Land*, Melbourne: Macmillan.

Tonkinson, R. 1970. 'Aboriginal dream-spirit beliefs in a contact situation: Jigalong, Western Australia', in R.M. Berndt (ed.), *Australian Aboriginal anthropology*, Perth: University of Western Australia Press.

—— 1974. *The Jigalong Mob: Aboriginal victors at the Desert Crusade*, Menlo Park: Cummings.

—— 1978. *The Mardudjara Aborigines: living the dream in Australia's desert*, New York: Holt, Rinehart and Winston.

—— 1980. 'Review of "Social Organization in Aboriginal Australia" by W. Shapiro', *American Anthropologist*, 82, 702–3.

—— 1984. 'Semen versus spirit-child in a Western Desert culture', in M. Charlesworth *et al.* (eds.), *Religion in Aboriginal Australia: an anthology*, Brisbane: University of Queensland Press.

—— 1986. 'Egalitarianism and inequality in a Western Desert culture', paper delivered at AIAS Biennial conference, Canberra.

—— 1987. 'Mardujarra kinship', in D. Mulvaney and J. White (eds.), *Australians to 1788*, Sydney: Fairfax, Syme and Weldon.

Turnbull, C. 1966. *Wayward servants: the two worlds of the African Pygmies*, London: Eyre and Spottiswoode.

Turner, D. and P. Wertman 1977. *Shamattawa: the structure of social relations in a northern Algonkian band*, Ottawa: National Museums of Canada.

Urban, G. 1986. 'Ceremonial dialogues in South America', *American Anthropologist*, 88, 371–86.

VanStone, J. 1985. *Material culture of the Davis Inlet and Barren Ground Naskapi: The William Duncan Strong collection*, Chicago: Field Museum of Natural History.

Verdon, M. and P. Jorion 1981. 'The hordes of discord: Australian Aboriginal social organization reconsidered', *Man*, 16, 90–107.

Vincent, S. and J. Mailhot 1982. 'Montagnais land tenure', *Interculture*, 75–6, 61–9.

Vinnicombe, P. 1975. 'The ritual significance of eland (*Taurotragus oryx*) in the rock art of southern Africa', in E. Anati (ed.), *Les religions de la préhistoire*, Capo di Ponte: Centro Camuno di Studi Preistorici.

—— 1976. *People of the eland*, Pietermaritzburg: University of Natal Press.

von Sturmer, J. 1978. 'The Wik region: economy, territoriality and totemism in western Cape York Peninsula, north Queensland', PhD dissertation, University of Queensland.

—— 1984. 'A critique of the Fox report', in *Aborigines and Uranium*. Canberra: Government Printer.

Warner. W.L. 1937. *A black civilization*, New York: Harper and Row.

—— 1958. *A black civilization* (revised ed), New York: Harper and Row.

Webb, T. 1933. 'Tribal organization in eastern Arnhem Land', *Oceania, 3*, 406–17.

Weber, M. 1947. *The theory of social and economic organization*, New York: Free Press.

Weiner, A. 1985. 'Inalienable wealth', *American Ethnologist, 12*, 210–27.

Werner, A. 1908. 'Bushman paintings', *Journal of the Royal Anthropological Institute, 7*, 387–93.

Westermarck, E. 1926. *Ritual and belief in Morocco, Volume 1*, London: Macmillan.

White, I. 1970. 'Aboriginal women's status resolved: a paradox', in F. Gale (ed.), *Women's role in Aboriginal society*, Canberra: Australian Institute of Aboriginal Studies.

White, Jr. L. 1967. 'The historical roots of our ecological crisis', *Science, 155*, 1203–7.

Wiessner, P. 1980. 'History and continuity in !Kung San reciprocal relationships', paper presented at the Second International Conference on Hunting and Gathering Societies, Quebec.

—— 1982. 'Risk, reciprocity and social influences on !Kung San economics', in E. Leacock and R. Lee (eds.), *Politics and history in band societies*, Cambridge: Cambridge University Press.

Wild, S. (ed.) 1986. *Rom: an Aboriginal ritual of diplomacy*, Canberra: Australian Institute of Aboriginal Studies.

Wilkinson, R. 1926. *Papers on Malay subjects: supplement: the aboriginal tribes*, Kuala Lumpur: Federated Malay States Government Press.

Willcox, R. 1984. 'Meaning and motive in San rock art — the views of W.D. Hammond-Tooke and J.D. Lewis-Williams considered', *South African Archaeological Bulletin 39*, 53–7.

William, N. 1982. 'A boundary is to cross: observations on Yolngu boundaries and permission', in N. Williams and E. Hunn (eds.), *Resource managers: North American and Australian hunter-gatherers*, Boulder, CO: Westview Press.

—— 1983. 'Yolngu concepts of land ownership', in N. Peterson and M. Langton (eds.), *Aborigines, land and landrights*, Canberra: Australian Institute of Aboriginal Studies.

—— 1985. 'On Aboriginal decision-making', in D. Barwick, J. Beckett and M. Reay (eds.), *Metaphors of interpretation*, Canberra: Australian National University Press.

—— 1986. *The Yolngu and their land: the system of land tenure and the fight for its recognition*, Canberra: Australian Institute of Aboriginal Studies.

Willis, R. 1974. *Man and beast*, London: Hart-Davis, MacGibbon.

Wollheim, R. 1968. *Art and its objects*, Harmondsworth: Penguin.

Woodburn, J. 1968. 'An introduction to Hadza ecology', in R. Lee and I. DeVore (eds.), *Man the hunter*, Chicago: Aldine.

—— 1972. 'Ecology, nomadic movement and the composition of the local group among hunters and gatherers: an East African example and its implications', in P. Ucko, R. Tringham and G. Dimbleby (eds.), *Man, settlement and urbanism,* London: Duckworth.

—— 1978. 'Sex roles and the division of labour in hunting and gathering societies', paper presented at the First International Conference on Hunting and Gathering Societies, Paris.

—— 1979. 'Minimal politics: the political organization of the Hadza of North Tanzania', in P. Cohen and W. Shack (eds.), *Politics in leadership: a comparative perspective,* Oxford: Clarendon Press.

—— 1980. 'Hunters and gatherers today and reconstruction of the past', in E. Gellner (ed.), *Soviet and Western anthropology,* London: Duckworth.

—— 1982a. 'Egalitarian societies', *Man,* 17, 431–51.

—— 1982b. 'Social dimensions of death in four African hunting and gathering societies', in M. Bloch and J. Parry (eds.), *Death and the regeneration of life,* Cambridge: Cambridge University Press.

—— 1988. 'African hunter-gatherer social organization. Is it best understood as a product of encapsulation?', in T. Ingold, D. Riches and J. Woodburn (eds.), *Hunters and gatherers I: History, evolution and social change,* Oxford: Berg.

Woodbury, A. 1984. 'Eskimo and Aleut languages', in D. Damas (ed.), *Handbook of North American Indians, Volume 5,* Washington, DC: Smithsonian Institution.

Worl, R. 1980. 'The North Slope Inupiat whaling complex', in Y. Kotani and W. Workman (eds.), *Alaska native culture and history,* Suita, Osaka, Japan: National Museum of Ethnology.

Yates, R., J. Golson and M. Hall 1985. 'Trance performance: the rock art of Boontjieskloof and Sevilla', *South African Archaeological Bulletin,* 40, 70–80.

Index

Names

Subjects

Notes on the Contributors

Jon Altman Jon Altman's *Hunters and Gatherers Today*, a study of an 'outstation' community in northern Australia, has been recently published by the Australian Institute of Aboriginal Studies.

Alan Barnard Alan Barnard is co-author of *Research Practices in the Study of Kinship* (Academic Press). His papers on hunting and gathering societies in general, and on the Bushmen in particular, have been published in the *Annual Review of Anthropology*, *Africa* and other journals and collections.

Ernest S. Burch, Jr. Ernest Burch's numerous papers on the North Alaskan Eskimo are based on fieldwork carried out over a period of twenty years. His book, *Eskimo kinsmen*, was published by West Publishing Company.

Kirk Endicott Kirk Endicott has researched and published extensively on the Batek of Malaysia. The Clarendon Press has published his *Batek Negrito Religion* and *An Analysis of Malay Magic*.

Thomas Gibson Thomas Gibson's *Sacrifice and Sharing in the Philippine Highlands*, based on fieldwork among the Buid of Mindoro, was recently published in the London School of Economics monographs series. He also has papers in *Man* and other journals and collections.

Lee Guemple Lee Guemple's monographs on the Canadian Inuit include 'Inuit Spouse Exchange' (Chicago University) and 'Inuit Adoption' (National Museums of Canada). He is also the editor of *Alliance in Eskimo Society* (American Ethnological Society) and the author of a large number of papers.

Mathias Guenther Among Mathias Guenther's many publications on the Bushmen are *Bushman folktales (Nharo and / Xam)* (Franz Steiner Verlag Wiesbaden, Stuttgart) and *The Nharo Bushmen of Botswana* (Helmut Buske Verlag, Hamburg).

Tim Ingold Tim Ingold's books include *Hunters, Pastoralists and Ranchers* and *Evolution and Social Life* (both Cambridge University Press) and *The Appropriation of Nature* (Manchester University Press). He is the editor of *'What is an Animal?'*, recently published by Unwin

Hyman. He was Malinowski Memorial Lecturer in 1982, and Curl Lecturer in 1989.

Ian Keen   Ian Keen has published many papers on the Yolngu of Arnhem Land, including 'How some Murngin men marry ten wives' (*Man* 1982).

Corinne A. Kratz   Corinne Kratz has written a number of papers on the Okiek of Kenya. She is currently completing her PhD thesis at the University of Texas.

J.D. Lewis-Williams   David Lewis-Williams is a leading authority on San (Bushman) aesthetic culture. Among his many publications are *Believing and Seeing: symbolic meanings in southern San rock art* (Academic Press) and *The Rock Art of Southern Africa* (Cambridge University Press).

Howard Morphy   Howard Morphy is the author of *Journey to the Crocodile's Nest*, published by the Australian Institute of Aboriginal Studies, and he has just finished editing *Animals into Art*, to be published by Unwin Hyman. He was the winner of the 1987 J.B. Donne Prize for the anthropology of art for his paper, 'From dull to brilliant: the aesthetics of spiritual power among the Yolngu'.

Fred Myers   Fred Myers's *Pintupi country, Pintupi self*, was recently published by Smithsonian Institution Press. He is also the author of many papers on Australian Aboriginal society.

Nicolas Peterson   Nicolas Peterson has published many papers on the Australian Aborigines, in *Man, American Anthropologist* and elsewhere. Among the books he has edited is *Tribes and Boundaries in Australia*, and his *Australian Territorial Organisation* recently appeared as an *Oceania* monograph.

David Riches   David Riches's comparative study, *Northern Nomadic Hunter-Gatherers* is published by Academic Press. He is editor of *The Anthropology of Violence* (Basil Blackwell), and his papers on the Inuit Eskimo have been published in *Man* amd other journals and collections.

Colin Scott   Since the completion of his PhD thesis at McGill University on the James Bay Cree, Colin Scott has published many papers on contemporary Canadian Indians.

Henry S. Sharp   In 1988 the Smithsonian Institution Press published Henry Sharp's *The Transformation of Bigfoot: maleness, power and belief among the Chipewyan*. He is also the author of *Chipewyan marriage* (National Museums of Canada) and numerous papers.

Robert Tonkinson   Robert Tonkinson is the author of *The Jigalong Mob: Aboriginal victors of the Desert Crusade* (Cummings), *The Mardujarra Aborigines* (Holt, Rinehart & Winston), and many papers on Australian Aboriginal society.

James Woodburn   James Woodburn's extensive publications on the Hadza of Tanzania, and on the comparative analysis of hunting and gathering societies, include his Malinowski Memorial Lecture, 'Egalitarian societies' (*Man* 1982), and 'Hunters and Gatherers: the material culture of the nomadic Hadza' (British Museum).